D1663527

The Urban Question in Africa

RGS-IBG Book Series

For further information about the series and a full list of published and forthcoming titles please visit www.rgsbookseries.com

The Urban Question in Africa

Uneven Geographies of Transition

Pádraig R. Carmody
James T. Murphy
Richard Grant and
Francis Y. Owusu

WILEY

Registered Office(s)
John Wiley & Sons, Inc., 111 River Street, Hoboken, NJ 07030, USA
John Wiley & Sons Singapore Pte. Ltd, 1 Fusionopolis Walk, #06-01 Solaris South Tower, Singapore 138628

For details of our global editorial offices, customer services, and more information about Wiley products visit us at www.wiley.com.

Wiley also publishes its books in a variety of electronic formats and by print-on-demand. Some content that appears in standard print versions of this book may not be available in other formats.

Library of Congress Cataloging-in-Publication Data
Names: Carmody, Pádraig R., author. | Murphy, James T., author. | Grant, Richard, author. |
   Owusu, Francis Y., author. | John Wiley & Sons, publisher.
Title: The urban question in Africa : uneven geographies of transition / by Pádraig R. Carmody, James T. Murphy, Richard Grant, and Francis Y. Owusu.
Description: Hoboken, NJ : Wiley, 2024. | Series: RGS-IBG book series | Includes bibliographical references and index.
Identifiers: LCCN 2023021898 (print) | LCCN 2023021899 (ebook) | ISBN 9781119833611 (hardback) |
   ISBN 9781119833628 (paperback) | ISBN 9781119833659 (epdf) | ISBN 9781119833642 (epub) | ISBN 9781119833635 (oBook)
Subjects: LCSH: Urbanization--Africa. | Urban policy--Africa. | Community development, Urban--Africa. |
   Africa--Economic conditions.
Classification: LCC HT384.A35 U77 2024 (print) | LCC HT384.A35 (ebook) | DDC 307.76096--dc23/
   eng/20230512
LC record available at https://lccn.loc.gov/2023021898
LC ebook record available at https://lccn.loc.gov/2023021899

Cover image: Courtesy of James T. Murphy
Cover design by Wiley

Set in 10/12 and PlantinStd by Integra Software Services Pvt. Ltd, Pondicherry, India

For our families and friends.

Contents

Series Editor's Preface

The RGS-IBG Book Series only publishes work of the highest international standing. Its emphasis is on distinctive new developments in human and physical geography, although it is also open to contributions from cognate disciplines whose interests overlap with those of geographers. The series places strong emphasis on theoretically informed and empirically strong texts. Reflecting the vibrant and diverse theoretical and empirical agendas that characterize the contemporary discipline, contributions are expected to inform, challenge and stimulate the reader. Overall, the RGS-IBG Book Series seeks to promote scholarly publications that leave an intellectual mark and change the way readers think about particular issues, methods or theories.

For details on how to submit a proposal please visit:
www.rgsbookseries.com

Ruth Craggs, *King's College London, UK*
Chih Yuan Woon, *National University of Singapore*
RGS-IBG Book Series Editors

Acknowledgements

Many people made this book possible. We thank all our interview participants for their time and insights. We are also grateful to the RGS-IBG book series editors and board for their comments; particularly Wooh Chih Yuan who shepherded this project through and for his and Ruth Craggs comments on it, which have substantially improved it. We are also grateful to the proposal and manuscript reviewers who provided very helpful comments to allow us to develop the project into a book. We thank Alex Sphar and Mwangi Chege for their assistance with some of the field research. Some of the research for this book was funded by the University of Johannesburg, the US National Science Foundation [BCS-0925151], and Regional Studies Association [MERSA 2017] for which we are grateful. Many people have commented on parts or all of the book. We thank Ayona Datta, Andrew McLaran, Julie Silva, Chris Rogerson, Julia Giddy, Kate Meagher, Laura Mann, Federico Cugurullo, Mike Morris, Martin Oteng-Ababio, Paul Stacey, Michael Osei Asibey, and Owen Crankshaw for their comments. Pádraig Carmody and Richard Grant also thank Jayne and Chris Rogerson for their advice and guidance on sources, and their hospitality. Any errors of fact or omission are of course ours.

We are also grateful to publishers for allowing us to base some chapters on previously published material.

Chapter 6 is derived, in part, from an article published in *the African Geographical Review* on the 24th of April 2019, available online:

Pádraig Carmody and Alicia Fortuin, "Ride sharing, Virtual Capital and Impacts on Labor in Cape Town, South Africa," *African Geographical Review* 38(3), (2019) 196–208.

Other chapters draw on parts of the following publications, which are reproduced by permission.

Pádraig Carmody and Francis Owusu "Neoliberalism, Urbanisation and Change in Africa: The Political Economy of Heterotopias," *Journal of African Development* 18(1), (2016) 61–73.

Richard Grant, Pádraig Carmody and James Murphy "A Green Transition in South Africa? Sociotechnical Experimentation in the Atlantis Greentech Zone," *Journal of Modern African Studies*, 58(2), (2020) 189–211.

James T. Murphy (2020) "Greenfield cities in Africa: A recipe for generative urbanization," *Regions e-Zine*, on-line only. DOI: 10.1080/13673882.2020.00001059.

Pádraig Carmody and James T. Murphy "Generative Urbanisation in Africa? A Sociotechnical View of Tanzania's Urban Transition," *Urban Geography*, 40(1), (2019) 128–157.

Pádraig Carmody and James T. Murphy "Chinese Neoglobalisation in East Africa: Logics, couplings, and impacts." *Space and Polity*, 26(1), (2022) 20–43.

James T. Murphy "Urban-economic geographies beyond production: Nairobi's sociotechnical system and the challenge of generative urbanisation," *ZFW–Advances in Economic Geography*, 66(1), (2022) 18–35.

James T. Murphy, Pádraig Carmody, Francis Owusu and Richard Grant, "The Impact of China on Urban Africa," *Handbook of Emerging 21ˢᵗ Century Cities*, Kristine Bezdecny and Kevin Archer (eds). London, Edward Elgar, (2018) 106–127.

We also thank the referees and editors for these journals and book chapter for their comments. We also thank the staff at Wiley Blackwell.

Pádraig R. Carmody, James T. Murphy, Richard Grant and Francis Y. Owusu
Dublin, Ireland, Worcester, MA, Miami, FL, and Ames, IA, USA.

List of Abbreviations

3D printing	three-dimensional printing
4IR	Fourth Industrial Revolution
AfCTA	African Continental Free Trade Area
AfDB	African Development Bank
AGOA	African Growth and Opportunity Act
AgTech	Agricultural Technology Companies
App	mobile phone application
AG	Atlantis Greentech (special economic zone)
AI	Artificial Intelligence
ANC	African National Congress
AU	African Union
AUC	African Union Commission
ASEZ	Atlantis Special Economic Zone
AUC	African Union Commission
BAIC	Beijing Automobile Industrial Corporation
BBC	British Broadcasting Corporation
BPO	Business Process Outsourcing
BRI	Belt and Road Initiative (of China)
BRT	bus rapid transit
CBD	Central Business District
CBO	Community-Based Organizations
CCT	City of Cape Town
CIP	Competitiveness International Performance
COP	Conference of the Parties of the United Nations Framework on Climate Change
CO_2	Carbon dioxide
COSATU	Congress of South African Trade Unions
DA	Democratic Alliance
DRC	Democratic Republic of Congo
DTI	Department of Trade and Industry (of South Africa)

EBA	Everything But Arms
EPZ	Export Processing Zone
ETCZ	Economic Trade and Cooperation Zone
EU	European Union
EVD	Ebola Virus Disease
EXIM Bank	Export-Import Bank (of China)
FDI	Foreign Direct Investment
FinTechs	financial technology companies
GDP	Gross Domestic Product
GE	Green Economy
GEP	Green Economy Progress
GIIF	Ghana Infrastructure Investment Fund
GIN	Global Innovation Network
GIZ	*Deutsche Gesellschaft für Internationale Zusammenarbeit*
GPN	Global Production Networks
GPTs	general purpose technologies
GR	Gestamp Renewables
GRA	Ghana Revenue Authority
GVC	Global Value Chains
HBEs	home-based enterprises
ICT	Information and Communication Technologies
IDC	Industrial Development Corporation (of South Africa)
ILO	International Labour Organization
IMF	International Monetary Fund
IPPs	independent power producers
IS	Informal sector
ISI	Import Substitution Industrialisation
IT	Information Technology
ITS	intelligent transport system
j-vs	joint ventures
KTDA	Konza Technopolis Development Authority
LPG	Liquid Petroleum Gas
MLP	multi-level perspective
mt	metric tons
MTechs	medical technology companies
MVA	manufacturing value added
NDC	Nationally Determined Contribution
NEUPs	New Economic and Urban Powers
NGOs	Non-Governmental Organizations
NUMSA	National Union of Metalworkers of South Africa
NUPs	National Urban Policies
OECD	Organization for Economic Cooperation and Development
OPEC	Organization of Petroleum Exporting Countries
PAGE	Partnership on Action for Green Economy

PPP	public-private partnership
PV	photo-voltaic
R&D	research and development
R&R	refurbishing and recycling
REDD+	Reduction of Emissions from Deforestation and forest Degradation (plus community benefit)
REIPP	Renewable Energy Independent Producers Programme (South Africa)
RETs	Renewable Energy Technologies
RVCs	Regional Value Chains
SACCO	Savings and Credit Cooperative Organization
SADC	Southern African Development Community
SAP	Structural Adjustment Programme
SAREBI	South African Renewable Energy Incubator
SARTEC	South African Renewable Energy Technology Centre
SCP	Sustainable Consumption and Production
SDGs	Sustainable Development Goals
SDI	Slum Dwellers International
SEZ	Special Economic Zone
SIM	subscriber identity module
SGR	Standard Gauge Railway
SME	small and medium enterprise
SNM	strategic niche management
SOE	State-Owned Enterprise
SSA	Sub-Saharan Africa
SSC	South-South Cooperation
STI	Science, Technology and Innovation
STS	Science, Technology and Society
TIS	technological innovation systems
TM	transition management
UAE	United Arab Emirates
UIS	urban informal sector
UK	United Kingdom
UN	United Nations
UNCTAD	United Nations Conference on Trade and Development
UNDRR	United Nations Office for Disaster Risk Reduction
UNECA	United Nations Economic Commission for Africa
UNEP	United Nations Environment Programme
UNESCO	United Nations Educational, Scientific and Cultural Organization
UN HABITAT	United Nations Human Settlement Programme
UNICEF	United Nations Children's Fund
UNIDO	United Nations Industrial Development Organization
USA	United States of America

WASH	water, sanitation and hygiene
WCG	Western Cape Government
WCISP	Western Cape Industrial Symbiosis Programme
WCP	Western Cape Province
WHO	World Health Organization
WIEGO	Women in Informal Employment: Globalizing and Organizing
ZAR	*Zuid-Afrikaanse Rand* (South African rand)

Introduction: Urban Transitions in Africa

Since 2007, most of the world's population has lived in urban settings for the first time in human history. Africa is the last (inhabited) predominantly rural continent, but it's most rapidly urbanizing one. It is undergoing an "urban revolution" (Parnell and Pieterse 2014) unlike that seen anywhere else in the world for reasons that will be elaborated later. What this means for development outcomes and pathways is one of the most pressing questions facing the region.

Africa's urbanization rate is rising steadily, and this will continue in coming decades (see Figure I.1). The geographical distribution of urban agglomerations is widespread, and some estimates suggest more than 50 cities on the continent have populations greater than one million people (see Figure I.2). Lagos and Kinshasa alone are thought to hold approximately 14 million people each (United Nations Department of Economic and Social Affairs 2018), although some estimates put the formers' population at over 20 million. Many cities in the region have populations which have grown rapidly in recent decades. For example, Kinshasa added 8.2 million people between 2000 and 2020; Lagos added 354,000 per annum, and a few even tripled their population numbers since 2000 (e.g., Luanda and Dar es Salaam). However, some of the fastest growth rates of all (7.3% per year 2015–2020) are registered for smaller urban settlements such as Gwagwalda (Nigeria), Kabinda (Democratic Republic of Congo [DRC]), and Mbouda (Cameroon) (Satterthwaite 2021). Some observers posit that thirteen of the world's twenty largest cities will be in Africa by the end of this century, with Lagos potentially being the first city with more than 100 million people (Hoornweg and Pope 2017).[1] As Figure I.2 demonstrates, urban growth will be

The Urban Question in Africa: Uneven Geographies of Transition, First Edition. Pádraig R. Carmody, James T. Murphy, Richard Grant and Francis Y. Owusu.

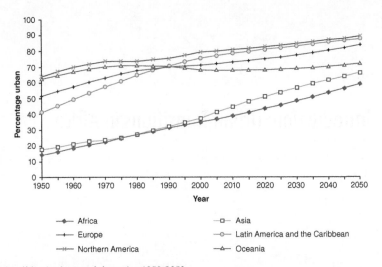

Figure I.1 Urbanization trends by region 1950-2050.

Source: UNDESA, 2019 / United Nations / Licensed under CC BY 3.0.

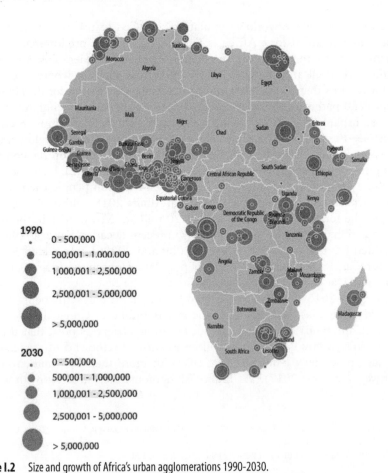

Figure I.2 Size and growth of Africa's urban agglomerations 1990-2030.

Data source: World Population Prospect-UNDESA GISS/ACS/ECA 2016; Original figure modified from United Nations Economic Commission for Africa [UNECA], 2017.

highly significant throughout the region and not only in mega, primate, or large cities but in secondary agglomerations as well. By 2050 it is estimated that 70% of all Africans will be urbanites (Paller 2019).

While official statistics on urban growth rates remain somewhat specious – based on inconsistent vital registration systems and irregular censuses, United Nations [UN] projections, and sample surveys – it is clear that municipal leaders and policymakers in most African cities face very significant challenges with respect to delivering vital collective goods and services (e.g., water, housing, energy). Common to almost all cities is the reality that municipal governments' budgetary, bureaucratic, and technical capacities are insufficient to effectively manage the "urban revolution." For example, only 5% of Kinshasa's huge population has sewer connections and Lagos' municipal leaders grappled with an estimated 1,353 (new) in-migrants per day in 2020–2021; giving a growth rate of approximately 3.5% per year (Macrotrends 2021a). In Nairobi, nearly 60% of the city's population lives in informal settlements that occupy only 6% of the land area (Bird et al. 2017; Talukdar 2018). Providing housing, sanitation, education, and job opportunities for burgeoning populations is incredibly challenging, even if, as the case of Lagos, some cities have relatively/more effective urban governance systems (Cheeseman and de Gramont 2017).[2]

Historically, urbanization is most often a process associated with structural economic transformation, whereby countries shift from reliance on primary sectors, such as agriculture, to manufacturing and other secondary industries (e.g., construction) that benefit from the scale and scope economies that cities can provide. Such transitions can generate formal employment, create new trading opportunities, and base industries, and facilitate social upgrading in terms of improved incomes and access to services. In Africa today, however, generative pathways such as these remain generally elusive as the region has not experienced sufficient growth in manufacturing sectors and other value-adding industries capable of providing employment for rising urban populations; the discourse of "Africa Rising" notwithstanding (Carmody et al. 2020). Instead, urbanization without industrialization has become the norm in most of the region's countries; marked, in particular, by an expanding informal economy where approximately 85% of Africans currently work (Choi et al. 2020). Furthermore, many African cities are "imploding" due to infrastructure overload, marked by a general lack, and highly uneven distribution of, basic services and collective goods (e.g., water, sanitation, housing).

Such conditions coexist with the increasing integration of Africa's cities and economies into the world economy through trade, financial flows, information-communication technologies (ICTs), and migration. Economic growth has accompanied this process in most countries, but wealth and welfare distributions have been highly uneven. As Abdul Malik Simone (2001: p. 17) explains:

> as the "insides" of African cities are more differentially linked to proliferating networks of accumulation and circulation operating at also increasingly differentiated scales, this uncertainty [for most of the population] is "materalized."

In response to this precarity, networks of social support play a vital role, making people a type of "infrastructure" (Simone 2004). As one respondent for another study noted "we don't have insurance here, you see, we make connections and friendships, it's our insurance" (quoted in Joelsson 2021: p. 144). Social capital, relationships, and networks thus serve as vital means for the urban poor to manage material deprivations associated with uneven development, creating "a moral economy in the sense that the maintenance of social relationships often outweigh[s] the importance of profits" (Newell 2012: p. 3). Africa's urban poor deliberately create their own social capital in work realms, where jobs must be "invented," and reside in the region's burgeoning informal economies (Grant 2010).

Simone (2022, p. 4) has more recently developed a more encompassing theory of the "surrounds" to better explain the urban milieu. This he says can be thought of as urbanization from the bottom up, most visible in urban peripheries undergoing (re)development. "These are spaces of intensive contiguity of the disparate – disparate forms, functions and ways of doing things." They are a "mode of accompaniment" to more formal urbanism.

Paradoxically, however, African cities are also sites for hyperdifferentiation (Grant and Nijman 2004) and hyperaccumulation and wealth generation for elites and growing middle classes. As a result, many cities have experienced construction booms and real estate speculation in middle and high-income markets, physically manifest in the development of shopping malls, gated communities, and luxury housing projects that do little to ameliorate, or may even exacerbate, the material challenges facing the poor (Murphy and Carmody 2019; Murphy 2022), generally marked by extreme social and spatial polarization (Grant and Nijman 2004). For example, the redevelopment of Lagos' urban waterfront was enabled in part by the partial destruction of Makoko, a floating slum built on stilts on an area partly reclaimed from the water by compacting sand, wood shavings, and rubbish. The results were devastating to some of the long-time residents of the settlement and fisherfolk such as Elebiomayo Folashade, who had been a relatively well-off woman living there:

> They destroyed my boats and my husband's boats and now I cannot pay the school fees, so the children have been withdrawn from school," she says. "I am old – what am I going to do now? (Leithead 2017: p. 7).

The Lagos state government has had a "war" and "kick against indiscipline" policies directed against informal residents, such as the mass displacement at Oshodi market in 2009 (Omoegun 2015). Violent displacements of urban residents are often undertaken by the military or police, but also in some cases by armed private companies such as the infamous "Red Ants" in South Africa, allowing for "accumulation by repossession" (Cooper and Paton 2021). Such uneven developments are widening inequalities and further complicating attempts to improve the distribution of vital collective goods and services. Thus urban "renewal" and "urbicide" (Coward 2009) are often two sides of the same coin, despite the plaudits the urban management of Lagos has received (see Cheeseman and de Gramont 2017). However, displaced urban residents may also "take back" spaces from which they have been displaced through informal street trading, for example (Gillespie 2017). Residents in informal settlements may also appropriate or repurpose infrastructure to their own ends as well, so are far from completely powerless as is often depicted in the literature.

The circumstances facing Africa's cities today can be understood in part as a symptom of what Fox and Goodfellow (2022) term "late urbanisation." Countries and regions, especially in the Global South, that are urbanizing later than the core economies face particular challenges that were not the case for early urbanizers. Improved life expectancies and mobilities have greatly increased the pace and depth of population growth in cities, creating levels of congestion that make planning extremely difficult. Southern/African cities are also subject to the forces of hyperglobalization (especially financialization, informationalization, inward foreign direct investment [FDI], and the rise of platform economies) which play key, yet often volatile, roles in shaping urban development trajectories and possibilities.[3] At the same time, new environmental and public-health threats – namely climate change, COVID-19, and other disease outbreaks – are adding additional, global, and existential challenges which will need to be managed/addressed in the coming years.

In the face of this complex array of issues and multiscalar drivers of urban change, many "late" African/Southern cities face governance challenges stemming from what Fox and Goodfellow (2022) term "centripetal state politics" that has situated control over urban development in the hands of national agencies, rather than municipal governments and the realities of entangled governance combining, market, formal, and informal logics (Stacey et al. 2021). The result of this is that municipal governments often lack the authority, political power, finance, and technical capabilities to plan and manage cities in ways that improve their internal workings to the benefit of all residents; forced instead to cede control to domestic and transnational actors that prioritize the growth and exchange value production potential of cities (i.e., what they can do to spur national development first and foremost). However, urbanization is also highly variegated across the continent, including within the same cities. For example, suburbs are complex places with their "economic multi-nodality, multi-directional movement of patterns and multiple governance arrangements, which complicate concepts of peripherality" (Meth et al. 2021: p. 34) and confound generalizations about urban Africa. The growth of Africa's towns and smaller cities is also transforming the region. For example, as Kisumu, Kenya has grown, Nyamasaria has become part of the city. Mr. Aloo, an urban landowner, is building two houses on his land [in Nyamasaria]. He will rent them out, "hopefully to God-fearing people," for US $62 each per month, "'more than twice the going rate five years ago. Now it is urban,' he says, 'this is a prime area'" (The Economist 2023: p. 1).

All told, Africa's urban transition is complicated and co-constituted by its entanglements with global geopolitical, geoeconomic, and "natural" forces that are combining to shape potential urbanization pathways and the prospects for sustainable development. As Horner and Hulme (2019) and Horner (2020) argue, the prospects for development are no longer simply a matter of international relations between countries (esp. North-South), but are instead determined in large part by diverse, global factors. Such meta-trends – including financialization, digitalization, climate change, China's rise, migration, and South-South trade – have intensified the interconnectedness of places and created multipolar forms of globalization that transcend the North-South divides of old. In this context, the development prospects for cities are shaped by forces and contingencies well beyond their immediate control or the ambit of municipal planning strategies.

The rise of China and other new centers of global production, for example, has put competitive pressure on urban-based manufacturers at the same time as it has opened new sources of investment flows into African cities. Importantly, globalized production is implicated in the climate emergency the continent, and its cities, face. Globally uneven geographies of vaccination also contribute to the development of a COVID-19 "pandemic structure" (Carmody and McCann 2022), which allows for new variants to emerge, recursively shaping urbanization pathways. In terms of urban planning, traveling technocrats and consultants, mobile policies, and transnational relations play an increasingly important role in shaping urban governance. As Robinson (2022: p. 90) notes:

> In many poorer and middle-income cities, powerful external agents, such as the World Bank, international NGOs and visiting consultants are an important part of any "urban regime."

In this context, established (western based) teleologies and stage models (e.g., Walt Rostow's *Non-Communist Manifesto*) for translating urbanization into widespread, distributive, and sustainable forms of development will not offer magic bullets for late urbanizers in the region. Needed instead are novel, experimental, and/or creative approaches to urban planning and management that balance the desire for economic growth with the need to manage/reduce congestion, inequality, and poverty levels to the benefit of all residents. The development of such strategies demands multidimensional perspectives on African cities and their functions internally and externally, and comparative insights from across the continent in order to determine the drivers, geographies, and contingent features that can enable (or prevent) more sustainable and just urban transitions.

This book seeks to contribute to this agenda through a focus on two of the most significant urban questions facing Africa today. First, what do current meta-trends (e.g., global geopolitical and economic changes, the climate crisis, COVID-19) mean for African cities and the continent's development more broadly? Second, can African cities help generate widespread developmental transformations or will their growth simply reinforce "parasitic," unequal, and/or extractive relations with and from rural areas and to the global economy?

To answer these questions, we theorize and empirically assess the tendencies, nature, diversity, and complexity of urbanization on the continent. Our approach centers on a novel conceptualization of cities that views them as sociotechnical systems constituted through three overlapping sociotechnical regimes: those of production, consumption, and infrastructure. Scholarship on sociotechnical systems encompasses a diverse field of scholars and practitioners and we add to this body of knowledge with urban African insights from a spatial perspective; contributing significantly to urban-economic geography and the emergent subfield on the geography of sustainability transitions (see Sengers and Raven 2015; Truffer et al. 2015). Our analytical framework integrates concepts and concerns from economic geography (e.g., transnational couplings, agglomeration, exchange value), urban geography (e.g., regime theory, governance, use value of cities), sociotechnical transitions scholarship (e.g., sociotechnical regimes), and practice-based epistemologies (see Jones and Murphy 2011) in order to examine and compare African cities in relation to different functional realms (e.g., consumer markets, manufacturing facilities), and with regard to the role that (geo)economic/political relations and multiscalar forces are playing in shaping their evolution. In doing so, we seek to provide a more holistic perspective on African cities today, one that shifts debates/ dialogues on the urban question beyond one-dimensional perspectives (e.g., the need to develop agglomeration economies) by capturing the links between production, consumption, and infrastructure-related activities and their governance: the central question being what Africa's ongoing urban transition means for development across the continent, and within its countries and cities.

Urban Transition Trajectories in Africa: Generative or Parasitic?

Urban areas are also highly monetized, and the lives especially of the poorest residents are determined almost entirely by market forces. Money thus becomes the focus of the city dweller's attention: the means by which relationships are negotiated, the measure of success, and a necessary condition for well-being (Stark and Teppo 2022: p. 1).

Africa's ongoing urban transition is a key driver of development trends in the region, manifest in rapid demographic shifts and associated major socioeconomic changes (AfDB et al., 2016). As cities grow, rents increase, reducing returns to labor and (non-rentier) capital and compromising more distributed consumption and productive investment (Obeng-Odoom 2016). Nonetheless, urbanization itself accounted for roughly a third of economic growth on the continent over the past two decades (OECD, United Nations Economic Commission for Africa, & African Development Bank 2022). Thus, critical questions arise as to whether or not generative urbanization is occurring in Africa.

As urbanization accelerates, many cities have become more deeply enmeshed in global networks of finance, trade, information, and geopolitics that significantly shape the nature and implications of globalization for national development – indeed some argue that this is a form of distantiated, planetary urbanization (Brenner 2015), although others argue that African urbanites still view them as bounded places (Schindler 2017). Cities that are able to more successfully integrate themselves into these networks do so through a "multidimensional infrastructure of connectivity" (Castells 2010: p. 2741) that facilitates the attraction of investment and industrial upgrading, and enhances produced exchange values of the city, while retaining value locally in the form of improved collective goods (e.g., schools, infrastructure) and widespread welfare distribution. Successful integration is largely dependent on particular forms of "spatial performativity" (Aberg and Becker 2021), social connections, and forward-thinking policy choices rather than a more passive dynamic of "natural outgrowth" through factor endowments. Generative dynamics such as these are a critical means through which the growth of cities can translate into widespread/ distributive development within them and nationally.

Despite the arguments of urbanization advocates or boosters (World Bank 2009), high rates of chronic poverty and rising inequality levels have accompanied the growth and spread of cities in Africa (Beegle et al. 2016). As such, significant questions remain as to whether and how a generalized generative urbanization dynamic can emerge so that the region's cities serve as central drivers of progressive socioeconomic transformations. At present, urban transitions appear to be more "parasitic" in nature as cities serve as key nodes or hubs for processes of extraversion – the extraction of wealth and "surplus value" from rural areas or offshore through unequal exchange or exploitative trade relations (e.g., see Hoselitz 1955; Lipton 1977; Smith 1987; Bayart and Ellis 2000; Wuyts 2001; Murphy and Carmody 2019).[4] Such parasitism, sometimes associated with the "plunder economy" (Cramer 2006), has been a feature of African underdevelopment for centuries. For example, the Royal African Company, which was founded by the future British king, James II, paid 300% dividends on the 70,000 slaves it shipped between 1680 and 1688, even though only two-thirds of them made it alive (Bassey 2012), contributing to urban development and industrialization in Britain (Williams 1994).

Surplus value is being further extracted offshore through intraversion (Murphy and Carmody 2015): a process through which cities serve as gateways for the flow or dumping of imported goods into domestic markets, to the detriment of endogenous industrial development. Intraversion may be further facilitated by infrastructure development such as when foreign aid or loans (e.g., through China's Belt and Road Initiative [BRI]) are used principally for logistics hubs (e.g., ports) and transportation projects (e.g., railways, motorways) that expand, and speed-up import flows. Parasitism is also associated with the "splintering" of urban infrastructures, labor markets, and services such that there are high levels of inequality with respect to employment, essential utilities, and social services (Graham and Marvin 2001; Jaglin 2008; Swilling 2014). Splintering occurs when there is insufficient redistribution or investment in infrastructure and social services such that the poorest urbanites and recent migrants are forced to rely on informal, *ad hoc*, inefficient, and low-quality alternatives to meet their basic needs. In Africa today, parasitic urbanization appears to be the norm, marked by a threefold dynamic of extraversion, intraversion, and splintering such that urban population and economic growth occur at the expense or neglect of endogenous industrial development, widespread formal employment opportunities, and a more even, just, and adequate distribution of collective goods and basic services.

Through our sociotechnical systems approach we assess the generative or parasitic tendencies of African cities today as being determined by the development trajectories of their production, consumption, and infrastructure regimes. These regimes are constituted by/through forms of governance, embedded practices, inter-regime interdependencies, and multiscalar relations that shape the pace and direction of urban development through the creation of exchange value in global, regional, and national markets, and use value locally through the provisioning of collective goods, services, amenities, and the consumption of nonbasic goods. Generative urbanization becomes possible when regimes are practiced, governed, networked, and interrelated in ways that progressively transform the immanent (structural, relational) conditions that produce negative development outcomes (e.g., neocolonialism, extraversion, unequal exchange, and/or parasitic accumulation via kleptocracy and a process of "looting" that links African's political elites to financial and technocratic expertise abroad that sustains financial outflows from the region, and in the worst cases, drains economies (Bond 2006).

Beyond the question of whether cities are driving progressive or regressive forms of development, this book is timely given the ongoing evolution of the global economy, the rise of new geopolitical powers (e.g., China, India), and other global drivers of socioeconomic restructuring (e.g., climate change, COVID-19, the fourth industrial revolution [4IR]). These meta-trends are profoundly changing the nature, meaning, and developmental significance of cities globally; highlighting the importance of urban processes for "globalized" socioeconomic transformations, for better or worse. For example, we are seeing the emergence of new urban forms such as open, local distributed manufacturing (i.e., local manufacturing) as a form of decentralized production practiced by enterprises using a network of geographically dispersed facilities coordinated using ICT (Wells et al. 2020; Corsni and Moultrie 2021). Transformations such as these offer the potential for African cities and economies to forge new developmental pathways if the forces driving them (e.g., geopolitical, technological, financial) can be managed in ways that can create transnational couplings that capture and distribute value in the continent.

In short, the question of how to make cities work better as drivers of socioeconomic and spatial wealth distribution is an existential one for the hundreds of millions of Africans who have yet to reap the material rewards meant to accompany economic globalization. This, in essence, is one of the pressing urban questions that binds the chapters of this book together, one that demands multiple focal areas, perspectives, and comparisons in order to begin to understand the challenges to, opportunities for, and effective policies to guide development trajectories.

Assessing the Urbanization-Globalization-Industrialization Nexus

There has been substantial debate in the literature in recent years as to what constitutes "the urban." Some argue that what happens in, and decisions taken in, cities largely determine what occurs in rural areas globally (for example, whether or not to establish a new mine or plantation) and that consequently we live in an era of "planetary urbanisation" (Brenner 2015). Thus, there is no neat division between the urban and the rural, as has been posited in much of the earlier literature, and in many cases urban and proximate rural hinterlands morph into peri-urban environments, where it is unclear whether urbanization is extending into rural spaces or urban areas are being ruralized or processes are being recombined? The urban is instead what we view as a context constituted not only by actors, institutions, and processes in city sites and locations, but also by multiscalar forces and translocal relations that shape urban development pathways in significant ways.

As noted above, urbanization has been historically intertwined with economic development as the productive sectors in cities "pull" rural people in for employment opportunities. More recently, however, urban population growth has been driven principally by a demographic boom in cities (i.e., natural increase) and in-migration of rural people in response to crises and livelihood struggles across much of the continent (Moyo 2019); not formal employment opportunities. The net result is that growing numbers of urban residents live in poverty, with more than half forced to dwell in slums or informal settlements (Tusting et al. 2019), even as housing conditions by and large improved on foot of generally revived economic growth associated with the recent (2003–2014) commodity boom or super-cycle.[5] In short, urban production realms (e.g., manufacturing industries and urban real estate) are out-of-sync with the demographic changes at work across the region.

At the same time, Africa's consumers have become increasingly powerful and attractive to foreign investors, especially in retail sectors. Such improvements, however, have been highly uneven in their realization. Most African cities have experienced the growth of middle classes, building booms, and foreign direct investment (FDI) into speculative real estate markets; forces that have improved housing conditions for the wealthy and many middle-class residents while doing little to address informality and poverty for the majority of people (Grant 2009). Such trends have thus exacerbated inequality and fragmented many cities into enclaves of wealth and accumulation, and areas of poverty and immiseration, sometimes expressed in extreme social and spatial polarization (Unequal Scenes 2021). Gillespie and Schindler (2022) relate Africa's infrastructure-led urbanization (in Ghana and Kenya) to the emergence of vast extended urban landscapes characterized by the outward expansion of major cities along transport corridors, the integration of national urban systems into transnational urban regions, and the rapid urbanization of peri-urban and rural areas. They highlight the case of the Abidjan-Lagos Corridor, an extended urban axis straddling five West African states along a coastal highway, as well as a different spatial formation in East Africa - the Lamu Port, South Sudan, Ethiopia Transport Corridor – with a north–south axis connecting Nairobi and Ethiopia and an east–west axis linking Lamu on the coast with South Sudan.

Demographic change in African cities has also been driven by the "pull" factor of better infrastructure. On the continent 40% of city dwellers have access to improved sanitation and 87% to improved water sources as compared to 23 and 56% respectively in rural areas (Cartwright et al. 2018). Yet, infrastructure provisioning remains woeful inadequate in most cities where poor housing conditions (esp. in slums), traffic congestion, inadequate basic services (e.g., water, sanitation, energy), and polluted environments ensnare the majority of residents. Beyond continued, rapid population growth, these challenges have been and are being magnified by the ongoing global climate and public health/COVID-19 crises which are making living conditions even more difficult for the poor (Moore 2015; Wilkinson 2020).

How can we make sense of these developments? Urbanization is a continuing, and in Africa, accelerating meta-trend, but what does it mean for the future of the continent? Should we expect that development pathways will advance in lock-step with growing cities and the scope and scale economies that accompany them? The mutually reinforcing westernized teleology of the urbanization-industrialization-development nexus is deeply embedded in the ideations, assumptions, and policy frameworks of mainstream development institutions (e.g., World Bank 2009) even though such frameworks often fail to account for the situatedness of Southern cities in the current era of (de)globalization and late urbanization. As noted above, Africa's cities and urban transitions are being heavily influenced by other meta-trends that are transforming the international system and challenging developmentalist models that privilege the role that internal/national factors and forces (e.g., fiscal and monetary policy, institutions, markets) play in creating the necessary conditions for growth and distribution. These trends include deindustrialization, informalization, financialization, 4IR, the continuing rise of China, and global environmental change; topics that will be dealt with in this book.

In relation to these meta-trends paradoxes abound. For example, because of new technology, the growth in demand for fin-tech (financial technology, such as mobile payments systems) has sky-rocketed. Sub-Saharan Africa now boasts four fin-tech "unicorns" – companies valued at over a billion US dollars each – with Flutterwave from Nigeria being the latest of these (Collins 2021; Lewis 2021a).[6] African cities such as Lagos and Nairobi are significant sites of tech-driven innovation (Oranye 2016), which has imbricated them as nodes in global innovation networks (GINs) (Cooke 2017), but without making a significant difference to local urban social challenges (namely employment generation) as these cities or their firms are not articulated with GINs in straightforward or unproblematic ways. For example, Africa's most iconic "unicorn" – Jumia, the Lagos-based online marketing company – has struggled in recent years as its losses rose 34% (to $246m) in 2019, the eighth straight year without profits (BBC 2020). Its stock price on the New York Stock Exchange subsequently collapsed and it was forced to close operations in three African countries. As is also the case with Flutterwave, whose headquarters are in San Francisco, critics have questioned how African Jumia is. As noted in a recent BBC article:

> Jumia's public claim to African-ness is tenuous because its headquarters are in Berlin, Germany, its Technology and Product Team in Porto, Portugal, and its senior leadership in Dubai in the United Arab Emirates (UAE). Critics see it as an exploitative Western company that conveniently co-opted an African identity to extract as much value as possible and profit off the continent (BBC 2020).

While there are other widely noted tech start-ups out of Nigeria, such as Andela (an accelerator for software developers) (Anwar and Graham 2022), an additional concern that relates to urbanization is the fact that only about 10% of African gross domestic product (GDP) is produced by the manufacturing sector. Some (e.g., Choi et al. 2020) view this as an advantage given the rising competitive displacement of labor by robotics and other technologies of the 4IR; circumstances that will thus be less pronounced in Africa than in other world regions. However, existing economic and industrial marginalization (deindustrialization in some cases) may simply be compounded, resulting in further urban involution (Armstrong and McGee 1968) as rates of investment remain low and labor continues to be absorbed in burgeoning informal economies marked by low levels of productivity (Myabe 2019).[7] However, informal enterprises in some instances operate with "unfair" advantages (avoiding regulations, lack of obligations to pay taxes, and regulated wages) over small formal firms that produce for domestic markets, thus further inhibiting the latter's development (Mbaye et al. 2020).

In South Africa, generally taken to be the most industrially advanced country on the continent, investment as a proportion of GDP fell from over 34% in 1981 to less than 19% in 2017 (World Bank 2021a), despite the purported "Africa Rising" phenomenon which was meant to be transforming the continent economically (Taylor 2016). This decline in the relative level of investment is reflective of the largely autonomous development of the trade and financial sectors or circuits of capital on the continent. This development is centered on cities as centers of trade and finance, and associated capital leakages through imports and financial flows (Carmody 1998), now increasingly facilitated through ICTs. Nairobi, for example, is taking inspiration from Dubai by focusing on financial services, real estate, and consumption as the desired engines for growth (Upadhyaya 2020). Such strategies can enable short-run, often speculation-driven accumulation by elites and foreign investors, but they do not provide the foundations for long-term industrial transformation. In fact, gross capital formation for Sub-Saharan Africa (SSA) was 22% in 2019, compared to 44% in 1981 – a halving (World Bank 2021b).[8] Moreover, such strategies will not enable the sub-continent to move from factor- to investment- and innovation-driven growth, claims to the contrary notwithstanding. Consequently, while Africa is increasingly an information society, it is not a knowledge economy (Carmody 2013), with profound implications for its cities.

Ultimately, productive economic transformation of Africa's cities is unlikely absent significant gains in quality jobs in the formal sector, and/or targeted policy supports to enhance the skills, capabilities, and technologies of groups of workers and managers in the informal economy. Such policies would also need to tackle the structural drivers of informality (e.g., welfare systems, labor regulations) and create more inclusive/productive economies through digital, political, and grassroots innovations (esp. in basic services such as water, sanitation, energy, and transport) that can help to pull urban residents out of survival-driven, precarious, and informal livelihood strategies. The combined emphasis would thus need to address issues of the exchange value of the goods and services that cities produce/provide, and the use value of the city for all residents – manifest in the amenities and basic services available to them. As we elaborate below, our view is that it is vital to examine cities in a manner that integrates these concerns through a three-dimensional perspective focused on the operation, governance, and interrelationships of/between what we describe as production, consumption, and infrastructure regimes in African cities.

Structure of the Book

The remainder of the book is structured into ten chapters that offer an in-depth analysis of urban transitions in Africa today. Chapter 1 explores different conceptions of the urban and their development in, and applicability to, African experiences to argue the case for a new theoretical approach to urban development. After laying out the dimensions, nature and scale of urbanization on the continent, it then develops the theoretical framework for analysis which threads through the book: that cities are sociotechnical systems constituted through three overlapping regimes related to production, infrastructure, and consumption. These regimes are institutionalized, materialized, embedded, and practiced in ways that shape development outcomes and the prospects for progressive urban transitions. In African cities, regimes are often fragmented, heterogeneous, and subject to informalization; characteristics that challenge their developmental potential in highly significant ways. We elaborate this theoretical framing in this chapter and the remainder of book analyzes diverse thematic areas through the lens of this framework.

Chapter 2 explores the nature of urban-industrial development in Africa today, focusing particularly on production regimes. Manufacturing is historically the key sector in the transformation of (urban) economies onto higher productivity/value-added paths that are generative of distributed welfare gains. However, the nature of African cities and their production regimes has been heavily shaped by their colonial and postcolonial history. Under colonialism cities served primarily administrative functions, as centers of political control, and as trans-shipment points for exports of raw materials and imports of manufactured goods.[9] Import substitution policies, postindependence, tried to reverse this economic and ideational legacy, but were overwhelmed by the debt crisis of the 1980s and subsequent neoliberal programs of austerity sponsored by the World Bank and International Monetary Fund (IMF) which devastated "infant industries." These policies resulted in decades of stagnated or declining manufacturing value-added (MVA) in most countries; conditions that sometimes persist today. The chapter assesses contemporary manufacturing in Africa, highlighting key trends such as recent experiments with Chinese-financed special economic zones (SEZs) and the challenge of onshoring transnational manufacturing firms. This chapter further explores the prospects for the 4IR to enable industrial transformations in cities, arguing for national urban policies as key strategies to facilitate such transitions. The chapter closes with a discussion of why manufacturing matters, focusing on emerging opportunities such as linkages to extractive sectors and the 4IR.

The rise of China and other emerging economies (e.g., India, Turkey) is a key meta-trend marking the global political economy today. China, in particular is now playing a central role in shaping urbanization dynamics in Africa, given its rapidly growing economy, environmental impact and its exportation of urban development ideas, particularly through infrastructure construction and new-build city investments (Zheng, 2021). Chapter 3 explores the direct and indirect impacts of China (especially) on urban development in Africa, from the creation of SEZs, to competitive displacement of local manufacturers and the construction of new housing developments and large infrastructure projects associated with the BRI. The urban impacts of China (especially) on the continent are contradictory and locally mediated, but nonetheless with clear tendencies coming into view, including its increasingly control over production regimes, its significant influence on infrastructure regimes, and the role that Chinese importers, traders, and markets are playing in consumption regimes.

Urbanization is at once both an intensely localized and globalized phenomenon. In recent decades successful national and urban development imaginaries, often based on the experience of Dubai and driven by externally-funded developers, have circulated through transnational policy networks. Chapter 4 explores attempts to reimagine and implement "fantasy urbanism" (Watson 2014) on the continent, drawing on a variety of proposed, implemented, and failed new-build city developments (e.g., Eko-Atlantic [Nigeria], Hope City [Ghana], Konza Technopolis [Kenya]). The nature of planning processes behind these developments, the theory undergirding them, and their concrete impacts are assessed. The chapter examines the visions associated with new-build cities and their implementation impacts on production, consumption, and infrastructure provisioning. It finds that such "heterotopic" developments do not address the challenges facing most African city residents but rather exacerbate tendencies toward splintering, regime fragmentation, and intraversion. They represent attempts at connection to the global economy through erasure, and while they often fail to be realized they nonetheless impact urban and peri-urban populations, through displacement for example.

The vast majority of Africa's working population is employed in the informal sector and the dearth of formal sector jobs in most cities means that such conditions are likely to persist for decades to come. Chapter 5 explores the evolving nature of the urban informal economy, through the lenses of its role in the creation and/or fragmentation of production, consumption, and infrastructure regimes. Attention is also paid to its inertia (e.g., lack of policy innovation for informal food and other markets), attempts to manage and formalize it, and the emergence of relatively new subsectors, such as e-waste processing. The informal sector has recently been heavily affected by the "perfect storm" of COVID-19 pandemic containment strategies, modest or declining economic growth, and fragile health systems that often bypassed or disregarded it. The nature and developmental impacts of these phenomena are explored through a case study of Agbogbloshie, Ghana. Whether or not economic and social upgrading can occur leading to the transformation of the urban informal sector (UIS) is also explored with a focus on the prospects for 4IR and makerspace innovations.

Capital and labor are inter-constitutive and in long-term dynamic tension. Historically capital has sought to increase profits through reducing the power of labor through strategies such as union-busting and off-shoring. The emergence and profusion of the internet has changed capital-labor relations and allowed for new forms of distantiation. This has given rise to the emergence of new forms of "virtual capital" in infrastructure and consumption which "extract" or "release" value from assets they do not own and labor they don't directly contract or manage. Chapter 6 explores the nature of the emerging "gig economy" in urban Africa, with a particular focus on labor. Empirical material from a survey of Uber and Bolt drivers in Cape Town is presented. Whether this hybrid (in)formal economy can be reformed to offer decent, stable work and the implications of this for urban regimes is also explored later.

Cities are much more than sites of production, and truly generative urban transitions must enhance their use value as manifest in the quality of life available to most urban residents. Well-distributed and good quality collective goods (e.g., education, public health, housing, safety) and basic services (e.g., water, energy, transportation, and sanitation) are essential as they enable residents to live healthy, productive lives that make social mobility possible. Chapter 7 examines the scope and scale of the challenges associated with infrastructure regimes, such as the difficulties associated with basic service provisioning, the spatial splintering and fragmentation of infrastructure access along class lines, and the tensions between growth, distribution, and justice as it relates to universal needs. The discussion further highlights the impacts of global meta-trends on the development, resilience, and prioritization of vital services and infrastructures, and the political-economic challenges to pro-poor planning. Suggestions on the requirements and elements for more inclusive infrastructure regimes are also presented.

African cities face massive and interconnected challenges, ranging from employment to infrastructure and housing provision. The rapid growth of cities on the continent is also, as noted earlier, reflective of rural crises across much of the continent, which will accelerate in the context of climate and other ecological disruptions. Chapter 8 explores the nature of climate-related and public health threats to African cities that are creating existential hazards for residents and economies. The discussion focuses particularly on the "riskscapes" associated with climate change and its impacts (e.g., sea level rise, drought, flooding), as well as public health challenges associated with Ebola and COVID-19. The analysis assesses their implications for urban sociotechnical regimes and discusses means for improving adaptation and resilience management strategies in African cities.

Some consider sustainable development to be an oxymoron given the carbon-intensity of current (global) growth models. Nonetheless there are several ambitious green economy initiatives across the continent, including green SEZs. Chapter 9 explores the nature of urban green economy initiatives on the continent and the extent to which they have the potential to fundamentally alter its urban regimes. The nature of these processes and the construction of the policy networks required for their implementation are explored through a case study of the Atlantis greentech SEZ outside of Cape Town, South Africa. While many of these initiatives are incipient, the extent to which they represent innovations which can be up-scaled and mainstreamed is also examined. The chapter further explores potential linkages between the green economy and the urban informal sector.

The final chapter (10) assesses the prospects for generative urban transitions in Africa. It first summarizes and integrates the key findings from earlier chapters in order to provide a generalized assessment of the key challenges facing African cities today. It then argues for a focus on constraints, capabilities, governance, and resilience strategies as crucial factors that can enable urbanites, states, and municipal governments to overcome the constraints preventing sustainable, progressive urban transitions. Constraints, capabilities, governance, and resilience strategies are assessed in relation to production, consumption, and infrastructure regimes, with promising policy approaches highlighted. The chapter/book concludes by making the case for our sociotechnical approach to the study of pressing urban questions in Africa and beyond; one that offers a framework for comparative, situated, and systematic studies of cities globally.

Notes

1 However, some view these predictions regarding Lagos' growth as being extreme (Satterthwaite 2017a).
2 If it were a country, Lagos would have the fifth biggest economy on the African continent (Patey 2020).
3 As we detail later, China's influence in Africa is especially significant in relation to these forces.
4 Some dispute the universalizing narratives of extraversion, arguing for greater complexity. For example, in relation to Uber's operations in Cape Town, South Africa (Pollio 2019, p. 772) notes that "what emerges, instead, is a complex arrangement of calculations and rationalities that are activated through the platform in relation to the unique geography of, in this case, a postcolonial, post-apartheid capital." Thus, African actors' power or "agency" is central to the determination of developmental outcomes.
5 One of the paradoxes of African development in recent decades has been a reduction in the proportion of people living in poverty, even as the absolute number of the poor has increased (Beegle et al. 2016).
6 Notably, Flutterwave is now headquartered in the US while remaining Nigerian-owned. The other unicorns are Fawry, Jumia, and Interswitch.
7 For example, the marginal productivity of labor in street hawking or selling is zero, as output is not increased by the addition of another worker, but returns may be depressed for others (Ravenhill 1986).
8 Relatively high rates of economic growth in the early years of the new millennium were driven largely by higher primary commodity prices.
9 For some European colonial academics "Africans were not simply migrants into urban towns but into European culture and civilization, forcing both a brutal acceleration of their historical development that left them psychologically disoriented and in need of European guidance" (Clémens 1955 cited Larmer 2021: p. 50).

Chapter One
(African) Cities as Sociotechnical Systems: A Conceptual Approach

Introduction

Our approach to analyzing urban questions in Africa is a systemic, sociotechnical one. Cities are conceptualized as sociotechnical systems constituted by configurations of institutions, actors, technologies, and practices that govern the socioeconomic processes that shape welfare distributions, built environments, production activities, consumption patterns, and flows of materials, people, and capital into, and out of, an urban area. Such a perspective enables us to examine urbanization pathways in Africa in a more comprehensive manner than other approaches to better account for the role of intra-urban interrelationships (e.g., between formal and informal economies and combinations of the two) and the influence of multiscalar factors (e.g., investment flows, climate change) on the evolution of cities.

In taking a sociotechnical-systemic view we avoid the kinds of abstract, essentializing, overly functionalist, static, and/or teleological perspectives found in some (sociotechnical) urban systems scholarship. Such works draw on complexity theory, ergonomics, central-place theory, diffusion of innovations, and/ or management science in order to understand how cities should be planned, managed, interconnected, and optimally "coded" through modeling approaches

The Urban Question in Africa: Uneven Geographies of Transition, First Edition. Pádraig R. Carmody, James T. Murphy, Richard Grant and Francis Y. Owusu.

that break down their functions into interactions between individual elements (e.g., actors, markets, service centers) within the city, and between cities/regions (Berry 1967; Van der Laan 1998; Bretagnolle et al. 2009; Patorniti et al. 2018; Bedinger et al. 2020). Instead, we go beyond the abstraction and methodological individualism that is built into these approaches, taking inspiration from heterodox and substantivist perspectives in urban-economic geography (e.g., Truffer and Coenen 2012; Peck 2017). Our view of an urban "system" – i.e., "an entity of interdependent elements and factors" (Van der Zwaan 1975: p. 149) – is thus dynamic, contingent, geographically situated, and historically shaped by the conjunctures of multiscalar forces, formations, and relationalities (Peck 2017; Hart 2018; Murphy and Carmody 2019; Werner 2019). This approach is particularly attentive to the role that place-specificity, transnational flows and connectivities, and multiscalar forces play in shaping urban-regional development trajectories. As such, it is epistemologically "open" in the sense that cities in Africa are not essentialized in relation to a developmentalist teleology (e.g., see World Bank 2009) that views urbanization as progressing along a universal pathway, but taken on their own terms as contested, contingent, and shaped by context-specific features such as histories, cultures, institutions, and transnational relations.

Beyond concerns about place-specificity, we are also keen to generalize about, and compare, cities and urban systems across cases. To do so, we adopt a critical realist perspective that recognizes that there are immanent/structural forces common to all cities, but which are variegated in place in response to the contestations, contingencies, and context-specific features noted above (see Lawson 1997, 2003).[1] The goal here is to identify those variegations which are more/less conducive to progressive (broadly developmental) forms of urbanization, determine how/why these emerge or are prevented from emerging, and subsequently conduct a meta-analysis that identifies general patterns, processes, and possibilities associated with urban transitions in Africa today.

Having a more open yet comparable perspective on urban systems and their evolution is especially important when studying cities in postcolonial regions like Africa. This is because northern perspectives on urban development processes and the fundamentals regarding what makes cities work (or not), have dominated or "colonized" mainstream views of what to look for and see when examining urban questions in the Global South; largely erasing the role of history and geographical difference. Decades of postcolonial scholarship have shown how Southern cities are not simply situated at stages of Rostovian, modernist development trajectories but are vibrant, complex, and often hopeful sites for innovation, experimentation, and novelty with respect to socioeconomic development (e.g., Bishop et al. 2003; Simone 2004; McFarlane 2010; Roy and Ong 2011; Schindler 2017; Myers 2020). Furthermore, scholars are reevaluating urbanism because it is changing so quickly itself (Myers 2020).

Importantly, the postcolonial turn in urban-economic geography is also a comparative project that seeks to explicate the heterogeneity, diversity, and contingent features of cities and urban development processes globally (Robinson 2004, 2016; Peck 2015). One objective of comparative urban research is to substantiate and compare the precarious, unexpected ways in which neoliberalism – often characterized as a universalizing and monolithic phenomenon – translates into, articulates with, and/or is produced within particular places (Hart 2002: Peck 2017). In doing so, postcolonial geographers strive to identify spaces of possibility and strategies for resistance, while documenting the pernicious, adaptive, and expansionist tendencies of globalizing neoliberal capitalism.

The comparative urbanisms project is not without its limitations, particularly in relation to the conjunctural approach advocated by some (Peck 2017; Hart 2018; Werner 2019). Following Robinson (2011: p. 5), conjunctural analysis can be described as an "encompassing" method in that "common systemic processes" (e.g., neoliberalism) are *a priori* presumed to be dominant in shaping development outcomes, but in differentiated ways across cases. What this means is that

> differently placed cities illuminate the wider system and processes, but comparison across these different experiences has been limited and, in fact, discouraged by the *a priori* assumption of systemic differentiation (Robinson 2011: p. 7).

In other words, the focus is on "common" processes, not the contingent differentiations between cities and their development. Although it is possible to zoom in, conjuncturally, to the details or "inner movements" of historical periods and urban-regional development dynamics (Rosenberg 2005), the explanatory emphasis remains on the higher-order mechanisms of capitalism. As such, while conjunctural analysis can tell us much about variegations of neoliberalism in particular places/regions, it remains pitched at a rather abstract conceptual level – that of the capitalist system. It thus fails to tell us much in generalizable and comparable terms about urban processes and their relationships to uneven development outcomes. The challenge is thus to find a middle ground or meso-level approach; one that can account for the immanent forces of capitalism while unpacking, analyzing, and comparing urban processes and functions in and between places.

In response to such concerns, we develop and apply a mid-level conceptual framework that can facilitate more grounded and durable comparisons of African cities and their evolution. We face a circumstance where we have a relatively small number of empirical cases (i.e., select African cities), and many variables (e.g., related to production, consumption, and infrastructure). In response, we develop and deploy a conceptual framework that refines our focus to reveal generalized processes, structures, and outcomes.[2] Drawing on sociotechnical and sustainability transitions frameworks (Geels 2002, 2004; Hodson and Marvin 2010; Frantzeskaki et al. 2017), and recent intersections between the field and urban-economic geography (Truffer and Coenen 2012; Murphy 2015, 2022; Schwanen 2018; Murphy and Carmody 2019; Grant et al. 2020), we conceptualize cities as sociotechnical systems constituted by three overlapping sociotechnical regimes that govern and guide their evolution – those of production, consumption, and infrastructure. Our approach focuses on to the ways in which these regimes and their couplings vary, thereby shaping outcomes. Given that the fieldwork for this book is drawn from a variety of cases over the course of approximately a decade we deploy this framework flexibly and do not engage in systematic cross-city comparison, which is perhaps work for another book project. Rather in this book we seek to illuminate the ways in which this framework enhances our understandings of the nature, functioning, and developmental outcomes of the cities under consideration.

As we discuss below, regimes are stabilized but often fragmented configurations of actors, institutions, practices, and technologies that govern and guide urbanization pathways and the development outcomes that accompany these. They are coupled to, interdependent on, one another and shaped significantly by multiscalar forces and trans-urban relations (e.g., to climate, global finance, FDI) that help to produce cities. All told, viewing cities as systems governed by sociotechnical regimes and their interrelationships provides a means to bound off cities as analytical objects, but in a manner that retains an openness to contingent, unexpected, and place-specific variegations in urban processes and development trajectories, and an awareness of their relational production. This approach is thus not intended to be "strong theory" per se, but rather an epistemological strategy that can enable a meta-analysis of urbanization dynamics, outcomes, and pathways.

This chapter's primary purpose is to work through this conceptual approach; one that is empirically illustrated and applied in the remainder of the book. Before doing so, we first clarify what we view as the urban (question) and offer a condensed review of urban-economic geography conceptualizations of cities and the drivers of their development. We focus particularly on the limits of these approaches as a means to better understand urbanization dynamics in Africa today. We then make the case for, and elaborate our approach, highlighting how it can explicate the underlying urban processes and relations that determine whether urbanization pathways are generative of progressive, distributive development outcomes; or whether cities are growing in a parasitic manner that heightens inequality and channels the material gains of urbanization offshore and/or to a narrow group of domestic elites.

The Urban (Question) in Africa: A Review of the Literature

Before we elaborate on our conceptual approach, it is essential that we explicate what is meant by the "urban" and what urban questions are central to this book. Urban studies and geography have a long history of defining, examining, and debating what constitutes the urban, how and why cities came to be, their form and function, and what urbanization "does" for socioeconomic development. With respect to Africa, understandings of cities and their development has traditionally been framed in relation to the experiences of Europe and the United States of America (USA). However, recent work has challenged westernized concepts and theories, calling for uniquely Southern, comparative approaches that recognize the diversity of urban forms and functions; which can serve as the basis for alternative concepts and theories. Indeed, in the scholarly terrain, "Southern cities in general and African cities in particular are beginning to gain more traction" (Guma and Monstadt 2021: p. 360). Here we review the scholarship on cities and urban development from urban-economic geography and African studies.

Economic Geographies of Urban Development

Early perspectives viewed the emergence of cities as a natural, logical means to organize economic space and efficiently distribute goods and services through a hierarchy of central places (Christaller 1966 [1933]). Within cities and regions, land markets would similarly and productively distribute services, industries, and residential areas through rent differentials radiating out from a central business district (CBD) or urban core (Alonso 1960; Von Thünen, 1966 [1826]). Alongside these demand-driven or consumption-oriented explanations, other theories focused on the productive capacities of cities, highlighting the importance of agglomeration as a means to create positive externalities or spillovers (e.g., Marshallian, Jacobian) through urbanization and localization economies (Lösch 1954 [1940]; Jacobs 1969; Scott and Storper 2003; Duranton and Puga 2004; Van der Panne 2004; Turok and McGranahan 2013). Successful agglomeration is not viewed as a purely "natural" process driven by population growth, but one that requires the right institutions, planning strategies, and infrastructures able to reduce congestion, ameliorate market failures, and improve the city's connectivity transnationally and domestically (Davis and Henderson 2003; Turok 2013; AfDB et al. 2016; UN-Habitat 2016). Agglomerations in cities are thus seen as growth poles able to generate competitive advantages for industries and drive national development processes, albeit in an uneven manner (World Bank 2009; Duranton 2015). Viewed from this perspective, the urban-economic challenge in Africa is thus how to develop ways and means to more effectively manage and guide the forces of agglomeration to support industrial growth and the dynamic of cumulative causation in city-regions (Venables 2009; 2018; World Bank 2009).

The agglomeration perspective on cities and their development remains dominant in much of economic geography with recent work examining the mechanisms through which city-regions realize positive externalities. These nuanced views on the evolution of the assets, relationalities, and couplings needed to successfully "globalize" regional development highlight the depth of the challenges facing African cities even in contexts where agglomeration economies and industrial clusters exist. Urban development thus needs to be understood in multiscalar terms, as a process that is contingent on the scope, scale, and quality of external relations, not simply an internally driven process of kick-starting cumulative causation. Establishing and sustaining the right kinds of linkages remains a central development challenge facing African economies today.

Beyond these established ideas, economic geographers have specified key processes, resources, and relationalities that make city-regions more or less successful. At the intra-urban or regional scale, places can develop innovative, globally competitive industries through the emergence, maintenance, and augmentation of critical, embedded assets and relations able to support learning and knowledge accumulation. Such assets include: relational infrastructures (Storper et al. 2015); "thick" layers of complementary and interrelated institutions in support of industries (Amin and Thrift 1994); "untraded interdependencies" (conventions, rules, practices) that enable firms to acquire, integrate, and produce new forms of knowledge (Storper 1995); industrial environments that are "buzzing" with ideas (Bathelt et al. 2004); functional entrepreneurial ecosystems (Iacob et al. 2019); and complementary competencies (i.e., related and unrelated variety) shared between different sectors in the same region (Frenken et al. 2007; Boschma and Iammarino 2009).

At the inter-urban or transnational scale, geographers have also highlighted the importance of positionality in relation to, and/or couplings with, lead firms, cities, regions, and centers of innovation in the global economy. Such relationalities are manifest in world-city networks (Taylor 2005; Acuto and Leffel 2021), global production networks (GPN) and value chains (Coe et al. 2004; Breul and Diez 2018), and the "pipelines" of knowledge and information flow that connect a region's firms to new/novel ideas (Bathelt et al. 2004; Bucholz and Bathelt, 2021).

While economic geographers have made significant advancements to our understandings of what constitutes cities and makes urbanization more or less developmental, challenges persist. For our purposes, a major concern is the need to think about urban development in a much broader manner, as a process whereby residents fundamentally seek to improve their quality of life and experience social mobility for themselves and their families. Successful, progressive forms of urbanization are not simply about the growth and competitiveness of industries but about livelihoods and the material conditions that residents experience in their lifeworlds; a consideration that is often ignored except as it relates to attracting particular types of workers to productive sectors (e.g., creatives). Urban geographers attend more readily to livelihood and quality of life concerns (e.g., see Brenner et al. 2009) but such works often have the opposite problem, an underappreciation or poor accounting for the economic, as it were. Needed are frameworks that bridge these concerns and develop richer accounts of the development dynamics and outcomes accompanying urban transitions. One way to consider development in a broader sense is to bring (back?) questions about consumption into our frameworks – that is how urbanization changes the consumption possibilities available to all urban residents, especially food, housing, wage goods, basic services, and savings possibilities.

Radical, Planetary, Comparative and Postcolonial Urbanisms

Other debates and dialogues cover a wide, diverse, and often complementary range of emerging concepts and epistemologies including: planetary or extended urbanization (Brenner and Schmid 2015), assemblage urbanism (McFarlane 2011), postcolonial and decolonial urban theory (Lawhon and Truelove 2020), "late" urbanization (Fox and Goodfellow 2022), and conjunctural urbanisms (Peck 2017). A concern of several of these projects is how to frame and conduct robust comparative analyses that will advance urban theory in ways that move it beyond what Robinson (2013: p. 659) terms "the inheritance of modernity"; that is, in part, that only the most "modern" cities "count" for advancing theories. Instead, it is more useful to consider that we live in a world of diverse, complex cities whose study can reveal contingent variegations and differentiations that transcend developmentalist teleologies (Robinson 2016).

Radical scholars have problematized the urban and urbanization processes as core features of modern capitalism. Here the urban is a social and material formation that enables capitalists to concentrate wealth and political power spatially and exert control over national space (Harvey 1973; Castells 1977). City-regions scale up the (industrial) means of production, accelerate "surplus value" accumulation, and concentrate more easily exploitable pools of labor (through industrial reserve armies) as workers migrate to cities in search of wages (Peet 1975). Central to these dynamics is economic growth driven by the exchange value of what is produced in cities; determined in large part by a city's ability to attract capital from the outside through glocalization and other strategies (e.g., growth coalitions) that make them attractive to speculative and other investments (Molotch 1976; Molotch and Logan 1985; Harvey 1989; Smith 2002; Swyngedouw 2004). In contrast to use value – such as the amenities and quality of life available locally to residents – exchange value has become the *de facto*, central logic through which cities operate under (neoliberal) capitalism, although elites can use their political power to maintain or enhance their local use values through engagements with municipal and national governments.

As has been highlighted for decades, the capital flows associated with exchange value are often distributed in highly uneven ways given they are largely controlled by private sector actors in conjunction with political elites, thus limiting their impact on the city's use values and socioeconomic concerns such as poverty, inequality, and immiseration. The net effect is the "splintering" or fragmenting of many cities into hyper-globalized enclaves of accumulation and wealth, and disconnected, and/or adversely incorporated ("excluded") spaces marked by poverty and low-quality collective goods and services (Graham and Marvin 2001; Swilling 2011). Such circumstances compound previous patterns of structural inequality (e.g., under colonialism in Africa) and have historically resulted in the creation of what have been called "parasitic" cities (Hoselitz 1955). Such cities engaged in unequal trade with their hinterlands (i.e., urban bias) and/or served as entrepôt for foreign manufactured imports – generally of consumption goods, resulting in a transfer of surplus overseas and the stagnation of manufacturing activities locally: the net result being intensely uneven development within these cities. Splintering effects and parasitic tendencies are highly visible throughout Africa and the Global South today, manifest in the stark contrasts between the living conditions faced by populations living in informal settlements or slums, and those able to afford luxury housing, gated communities, and high-quality infrastructure (Jaglin 2008; Silver 2015; Dias 2021).

Beyond political-economic, structural views on contemporary urbanization processes, some scholars have posited that we are in an age of "planetary urbanization" as the world's population becomes increasingly urban-based. In this context, longstanding categories such as the city, rural, and urban have become increasingly irrelevant or "obsolete" in relation to their explanatory power regarding development processes and outcomes (Brenner and Schmid, 2012).[3] This is due to the expansion and dispersal of urban processes and inter-urban relations at a global scale, with virtually no locations or places remaining untouched by them. As Brenner and Schmid (2012: p. 12, italics in original) note:

> This situation of *planetary urbanisation* means, paradoxically, that even spaces that lie well beyond the traditional city cores and suburban peripheries – from transoceanic shipping lanes, transcontinental highway and railway networks, and worldwide communications infrastructures to alpine and coastal tourist enclaves, "nature" parks, offshore financial centres, agro-industrial catchment zones and erstwhile "natural" spaces such as the world's oceans, deserts, jungles, mountain ranges, tundra, and atmosphere – have become integral parts of the worldwide urban fabric. While the process of agglomeration remains essential to the production of this new worldwide topography, political-economic spaces can no longer be treated as if they were composed of discrete, distinct, and universal "types" of settlement.

A central point of this thesis is that there is a need for new concepts, methodologies, and empirical foci in urban studies if scholars are to accurately capture and understand the drivers of uneven development globally (Brenner 2018; Schmid 2018). This is an ambitious agenda and one that has been critiqued from several perspectives (e.g., Storper and Scott 2016; Ruddick et al. 2018). In Africa, planetary perspectives have been by-and-large limited in application, with a few cases that examine the links between cities and extractive, rural economic sectors (e.g., Lesutis 2021), and those which deploy African cases (and postcolonial thinking) to challenge the universalizing tendencies of planetary urbanization (e.g., Myers 2018).

Urban theory has also taken on poststructural inspirations, particularly from the assemblage theories of Deleuze and Guattari (1988) and DeLanda (2006). In this view, cities are viewed as sociomaterial configurations of relations, histories, actors, and associations that contingently stabilize them in ways that generate path dependencies and entrench inequalities (McFarlane 2011a; 2011b). Rather than *a priori* essentializing which of these features is more or less significant, assemblage as method calls for thick, ethnographically inspired descriptions and "tracings" of urban sites and situations in order to reveal the ways and means in which cities, and the development outcomes they shape, are held together (McFarlane 2011b; Baker and McGuirk 2017; Boy and Uitermark 2017). By doing so, it is possible to understand the contingent, oft fragile nature of seemingly omnipotent urban processes (e.g., that plural interests are united around economic growth) and to identify new/novel points of political engagement able to challenge or transform such fixities and path dependencies. Unlike planetary views, assemblage thinking has been taken up by Africanist scholars in significant ways given its capacity for inclusion and to account for a greater diversity of actors, processes, and relations shaping urban development processes today (Splinter and Van Leynseele 2019; Korah 2020; van Greunen 2021). As Robinson (2022, p. 4) notes "the urban can be thought of as composed of a multiplicity of **differentiated** (repeated) outcomes" (original emphasis). The urban is thus both "universal" and particular or as Schmid (2015 cited in Robinson 2022), following Hegel, would have it "individual." Nonetheless cities in the Global South may share some tendencies and characteristics (Schindler 2017).

Finally, postcolonial and decolonial scholars have engaged significantly with urban theory – advancing uniquely Southern perspectives on cities while questioning the utility, applicability, and potentiality of western theory for the Global South (Bishop et al. 2003; Robinson 2004, 2022; Parnell and Robinson 2012; Roy 2016; Schindler 2017; Goodfellow 2022). Beyond critiquing the urban theory "canon," postcolonial urbanists further argue for a comparative project, one able to account for, describe, and substantively interrogate diverse variegations of cities globally as a means to decenter and dismantle taken-for-granted, western "truths" about urbanization pathways (Myers 2011, 2014; Robinson 2011, 2016; Lawhon and Truelove 2020). Moreover, some contend that studies of African and other "Southern" cities can serve as sites for theorizing back to the core/ west regarding the nature of the urban and how cities evolve and develop in the contemporary world system (Myers 2011, 2018; Lawhon and Truelove 2020). All told, comparative research can facilitate a sharing of experiences in order to understand generalized trends, contingent differentiations, and context-specific factors that make cities more or less generative.

Urban Studies and Theory in/for Africa

Specific to Africa, there are three significant focal areas where the region's cities are seen as exceptional places and objects of (comparative) analyses; contexts that demand particular solutions to the urban question and from where urban theories can be advanced to challenge the urban studies "canon." Our focus here is by no means exhaustive but is instead concerned principally with works that seek to address imminent and immanent development challenges in African cities today.

The first are perspectives that view African cities as places in need of new (non-Western) policies and planning strategies to understand and more effectively manage the processes and multiscalar relations shaping them. Emblematic of this work is Parnell and Pieterse's (2014) volume *Africa's Urban Revolution* which took stock of the urbanization trends in Africa and addressed a wide array of issues and policy options (e.g., infrastructure, education, food security, culture). The net result was an in-depth empirical assessment of conditions on the ground coupled to an array of policy and planning ideas to help address the development challenges African cities face. This kind of work typifies much of the Africa-specific urban literature – research and analyses that offer context-sensitive assessments of cities in the region that are focused on particular challenges such as housing (e.g., Migozzi 2020), informality (e.g., Azunre et al. 2022), sustainability (e.g., Smit and Musango 2015), congestion (e.g., Rajé et al. 2018), hazards (e.g., Amoako and Inkoom 2018), infrastructure (e.g., Silver 2015), industrial development (e.g., Adunbi 2022), and urban governance (e.g., Goodfellow 2018), among others. An extensive array of works of this type are drawn on throughout this book in relation to the meta-trends and urban conditions we document and analyze.

As second area of interventions is focused on more conceptual and theoretical concerns, namely how "ordinary" African cities challenge the Western theoretical canon and highlight the need for alternative urban theories and planning strategies (Myers 2011). This work has, in part, deepened the comparative urbanism project in Africa as exemplified through the work of Myers (2014), Goodfellow (2022), and Robinson (2022), among others. Informality and the "informal city" are common sites of interrogation, seen not as temporary or illegitimate, but as hopeful arenas through which livelihoods are realized and many urbanites claim rights to the city (e.g., land, housing) through diverse governance arrangements, networks, and negotiations with the state and other actors (Hansen and Vaa 2004; Simone 2004, 2022; Lindell 2009; Myers 2011; Lindell et al. 2019). Formalization in the Western sense is thus not seen as the inevitable, necessary pathway for urban transitions but as a potentially pernicious form of assimilation that will disempower and further marginalize the agencies of lower-income urbanites (Kamete 2018). Informality needs to instead be reconsidered and legitimated as a vital means for urbanites to achieve and practice their "citizenship," as a human rights and social justice concern, and as a potential pathway for bottom-up industrialization (Brown et al. 2010; Myers 2011; Kraemer-Mbula and Monaco 2020; Lemanski 2020). As Myers (2011: p. 194) notes, this is not to suggest that informality be "blindly championed" but to call for concepts and theories that can better capture and assess the relationalities at work (e.g., formal-informal, social networks) in producing urban space in Africa. A key goal here is to enable the poor and majority populations to have a real say in the decision-making processes that shape their welfare, livelihoods, and prospects for social mobility.

A third, and related, area of African-centered research are postcolonial calls for a "worlding" of cities in the Global South (Simone 2001; Roy and Ong 2011;

McCann et al. 2013). In simple terms, as Burns et al. (2021) note, "'worlding' denotes the ways that cities assert their local economy and culture as positioned within global flows of capital, people, and information." Such assertions are, in one sense, manifest in the "mass dreams" of urbanites in Southern cities through which worldviews are produced by the subaltern (McCann et al. 2013). As Simone (2001: p. 23) notes, worlding is a "constantly unstable and precarious practice" but one that can produce opportunities and generate transnational relations and new forms of urban experimentation and governance that "operate outside increasingly outmoded laws and regulatory systems." The "worldliness" of African cities – these dreams, experiments, multiscalar relations, and opportunities – emerges out of the particular historical, political, social, economic, and cultural entanglements that Northern urban theory simply fails to capture (Mbembé and Nuttall 2004). This failure is crucial in that it produces only partial views of urban processes and possibilities in Africa; ideas built on "paper-thin" assumptions that lead to policy prescriptions doomed to fail at the outset (Pieterse 2010: p. 206). Needed instead are in-depth, grounded, and context-sensitive explorations of African cities "cityness" or "worldliness" on their own terms rather than as they relate to essentialisms emanating from the Western canon (Pieterse 2010). In doing so, the "worlding" project strives to (re)theorize African and Southern cities in order to develop, per McCann et al. (2013: p. 585):

> new understandings of the political processes, those that exceed and elude the standard formats of social mobilization or subaltern resistance and instead are complex compositions – or assemblages – of collusions and subversions in the interstices of global urbanism.

Such knowledge can help to identify novel, place-based pathways for changes in urban governance and the role that translocal, transurban, and transnational relations play in shaping the contestations over, and possibilities for African cities.

Conceptualizing the Urban Question in Africa

Our approach to the urban question in Africa is inspired by, and situated in relation to, these perspectives. We recognize that African cities are central places for consumption and production, where agglomeration economies play a key role in shaping their development. We understand the importance of situating urban-regional processes at the conjunctures of substantive historical, political-economic, social, and global forces that structure and guide the evolution of cities through institutions, power relations, interdependencies, and exchange relations. We acknowledge the planetary nature of urbanization in Africa today, recognizing that that the development of cities is entangled with seemingly non-urban, multiscalar processes (e.g., extractive industries, climate change, rural livelihoods) that shape the flows of capital and people into cities; calling into question the utility of long-standing concepts and theories to explicate the drivers and rationales of urbanization pathways. We view African cities as constituted sociomaterially, assemblages of heterogeneous actors, artifacts, structures, practices, histories, meanings, and identities that produce variegations of cities and the urban across the region. Finally, we take heed of postcolonial calls for urban theory that are based on the lived, historical experience of African cities; their "citynesses" as it were.

Ontologically, this may seem like an impossible row to hoe – integrating this wide range of oft-conflicting perspectives on the urban and urban questions. This is not our objective, however, as we seek instead to advance an epistemological approach for examining and comparing cities in a manner that advances understandings of the general mechanisms, relationships, materials, and structural features that shape urbanization pathways and their development implications in Africa today. As such, we are not able to provide a singular answer to the question of what constitutes the urban or what cities are by their nature, but to instead identify, explicate, and compare the key (multiscalar) drivers of their development with an eye to assessing whether, why (not), and where there are generative or parasitic urban transitions playing out in Africa today.

We do so through a mid-level conceptual approach that elucidates and operationalizes the systemic, everyday features of all cities in order to enable a comparative, meta-analysis of urbanization pathways in Africa. This approach comes with tradeoffs, particularly with respect to some of the detail related to our empirical discussions of individual cities and urban-regional contexts. Ultimately, however, we compromise some detail so as to strengthen the generalizability and explanatory power of our meta-analyses of urban questions in Africa today. Our distinctive contribution is to bring together insights from science technology and society (STS) studies and economic geography with a critical awareness derived from postcolonial and poststructuralist approaches to the importance of history, context, difference, and relationality. The differences and different experiences of African cities are a result of the concatenation of "global forces," such as colonialism, experienced in much the same way across the continent, and distinctive local and national politics and political settlements and policy regimes (Goodfellow 2022). These contextual politics and assemblages result in different types of urban regimes at a city scale and among those of production, infrastructure, and consumption. However, recursively the regimes we identify also have and develop their own dynamics and interactions, in turn influencing politics, policy, and implementation.

(African) Cities as Sociotechnical Systems

Our conceptualization of cities and their evolution is informed by the literatures above and the extension of these ideas into the realm of sociotechnical systems studies. Sociotechnical systems research has long been concerned with the evolution of sector-specific systems that produce and distribute essential goods and services such as energy, water, transportation, and sanitation, particularly in city-regions (Hughes 1987; Coutard, 2002; Geels 2002, 2004, 2005). These systems are constituted not solely by artifacts or technologies but also include diverse actors (e.g., consumers, engineers), organizations (e.g., utilities, firms), institutions (e.g., rules, regulations), and imaginaries or logics (e.g., efficiency, optimality) that determine their operation and evolution. Beyond unpacking and examining these constitutive features, a key concern is sociotechnical transitions – the ways and means through which these systems evolve and change, and whether or not such transitions are more sustainable, just, and distributive (Geels 2002; Geels and Schot 2007; Hodson and Marvin 2010; Coenen et al. 2012; Markard et al. 2012; Truffer and Coenen 2012; Murphy 2015; Köhler et al. 2019). Economic geographers have drawn on and contributed significantly to this literature given its relevance for analyzing industrial and regional development pathways (Coenen et al. 2012; Truffer and Coenen 2012; Murphy 2015; Boschma et al. 2017; Steen and Hansen 2018; MacKinnon et al. 2019; Binz et al. 2020). In Africa, the approach has been applied to studies of sectoral transitions in cities including studies of sanitation systems in Nairobi (van Welie et al. 2018; Van Welie et al. 2019), green industry initiatives in Ethiopia (Okereke et al. 2019), energy transitions in Ghana, Kenya, South Africa, and Uganda (Boamah and Rothfuß 2018; Ambole et al. 2019), and development pathways in Dar es Salaam and Nairobi (Murphy and Carmody 2019; Murphy 2022).

Conceptually and in application, sociotechnical transitions research has focused on four overlapping areas of inquiry: strategic niche management (SNM), transition management (TM), technological innovation systems (TIS), and the multilevel perspective (MLP). SNM and TM are more applied, policy-oriented, approaches that examine how policy, planning, and technology management can facilitate the uptake and mainstreaming of new, more sustainable innovations and the subsequent transitions these can enable (Kemp et al. 1998, 2007; Loorbach 2007; Schot and Geels 2008; Ruggiero et al. 2018). TIS, in contrast, takes a more supply-side approach to sociotechnical transitions, focusing particularly on industry/sector-specific innovation development processes and the mechanisms through which new, more sustainable technologies diffuse globally (Bergek et al. 2008; Walrave and Raven 2016; Markard 2020).

Lastly, and arguably most significantly in terms of uptake, the MLP entails a multitiered view of sociotechnical systems and their evolution, focusing particularly on the interactions between sector-specific regimes, societies (landscapes), and niche innovations (Geels 2002, 2005; Genus and Coles 2008; Sorrell 2018). Sociotechnical regimes are at the center of this approach – stabilized, but dynamic, configurations of actors, artifacts, rules, norms, meanings, and beliefs that govern and guide the evolution of sectoral systems (Geels 2004; Markard et al. 2012; Sorrell 2018). Sociotechnical transitions occur when regimes are reconfigured in response to societal (landscape) changes, the uptake of niche innovations, and/or through intra-regime dynamics that reconfigure their core features.

We extend these frameworks and applied works to examine the evolution of cities more generally, moving beyond the focus on singular services or sectors. Specifically, we expand the concept of a sociotechnical regime to account for the core features and functions of urban (sociotechnical) systems, namely their role in production, consumption, and the provisioning of vital infrastructures. As Figure 1.1 shows, we view cities as sociotechnical systems constituted by overlapping, interdependent regimes associated with production, consumption, and infrastructure. Production regimes are configurations of firms, workers, factories, technologies, and urban areas that produce goods and services for local and nonlocal distribution/sale, thus playing a central role in determining exchange values in the city. These regimes include both formal and informal enterprises, with the latter playing a particularly significant role in most African cities. Consumption regimes are closely entwined with production regimes and manifest in urban marketplaces, shops, consumers, retail/wholesale firms, distributors, and other actors/artifacts that enable residents to meet their needs. These regimes also include the consumption of collective goods and services associated with public welfare (e.g., education, healthcare), urban amenities (e.g., parks), and householding functions (e.g., electricity, water, sanitation, and housing).

Integral to both production and consumption regimes are infrastructure regimes – a conceptualization most clearly aligned with sociotechnical transitions research, but one we expand to account for multiple sectors (e.g., water, transport, energy) at the same time. Infrastructure regimes produce, distribute, regulate, and control essential goods and services for producers and consumers, manifest as configurations of utilities, agencies, technologies, markets,

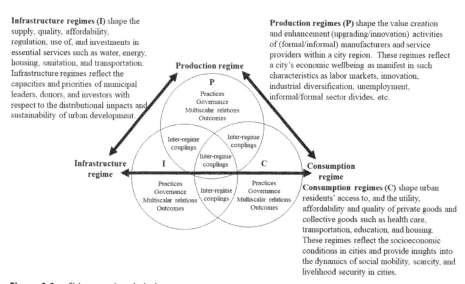

Infrastructure regimes (I) shape the supply, quality, affordability, regulation, use of, and investments in essential services such as water, energy, housing, sanitation, and transportation. Infrastructure regimes reflect the capacities and priorities of municipal leaders, donors, and investors with respect to the distributional impacts and sustainability of urban development.

Production regimes (P) shape the value creation and enhancement (upgrading/innovation) activities of (formal/informal) manufacturers and service providers within a city region. These regimes reflect a city's economic wellbeing as manifest in such characteristics as labor markets, innovation, industrial diversification, unemployment, informal/formal sector divides, etc.

Consumption regimes (C) shape urban residents' access to, and the utility, affordability and quality of private goods and collective goods such as health care, transportation, education, and housing. These regimes reflect the socioeconomic conditions in cities and provide insights into the dynamics of social mobility, scarcity, and livelihood security in cities.

Figure 1.1   Cities as sociotechnical systems.
Source: From Murphy and Carmody, 2019.

buildings, plans, and other elements that shape their evolution. Because infrastructure provisioning reflects the priorities of economic and political elites, these regimes will often be highly fragmented or splintered in African cities as many residents face shortages, limited accessibility, and/or poor quality, informal services while others have access to "modern," high-quality, and formalized ones.

Each regime, and the urban sociotechnical system as a whole, is stabilized and its evolution guided by four core features – practices, governance, multiscalar relations, and inter-regime couplings. **Practices** are the taken-for-granted, everyday ways in/through which regimes function, constituted by actors, relations, rules, norms, expectations, meanings, behaviors, power relations, technologies, materials, spaces, scales, and temporal dimensions that are bundled together in sociotechnical regimes (Geels 2004; Schatzki 2005; Jones and Murphy 2011; Hui et al. 2017). An *in situ* analysis of core or central practices reveals insights into the other features of urban regimes and systems. **Governance** is manifest in the institutions, markets, rules, rationalities, hierarchies, subjectivities, networks, and governmentalities that incentivize, subsidize, sanction, and/or obstruct particular practices and structure regimes. **Multiscalar relations** are connections, flows, and ties that link regimes, and cities more generally, to national, regional, and global markets, transnational corporations, investors, diasporas, information, and technologies that shape and help to govern production, consumption, and infrastructure-related practices. Within cities, regimes are interrelated through **couplings** that create complementarities, constraints, relations, and/or interdependencies between them. Inter-regime couplings can be functional in nature, as when the output from the production regime is consumed in local markets, or they can be structural, manifest in circumstances where regimes share common actors, materials, institutions, infrastructures, and spaces (e.g., when a common electricity utility serves producers and consumers).

Epistemologically, we take a substantivist approach to the study of regimes and their constitutive features/evolution, entering into the study of sociotechnical systems from a number of perspectives, including production, consumption, and infrastructure. The framework is operationalized through grounded research that draws on the authors' primary data from Ghana, Kenya, South Africa, and Tanzania, and secondary sources from throughout SSA. All the authors have undertaken extensive research in these contexts, which are drawn from "subregions" across the continent; namely Western, Eastern, and Southern Africa, thereby ensuring diversity, if not representativeness. Specific methods varied and included in-depth interviews, surveys, and direct observations during multiple field visits. These primary data are supplemented and triangulated through extensive and intensive engagements with the relevant literatures, as demonstrated below in individual chapters and in the book's lengthy bibliography. Where and when relevant we discuss specific methods but the primary focus here is on detailing the main findings relating urban development in Africa to key meta-trends (e.g., the rise of China, new-build cities). These findings are by-and-large drawn from prior published works (see the acknowledgments) but integrated and compared here such that we go beyond the limitations of individual case studies.

Our varied research interests, sites, and periods of fieldwork have by necessity shaped the focus on the book and the topics examined therein, such as the impact of China or the nature and function of the gig economy, for example. However, research is a social and reflexive process, and we are confident that through our theme selection we have identified some of the most important urban developmental issues, and their diversity, on the continent today. We interrogate them through the lens of our sociotechnical systems framework which allows us a unique perspective through which to access the issues and their wider impacts. In doing so, we take stock of core or central practices that stabilize and guide regimes in African cities, and then "zoom out" from these to develop working, generalized, and empirically grounded narratives regarding contemporary urban processes and patterns (Nicolini 2009). In doing so we articulate and compare the immanent processes, relations, and flows that shape urbanization pathways, identify sources of lock-in or obduracy that create barriers to progressive change, and/or highlight factors or features that might facilitate regime transitions: a core concern being whether, where, and why generative or parasitic forms of urbanization are playing out in the continent today, focusing particularly on the wheres and why-theres of these dynamics as they relate to particular economic activities, transnational relations, socioeconomic issues, and environmental challenges.

Applying the Approach

The remainder of the book broadly deploys this approach to examine a number of pressing urban questions facing Africa today. Our focal topics demonstrate the diverse ways in which the conceptualization can be utilized as we examine cities from a number of vantage points that address different urban questions through a common lens. Rather than attempt to capture the entirety of urban sociotechnical systems through a singular analysis, we instead focus each chapter on one or two regimes and their relationships to one another. The book's conclusion (Chapter 10) then brings together these analyses to assess and explicate potential pathways along and through which generative urban systems might emerge to create and distribute sustainable development outcomes within African cities and countries. In terms of broad organization, Chapters 2–7 primarily address socioeconomic development and urban planning issues, while Chapters 8–9 take on environmental/health concerns as critical urban-economic questions.

In specific terms, we apply the sociotechnical systems framework as follows. Chapter 2 looks at production regimes through an analysis of urban-manufacturing industries, asking whether urbanization without (high-levels of) industrialization is Africa's fate and whether/how widespread industrial development and upgrading might occur. Chapter 3 examines the role that multiscalar/transnational relations are playing in urban development, focusing specifically on the role that China is playing in shaping production, consumption, and infrastructure regimes. Chapter 4 explores notions of "fantasy urbanism" as they are being promoted and enacted in Africa, asking whether it is possible to achieve generative forms of urbanization by planning and building sociotechnical systems from scratch, or whether this simply deepens fragmentations and inequalities. Chapter 5 interrogates the informal/formal economy question, examining whether and how the regimes associated with each "system" might be better integrated and legitimized such that urban livelihoods can be made more resilient, viable, and sustainable. Chapter 6 looks at Africa's emerging "gig" (platform) economy, one that has been facilitated by the rapid absorption of ICTs into production and consumption regimes, and whose constitution and functioning raises critical questions as to its impacts on livelihoods and urban economies. Chapter 7 examines infrastructure regimes, detailing the scope and scale of the challenges of providing basic services to rapidly growing urban populations, many of whom reside in informal settlements.

Our focus then shifts to more explicitly environmental/health considerations, both in terms of the impacts of these on the evolution of urban sociotechnical systems, and in terms of the prospects for green urban economies in the coming decades. Chapter 8 examines how urban sociotechnical transitions are driven in part by the environmental risks that drive rural-urban migrations, and how infrastructure regimes (in particular) in cities are being challenged by increased temperatures, floods, sea-level rise, and public health issues (e.g., COVID-19). Chapter 9 then takes a productivist view of the urban-environment nexus, examining the prospects for transformations of production regimes through the adoption of green logics, rules, practices, markets, subjects, and modes of governance.

Notes

1 In an ontological and epistemological sense, our approach is aligned with critical realist thinking, particularly the work of Tony Lawson (1997, 2003). For Lawson, and in simple terms, system "openness" means that our conceptual frameworks and analytic methods can provide opportunities for alternative, unexpected explanations and outcomes (contrasting demi-regularities) to emerge that can then be "retroductively" used to advance theories. Openness is thus in stark contrast to hypothetico-deductive modeling exercises that close off, contain systems (e.g., economies, city-regions) in ways that only allow for predetermined causalities.

2 As Robinson notes (2022: p. 63), "The fundamental methodological challenge of qualitative variation finding is, according to Lijphart (1971), the difficulty of having few cases and many variables."

3 The notion that the world is urban is not an entirely new premise but one that was first raised by Henri Lefebvre (2003 [1970]).

Chapter Two
Urbanization with Industrialization?
Manufacturing in African Cities

Introduction

Traditionally manufacturing has played a key role in the economic growth of developing countries. A virtuous circle between economic development and urbanization sketched in an extensive body of economics, development studies, and urban research (Rostow 1960; Venables 2010; Glaeser 2013; Gollen et al. 2016) has not materialized for the African region. As noted earlier, economic geographers have long linked industrial progress to the emergence of agglomerations, such as cities and clusters, which create scale and scope economies and serve as central places to drive national development processes (Christaller 1966 [1933]; Jacobs 1969; Scott and Storper 2003). According to this teleology, as countries develop, people move out of rural areas and agricultural activities into cities, where they engage in formal manufacturing and services. However Africa appears to be an exception, where "urbanization without industrialization," "premature industrialization," "underindustrialization," "late urbanization," and "premature deindustrialization" prevail as this dynamic has yet to be realized to a large extent (Gollin et al. 2016; Rodrik 2016; Fox and Goodfellow 2022; Lopes and Willem te Velde 2021).

The Urban Question in Africa: Uneven Geographies of Transition, First Edition. Pádraig R. Carmody, James T. Murphy, Richard Grant and Francis Y. Owusu.
© 2024 John Wiley & Sons Ltd. Published 2024 by John Wiley & Sons Ltd.

Tables 2.1 and 2.2 provide an overview of the structure of Sub-Saharan African economies, the significance of cities, and the region's trade profile between 2010 and 2019; pre-COVID-19 and during a phase of general economic growth on the continent (a la "Africa Rising"). Presently, Africa has the lowest manufacturing output per capita of any inhabited planetary region. The commodity boom of the first decade and half of the twenty-first century occluded the fragility of Africa's manufacturing sector, and the continent's heavy dependence on manufactured imports, accounting for 65% of

Table 2.1 Sub-Saharan Africa's economic structure and urban population profile (2010 and 2019).

	2010	*2019*
Agriculture, forestry, and fishing, value added (% of GDP)	15.9	16.5
Manufacturing, value added (% of GDP)	9.8	11.0
Services, value added (% of GDP)	50.9	50.2
Employment in agriculture (% of total employment)	58.2	52.9
Employment in industry (% of total employment)	9.8	10.7
Employment in services (% of total employment)	32.0	36.4
Urban population (% of total population)	36.0	40.8
Urban population growth (annual %)	4.3	4.0

Source: Adapted from World Bank, 2023.

Table 2.2 Sub-Saharan Africa trade profile (2010 and 2019).

	2010	*2019*
Exports of goods and services (% of GDP)	29.5	22.8
Agricultural raw materials exports (% of merchandise exports)	2.9	2.7
Food exports (% of merchandise exports)	13.7	13.5
Fuel exports (% of merchandise exports)	38.0	37.9
Ores and metals exports (% of merchandise exports)	14.6	15.1
Manufactures exports (% of merchandise exports)	28.9	24.0
Imports of goods and services (% of GDP)	28.7	26.3
Manufactures imports (% of merchandise imports)	67.7	65.0

Source: Adapted from World Bank, 2023.

merchandise imports in 2019. Economic output, in terms of value added, is principally accounted for by the service sector which includes informal commercial enterprises in cities in addition to formal sector and government jobs. Primary sector work still accounts for over 50% of employment based on ILO estimates with agriculture, forestry, and fishing outpacing manufacturing in terms of their value added.

Exports, as a percent of GDP, declined between 2010 and 2019 with the dominance of extractive industries in Africa's merchandise export profile clearly apparent. In 2019, agricultural raw materials, food, fuel, and mineral/metal exports combined accounted for 69% of all merchandise exports, with manufactures making up only 24%, down from 29% in 2010. While there is modest evidence of splinters of manufacturing diversification in higher technology automotive and chemical exports, and limited upgrading in agro-processing global value chains (GVCs) in some sectors (e.g., horticulture in Kenya; coffee in Rwanda), manufacturing growth has not been on a pace with urbanization (Qiang et al. 2021). In fact, manufacturing value-added on the continent has been in decline or stagnant since the 1980s; down from 25% of GDP in 1981 to 11% in 2019 (World Bank 2022). In contrast, manufactured imports constitute nearly two-thirds of merchandise imports in terms of their value. The net result is a significant expansion of employment in the service (esp. commercial) sector from 2010 to 2019 (up over 4% to 36% of total) whilst industrial job creation remained stable/stagnant (less than 1% growth); making up only about 11% of total employment in 2019.

Urbanization rates remain high, at 4% per annum growth in 2019, however, despite the fact that industrialization and the concomitant creation of manufacturing jobs has not materialized in cities to the extent needed. The basis of the region's economic development context, particularly production regimes in cities, has thus led to a questioning about whether Africa's urbanization is "abnormal" (Obeng-Odoom 2010), and whether the continent's cities can move beyond historical legacies, inadequate manufacturing experimentation and development, and transition toward more sustainable forms of industry. Such transitions depend largely on whether urban production regimes can be reconfigured, regoverned, and transformed into centers of innovation and widespread generators of employment in a diverse range of industrial sectors.

International policymakers and African governments recognize the fundamental need for industrialization (UNIDO 2020). Successive UN General Assembly resolutions have proclaimed the first, second, and recently, the third industrial development decade for Africa (2016–2025). The UN's sustainable development agenda has a specialized goal (Sustainable Development Goal [SDG] 9) that aims to build resilient infrastructure, promote sustainable industrialization, and foster innovation. The African Union's development plan, Agenda 2063, reiterates the importance of transformation, growth, and industrialization of African economies through value addition to natural resources (African Union 2015). UNECA's Economic Report for Africa (2017) calls for more attention to the urbanization-industrialization nexus, and to move beyond conceptualizing industrial and urban policy as separate domains. All told, Africa's current manufacturing base and profile raises key questions regarding its relationships to urbanization, including: a) how can urban production regimes serve as enablers for manufacturing in African cities?; and b) how might the manufacturing sector be incorporated into a sociotechnical transition such that industrial and technological upgrading takes place?

The chapter interrogates these questions as follows. The next section provides a thumbnail sketch of the role of manufacturing from colonial times to the present. Africa's history with industrialization has some similarities to the historical experiences of other world regions, but also important divergences. We then present some stylized empirical details that shape the contemporary geographies of, and possibilities for, manufacturing-driven production regimes in African cities. Next, we assess international developments such as the influence of China on Africa's urban-industrial development and the potential for the Fourth Industrial Revolution (4IR) to drive innovation and industrialization in the region. In the final section, we discuss needed changes to production regime governance, particularly through National Urban Policies (NUPs), and the prospects for interventions such as these to create the conditions for a sociotechnical transition in manufacturing.

Historicizing Africa's Manufacturing Path Dependencies

Africa has a long indigenous, artisanal manufacturing tradition; generally small in scale and scope, and largely informal. Prior to colonialism its two most important sectors were textiles and ironwork (Austin 2017). Successive colonial, early post-independence, and neoliberal policy environments have not resulted in the development and emergence of a broad-based African manufacturing sector. Indeed, each of these eras stymied Africa's manufacturing environment in distinct ways.

Spatial planning of the colonial era sought to confine manufacturing in proximity to the indigenous zone, away from European areas, and it remained small, while colonial economic geography pivoted around natural resources, cash crops, ports, railways, and warehouses (Grant and Nijman 2002). As domestic consumer demand increased, in time, for consumer, healthcare products and construction materials, it was generally not satisfied by domestic manufacturing producers but from trading companies linked to manufactures in Europe (Lopes 2019). Domestic manufacturers concentrated on brewing, confectionary, cotton, textiles, furniture, and footwear for small domestic markets. By-and-large at independence the manufacturing sector throughout Africa was meager, high cost, largely producing manufacturing outputs of low international quality, and locked-in to a narrow range of products (Riddell 1993). Its fragility was apparent in the weak interlinkages with other productive sectors of the economy, with the exceptions of agriculture and minerals processing.

After independence, efforts to facilitate a sociotechnical transition to (urban-based) domestic manufacturing saw many African governments implement import substitution industrial strategies (ISI). Such industrialization efforts typically led to the development of large-scale, often capital-intensive manufacturing industries owned and managed by the state i.e., state-owned enterprises (SOEs) with infant industry protections and investments in supporting infrastructures (transport and energy) aimed at achieving self-sufficiency in the production of domestic consumer and producer goods (e.g., electrical, electronic, and machinery), rather than export manufacturing (Kilby 1975). ISI strategies in the region, however, locked manufactures into modest domestic markets and a high degree of technological dependence on foreign know-how. This often meant that domestic factor endowments were grossly neglected and value-added remained low because products incorporated high import content (Lopes 2020). Making matters worse – in order to facilitate the import of required intermediate products for protected industries – governments overvalued currencies, creating protected enclaves of domestic, inefficient, and monopolistic industries (Lopes 2019).

Related to ISI strategies, the nationalization of industries was also common in the immediate post-independence period. Some African countries not only nationalized foreign multinationals but also indigenized properties of foreign merchants (e.g., Nigeria, Zaire, Ghana, Uganda, and Kenya) to distribute them to domestic firms (Lopes 2019: p. 87). The number and size of SOEs increased dramatically so that by the 1970s they accounted for 17% of African economies' GDP and one-quarter of formal employment (Lopes 2019: p. 88). Consequently, private capital retreated while medium, small, and informal firms engaged in light manufacturing in cities. By 1985 it was widely acknowledged that many SOEs were overstaffed, largely inefficient in allocating resources, generally lacking in technical skills, and highly dependent on loans from state-owned banks, with many operating at a loss (Lopes 2019). The concentration on consumer rather than intermediate or capital-intensive manufacturing had also generally faltered. Venables (2010) further adds that the fragmentation of urban structure and thin domestic markets adversely affected African manufacturing productivity and impeded the development of major international manufacturing centers of the type that contribute to the performance of high growth economies. All told, Africa's ISI experiments were stymied by state-led production rather than supported by it (Lopes 2019). Urban production regimes consequently became locked into manufacturing activities dominated by informal practices and modes of governance, and characterized by low levels of productivity with little or no export potential.

Despite the failures of ISI policies and SOEs, significant, albeit informal manufacturing hubs emerged in African cities (e.g., Nairobi [Kenya] in apparel and metalwork; Nnewi [Nigeria] in auto parts manufacturing, Dar es Salaam

[Tanzania] in garments, leather shoes, textiles, and garments in Addis Ababa [Ethiopia]) (Sonobe and Otsuka 2011). Emblematic of this was Suame Magazine (Kumasi, Ghana) which emerged in the 1970s and 80s and became a major vehicle and machinery parts hub serving a market that could no longer source imports as result of foreign exchange scarcity. Ghanaian entrepreneurs became adept and innovative at fabricating suitable spares, customizing and precision manufacturing for autos, food processing, agricultural equipment and inventing new equipment for light manufacturing (McCormick 1999; Adu-Gymfi and Adjei 2016). At its peak Suame Magazine hosted approximately 12,000 small businesses and 200,000 artisans (Adu-Gymfi and Adjei 2016: p. 3). To date, Africa's informal manufacturing centers like Suame are deeply embedded in, and central to, urban production regimes but typically remain overlooked in industrial policies.

The structural adjustment era from the mid-1980s ended national experiments in state-controlled industrialization (Riddell 1993) and ushered in experimentation with liberalization policies and FDI promotion. One of the purported aims of these policies was to kick-start the manufacturing sector with aspirations to replicate Asian experiences; such as the promotion of export processing zones (EPZs). Most EPZs developed by African governments, however, failed to take off (Mauritius as an early promoter was an exception), largely because of the relative lack of technological capabilities (Lall and Kraemer-Mbula 2005), supporting infrastructure, poor coordination with national/urban policy environments, high costs, and less productive African labor (Farole 2011).

Economic liberalization coincided with rapid urban population growth, but this did not correspond with formal employment growth able to absorb the growing labor force into manufacturing (Rodrik 2014). Indeed, the structural adjustment program (SAP) period was marked by intensified competition from imports (cheaper textiles and garments from Asia), rising production costs, lack of manufacturing technical expertise, higher interest rates and lack of working capital put considerable pressure on Africa's manufacturing firms. Since the mid-1990s the growth of manufacturing firms has fallen or remained flat in every country, except Uganda (Newman et al. 2016), deindustrialization is evident in several countries (e.g., Burundi, Chad, Malawi), and urban production regimes are increasingly marked by growing numbers of small-scale, informal enterprises, many of which eschew manufacturing for petty trade and other commercial/retail services (Clark 2019).

Africa's Present-day Manufacturing Horizon

Considerable structural challenges face manufacturing production regimes in African cities today, raising critical concerns about the sector's readiness. Our focus on manufacturing is justified by its generally urban location and its specific features, such as economies of scale, employment multiplier effects, backward and forward linkages and potential for innovation, including as a catalyst for the development of consumption and infrastructure regimes (Zhang 2015). Competitiveness International Performance (CIP) rankings provide a snapshot of the ability of African countries to produce manufactured goods competitively. In 2020 South Africa was the top ranked African country at 52nd globally, and only six African countries were ranked in the top 100 (see Table 2.3). Most recorded low performances, with 6 out of the bottom 10 countries from SSA. Path dependencies, industrial policy failures, lock-ins, and various infrastructure regime impediments (e.g., high trade costs associated with poor logistics infrastructure and cumbersome trade procedures) inhibit a manufacturing sociotechnical transition. Most countries of the region are marginal nodes in GVCs (exceptions are Mauritius, Nigeria, and South Africa), primarily based on the export of un- and semi-processed raw materials and intermediate goods. Production regimes in the region are currently locked into the production of resource-based manufactured goods and low-technology products. Such specializations are unlikely to create large-scale formal employment opportunities in cities, and are by-and-large unable to produce benefits such as domestic value-chain linkages, knowledge spillovers, and other externalities that might stimulate industrial upgrading. All of this has important implications for the development, growth, and sustainability of production regimes in African cities where most manufacturing is based.

Africa faces a macro environment with significant headwinds. Deglobalization in some industrial markets may impede the growth of Africa's share of manufacturing exports (Carmody 2020). Recent deglobalization impulses emanate from the tilt toward protectionism because of the rise of right-wing populism, disruptions from the COVID-19 pandemic, the ongoing war in Ukraine, and rising anti-consumerist tendencies in some countries and communities. Already some reshoring of manufacturing production is occurring, and the restructur-

Table 2.3 Africa's Competitive Industrial Performance Rankings: SSA countries in the Top 100 countries in the world.

		Global Rank 2020	Global Rank 2012	Change 2012–2020
1.	South Africa	52	48	–
2.	eSwatini	83	82	–
3.	Mauritius	87	88	+
4.	Botswana	89	91	+
5.	Namibia	97	92	–
6.	Nigeria	99	85	–

Source: Adapted from UNIDO, 2020.

ing global supply chains looks likely to continue with calls for more sustainable industrial production and trade to transition toward zero emissions internationally (Maglableh 2021).

Outside of the extractive, and to some extent the hospitality sectors, African cities have difficulties attracting foreign investors to their production regimes (Newman et al. 2016: p. 36). This may be changing, however, as activist approaches to catalyze industrial development are returning through the promotion of labor-intensive manufactured exports (e.g., in Ethiopia) and value chain upgrading (e.g., Kenya, Mauritius, and South Africa). For example, Ghana is developing value-addition; applying national resources within local value chains to enhance within country processing (e.g., of shea butter) and promoting new industries (e.g., petrochemicals, fertilizer, LPG [liquid petroleum gas] cylinder production) on the back of the new oil and gas sector. Other trends may stimulate African manufacturing output. Importantly, green manufacturing is being emphasized by the African Union (AU) and in various national industrialization strategies (Chapter 9 provides a more detailed discussion). Shifts within the Chinese economy (rising labor costs, upgrading of its within-country manufacturing, and curbs on brown industrialization) are also touted as opportunities for Africa to serve as an export platform for light manufacturing; a process facilitated by the region's integration into the Belt and Road Initiative (BRI; see Chapter 3) (Yuan Sun 2017). The region's trade concessions from the United States (e.g., the African Growth and Opportunity Act – AGOA) as well as the European Union (e.g., Everything But Arms – EBA) are also considered favorable. Moreover, a projected doubling in the size of African markets by the end of this century, coupled with its emerging middle-classes, is expected to increase demand (Grant 2015), although perhaps not to the extent expected given the uncertainties regarding what constitutes the middle class (Melber 2022).

In addition, there are new possibilities for an Africa-wide market, potentially stimulating intra-regional trade and opening possibilities for the greater development of regional and domestic manufacturing value chains are anticipated (Barrientos 2022). To date SSA has been more heavily involved in GVCs than in regional value chains (RVCs). The intensifying of RVCs driven by new technologies and shifting global economic governance away from multilateral to bilateral and regional frameworks may change this, particularly with enactment of the AfCTA and strategic diversification by African firms (Barrientos et al. 2016). Besides boosting international trade and investment in the region, this may recalibrate intra-African trade through an acceleration of trade in final goods, a dynamic that may stimulate manufacturing in cities and enable economies of scale hitherto unrealized because of relatively small national markets (Songe 2019). However, this will likely disproportionately benefit stronger industrial economies, such as South Africa unless a planned, "developmental regionalist" approach is adopted (Ismail 2019; Barrientos 2022).

Assessing the urban question in Africa demands significant consideration of manufacturing's contemporary and future role in shaping urban transitions – the possibilities and challenges it presents as a pathway for more progressive and distributive developments in the region's cities. The discussion that follows focuses on two key trends that are, or will shape(ing) urban production regimes in the coming years. The first is the influence of China on the prospects for African owned/operated manufacturing enterprises to emerge, expand, and diversify. The second relates to the implications of the 4IR – especially ICTs – for the development of urban production regimes.

The China Factor in African Manufacturing

In the early 2000s, China accounted for about 4% of the global economy versus 11.9% now (World Bank 2021a). Its rise as an economic superpower reflects the success of the development policy initiatives of its state which facilitated increases in FDI and domestic economic growth. Over 90% of African exports benefit from a unilateral tariff exemption into the Chinese market (Diawara and Hanson 2019). An important exception to the general trend of raw material exports is South Africa, where manufacturing goods comprise about 50% of total exports to China (Goetz 2019).

Despite such incentives, China's main impact on manufacturing in Africa has been vis-à-vis imports that often hinder the development of African manufacturing (Brautigam and Xiaoying, 2011; Carmody et al. 2020; Black and Yang 2021; Ogbonna 2021). There is evidence of the competitive displacement of local manufacturers who cannot compete with lower cost/higher quality, subsidized Chinese imported products (Senghaas 1985; Dobler 2008). In particular, many African textiles and apparel industries have been decimated, with some exceptions (e.g., Ethiopia and Mauritius), and the region has continued to export cotton as a raw material rather than engage in domestic manufacturing for the most part. Indeed, China's role in textile and apparel GVCs has intensified competition for cotton as Benin, Mali, and Burkina Faso supply China with 20% of its supply (Diawara and Hanson 2019). Chinese manufactures also increase competition in "third country" export markets, such as the US or Europe (Kaplinsky 2008).

The urban consequences of Chinese engagement are multifarious and will be described in greater detail in Chapter 3. Though Chinese FDI in manufacturing, largely in urban Africa, may create jobs directly, it also plays a role in outcompeting local producers for bank loans, skilled labor, and other production factors. Transfers of Chinese manufacturing equipment are welcome given that they are more affordable and contextually appropriate for production and infrastructure regimes in Africa. However, this often comes without high skills transfer and this equipment is neither as durable nor cutting edge as that which is associated with global best practices (Jenkins 2019). Industrial innovation and universities are severely underfunded in Africa so the reliance on imported technologies and parts is a concern.

Chinese economic zones in Africa have generally failed to meet anticipated impacts of bringing future-oriented design, high-standard infrastructure, and world-class professional management to facilitate economic growth. Initial plans for 50 Chinese zones failed to materialize. An early assessment of six operational ones showed little transfer of knowledge and no links to Africa's development objectives (Bräutigam and Xiaoying 2011). More recent research shows that, by-and-large, Chinese and other SEZs are poorly linked to domestic suppliers beyond the zones themselves, as investing firms continue to import inputs from abroad (Frick and Rodriguez-Pose 2022). For example, the Chinese established Economic Trade and Cooperation Zone (ETCZ) in Mauritius has not been a success even though that country has its own impressive history with EPZs. Assessments of Sino EPZs in Nigeria (Ogbonna 2021) and Chinese plants within South Africa's SEZs (Black and Yang 2021) indicate predominantly assembly of already manufactured products from China with limited opportunities for domestic firms to supply inputs.[1] One survey of a thousand Chinese firms in SSA found that less than half of inputs were locally sourced (Yuan Sun et al. 2017).

Some argue that as labor costs rise in China, industrial offshoring to Africa will be a major source of growth and development on the continent (Yuan Sun 2017; Lin and Xu 2019). China is currently the world's leading exporter of clothing, accounting for one-third of the total (Altenburg et al. 2020). While it is important to take advantage of this possibility, there is little evidence to date of widespread "industrialization by invitation" on the continent. Africa accounted for only 7% of China's outward FDI in 2015; rising to approximately 10% in recent years (Jenkins 2019). France, the Netherlands, the US, and the UK are more important investors in Africa than China in terms of FDI stock (UNCTAD 2019b). Some skeptics contend that "Alibaba industrialization" is far more likely to emerge whereby African small and medium-sized enterprises (SMEs) supply components and basic services to China as only parts of the production process are outsourced (e.g., in clothing sewing and basic cutting which takes place in Africa), while more sophisticated production remains in China and/or Asia. According to Simons (2019) this type of industrialization is "powered by a worldwide revolution in modular plant design, multipurpose machinery, efficient small-batch production, global SME-SME engagement, new forex transfer practices, and the growing strategic transformation of China's late-phase industrial players." A dramatic example was the development of Ghana's Kantanka automobiles, marketed "as made in Ghana," but all parts are from China (Simons 2019). This genre of industrialization might have most potential for informal manufacturing to evolve and link with industrial production chains.

Also of concern is the fact that labor costs in Africa may not be a sufficient enticement to low-cost manufacturing relocation. Jenkins (2019) notes that wages in manufacturing are higher in South Africa and Mauritius, Zambia's are similar to China's, and only countries such as Tanzania and Ethiopia offer lower labor costs. Landlocked Ethiopia has other cost disadvantages (Altenburg et al. 2020), and conflict in the Tigray region and spillover to Amhara regional state threatened to disrupt rail transport of manufacturing apparel and metal manufacturing exports, especially from the manufacturing center of Kombolcha. Such realities cast doubt that Beijing is the main enabler of manufacturing in Africa, and that the Chinese model of urbanization and low-tech manufacturing is being diffused into the continent.

China's macroeconomic effects and Africa's trade deficits are also consequential. Most Chinese exports to Africa are manufactured consumer products, e.g., clothing and electronics, while the continent exports mostly primary products to China, which has relatively little effect on urban industry and production regimes. Beijing now runs a trade surplus with most African countries, particularly since the commodity price bust of 2014. Running trade deficits necessitates taking on debt, and, if this cannot be serviced, adopting austerity policies which also affect the demand for local manufacturers. In 2020, Zambia, which is heavily indebted to China, defaulted on its debts (Williams 2020). All told, it is still too early to assess if Africa's integration into Chinese value chains and FDI flows through the BRI initiative will result in substantial export manufacturing benefits for African cities, although the impacts are likely to be highly uneven depending on existing national policy regimes and how different governments "negotiate China." In any event, there has been a dramatic contraction in infrastructure lending in recent years and attracting FDI may be more difficult post-COVID-19, even if China continues its (now somewhat faltering) ascent in the international system, suggesting the importance of developing other sources of inclusive growth in cities (Carmody and Wainwright 2022).

The Fourth Industrial Revolution (4IR)

Other meta-trends beyond the rise of China will also shape the nature, geography, and impact of global investment and urban-based manufacturing in Africa, including artificial intelligence (AI) and associated technologies: the "globotics upheaval" (Baldwin 2019) that is commonly associated with the 4IR.[2] Optimism abounds for some with the 4IR discourse being taken up as the next "best thing" for African industries and economies. As Dr. Amani Abou-Zeid, the African Union Commissioner for Infrastructure and Energy noted: "All the stars are aligned for Africa to take advantage of Revolution 4.0 and digitalization" (World Bank 2019a; Anwar and Graham 2022: p. 4). However, and importantly, as Sutherland (2020: p. 246) notes:

> 4IR is a rhetorical rather than an analytical device…the framework of general purpose technologies (GPTs) is more useful for policymakers, allowing them to focus on particular technologies (e.g., 3D printing) and skills training (e.g., data analytics).

While the 4IR discourse promises radical, innovative (possible) transformations to production regimes in places long left behind by the global economy – e.g., African cities – the tradeoffs and contingencies remain significant.

Robotics and 3D printing are, in effect, reducing the labor cost component of production facilitating near or reshoring to advanced economies, potentially discouraging manufacturing FDI in the Global South, and thus making it more difficult for African cities to industrialize. According to a study by McKinsey Global Institute (2018, cited in Sutherland 2020) demand for physical and manual skills will drop by 14% by 2030 in many countries. Although presently technology is not sufficiently sophisticated/cost-effective to make it a major challenge to more labor-intensive methods in the clothing industry (a "gateway" industrial sector) given "what is technically feasible is not always also economically profitable" (Monga, 2017: p. 9 in Cilliers 2018: p. 17; Altenburg et al. 2020). While there is still a window for Africa to industrialize via the globotics channel, the more likely pathway will be based on "low-cost labour in assembly-type manufacturing" (Naudé 2017: p. 4). Problematically, however, this low road to industrialization is exploitative of labor, with no guarantees of long-term success and industrial upgrading (Selwyn and Leyden 2022). Moreover Africa's slow demographic transition (Rotberg 2020), and rapidly growing urban populations, means that greater surplus labor may further subvert production regime transitions given that the employment intensity of manufacturing is in decline compared to when Asia underwent its most rapid manufacturing growth (Fox et al. 2017; Cilliers 2018).

The spatial dynamics of liberalization, globalization, and offshoring in the context of the 4IR have also generated reactionary backlashes (e.g., right-wing populism, protectionism, nearshoring, friendshoring) in some developed economies, such as the United States and the United Kingdom (Gereffi 2018; Kiely 2020). Baldwin (2019) predicts that these tendencies will intensify as middle-class professions are gutted by 4IR technologies, generating further protectionist pressures, including for service sector jobs, and making replicating the export-oriented manufacturing success of some East Asian economies even more difficult for Africa's latecomers (Carmody 2020). In any case, new models of industrialization may be more domestically and regionally focused and critically, greener. However, importantly, exports remain key to unlocking the foreign exchange constraint on growth.

There is no single impact of the 4IR on African cities, but rather it will be differentiated based on economic structures, existing production regimes, government capabilities, and local entrepreneurs. For some established industries, such as the automotive sector in South Africa, robotization promises major disruption (Sutherland 2020). Meanwhile, new ICTs continue to facilitate offshoring for basic service functions or sectors, such as call centers, to developing countries; offering potential to attract more of this economic activity (Benner 2006). Both Ghana and Kenya were recently rated higher than Ireland as preferred locations for offshore services work (Kearney 2019 cited in Anwar and Graham 2022).

The declining value of the South African rand since 2008 has made South Africa globally competitive for entry-level business process outsourcing (BPO) work, at the cost of relatively low returns to labor, but scheduled electricity disruptions, i.e., "load-shedding," is a major hindrance.

Baldwin (2019) further contends that in the future manufacturing will become less traded and more jobless as AI and the 4IR replaces the "manu" with "robofacuturing," dramatically transforming global activities, but with variations across industries (e.g., autos are more amenable to robotics than apparel) (Hallward-Driemeier et al. 2018). Africa's twenty-first century development journey may therefore be more like India and/or the Philippines and less like China based on cross border traded services as wealthy countries export service jobs in "telecommuting" and "telemigration" (whereby people may sit in African locations, for example, but work in offices/companies outside the region). Call centers and processing of basic business services are being promoted in many cities (e.g., Accra, Cape Town, Johannesburg, Nairobi, Port Louis) and countries. As Rotberg (2020: p. 265) notes in the case of Madagascar:

> Madagascar is one of Africa's surprising Internet commercial successes because of low wages, excellent French literacy, and a relatively fast Internet. In 2019, more than two-hundred business processing and outsourcing firms employed as many as 15,000 Malagasy workers, mostly in Antananarivo.

In contrast, Benner (2006) highlights high relative wages, problems with broadband infrastructure, unreliable electricity supply, and perceived issues with the clarity of African-spoken English for those in Europe and that US which means that only a few African locations recorded success (e.g., South African cities for British-based outsourcers, Port Louis, Mauritius with its bilingualism in French and English). These places, however, often serve as niches for second-mover companies seeking smaller operations compared to the multi-thousand worker call centers in Indian cities.

While there is little doubt regarding the success story that is ICT diffusion in Africa, especially mobile phones, the integration of these technologies into urban production regimes has been slow and often rather superficial. Murphy and Carmody (2015) highlight that while ICTs have been transformative to the consumer and fintech sectors, deeper data processing and management by African firms is often not evident even in the age of the 4IR; a phenomenon they term "thintegration." At the same time, new, ICT-enabled vehicles for external intervention and intermediation into African markets, such as quasi-monopolistic booking and shopping websites, may be further marginalizing African firms and industries (Murphy and Carmody 2015), with Amazon now setting up its African headquarters in Cape Town, for example (Akindele 2021).

The 4IR, technology-driven agenda also promotes "smart city" projects which are alluring to promotors and those preoccupied with rebranding African cities and Afrofuturist visions of the region. In development and implementation, however, these projects have been extremely limited in their conceptualization of the city and regarding their practical alignment with extant urban regimes (see Chapter 4). As a result, smart city projects have an abysmal track record, with Cuggurollo (2022) describing them as "Frankenstein Urbanism" or "the ICT incarnation of neoliberal urbanism" whereby large companies take over management functions to the detriment of "non monetizable urban issues" such as the use value of cities as manifest in the quality of infrastructure and consumption regimes (Watson 2015; Cugurullo 2021: p. 47). In fact, these projects can shape (ICT-driven) infrastructure regimes in significant ways that contribute not only to the extraction of profits through speculative investments in built environments, but also now through data mining, thereby undermining "industrialization without smokestacks" (Newman et al. 2016; Guma and Monstadt 2019) through "digital colonialism" by foreign tech companies.

The market for apps development and start-ups is booming in Lagos,[3] Nairobi, Johannesburg, Cape Town, Accra, and other cities, where incubators and accelerators have emerged (e.g., Nairobi's I-Hub) and which support the development of local technological solutions and start-ups: FinTechs, AgTechs, and MTechs[4] are flourishing. But, beyond these start-up ecosystems, substantial issues with (digital) literacy and skills remain. For example, according to Choi et al. (2020: p. xix):

> Kobo360 and Lori Systems have each invested in cashless, paperless, mobile-based on-demand trucking logistics technologies that have created new and better functioning markets. Mobile technologies are alowing young entrepreneurs to use various digital platforms to access larger markets. Of course, the risk of large sections of the poor, the low-skilled, and the uneducated being left behind in a so-called digital divide looms large as more than 60 percent of the labor force is made up of ill-equipped adults and almost 90 percent of employment is in the informal sector.

Moreover, while app development has shown signs of success in some areas (e.g., Ushahidi, M-Pesa in Kenya), it has by-and-large not resulted in widespread formal employment generation given, in part, the fact that when hardware manufacturing is needed to support an app (e.g., "tap" payment systems), production is almost inevitably outsourced outside Africa for cost and quality reasons (Murphy 2022).

While the competitive displacement of labor by robotics and other technologies of the 4IR will be less pronounced than that in other world regions, existing marginalization may be further entrenched and compounded as rates of investment in manufacturing remain low. As noted earlier, South Africa has struggled to increase investment as a proportion of GDP despite being the most industrially advanced country on the continent. Furthermore, the 2021 urban riots in response to the jailing of former President Zuma did not spare factories and has likely further eroded investors' confidence. This decline in the relative level of investment is reflective of the autonomous development of the trade and financial sectors or "circuits of capital"[5] on the continent and associated capital leakages through imports and financial flows (Carmody 1998), now increasingly facilitated through ICTs (Steel 2021). Gross capital formation for SSA was 24% in 2021, compared to 44% in 1981 (Word Bank 2022).[6] This has made it impossible for cities in the region to move from factor-driven to investment/innovation-driven growth. Consequently, while Africa is increasingly an information society it is not a knowledge economy (Carmody 2013).

The likely impacts of 4IR on African industries will reach beyond cities and manufacturing. For example, mining is increasingly being robotized to allow for access to deeper and more marginal ores, and to reduce workplace injuries (and associated costs) (Anglo-American 2013), and this industry historically had major impacts on the development of urban systems in large parts of Africa (Bryceson and MacKinnon 2012). Robotization will thus reduce demand for labor at the mine face, while supporting some higher skill jobs in maintenance and management. The agricultural sector may be substantially impacted as well and the "4IR could drive agricultural mechanisation through the application of robotics, genetics and automation" (Ayentimi and Burgess 2019: p. 645), potentially displacing labor, and propelling further rural to urban migration. Lastly, as discussed in Chapter 6, the 4IR may further facilitate a shift away from discrete categories of formal and informal economies toward hybrid urban production regimes that fuse elements of both such as digital platforms such as Upwork Global and Kuhustle (Nairobi) that enable freelance African workers to gain contract work from outside of home countries.[7]

Transforming Manufacturing? Governance Challenges and Opportunities

African manufacturing firms face multiple obstacles to becoming competitive in international markets. Global political economy and technological meta trends mentioned above, as well as developments within states and cities, affect their international competitiveness. Poor investment climates, unreliable and weakly integrated infrastructure, aspatial planning strategies, and uncontrolled sprawl in many African cities are major impediments as is the highly competitive international environment where much "product space" (Hidalgo et al. 2007) has been exhausted.

African cities are often internally disconnected: their inhabitants may have little opportunity to interact with each other due to factors including fragmentation, low and variable population densities, poor infrastructure, congestion, and high travel times. Lall et al. (2017: p. 118) emphasize how the lack of strategic and integrative planning helps to produce such conditions to the detriment of workers, firms, and everyday living conditions. These constraints discourage innovative productive regimes and impede the realization of agglomeration (scope) and urbanization (scale) economies, thus resulting in the inability of many African manufacturers to compete in export markets (Venables 2010; Lall et al. 2017). Governance is thus a crucial concern, one that demands forward thinking policies and institutional reforms.

Rethinking the Governance of Production Regimes: National Urban Policies

A promising development in governance is governments crafting national urban policies (NUPs)[8] as instruments through which they can upgrade production regimes. NUPs are particularly important in Africa, where local resources and the capacity to benefit from rapid urban growth are often weak, and layers of policies, initiatives, unfinished and/or absent plans have frustrated attempts to develop coherent, inclusive, and effective forms of urban-industrial governance. NUPs can bring greater coherence and legitimacy to authorities and agents in cities and – critically – recalibrate the balance of power shared by different levels of government, SOEs, civil society, and the private sector (Cartwright et al. 2018). Importantly, NUPs embrace multilevel governance and many plans embrace cross-cutting economic and development themes. As of 2021, twenty SSA states had formulated an NUP. Table 2.2 ranks NUPs in Africa in terms of their efficacy in integrating economic development, spatial structure, and urban planning. Mauritius, Rwanda, and South Africa have formulated the most comprehensive cross-cutting NUPs,[9] followed by Kenya. By contrast, Ethiopia's 2013 NUP is rated as low in virtually all categories.

Implementing NUPs effectively requires a sound institutional framework to coordinate urban and industrial development planning. If planning in both domains is to be linked, multiple sectors, subsectors, and actors need to be part of the planning process and the execution of policies. This mechanism should also provide opportunities for consulting with and involving private stakeholders, notably leaders in manufacturing and real estate. Most cities, beyond South Africa, have little local economic planning experience and where they do, are too limited in territorial and substantive scope to a specific industrial district(s), which limits their broader impact. Thus, coordination at the national level to align urban and industrial priorities should involve subnational authorities and be accompanied by technical, financial, and institutional support. However, and importantly, NUPs are only as good as their implementation. Navigating the complexities of the urbanization-industrial nexus – evaluating policy options and trade-offs, designing good policy and integrated spatial strategies, and measuring their impacts – requires evidence-based studies that rests on quality urban data (Cartwright et al. 2018).

Table 2.4 National Urban Policy Rankings for select countries – 2021.

National Urban Policy

	Economic development	Spatial structure	Human development	Environmental sustainability	Climate resilience
Cape Verde	Extensive	Extensive	Extensive	Moderate	Moderate
Congo Republic	Extensive	Low	Low	Low	Low
Djibouti	Extensive	Extensive	Extensive	Low	Low
Kenya	Extensive	Moderate	Extensive	Extensive	Extensive
Mauritius	Extensive	Extensive	Extensive	Extensive	Low
Rwanda	Extensive	Extensive	Extensive	Moderate	Moderate
South Africa	Extensive	Extensive	Extensive	Extensive	Low

Source: Adapted from UN-HABITAT, 2021.

Unfortunately, these kinds of data are often scarce in African cities, but for a qualitative assessment see Table 2.4.

Lal et al. (2017) contend that urban plans need to be innovative, more adaptable, and that they should strategically allow for more optimal use of land, arguably a mammoth task with the coexistence of multiple land ownership systems in African cities. Well-planned and forward-looking infrastructure regime improvements (e.g., transportation, energy) are also essential and these upgrades require better functioning institutions and enhanced governance capabilities. African institutional structures should thus lead, not lag, urban infrastructure regimes if the region's cities are to become better connected, more efficient, and more inclusive for their inhabitants whose skills will be critical to sustainable transformations of manufacturing production regimes (Lal et al. 2017: p. 157).

While there is no single recipe for manufacturing success, and no one-size-fits-all for African cities, policy packages might concentrate on important criteria including (modified based on Mcmillan et al. [2017; p. 28] and with our own additions):

- Continued improvements in soft capital, including sound macroeconomic management, stronger investment climates, support for the private sector, and development of public infrastructure;
- Investing in education and training programs and building relevant skills and ecosystems;
- Hard infrastructure spending and upgrading and integration of broadband, port, and transportation systems;
- An export push, including regional trade integration and RVCs;
- Agglomeration through building and operating successful EPZs, SEZs, and industrial parks;

- Active FDI promotion and building linkages among diverse local firms and utilizing joint ventures strategically;
- Supporting local small and medium enterprises to enhance productivity and access and absorb advanced technology and long-term finance to help them venture into new or more sophisticated products;
- Improve import and export logistics and intra-city and international accessibility, delivery, and export time to markets;
- Improved coherence and implementation coordination by multiscalar institutions;
- Strengthen consultation and collaboration among government, the private sector, industry, and business organizations and informal manufacturing firms[10];
- Mainstream/fuse all manufacturing firms into a coordinated/integrated industrial and technology policy that is supported by business, government, research institutions, donors, nongovernmental organizations (NGOs), and the education and legal system.

Pathways for Industrialization in African Cities

As indicated by the rise of NUPs, industrial policy is enjoying a revival throughout Africa. Even the IMF, for long one of the primary promoters of neoliberalism globally, has published on the principles of industrial policy (Cherif and Hasanov 2019). The scholarly literature reflects this trend, analyzing the prospects for industrialization in cities through integrated industrial and urban policies. Africa needs industrialization and its cities are well positioned to attract low-value manufacturing production given rising labor costs in Asia, at least to serve African markets. Lopes (2019) contends that rather than focusing on diversifying away from commodities, the focus should be on utilizing them as effective inputs to value-adding industrial sectors. A commodity-based focus offers immediate scope for MVA and creates opportunities to take advantage of backward and forward linkages domestically. Moreover, an important strategy for firms will be multiscalar, "strategic diversification" whereby they develop concurrent ties to domestic markets, RVCs, and GVCs in order to stabilize demand and develop capacities to compete in different market settings (Barrientos et al. 2016). Beyond these considerations, we now highlight a few other pathways for industrial growth and development in urban production regimes through manufacturing and other sectors.

To start with, there are increasing calls for smart specialization and capitalization of RVCs to facilitate Africa's potential upgrading in GVCs. Smart specialization is a urban-regional development policy which focusses on enabling the development of particular subsectors, building off regionally available resources

(Dosso et al. 2022). The shift in policy thinking can be traced to the 2006 Khartoum Summit and Africa's Science and Technology Consolidated Plan of Action, and the adoption of the Science, Technology and Innovation Strategy for Africa, 2024 (AUC 2014). The AU's Agenda 2063 refers to science, technology, and innovation (STI) as multifunctional enablers for achieving continental development goals. In Africa, awareness of the role of innovation has led to the elaboration of STI strategies. Preliminary mapping of innovation systems is taking place in several African countries, e.g., Côte d'Ivoire, Ghana, Rwanda (Yonagbo and Göransson 2020).

New industrial pathways may enable a breakthrough for Africa's manufacturing industries. For example, low-carbon technologies required for the 4IR require steady supplies of mineral and metals; more than is currently produced. Because generation systems are widely (spatially) distributed, approximately six times more iron and steel and seventy times more copper will be needed to transmit electricity generated for clean energy on a global scale (INRA 2021: p. 23). Moreover, wind and solar photovoltaic technologies and fuel cells, essential to power electric vehicles, will drive up demand for strategic minerals such as cobalt and lithium. Some of these minerals may be extracted through "urban mining" or "demanufacturing" (recycling of e-waste) (Phuluwa et al. 2020).

Africa is endowed with 42 of the 66 strategic minerals needed to drive the 4IR, so potentially huge opportunities exist to leverage the region as a global player in low-carbon technology (INRA 2021), although the problem of below-ground wealth and above-ground poverty is a persistent, structural challenge. The region provides two-thirds of global cobalt production, 80% of platinum, half of manganese production, one-third of bauxite, and 20% of uranium resources (INRA 2021: p. 23). Opportunities exist for DRC and Zambia, who combined account for three-quarters of global cobalt production; Namibia and Zimbabwe possess 100% of world cesium reserves and 89% of world's rubidium reserves, Namibia is the world's third largest producer of arsenic, and South Africa produces 70% of the world's platinum (INRA 2021: p. 23).

Given that Africa as a supplier of raw materials historically, has experienced adverse incorporation into the global economy, governments will have to learn to capitalize on the 4IR by more deeply integrating local content, resource industries, and value chains within the rest of the economy this time around, avoiding extractive enclaves (Phelps et al. 2015; INRA 2021). One possibility is for African states to designate these raw materials as "strategic" (INRA 2021) and to conduct external diplomacy around 4IR strategic minerals, aiming for a partnership of equals and more centrality in GVCs so that techno-specific knowledge can be created within Africa, most likely by joint ventures (j-vs).[11] Importantly, within the region strategic minerals need to be integrated into national sustainable development agendas whereby they become the catalyst for national and urban transformations as value chains link domestically sourced extractives productively with manufacturing exports.

Informal economy firms also have a role to play in productive structural transformation, a role that has been weak to date (Benjamin and Mbaye 2020). Marginalization from state/urban policies and supports are handicaps to the full development of informal enterprises. Research on informal firms in Tanzania found a significant similarity in labor productivity between formal and informal firms (Page et al. 2020). Page et al. (2020: p. 9) estimate a small, but significant, share of firms in the informal economy – about 10% – are relatively or highly productive. If the manufacturing sector grows these firms have the potential to grow with or as part of it. Research by Benjamin and Mbaye (2020) demonstrates that the degree of informality is correlated with productivity, where those firms closest to formality have the highest productivity and those which are completely informal the lowest. Policies and training programs to bridge to the formal economy are needed. Chapter 5 discusses these challenges in depth.

Beyond manufacturing, changes in transport costs and ICTs are shifting the boundaries of industry, creating services and agri-businesses that share many characteristics with manufacturing firms. In particular, there is potential offered by the agribusiness sector to improve its position along value chains in commodity-based industrialization ("the industrialisation of freshness") (Cramer et al. 2020). Like manufacturing, agribusiness products and services are tradable, have high value-added per worker, the capacity for learning and productivity growth, and some exhibit scale and agglomeration economies (Barrientos et al. 2016; Page et al. 2020). These "industries without smokestacks" may offer another pathway to transformed urban production regimes.

Conclusion

There is almost universal consensus on a wide array of factors that has held manufacturing back in Africa. Historical legacies, neglect of nurturing the potential of informal manufacturing, inconsistent roles played by states in production regimes, narrow conceptions of formal manufacturing as a separate policy domain, inadequate supporting (hard/soft) services, poor business climates, high costs, and deficiencies in technical and multilevel policy and governance capabilities stand out (Rodrik 2016). Infrastructure regimes too have played a significant role through, for example, electricity black and "brown outs" (where the voltage dips), a major issue in some countries in recent years, such as South Africa and Ghana. International meta-trends also add uncertainty and unpredictability to how the global economy will evolve. Despite the challenges, participation in manufacturing value chains is perhaps more important than ever before.

Manufacturing-led development does have a future in Africa cities, but its constitution and trajectory will be very different from the historical experiences of others. AfCTA, 4IR opportunities, and low-technology manufacturing, if capabilities can be improved and productivity enhanced, will provide a boost. Upgrading to more medium and high-technology manufacturing must also accelerate whenever possible. Some niche successes are observable, e.g., Rwanda in machinery, motor vehicles, processed food (Shepherd and Twum 2018), agro-processing in Ghana, greentech and motor vehicles in South Africa (Grant et al. 2020), pharmaceuticals in Mauritius (Mauritius and UNCTAD 2020), and "Alibaba industrialisation" among some SMEs (Simons 2019), although these subsectors alone are insufficiently catalytic in their respective urban sociotechnical systems. However, the range of options and possibilities is far more open than in the past. Especially needed are better industrial policy and coordination mechanisms, worker skills and training programs, improved informal-formal sector linkages, business incubators and accelerators, industrial groups, chambers of commerce, upgraded infrastructure regimes, and empowered consumers (consumption regimes) that generate demand for more domestic manufacturing and products produced with reduced carbon footprints; as opposed to manufacturing products in Asia and shipping and transporting them over long distances that involve port stops along the shipping route to various African marketplaces.

Industrial planning and its articulation and constitution through economic policy more generally is consequently of urgent importance for cities on the continent. Successful manufacturing production regimes will prioritize learning and capability development; both tacit and formal, imported and learned by being done (Lall and Kraemer-Mbula 2005). Government has a vital role to play in fostering the development of such innovation systems through support to infrastructure (regimes) supporting manufacturing, both hard and soft, and through the promotion of urban consumption (regimes) that can generate demand for domestically produced manufactures.

In a context of limited resources, choices have to be made regarding the extent to which social provisioning (use value) versus economic production and trade (exchange value) should be prioritized. How such decisions and prioritizations are arrived at will be an outcome of political struggles within cities and nations. Such objectives (i.e., use versus exchange value) are not mutually exclusive but rather synergistic – improved manufacturing sectors that compete successfully against imports and in RVCs and GVCS can capture value from external markets, generate employment, and improve tax revenues in/for cities whilst enabling social upgrading and supporting more resilient livelihood strategies (Mkandawire 2004). There needs to be a balance struck between the two, one that is achieved through political settlements arrived at inclusively with wide participation from civil society as well as states and private/foreign capital; negotiations and debates that make concerns about distribution and use value central to them.

Notes

1 Still, there are proposals to develop large-scale EPZ to attract Chinese industrial jobs. The largest of these being Coega EPZ in South Africa, Nelson Mandela Metro. Coega already accounts for the largest single manufacturing investment in Africa. The Beijing Automobile Industrial Corporation (BAIC) plant is 35% cofinanced by the South African State Industrial Development Corporation (IDC), and the joint venture (j-v) has ties with fourteen specialized auto dealerships in South Africa (Black and Yang 2021). There are plans to supply 100,000 vehicles to the African market, including electric ones that could potentially support a sociotechnical transition in clean and affordable transportation.

2 For Baldwin "globotics" is the combination of robotics, and associated technologies of AI, and globalization.

3 Shapshak (2019) identifies Lagos is the African leader with 40 tech hubs, the largest number in any African city.

4 Medical technological firms.

5 Outflows are not fully autonomized but only within the national space. Capital flight from Africa may be used for productive investment overseas, but it also represents a substantial loss to national economies, particularly if profits remain offshore.

6 High economic growth rates in the early years of the new millennium were driven largely by higher primary commodity prices.

7 Digital platforms can offer an on-ramp for informal firms to gradually formalize by finding suppliers and customers, using mobile money, drawing up contracts, etc. (Ng'weno and Porteous 2018). This would involve a different trajectory to urban survivalism and multiple modes of livelihood (Mustapha 1992). It might also include SEZs linking informal and the formal firms (Cross 2010).

8 NUPs emerged from Habitat III, 2016, as the policy instrument through which national governments engage and shape the urbanizing world.

9 Ranked by UN-Habitat (2021) as extensive based on a three-category ranking of extensive, moderate, and low.

10 Too often policymakers treat the informal economy as an entirety. Industrial and urban policies have not been inclusive of informal manufacturing. In the past, the informal sector was low on the agenda of policymakers, and the *status quo* is prone to inertia, unless driven by pressures from social movement actors and policymakers to transform their views and business practices in order to be more inclusive of informal manufacturing firms.

11 Botswana's diamond beneficiation, and Gaborone's improving role in GVCs, may serve as an example.

Chapter Three
The Impact of China and Other New Economic Powers on African Cities

Many infrastructure provisions by China are considered white elephant projects that reflect the interests and "urban fantasies" of African officials rather than the immediate needs of respective populations (Goetz, A. 2019: p. 190 / University of Ottawa Press).

China's influence has become genuinely global, partly through the integration of financial markets that have used their flexibility to debt-finance urban development around the world (Cain, 2017: p. 482 / Oxford University Press).

Introduction

The "rise" of China is an important secular process, altering the nature of the global political economy and manifest, for example, in "inter-regionalism" between China and Africa (Carmody 2010). There is now a voluminous literature on the nature of Chinese engagements on the continent, which has passed through a variety of phases or waves. During the pre- and immediate post-independence periods relations were mainly ideologically-based as China sought to support liberation movements across the continent. Perhaps the most well-known example of this cooperation, which is still in existence, is the Tanzam or TAZARA railway which allowed land-locked Zambia to divert its exports away from apartheid South Africa and route them through Tanzania's ports instead.

The Urban Question in Africa: Uneven Geographies of Transition, First Edition. Pádraig R. Carmody, James T. Murphy, Richard Grant and Francis Y. Owusu.
© 2024 John Wiley & Sons Ltd. Published 2024 by John Wiley & Sons Ltd.

Since then Chinese engagement on the continent has waxed and waned. When China became a net oil importer in 1993 this promoted the development of a "go out" strategy for its companies later that decade, where there were incentives provided by the central government for companies to invest overseas to source raw materials and energy for the economy, in addition to establishing markets and building up their international experience to enable them to become globally competitive. This orientation was further embedded, refined, and expanded through the BRI announced by the Chinese President in 2013.

The BRI has been conceptualized as a form of "third wave" South-South Cooperation (SSC). As Barton (2022: p. 1 citing Chaturvedi, 2016: p. 4) observes:

No longer content with operating in the shadows of the Global North, the business model undergirding "third wave" SSC – emphasiz(es) state intervention, Public-Private Partnerships (PPP), concessional financing, stakeholder symmetries and development effectiveness.

There has been much ink spilt on this project with some viewing it as a primarily geopolitical strategy to gain influence, largely through infrastructure construction overseas, whereas others highlight it as a "spatial fix" for the Chinese economy's problem of capital overaccumulation (Zajontz 2021; Carmody et al. 2022a). A more controversial allegation is that it represents a form of "debt trap diplomacy"; a means to project geopolitical and economic power by indebting recipients of BRI-driven aid/investments. The idea was initially developed in India, but has since become a global trope or meme; one which has been debunked (Bräutigam 2020). Nonetheless, the BRI has been associated with the creation of significant levels of debt (and dependency) in certain countries, such as Zambia and Djibouti, even if this was not the intention (Patey 2020: Carmody and Wainwright 2022). The project has thus experienced substantial global pushback as a result.

Afro-Chinese relations are deepened, embedded, and constituted through specific spatial forms and associated flows, ranging from infrastructural projects to SEZs and other less tangible interchanges (Lee 2009). China, or better Chinese-based actors, have multifold indirect impacts through flows of commodities and ideas into African cities (Harrison and Yang 2015; Kuo 2015); the latter being less spatially "visible," through technological standards for example, and less concentrated. This embedding, in-turn, influences the nature of relations and shapes African cities significantly through, for example, the competitive displacement of domestic manufacturers (Kaplinsky 2013; Bbaala 2015) and the facilitation of new spatial forms such as "Chinese" markets or shops. Embedded flows are furthermore dependent on relational infrastructure (Storper et al. 2015)[1] or what might be called social capital or *guanxi* (trust) with deepening potential.

Africa is largely caught between economic intra and extraversion. Intraversion is where imports, often from China, competitively displace local producers, whereas extraversion refers to the external orientation of African economies through natural resource exports, although the two co-constitute through the counterflow mechanism where receipts from exports are (partially) used to purchase imports, and imports of value-added products also serve the interests of external producers. This chapter examines the channels of causal "impact" on African cities from China and other "new economic and urban powers" (NEUPs), while acknowledging their relational coproduction, through flows of goods mediated by African traders, for example (Lee 2014; Large 2021). We demonstrate how commodities, investments, policy ideas, and political influences from Beijing and other NEUPs (e.g., India, Turkey, United Arab Emirates [UAE]) are influencing African cities through significant changes to production, consumption, and infrastructure regimes.

NEUP-African Relations Today: Key Channels of Impact

NEUPs, but particularly China, are having a significant impact on real estate markets, industries, infrastructures, and consumption patterns in African cities. No unilinear "impact" in Africa is identifiable, as NEUP/Chinese "inflected globalization" is also locally constructed (Hart 2002), even though general tendencies are observed due to some similarities in economic and governance structures (Jenkins 2019). The "impacts" of these factors play out differently depending on local context, state mediation, and negotiation (Ziso 2018; Jepson 2019). That said, four principal channels stand out: imports, infrastructure and other productive investments, housing and built environments and migration, travel, and knowledge flows.

Imports

The first channel is NEUP exports to Africa. Such flows are highly diversified in the forms of furnishings, clothing, electronics, machinery, chemicals, etc. and these commodities increasingly meet demand for wage goods (i.e., necessities), contributing to the entrenchment of "consumption-based cities" (Gollin et al. 2016). By some estimates, China has overtaken the European Union as Africa's largest trade partner, accounting for a quarter of its total (Mohseni-Cheraghlou 2021). India is now the continent's second largest single country trade partner, and the UAE accounted for US$50 billion of trade in 2019 – roughly 1/4th of China's from a country with only 1/1400th of China's population (Zaywa 2021); although many UAE-Africa exports comprise Chinese reexports. Many African traders prefer Dubai to source consumer goods because of greater relational (and geographic) proximity, better logistics, low taxes, and the opportunity to utilize the *hawala* (Islamic) money transfer system (Keshodkar 2014). Turkish trade with Africa rose from US$4.2 to US$23.5 billion from 2002 to 2019 (Karaoguz and Gurbuz 2021).

For "ordinary" urban Africans, Chinese and other imports are "transformative" by enabling everyday items (e.g., flip-flops, sunglasses) to circulate widely and cheaply in consumption regimes. However they may come with the concomitant displacement or crowding out of local manufacturers in production regimes (Edwards and Jenkins 2014; Jenkins and Edwards 2015; Jenkins 2019). As noted in Chapter 2, profits are channeled offshore through imports in African cities, but often without the spillovers of knowledge and capabilities in local industrial development commonly envisaged with trade liberalization, despite claims to the contrary (Yuan Sun et al. 2017; Obobisa et al. 2021).

In some cases, resource demand from China and other NEUPs is associated with domestic market formation, e.g., in the food and beverage industries in Angola (Wolf 2016, 2017), with some suggesting this should be the primary focus of economic policy (Jeppsen and Kragelund 2021). Where it exists, neopatrimonial governance by African leaders may be reinforced by Chinese-funded infrastructure spending as politically connected individuals reap significant monetary benefits from this (Wang and Wissenbach 2019; Wang 2022). Beijing's aid to African leaders' home regions nearly triples after the latter assume power (Dahir 2019).

Infrastructure and Other Productive Investments

A second channel of significance relates to Chinese investment in productive and extractive activities. In this case, investments in the (re)construction of infrastructure (especially transport) and the creation of SEZs (see Figure 3.1 for example) are arguably reproducing a more dynamic - economic extraversion (Amin and Pearce 1974; Bayart and Ellis 2000; Carmody and Murphy 2017). Such investments in infrastructure regimes facilitate the exportation of raw materials, such as from the copper-focused SEZ in Northern Zambia (Carmody and Hampwaye 2010), and support political alliance building and transnational dependencies. Extractive activities and SEZs remain poorly integrated with local industry; enclaved and transnationalized sites of capital accumulation (Giannecchini and Taylor 2018; Fei and Liao 2020) that serve instead to increase the efficiency of natural resource exports and facilitate access to "cheap" labor (Adunbi 2022). Such forms of adverse incorporation into GVCs are exemplified in Ethiopia which has substantial Chinese manufacturing investment, but the lowest wages for textile workers in the world – a shocking US $26 a month (Barrett and Baumann-Pauly 2019). Such wages, massively below the World Bank's absolute poverty line of US $2.15 a day, lead to skepticism about the role of Chinese FDI in reducing urban poverty (Selwyn and Leyden 2022). One visit to a Chinese car assembler in Ethiopia in 2012 revealed assembly of completely knocked down car kits, with no local content, taking place at that time (see Figure 3.2).

Figure 3.1   Eastern Industrial Zone, Addis Ababa, Ethiopia.
Photo credit: David Taylor (2012).

Figure 3.2   Knocked down car kits at Lifan Motors, Ethiopia.
Photo credit: David Taylor (2012).

Infrastructure, mining, and SEZ investments through foreign aid mechanisms (i.e., soft loans, grants) increased dramatically from 2006, with China providing nearly US $100 billion in financing to the region between 2000 and 2013 and US $24.2 billion for transport projects alone from 2000 to 2014 (Solomon and Iman 2017). Chinese funded infrastructural projects are often "misfits" that are rapidly "swallowed up" by the prevailing political economy (Goodfellow and Huang 2021). Infrastructure construction in cities creates demand effects and opportunities for local suppliers, although in many cases inputs appear to be sourced primarily from China, despite their being local sourcing mandates (e.g., in Kenya) (Murphy 2022).

Chinese-led infrastructure projects may also generate population displacement and consequent immiseration in and around cities. For example, outside of Dar es Salaam, a Chinese builder uprooted 1,000+ families to make way for an international airport that has never being completed (Rotberg 2020). In Nairobi, the construction of an expressway from the airport to the CBD displaced thousands of residents in the Mukuru slum (Ram 2021). The state, which approves or implements such displacements thus creates significant risks and livelihood challenges for the poor; marginalizing their ability to meet basic needs through the consumption regime. In South Africa local state officials need to feel they are in control of urban space and housing delivery programs and sometimes drive evictions (Levenson 2022). Such exclusions are echoed in other projects, such as the failed Modderfontein new city project in Johannesburg where the master planning process reflected instead a "distinctly South African urbanism" (Reboredo and Brill 2019: 9) even though extensive networks were created to help facilitate the project (Ballard and Harrison 2020). On the other hand where there is a highly visible Chinese presence, e.g., Derrick Avenue in Cyrildene, Johannesburg, it sparks imaginaries of "spatialised elsewhere" (Dittgen and Chungu 2023).

In the wake of COVID-19, recent data (Ray et al. 2020) reveal that overseas lending for infrastructure through China's two main policy banks – the China Development Bank and the Export-Import (EXIM) Bank – has all but collapsed. After peaking in 2016 at US$75 bn/year, lending from these banks fell to $4 bn in 2019 (Ray et al. 2020; Wheatley and Kynge 2020). Steep declines in Chinese commercial lending have also been registered (Inclusive Development International 2021). Furthermore, pre-COVID-19, China's flows of FDI to Africa fell by nearly 50% from 2018 to 2019 (Johns Hopkins CARI 2021). Ongoing Chinese investment contractions will have significant impacts on African cities and their production regimes, although it is uncertain whether these flows will rebound as COVID-19 abates. Some predict that although BRI financing has bottomed out for the time being, the initiative remains a geopolitical priority for China, with its next iteration to potentially shift beyond infrastructure as a principal focus:

> ...the Belt and Road Initiative hasn't died of COVID-19. On the contrary, Xi and other senior Chinese officials continue to trumpet the initiative. Their messaging is highly consistent: In 2021, China will start to wind down its new investment into traditional capital-intensive infrastructure, both at home and abroad.... Instead, the initiative will refocus on public health (especially vaccines), green technology, and digital services (Han and Freymann 2021).

Housing and Built Environments

A third channel of Chinese influence on African cities is through investments in housing and the urban built environment. As is detailed in Chapter 4, however, investments are typically the "greenfield" type – manifest in the development of "double" cities, built from scratch (Murray 2015) inspired by China's recent phase of urban evolution (Wan et al. 2020) or elsewhere, such as Dubai (Moser et al. 2021) – "urban fantasies" that reek of "hyper-modernity" (Watson 2014). In Angola, China was – prior to contractions in lending – "involved in the construction of new urban centres on a scale unequalled by any other foreign partner" (Benazeraf and Alves 2014). In 2008 the Angolan President committed to building 1 million homes and this led to the development of five new cities around Luanda built by Chinese contractors: Kilamba Kiaxi, Zango, Cacuaco, KM44 and Capari. Kilamba Kiaxi – see Figure 3.3 – comprising a built environment of 3.3 million m² in the first phase alone, was contested from the outset; protected by the Presidential Guard while it was being built, given the unrest that the project caused through its displacement of slum dwellers. One displacee (José Manuel), who recounted being dumped in an area with no housing or infrastructure, said "this country is evil" (quoted in Gastrow 2017). However, in such cases there may be profits to be made beyond property (re)development, particularly through displacement companies such as the infamous "Red Ants" in South Africa, for example (Johnson 2016).

Despite its intention to provide affordable housing, some of the new apartments in Kilamba Kiaxi cost more than US$100,000 dollars; a price that was completely unaffordable for displacees and indeed most Angolans, resulting in a "ghost town" (Cain in Redvers 2012). The Angolan government subsequently reduced prices and by 2015 Kilamba accommodated 70,000 inhabitants with

Figure 3.3   Rendering of Kilamba Kiaxi, Angola.
Source: Santa Martha / Wikimedia Commons / CC BY-SA 3.0.

functioning basic services including water, electricity, kindergartens, schools, sports fields, shops, restaurants, etc. Some heralded it as a clean, modern, and dreamlike "un-African" town" (Croese 2016: p. 20) that had alleviated a "four-hour commute through gridlocked downtown Luanda" and which offered the peace, order, and tranquility of a well-planned satellite city (Tao 2015). Others view the project as a tool for elite extraversion through which Angola's then president (dos Santos) was able to reward loyal supporters through kickbacks and other forms of favoritism (Wang 2022).

Other NEUPs are also having an influence on planning strategies and built environments. "Dubaisation" is epitomized in the sail outline of the *Burj al-Fatih* building in Khartoum, evoking the *Burj al-Arab* in Dubai (see Figure 3.4), and Nairobi's push toward financial services and high-end consumption as key drivers of urban development (Choplin and Franck 2010; Upadhyaya 2020). The adoption of such imaginaries and logics, when combined with the intensification of trade and investment flows from UAE, make Dubai an NEUP. In fact, Cochrane (2021:p. 1) speculates that "Dubai is the new business capital of Africa"; which significantly and at times visibly influences the nature of urban development there. Concretely, however, China has the most visible, and at times controversial, presence of the NEUPs in the region. China has consolidated its NEUP role through its network of companies, standards, technologies, migrants, trade, financial and investment flows, among others, through the global city network.

Figure 3.4 *Burj al-Fatih building* in Khartoum, Sudan.
Source: Francisco Anzola / Wikimedia Commons / CC BY 2.0.

For China, investments in housing and built environments are meant to serve as a symbolic showcase for its developmental state model. This is perhaps most clearly articulated in Ethiopia given Addis Ababa's status as a hub for pan-African political and economic relations, serving important continental roles as the headquarters of the Africa Union and United Nations Economic Commission for Africa (UNECA) and a major economic hub in the Horn of Africa. China has thus viewed Ethiopia as a place where it can showcase its developmental model through a combination of large scale, and sometimes symbolic, infrastructure projects (e.g., the new African Union headquarters, see Figure 3.5) and industrial development investments (Fei and Liao 2020).

Migration, Travel and Knowledge Flows

A fourth channel is migration and travel, shaping the nature and structure of African cities in multiple ways (Chen and Myers 2013). Sino-inflected micro and meso spaces within cities, such as China Towns (see Figure 3.6), reflect the immigration of Chinese entrepreneurs, traders, and workers, and construction workers often move from project to project. The increase of Chinese-owned and -operated enterprises is changing the social and cultural characteristics of African markets as well as serving as a critical conduit for imports (Dobler 2008). Racial tensions have

Figure 3.5   African Union headquarters in Addis Ababa.
Source: USAFRICOM from Stuttgart / Wikimedia Commons / CC BY 2.0.

Figure 3.6   Nairobi's China Town.
Photo credit: James T. Murphy (Author).

increased at times in both places, sometimes resulting in xenophobic outbursts, although there are also relations of conviviality and intermarriage, for example, between migrants and "host" communities (Wall Street Journal 2012; Lampert et al. 2014). Despite the negatives, the net result of these flows is an expanded and deepened imbrication between China and Africa across a variety of axes; going well beyond oft-discussed geopolitical relations (Mohan 2021).

At a micro-social scale, business interactions between Africans and Chinese people in cities are changing markets, transforming value chains linking the regions, and providing mechanisms for knowledge transfer (Mohan and Tan-Mullins 2009; Marfaing and Thiel, 2013). Thousands of Africans now work for Chinese firms and this is further influencing the organization of urban labor markets and the prospects for skill upgrading, while bringing Africans and Chinese into close working relations. These interactions and experiences can be mixed, with some more positive than others (Arseme, 2014; Jackson 2014; Lambert et al., 2014; Plummer 2019). Simultaneously, there is a well-documented migration and travel of Africans to China to organize trade deals; some of whom migrate on a more permanent basis (Bodomo 2010; Cissé 2013; Bork-Hüffer et al. 2014; Carling and Haugen 2021; Jordan et al. 2021).

Chinese influence on cities is further manifest in the transfer of policy ideas about urban and economic development; through a demonstration effect encouraging a less neoliberal, non-Western approach to planning more in line with the "new structural economics" with its focus on infrastructure investment (Lin 2012).

Some see this as feeding into to a new "infrastructure-led" development regime globally (Schindler and Kanai 2021), potentially having deleterious effects on national debt (Zajontz 2021), the urban fabric, and rights to the city in the Global South. All told, through these embodied flows knowledge, capital, and commodities move between Africa and China and the relational proximity between and coproduction of these places is enhanced significantly; often under conditions of precarity, but also diversity (Ofosu and Sarpong 2021).

As intimated in the list above these four channels are not necessarily or strictly ontologically separate, rather they interweave such that the forces driving Chinese- and NEUP-inflected urban change in Africa are multiscalar, diverse, and uneven with respect to their impacts on production, consumption, and infrastructure regimes. In some cases, channels may work at cross-purposes with one another, such as when large-scale investments in SEZs (channel 2) create industries that may crowd out smaller-scale enterprises such as those owned and operated by Chinese entrepreneurs (channel 4). This contributes to the spatially uneven pace and direction of urban development in Africa noted earlier – manifest in pockets of globalized accumulation or consumption located in close proximity to areas of extreme deprivation and poverty – accentuating uneven development (Grant and Nijman 2004; Murphy 2022).

Integrating the Channels and Their Impacts

Ultimately, these four channels shape urban development pathways through their influence on economic, cultural, and political processes. Economically, Chinese and NEUP investments are driving some growth, "industrialization,"[2] and innovation in the region – manifest in the impacts of intra/extraversion on urban consumption and production regimes, the development of infrastructure regimes, and feeding into the potential restructuring of several cities (e.g., Accra, Addis Ababa, Cape Town, Nairobi) into regional hubs for innovation. Culturally, particularly significant are emerging shifts in consumer preferences in direct response to Chinese imports and the rise of *baihuo* (general merchandise) businesses (Haugen and Carling 2005; Mohan and Lampert 2013; Murphy and Carmody 2015).

Cities are ultimately expressions of these and other causal channels and power relations (Soja 1976) and their spatial forms and developmental impacts reflect prevailing distributions of power within the networks and relations through which they are constituted. Given that African actors are often in weaker power positions than those originating from outside the continent, such as the Chinese state (Carmody and Kragelund 2016), it is perhaps not surprising that many African cities continue to primarily exhibit symptoms of "parasitism" instead of generative development in response to these channels.

Nonetheless, experiences vary significantly across the continent (Carmody 2017b), depending on the nature of, and social relations constituting, the state.

For example, Ethiopia was successfully diversifying its production regimes due in significant part to Chinese investment (Oqubay 2015)[3], with manufacturing growing at an average of 15% a year recently (Tomkinson 2016) before the civil war, with many new industrial parks. Ethiopia's industrial policy has been characterized by "multiple axes of strategic coupling" which have allowed for win-win outcomes among the social actors involved (Carmody 2017b). Thus, it is not possible to determine urban outcomes solely on the basis of the international structures that NEUPs rely on for capital, commodity, and other flows into the continent, as these are dependent on the nature of the (power) assemblages created among social actors and sociopolitical opportunity structures. A focus on China in this regard is particularly relevant to illustrate the contingent, relational, and contested nature of such entanglements in African cities today.

Sino-African Relations in Africa Today: Specific Forms and Regime Impacts

Urban Africa is in the process of being "put together" (Carmody and Kragelund 2016: p. 8) through transnational relationships and networks that give rise to projects, initiatives, and other development forms. Much of the content of these relationships is brokered and subsequently governed by pacts among Chinese and African elite state actors; but separate and different relations coexist in the informal economy, governed by local market traders, associations, and their milieus. Domestic civil society also functions and sometimes provides checks and balances on Chinese labor, wage, safety, and environmental practices and, in some instances, graft, corruption and tax avoidance (Dobler 2009). Power, therefore, exists in the conventional form of statecraft via bilateral arrangements, but also in transnational and intrastate relations involving non-state actors. The latter may lack transparency and defined or codified governance as firms, organizations, and individuals shape these engagements in ways that are beneficial to themselves (Carmody and Kragelund 2016).

Such relationalities complicate the role of agency in African urban transformation – making it a multiscalar, bidirectional, and distributed phenomenon. Accordingly, "African agency" is not in opposition to "Chinese power," since the two are inter-constitutive (Mohan and Lampert 2013; Carmody and Kragelund 2016: p. 9). Developments in China have increasingly important effects on African countries and cities through different channels. As detailed above, these channels include both China's direct impact as a trading partner, financier, investor, and source of knowledge, labor, and policy ideas, but also its indirect, meta-effects through its knock-ons on global economic activity, real global commodity prices, technological standards, and "global" interest rates, among others (Carmody et al. 2022b). Such channels of spillover and transmissions to specific African countries are contingently experienced, shaped by national policy frameworks, actor-specific coalitions, and networks, and by the resilience of urban economies.

It is the scale and speed of increased Sino-African ties that is momentous in restructuring African economies; especially manifest in cities. Shocks from China (e.g., lower-output growth, relocation of Chinese firms offshore) may get transmitted rapidly to African economies, such as China's unfolding real estate crash that may impact urban development in Africa; either shutting down operations or expanding them in the region to counter the mainland fallout. Fast policy transfer, learning from the Chinese development experience and city-building and its interurban influences also pose a challenge to the traditional conception of the urban rooted in national and colonial-national experiences (Myers 2014). Looking East is attractive to African city officials who want to participate in an alternative model of urban development to that driven by Western neoliberal imperatives – the "pull" factor is important in these exchanges (Otele 2016).

A new stream of Chinese migrants has relocated to Africa's cities and is participating in urban transformation. While the number of Chinese in Africa is a matter of contention and speculation, estimated at between 1 and 9 million (Cissé 2021), and evidence of new Chinese neighborhoods in Johannesburg, Lusaka, Nairobi and Dakar is discerned (Chen and Myers 2013; see Figure 3.6), Chinese immigration is increasing competition and prices in consumption regimes and sometimes forcing outmigration of Africans to the urban peripheries (Lampert et al. 2014).[4] Chinese entrepreneurs have set up large wholesale enterprises[5] (known as *baihuo*) in cities to break-down bulk imports of consumer goods into units that can be traded by a diverse array of African informal traders (Grant 2015). There is some evidence that African informal traders have been crowded out as a result of the now ubiquitous *baihuo*. As a result, relations between Chinese traders and domestic informal entrepreneurs fluctuate from cooperation to downright hostility and confrontation (The Post 2005 cited in Sautmann and Hairong, 2013; Mairfaing and Thiel 2013); sometimes caught up in xenophobic outbursts and reciprocal racism (Grant and Thompson 2014). At the same time, other Chinese entrepreneurs work cooperatively through local wholesalers and patrons who operate as silent partners; lending a helping hand to navigate cultural and ethnic barriers in host societies as well as local contacts (Mohan and Lampert 2013). Dittgen and Chungu (2019: p. 3, emphasis in original) argue that the "metaphor of the graft... a foreign *tissue* either accepted or rejected by the receiving body while simultaneously forming an integral part of the bigger structure, is also applicable to the study of 'Chinese spaces' in urban Africa."

The size of the region, the diversity of Chinese and African actors, and the different global economic articulations of African countries and cities are considerable. As noted above China is only one among the "new" powers (NEUPs) to deepen its economic engagement with the region. However, a more developed Sino-East African regional strategy appeared as Beijing's BRI geopolitical-economic grand strategy came to life, where major infrastructure and defense projects were concentrated. For instance, new ports in Tanzania, rail-lines in Kenya and across Ethiopia linking landlocked Addis Abba to Djibouti's port, naval facilities in Djibouti and industrial zones along the Suez Canal in Egypt are all intended to support this massive new trade network; although recently mired in controversy and pushback (see Patey 2020). All told, China's influence on urban sociotechnical systems in Africa is diverse, extensive, and, in some cases, intensive. We now assess the quality and trajectories through which production, consumption, and infrastructure regimes in cities throughout the continent are developing in partial response to, and through the influence of, Sino-African relations.

Production Regimes

With respect to production, the results are mixed and spatially uneven. Investments in ports, roads, rail systems, and communications infrastructure have reduced both the time and costs linking African producers to regional/global markets. Such developments could bode well for the prospects that home-grown industries in the region might begin to compete in, and innovate in response to, the global economy such that the dual-dynamic of intra/extraversion might be slowed or reversed. However, infrastructure also enables competitive imports and accentuates debt accumulation, potentially undermining future infrastructure and social investments. For instance, the Standard Gauge Railway (SGR) project cost 6% of Kenya's GDP (Van Staden et al. 2020) and for "every 7.8 tonnes of cargo transported from Mombasa inland on the SGR [Chinese loan financed Standard Gauge Railway], only 1.01 tonnes [are] railed back to the port for export" (Taylor 2020: p. 42).

In practice, Sino-African inter-regionalism is, at best, an uneven contributor to the development of base (i.e., export-oriented) industries in African cities. As detailed in Chapter 2, urban-based manufacturing has struggled despite there being some growth in MVA over the past decade; in some years faster than general economic output, reversing previous trends. Because manufacturing output declined by less than other sectors under COVID-19, in 2020 its relative share of the economy increased but this cannot be considered "industrialization" in the context of an overall economic contraction. The flood of imports from China and other Asian countries has often meant that domestic production of consumer durables is either relatively superfluous or untenable given the prices of imports (Taylor 2016), although in some cases there are major Chinese factories supplying domestic demand, such as the Lee Group flip-flop (sandal) factory which has "99.99"% market share in Nigeria (manager quoted in Yuan Sun 2017).

Production regimes are becoming increasingly based on domestic and transnational commerce; activities offering limited pathways for upgrading and value capture. Given that many states and municipal governments lack industrial development policies or resources to implement existing strategies, the development of value-added manufacturing or service sectors remains uncoordinated, sporadic; some market access opportunities from AGOA and EBA notwithstanding. Needed are state agencies and African entrepreneurs capable and empowered to strategically manage the articulation of African cities into GVCs/GPNs in ways that obligate foreign firms and state-owned enterprises to invest in local capabilities (e.g., skills, technology transfers). At present, such a dynamic seems unlikely given the competitive pressures spurred by Chinese imports and the lack of "political will" (conducive political opportunity structures) and capabilities in most African states.

While much has been postulated about the potential of Chinese SEZs and EPZs in Africa (Brautigam and Tang, 2011), most acknowledge that zone investment is scattergun and that take-off is generally far slower than anticipated (Carmody and Murphy 2022). Relocation of Chinese manufacturing offshore (due to higher wages and economic upgrading) no doubt offers possibilities for African countries to (re)develop a manufacturing base and participate in the global supply and logistics networks that serve Chinese trade flows. EPZs and SEZs could be a central engine of urban economic development but they also require improvements in infrastructure and skills development (UNCTAD et al. 2021). Thus far, the necessary investments in this aspect of production regimes is generally lacking, so that Africa is experiencing a form of low-productivity structural transformation based on informalization. Much the same as in the extensive plans to build satellite cities (see Chapter 4), there were an estimated 237 legally established SEZs in Africa in 2021, but less than half this number were fully operational, with the remainder being under construction or in the very early stages of development (UNCTAD 2021).

Consumption Regimes

With respect to consumption regimes, it is clear that the quantity and variety of goods available in African markets has increased with deepened Sino-African relations. However, rising inequality in the region is most glaringly apparent in cities marked by pockets of luxury consumption and widespread deprivation. This is partly indicative of the spatial unevenness of Africa's articulation into and exclusion from new investment flows, commodity chains, and GPNs, such as those concomitant with ties to China (Hickel et al. 2021; Selwyn and Leyden 2022).

As has historically been the case, extraversion encourages boom and bust cycles that transfer wealth both to the countries that extract and receive the primary benefits of these resources, and to political and economic elites in the countries the resources come from (Arezki et al. 2015). The latter group may invest some of this into African real estate, but much has historically been transferred offshore to financial havens and other investments (e.g., overseas real estate, boarding school/university fees) that generate few benefits for development back home. Extraversion can also be linked to urban bias, a phenomenon manifest, in part, by the extraction of value from rural areas as a means to support urban-industrial development and consumption by urban-based "elites" (Lipton 1977).

Further evidence of the effects of Sino-African relations on consumption regimes can be seen in the everyday markets where Africans buy wage and other goods; markets where intra/extraversion dynamics are quite visible. Here we see the impacts of heightened inequality manifest in the disjuncture between markets where goods are affordable for the majority of urban residents – many of whom live below the poverty line – and those desired by established elites and *nouveau riche* who have benefited disproportionately from commodity-driven extraversion. This results in bifurcated consumption regimes: on one hand marked by small-scale traders, *buihuo*, informal enterprises, secondhand markets, and cheap imports from Asia; the other manifest in securitized shopping malls, gated communities, high rises, and chain stores demanded by wealthy residents.

Low prices and profit margins associated with mass markets in urban Africa can put pressure on wages and reduce quality and safety standards in Chinese-owned factories. Such circumstances help sustain informal economies or justify low wages given many poor can still consume basic goods despite living in conditions of extreme deprivation (Wuyts 2001). Urban consumption regimes thus remain locked into a dualistic/unequal structure that limits the prospects for social upgrading and wealth distribution even in cases where growth rates are relatively high. As Fosu (2015) demonstrated, the translation of growth gains into poverty reductions is determined significantly by inequality levels. The greater these are, the less impact growth has developmentally.

Infrastructure Regimes

The third pathway for urban development is determined by the evolution of infrastructure regimes in cities. Relations with China have played a significant role in driving capital investments in transportation, shipping, energy, housing, and industrial infrastructure throughout the continent. While such investments have contributed in important ways to alleviating congestion, energy, and housing shortages, and other negative externalities that reduce the competitiveness of African cities and industries in international markets, their impacts are highly uneven with regard to the provisioning of collective goods and services.

First and foremost, Sino-African relations are supporting economically significant infrastructure investments. Ports, SEZs, railways, roadways, and other trade-related construction is needed in and in-between cities. The World Bank (2009) emphasizes that such investments can reduce economic distances associated with trade and foster the emergence of networks of primary and secondary cities able to spread the benefits of growth nationally. However, Pigato and Tang (2015) report that the creation of linkages with local economies and the linking of local suppliers/firms to Chinese value chains has proven especially challenging in Africa in part because bottlenecks in key African infrastructures remain. The continent has a net infrastructure financing deficit of between US $68 and 108 billion a year (AfDB 2018).

While qualitatively different in many ways than the investments made by the colonial powers a century or more before, the primary purposes of these new infrastructures, at least from the Chinese side, is to generate contracts for construction firms and facilitate the extraction of raw materials offshore, whilst simultaneously creating channels for imports to penetrate more widely. Chinese construction companies control almost 60% of the entire construction market in Africa (Tang 2020) and their horizon is largely short-term profit as opposed to a grand strategy or urban vision for the region (Haung and Chen, 2016); although those that are state, or evenly privately-owned, must accord or at least not conflict with the Chinese Communist Party grand strategy (Doshi 2021). Through the adoption of Chinese standards such investments not only "power transport" but transport Chinese power (Otiso and Carmody 2023). The pressing question for African states is how to develop means and strategies to better exploit productivity gains to the benefit of local firms and urban economies from infrastructural investments, without compromising them through excessive debt. Absent effectively designed and implemented industrial policy (e.g., through the NUPs discussed in Chapter 2), it is difficult to see how this might occur as most production regimes face an enduring crisis with respect to their long-term development. As a result, evolving Sino-influenced infrastructure regimes almost exclusively privilege exchange value via transnational commodity and capital flows over concerns regarding the quality of life, amenities, and basic services available to local residents (i.e., the use values of cities).

There are also social implications of infrastructure development, manifest in the quality of the collective goods and services available to most urban residents. While there have been some significant investments in housing projects, these have generally not served the needs of the poorest. Instead, these investments enable a kind of "instant urbanism" in sequestered enclaves of new island-like enclosures that have sprung up on the outskirts of existing African cities. Consequently Sino-African relations have had limited impact on the distribution and quality of essential public services such as education, water, and sanitation services to the majority of residents in cities. In fact, between 2000 and 2020, nearly 75% of all loans tied to aid projects went to the transportation, power, mining, and ICT sectors while only 9.2% was allocated to water, education, and other social services combined (Boston University Global Development Policy Center 2022). The net result has been a continued spatial splintering of urban infrastructure (Amin and Graham 1997; Graham and Marvin 2001; Jaglin 2008; Swilling 2014; Marr and Mususa 2021) with the built environments of most cities improving, but in a highly uneven manner. Sino-African relations are symptomatic and partly constitutive of this pathway, not determinative of it.

Conclusion

This chapter focused on the impacts of increased inter-regionalism between China, other NEUPs, and African cities. The impacts, particularly from China, on Africa's urban development are influenced by city-specific dynamics and multiscalar relations and operate through overlapping regimes. Importantly, we underscore the uneven nature and diverse experiences of African cities with regard to the production and infrastructure regimes and their potential retarding impact on sustainable and equitable urban growth. The impacts on production, consumption, and infrastructure regimes are generally quite pervasive across the continent, manifest in the strengthening of endemic dualistic and splintered urban structures which lies at the heart of the "varying and increasing levels of urban poverty, inequality, and inefficiency" in Africa's cities (UN-Habitat 2014: p. 37).

From a policy perspective, as African cities continue to grow economically and demographically, and Sino-African inter-regionalism deepens, ensuring pro-poor development outcomes, among other things, will require a new paradigm of sustainable urban governance that can counteract the negative aspects of Chinese and other NEUPs' power. A sustainable urban governance system would engage national governments, regional institutions, urban and diverse urban agents (Myers 2011; Obeng-Odoom 2017) and require strengthened capacities of city governments to provide public goods and services. Another prerequisite will be a more vibrant, stronger and competitive local private sector that can partner and/or compete with Chinese firms and entrepreneurs. The creation of a more empowered urban governance system capable of performing these functions in African cities is a political "choice" that national and municipal leaders have to face. This is, however, doubtful given the current and still largely pervasive neoliberal regime in the continent and no prior examples of how to realize sustainable urban governance in the region. An essential concern in this regard is to move beyond exchange value/growth/agglomeration as the sole drivers of successful urban transitions by embracing wider concerns about distribution, inequality, accessibility, and quality as it relates to collective goods and services in African cities; that is to foreground and focus on use-value considerations (Murphy 2022). How to harness the geopolitical and geoeconomic power of China and other NEUPs to achieve such gains is a crucial question moving forward.

Notes

1 Storper et al. (2015) use this term somewhat differently to refer to cross-membership of corporate boards.
2 In the sense that some of the investments are industrial sector, even if they do not change the general trajectory of deindustrialization.
3 Interestingly, this author was a minister in the Ethiopian government, having previously served as mayor of Addis Ababa, and was awarded "African mayor of the year." His ideas were then "scaled up" to inform national development policy.
4 Return migration to China also occurred after the 2014 commodity price bust, with approximately 150,000 Chinese migrants leaving Angola between 2013 and 2017 (Hancock 2017 cited in Large 2021).
5 But earlier we saw these are general purpose stores.

Chapter Four
Fantasy Urbanization in Africa: The Political Economy of Heterotopias

Introduction

Africa's rapid urbanization is at once both an intensely localized and globalized phenomenon. The continent is currently urbanizing faster than it did in the late 1990s and is expected to become the fastest urbanizing region from 2020 to 2050 (UN 2014). Although urbanization is often presented as a challenge to the development aspirations of African countries, the process itself is not necessarily a bad thing. Indeed, most analysts agree that urbanization can – and often does – contribute to, or precipitate, economic and social development. However a notable aspect of Africa's urbanization is that it has not been accompanied by substantial improvements in basic living standards for the majority of the urban residents. In 2018, nearly 248 million sub-Saharan Africans lived in slums, an average of about 56% of urban populations that account for almost all the current urban spatial growth in some fast-growing African cities (UN Habitat 2020). Moreover, poverty rates remain high in cities, particularly when adjusted to the rapidly increasing costs of living experienced over the past decade. Rent premia are high, even in slums, and urban residents in Africa typically pay 55% more for housing and 42% more for transport compared to other regions (Talukdar 2018; Page et al. 2020).

The Urban Question in Africa: Uneven Geographies of Transition, First Edition. Pádraig R. Carmody, James T. Murphy, Richard Grant and Francis Y. Owusu.

Urban development in Africa has also been influenced by global trends. For instance, the region's urbanization is occurring in the context of a global neoliberal regime of accumulation. However, neoliberalism seems incapable of addressing persistent urban problems in Africa, including inequality and poverty. Rather, one of the ways neoliberalism in Africa is mitigating the contradictions it generates has been the embrace of national and urban development imaginaries, that have resulted in a push for megaprojects and creation of "world city" developments or heterotopias (attempts to enact utopias). As noted earlier, these projects are popular current urban development ideas, based on the fascination with Dubai, Singapore, or Shanghai's urban development experiences and are promoted within transnational policy networks, and are driven by externally funded developers. Perhaps the most extreme planned new city is Akon City in Senegal, named for the music star, which will be a "real life Wakanda" (from the Hollywood film *Black Panther*), where residents will use cryptocurrency rather than ordinary specie for example (https://akoncity.com/about).

This chapter explores these attempts to reimagine and implement fantasy urbanism on the continent by assessing the nature of planning processes behind these developments, the theory undergirding them, and their concrete impacts. It also examines their visions of, and implementation impacts on, urban sociotechnical regimes. Empirical evidence from a variety of proposed, implemented, and failed developments, including touted new-build, smart/eco-cities like Eko-Atlantic (Lagos Nigeria), Hope City (Accra, Ghana), and Konza City (Nairobi, Kenya) are presented. We argue that these projects are imagined, and in some cases brought into being, through practices which are at odds with, or disarticulated from, the extant regimes that govern the experiences of most African urban residents and everyday informal practices, such as street trading or buying water. The projects, in essence, seek to create sociotechnical systems from scratch that are outward-oriented but disconnected or divorced from those associated with the realities of established cities. They thus represent attempts at connection to the global economy that seek to erase or leapfrog beyond Africa's extant urban conditions.

The Rise of Fantasy Urbanism in Africa

In an attempt to modernize African cities, make them competitive for international investments, and satisfy the ambitions of politicians who champion them, high profile urban developments, including new satellite towns and megaprojects, are reemerging in Africa. Many larger African cities have gone beyond the traditional land use plans and instead have developed master plans of new "future cities." According to Watson (2014: p. 215):

> Visions for these future cities reflect images of Dubai, Singapore, or Shanghai, although iconic building shapes from elsewhere in the world may be thrown in for

good measure. And while the glass tower buildings and landscaped freeways suggest a revived Corbusian modernism, the accompanying texts also promise that these plans will deliver the more fashionable eco-cities and smart cities.

These urban fantasy plans evoke the "Africa rising" narrative and draw on the idea that the continent represents the "last frontier" for investments and real estate development, especially after the post-2008 financial crisis (Watson 2014). However, the particular variegation of fantasy urbanism proliferating in African cities is driven less by local development needs and more by (neoliberal) global processes including the hybermobility of capital, the need for spatial fixes to manage overaccumulation in the core and emerging economies, and emergent, footloose policy mobilities that replicate and diffuse utopian visions regarding what cities can and should be.

The spread of neoliberal globalization has drastically shaped the way cities are developing across the globe. Neoliberalism in the African context was initiated through the imposition of SAPs from the early 1980s; which essentially transformed the state's role into a gatekeeper of the neoliberal project and market; attempting to ensure a stable investment climate and keeping in check those marginalized by the process (Peck and Tickell 2002; Afenah 2009). Globalization also refers to worldwide processes of functional interaction and integration among the people, companies, and governments of different nations that have intensified since the late 1980s; driven in part by international trade and investment and aided by information technology that make the world more integrated and therefore interdependent (Carmody 2015). Although related, the connections between globalization and neoliberalism are not straightforward – globalization is a much broader and more multidimensional process than the transnational economic transactions that undergird neoliberalism (Heron 2008; Litonjua 2008). What is clear is that cities play critical roles in both processes – they embody and reflect globalization writ large, and serve as primary sites where neoliberal policies are formulated, experimented with, promoted, diffused, and enforced.

The world economy is largely organized around and through cities, and so-called "world cities" play increasingly important roles in globalization (Taylor 2005). Indeed, cities are no longer mere points of production and exchange of goods and services; they have become places where people and products are linked to the wider world (Robinson 2006). As a result, the global urban system is dominated by a small number of world cities that have become command-and-control points for global capitalism. Although most world cities are in developed countries, other cities are increasingly playing significant roles in globalization and thus offer a powerful lens for comparative analyses (Robinson 2006, 2013, 2016). For instance, cities of the Global South are increasingly becoming central to capital accumulation globally, as centers of production (Shanghai), ownership (in the platinum industry, for example in the case of Johannesburg – see Surborg 2012) and as new markets for Northern and other transnationals through so-called "Bottom of the Pyramid" strategies, which seek to enroll the poor into GVCs through selling small packets of washing powder for example, as they cannot afford larger boxes (Hart and Christensen 2002; Landrum 2007).

Although African countries have embraced economic neoliberalization and globalization, their integration into the latter process been somewhat limited. For instance, and as highlighted in Chapter 2, the new international division of labor characterized by export processing manufacturing has by-and-large bypassed most of SSA because the region is perceived as lacking infrastructure, a sufficiently skilled human resource base, capacity for effective state intervention and relatively high real product wages, among other issues. The region's economies instead continue to serve largely as suppliers of raw materials, including oil and mineral exports, commodity, and low technology basic goods, and as markets for the importation of consumer and capital goods (Omokhodion 2006). According to some, cities in the Global South also serve as "holding centers" for populations that are surplus to the requirements and demands of global capital accumulation (Davis and Monk 2007). This point is germane in the SSA context, where the relationships between urbanization, industrialization, and development have been tenuous (Ravallion et al. 2007; Freire et al. 2014; Fox and Goodfellow 2022).

Urban production regimes in Africa have not historically been well integrated into the global economy and cities depend on the export of natural resources and agricultural products in order to import manufactured goods into consumption regimes. Moreover, poor public services, infrastructure, and inadequate city management all obstruct urban economic growth in the region. In addition, Africa's rapid (late) urbanization is occurring in a context of slums, poverty, and unprecedented levels of demographic pressure (Fox and Goodfellow 2022). Poverty, deprivation, crime, and general human insecurity have become more widespread in many African cities, especially in slums. This is partly a result of underfunding of the public sector and collective services. For example, Pikine, a city of about a million people in Senegal had a municipal budget of ten US dollars per person and one police officer per 10,000 residents in 2012, versus 42 per 10,000 in New York City (Myers 2016).

One of the ways in which African political and planning elites are seeking to overcome this legacy of urban underdevelopment, reflected in the prevalence of informality in African cities, is through the creation of new types of urban development and large infrastructural projects. These efforts, driven by profit and the desire to globalize African cities further, have taken a variety of forms ranging from SEZs, financial services centers, and megaprojects and are expected to modernize African cities and make them competitive to and for international investors.

In many ways, this rise of fantasy urbanism in African cities is also partly driven by the spread of global policymaking ideas and partly supported through funds from actors in NEUPs and old economic powers. For example, "Rendeavour – a constellation of British, New Zealand, American and Norwegian investors – is actively building seven new cities in Sub-Saharan Africa" (Korah et al. 2021). The trend involves the widespread adoption and emulation of the so-called best practices and models of urban policy and development from around the world, which promises to make such cities attractive for investment, more competitive, and in some cases, environmentally sustainable (McCann and Ward 2011)[1] . The result has been the creation of "world-class cityness" through mega urban development projects. Marcinkoski (2017) refers to this phenomenon as "speculative urbanisation" as these activities differ from more conventional urban developments because they are primarily for political and economic purposes, rather than to meet real (as opposed to artificially projected) demographic or market demands.

Although many of the new high-profile satellite cities and megaprojects are at, or stuck in, the planning stages, proponents do not seem to have learned from Africa's long experience with such projects (Cain 2014), such as new capitals such as Abuja (Nigeria), and Dodoma (Tanzania), although others such as Gaborone (Botswana), and Lilongwe (Malawi) have been more successful. New city projects also emphasize physical development, exacerbate social exclusion, disrupt informal settlements and businesses, and lack public involvement (Abubakar and Doan 2017). Indeed, the most high-profile urban developments of recent years have not been about restructuring the accumulation processes within extant cities but center on new types of additive urban development which ostensibly attempt to: 1) work from a *tabula rasa*, and 2) on that basis forge new connections with the international economy. These attempts at connection through erasure are heterotopic. According to Foucault (1984: p. 3), heterotopias are "a kind of effectively enacted utopia." As Marcinkoski (2017) argues, "what is most often being peddled as 'urban design' today in Africa is simply scaled-up reproductions of 'proven' urban formats, or dystopic renderings of new settlement as implausible architectural icons." These projects exacerbate deficient urban conditions by shifting severely limited capital resources away from more basic urban services and extant sociotechnical regimes.

Neoliberal Planning and Heterotopic Urbanism in Africa

Since planning as a profession derives its relevance from the state, neoliberalism and its focus on reducing the role of the state, has had significant implications for urban planning. From a neoliberal perspective, much urban planning is seen as distorting land markets and increasing transaction costs through bureaucratization of the urban economy (Wright 2013), although critical perspectives see planning as largely serving the needs of capital (Rankin 2009; Su and Qian 2020). According to Gleeson and Low (2000: p. 135), neoliberalism undercuts the very basis of planning as a tool for correcting and avoiding market failure and privileges a "minimalist form of spatial regulation whose chief purpose is to facilitate development." As Tasan and Baeten (2012) argue, planning is a prerequisite for neoliberal urban development precisely because a system based on market-oriented dynamics can only function if planning institutions regulate land-use decisions. Neoliberalism, therefore, presents many challenges to planners, including the effects of "down-sizing of local government, a simplification of public planning processes, and an emphasis on production and economic efficiency rather than redistribution and fairness" (Sager 2011: 180). As Keith and de Souza Santos note (2021: p. 4), planners in their daily realities confront the necessity of

> "least worst" interventions, the rationing of scarce resources and the clumsy solutions that not always work when confronting "wicked" problems. Yet all too often, this is something that scholars in the business of providing "golden bullet" solutions to single systems in transport dilemmas, building homes or city electrification overlook.

In other cases, in Kigali, Rwanda, for example, planning is used as a kind of "development weapon" to control people (Goodfellow 2022).

According to Afenah (2009: p. 3), the practical effects of neoliberalism on urban policy can be seen at various scales, "through the reorientation from redistribution to competition, institutional rescaling (giving greater powers to sub- and supranational levels) and through the revitalization of the urban economy through privatization, liberalization, decentralization, deregulation and increased fiscal discipline." These neoliberal challenges to core planning ideas have led some to question the concept of "neoliberal planning," stressing the contradictory relationship between them. For instance, Olesen (2014) argues that neoliberalization of planning has helped to compromise strategic spatial planning and to normalize neoliberal discourses in planning processes.

According to Tasan-Kok and Baeten (2012), as urban planning becomes increasingly neoliberal and "entrepreneurial," serious contradictions emerge. Fundamentally, this highlights the planner's impossible task of serving private profit-seeking interests (exchange value) while seeking the public betterment of cities (use value). Baeten (2012: pp. 206–207) argues that neoliberalism seems to have reduced urban planning "to a mere facilitator of 'market forces'" with urban dwellers increasingly unable to "lay claims on the city government to guarantee their well-being." The net result is that "[t]he city as right, as entitlement, is slowly being replaced with the city as possibility and opportunity" (Baeten 2012: pp. 206–207). All told, neoliberalism has weakened the planner's toolkit as the focus of urban planners across Africa seems to have shifted from making the city a decent place to live to a place of elite consumption and production, the benefits of which are meant to trickle down. As a result, and also a consequence of resource constraints, Africa planners have only tinkered at the margins of the enormous urban problems in the region, while often privileging risky mega-developments at the expense of upgrading extant regimes in ways that can more widely distribute development.

Emerging Heterotopias in Africa

Given the limitations on planning practice posed by the operation of a "free" market economy, cities around the world, including major African cities, are adopting other strategies to enhance their competitive advantages in attracting capital, tourists, knowledge workers, and other flows judged beneficial. Florida's (2002) work on the importance of the creative class and fostering urban amenities, services, and environments conducive to attracting them has been a particularly important driving force here. In addition, the rhetoric of "smart cities" has been similarly taken up, manifest in desires to create places where ICT, sensing/surveillance technologies, and big data are used to effectively integrate infrastructures, efficiently manage essential services (e.g., energy, traffic flow), and reduce the ecological footprint of urban sociotechnical systems (Batty et al. 2012; Angelidou 2015). Other ideations built into new-build city designs and plans include the development of new financial service sectors, technology and innovation hubs linked to higher education, globally competitive industries through inward FDI, and utopian living conditions for residents, far removed from the congestion and complexities of "old" cities.

In one sense, such visions are a welcome challenge to the notion that the continent should follow the West's lead when it comes to urban development. Afro-futurist, heterotopian cities offer the promise of leapfrogging beyond such pathways; a hopeful alternative to mainstream, modernist discourses focused on "catching-up." In practice, however, new-build urban developments have not lived up to the promises, have often stalled in their early stages of development, been mired in corruption, and/or remained woefully out of sync with the realities of extant urban regimes nationally. We now illustrate these circumstances through the examples of three new-build city projects – Eko-Atlantic (Lagos, Nigeria), Konza Technopolis (Nairobi, Kenya), and Hope City (Accra, Ghana) – that reflect the challenges of jump-starting urban transitions through utopian initiatives.

Eko Atlantic (Lagos), Nigeria

Eko-Atlantic, currently under construction on reclaimed land off the coast of Lagos, captures the heterotopian realities of new-build African cities today (see Figure 4.1). Lagos experienced spectacular population and spatial growth in the past four decades. Even though growth rates have slowed since the late 1980s, the city faces severe urban problems such as high rates of poverty and

Figure 4.1   Eko-Atlantic Skyline 2020.
SmartAfricanBoy / Wikimedia Commons / CC BY-SA 4.0.

inequality (UN-Habitat 2010). The city is also known for urban decay, as reflected in overcrowded housing, congested traffic, inadequate sanitation and social services, and a high unemployment rate, despite what is often touted as more effective city management in recent years. In addition, many residents are crowded into limited space threatened by sea-level rise, ocean surges, and extreme weather events. Despite these problems, Lagos remains the economic "pulse" of the largest economy in Africa; itself bigger in size than either Kenya's or Côte D'Ivoire's (Kazeem 2016). This has put pressure on urban infrastructure regimes and resulted in substantial rises in property prices in Lagos Island in particular, where many of the urban elite live (Global Property Guide 2014).

Inaugurated by former US President Bill Clinton and developed, perhaps uncoincidentally, by a substantial donor to the Clinton Foundation (Côté-Roy and Moser 2019), the Eko-Atlantic project is an attempt to rearticulate Lagos' relations with the global political economy so that it becomes a world city. Funded jointly by the Lagos state government, South EnergyX Nigeria Limited (a subsidiary of the Chagoury Group), and other African and international banks, Eko-Atlantic is being promoted nationally and internationally as a model of a public-private partnership (PPP). The project, which is being implemented by experienced international architectural design and engineering firms, is the highest-profile example of the so-called "ecocities" currently in vogue across Africa. In this case, Eko-Atlantic is presented as a green development that will protect Lagos from the storm flooding and rising sea levels through the Great Wall of Lagos sea revetment that is expected to help reverse coastal erosion and relieve some of the pressure on land and resources in Lagos that will accompany climate change (Grant 2015).

Eko-Atlantic is also marketed with a pro-business message: a world-class city that was touted as it going to be "the new financial epicentre of West Africa by the year 2020" (http://www.ekoatlantic.com). This "model city" will boast an infrastructure regime that is privately administered and supplied with electricity, water, mass transit, sewage, and security and will help "update and transform Lagos's notoriously bad international reputation as a poster-child of crime and urban dysfunction" (Grant 2015: p. 321). When completed, Eko-Atlantic will include 3,000 new buildings, zoned in 10 separate districts over 10 square kilometers on reclaimed land, complete with waterfront areas, tree-lined streets, efficient transport systems, and mixed-use plots that combine residential areas with leisure facilities, offices, and shops. It is projected to house many businesses, 250,000 residents, serve as the workplace for 150,000 people, and support an additional 190,000 commuters. Moreover, it is meant to attract significant levels of FDI that "will support a new urban development the size of the Manhattan" (http://www.ekoatlantic.com). Given it is still under construction with only a few residential towers and facilities built as of early 2022, it is difficult to know how these ambitions will come to fruition.

Nonetheless, Eko-Atlantic reveals important insights regarding the limitations on new-build cities as a solution to the urban question in Africa today. As Grant (2015) notes, there is a risk of abandoning other cities through the promotion of such detached new cities, or "city doubles" (Murray 2015), explicitly geared toward serving elites and international capital. Eko-Atlantic does not address the multifold problems of Lagos discussed above and may indeed exacerbate them through the diversion of resources, jobs, and tax revenues. For instance, it is doubtful that many jobs will be created in its production regime beyond those during the construction phase, unless the project's retail and business ambitions are fully realized: a tall order. Eko is, in fact, a form of "enclave urbanism" that is likely to be inaccessible to Lagos' informal sector whilst enabling Nigeria's super-rich to exploit the crisis of climate change to increase inequality and seal themselves off from its impacts; part of a broader global trend (Lukacs 2014; Buxton and Hayes, 2016; Korah et al. 2021).

Konza Technopolis (Nairobi), Kenya

Konza Technopolis is a "smart" greenfield city that is meant to play a central role in Kenya's industrial development (see https://www.konza.go.ke). Formally launched in 2013, the city is still in the first-stage of construction, on a 5,000 acre tract 60 km southeast of Nairobi. A highly ambitious project, Konza will be a "self-sustaining" city that will create an "innovation ecosystem" in support of three clusters of industrial activity: ICT and ICT-driven activities, life sciences research and development, and engineering. An Italian company is building the city's main infrastructure (e.g., roads, energy, waste, water), the Chinese government is investing in a data center on the site, and the Korean Economic Development Cooperation Fund (ECDF) has committed nearly $100 million to establish the Kenya Advanced Institute of Science and Technology (Kenya KAIST) there that will focus on training engineers and scientists. By 2030, it is hoped that Konza will help drive Kenya's economic diversification and upgrading, and attract significant FDI; employing 17,000 workers, having 200,000 residents, and boasting a world-class infrastructure that is sustainable and "smartly" managed. Its vision is utopian as aptly depicted in Figure 4.2.

As noted earlier in more general terms, there is something positive to be said for the radical and idealistic nature of the project and the desire of planners to have it develop autonomously. Leaders in the Konza Technopolis Development Authority (KOTDA) are unabashed boosters for the city to leapfrog Kenyan industries into creative, innovative, and high-value sectors. In fact, KOTDA views the project as central for the creation of a "Silicon Savannah" in Kenya, boldly advertised in its headquarters in Nairobi (see Figure 4.3). Moreover, there is the view that such a radical, forward-thinking plan is only possible through a greenfield project rather than within Nairobi city limits. As one of Konza's planners noted, "no one can fix Nairobi."

Despite the optimism and vision, however, Konza appears unlikely to achieve its goals unless three primary concerns are resolved. The first issue is the fact that Konza is, in many ways, a radical discontinuity with respect to Kenya's economic and

Figure 4.2   Konza Technopolis as imagined by its Planners (construction Kenya/Konza Technopolis Development Authority).
Source: URBAN GRAPHICS.

Figure 4.3   Konza Technopolis imagined as the Silicon Savannah.
Photo credit: James T. Murphy (Author).

industrial development, extant path dependencies, urban governance institutions, and the production regimes currently operating in its cities. While Konza's proponents view this as a major asset to the project, it is questionable as to whether, or how, FDI into Konza might create the kinds of proximities (e.g., institutional, material) needed to stimulate the development of linkages, spillovers, and upgrading processes beyond the Technopolis. Moreover, it is unclear where the related "varieties" of knowledge and capabilities exist between Konza's desired investments, and existing firms and industries in Kenya; interconnections that can prove essential for stimulating regional development (e.g., see Frenken et al. 2007). Such concerns are well documented by decades of regional studies scholarship and as of now it appears that Konza, at best, might become what Hardy (1998, p. 650) termed a "cathedral in the desert....[an] enclave of foreign capital with few linkages backwards or forwards."

A second issue relates to the costs and complexities of moving from planning to implementation. The KOTDA worked closely with a US-based consulting firm to develop its plans but these appear to have been, in some cases, woefully unable to account for the realities of actually getting things built and completed on the ground. Corruption-related issues have been especially challenging, manifest particularly in land grabbing and speculation by insiders familiar with where Konza was to be sited. Such practices drove up the costs of land and, in effect, helped to scare off investors who had expressed early interest. Another issue that has effected implementation has been the national government's support for the project and the shifting priorities of administrations since Konza was initiated. Such shifts, and the fact that barely 10% of the state funding promised has materialized, have made financing of the project inconsistent and slow, further discouraging potential investors (VOA News 2019). As of July

2019, only two international investors had committed, raising additional concerns about risks. All told, the realities of Konza's implementation have made many within and beyond Kenya highly skeptical.

The third issue also relates to risk perceptions. That is the chicken-egg challenge that greenfield projects like Konza face. Given that, like many new-build cities in Africa, it is located a good distance from a major city, there are questions as to how workers and firms might be convinced or productively enabled to relocate/commute. Public transportation linkages (the extant infrastructure regime) are poor and the new SGR linking Mombasa and Nairobi does not include a stop in Konza. Thus a key issue is whether investors are willing, and for how long, to wait for the city's population to grow, particularly with respect to the skilled workers and managers needed to support high-tech industries. At present, the plans to enable this to occur are, at best, vague, begging the question – if they build it, will they come?

HOPE City (Accra), Ghana

Hope (Home, Office, People, and Environment) City, Accra, Ghana, is the brainchild of the award-winning Italian architect Paolo Brescia with investment from RLG, a Ghanaian originating ICT company with headquarters in Dubai, and support from the Ghanaian government. Located about an hour's drive from central Accra in Prampram, Hope City is designed as a multidimensional city with six circulars that draws inspiration from the traditional compound houses of northern Ghana and contemporary living based on the Ghanaian communal values with residential, retail, ICT, business, leisure, and cultural life and projected to create 50,000 jobs, and host 25,000 inhabitants (Vourlias 2015). This $10 billion project was launched in 2013 by the Ghanaian president amid great excitement and was expected to be a beacon of hope for the rest of the continent (Kuuire 2017).

Like most of such planned projects across Africa, Ghana's Hope City faces an uncertain future. No work has begun on the project since its launch, and RLG Communications has been caught up in various scandals. In addition, Ghana's economic instability and decline in the value of the cedi since 2014 have raised doubts about the future of the project (Vourlias 2015). It has been reported that as of October 2021, the government was still looking for investors, raising concerns about whether "Hope City is dead" (Sabutey 2021). However, a more relevant question for our purposes is who would benefit from Ghana's Hope City? Given the expected high prices of the buildings, would we expect the project to benefit the elite in the tech market and outside companies looking for opportunities to expand their global reach, or would it cater to the needs of the many young Ghanaian developers and technology entrepreneurs looking to launch their projects? If the latter is the objective a more helpful approach from the government would have involved giving out more grants and scholarships and helping to build small tech hubs to inspire the average Ghanaian IT (information technology) person (Kuuire 2017).

Africa's Neoliberal Heterotopias: Generative or Exclusionary Enclaves?

We characterize these planned urban developments as utopian dystopias or heterotopias not only because they are unlikely to generate substantial economic benefits in the form of job creation, linkage, multiplier, or accelerator effects, but also because through their representations, micro-spatialities, and external foci they discursively erase the deepening contradictions of the urban agglomerations with which they are associated. As such, they can be seen as further examples of the unequalization of space and class associated with global neoliberalism, even as they attempt to reverse marginalization through greater integration into the global economy. As such, while the gaze of their planners/developers is utopian, the impacts may be partially dystopian – ultimately making them heterotopian in nature.

As noted earlier, Africa is undergoing a profound urban transformation and is charting its own, distinctive path to modernity (Chabal 2009). Current trends indicate deepening income inequality, with profound social, economic, and political ramifications of which these new-build projects are both reflective and constitutive. For instance, Johannesburg is the city in Africa with the highest Gini coefficient at 0.7, and it also has an extremely high crime rate, further incentivizing the construction of gated communities and urban heterotopias that enable elites to "manage" dystopian challenges by living in securitized enclaves. While the extent of crime should not be sensationalized or overplayed, structural violence (e.g., the enduring legacy of *apartheid*) begets direct economic violence, which results in deeper entrenchment of anomie and exclusion as reflected in the urban morphology of the city – i.e., urban splintering. This splintering no longer just manifests in gated communities, but as whole new cities being planned to discursively and spatially erase, bypass, or circumvent the often predominantly informal mode of reproduction and capital accumulation of the cities to which they are to be attached or articulated. They are to be hyperglobalized "spaces of (class) exception," sociotechnical enclaves linked to the global economy in ways distinctive from their "host" countries.

Campbell (2007: p. 141) writes that "similar to the way in which indigenous Kenyans were simultaneously needed [as workers] and rejected by the colonial city council in Nairobi, refugees and other African migrants now fill this ambiguous position." Utopias can never be achieved in practice, and their attempted construction results in new exclusions, as evinced by the cases highlighted above. However, exclusion or detachment from the reality of the host society can never be achieved, given heterotopic dependence on labor power for their construction and operation. Furthermore, in a dialectical interplay, revenge may be meted out to the neo-revanchist cities (Smith 1996) under construction through violent crime within and beyond their boundaries for their inhabitants. The class war, expressed by neoliberalism (Harvey 2005), then experiences contradictions and instability despite this attempted socio-spatial fix.

While some of the new heterotopias, either in the process of planning, or under construction, in Africa have their inspiration and finance from the "Global East," the longer-term question remains whether they represent a form of neo-developmentalism or neoliberalism? Whilst principally, presently they seem to be by-products of the latter, their futures are not set in stone. Although Africa is often written about, mistakenly, as marginal to the dynamics of global capital accumulation (which is ultimately dependent on natural resources), cities in Africa then are set to become, even more than before, some of the primary centers where the social and economic contradictions of neoliberalizing capitalism play out. However such urbanization, dialectically and partly through its contradictions, produces new opportunities for development. As such African cities, or many of them, represent a neoliberal frontier.

Rather than housing deficits, poor infrastructure, poverty, crime, or other symptoms being the main problems in African cities, it is their, and the global, mode of neoliberal capital accumulation and associated livelihoods which is the structural root of these symptoms. In the current round of urbanization in Africa, different forms of production (formal/informal) articulate, compete, and to some extent, conflict. Under national developmentalism the two circuits of the urban economy (formal and informal) were highly articulated and interdependent. Under the current round of neoliberal "glurbanisation" (Jessop 1997), there is an attempt being made through worlding practices (e.g., new-build cities) to restructure (some) space outward and, in the process, disarticulate further extant/established urban economies from the world system. These patterns of spatial restructuring, however, will be incapable of overcoming the urban crisis on the continent, because of their limited nature, lack of productive focus, and new exclusions they produce. A way to understand the potential roles of high-profile projects in the African context is through the sociotechnical systems lens.

These projects are directly or indirectly redefining the core features and functions of the urban sociotechnical systems of the cities/regions in which they are situated. For instance, they can be seen as part of the "global infrastructure turn," often driven by national governments, development banks, and private financiers, and therefore overshadowing metropolitan planning as a means of intervening in infrastructure regimes (Dobson 2017). This also reflects the centripetal state politics of many "late" urbanizers; a circumstance where national governments maintain control over municipalities under the guise of pursuing country-level development objectives (Fox and Goodfellow 2022). Although the push for infrastructure and mobilities has been justified by rapid urbanization, which is more pronounced in Africa, it is also driven by the growing consensus that infrastructure is fundamental to achieving national development. The question is, then, what do utopian cities actually do in terms of managing the demographic pressures of urban transitions, and who would benefit from them? At present, it appears that such projects principally serve as means for short-run, speculative accumulation and as enclaved spaces to enable elites to escape the messy/congested realities of extant/old cities. These projects have the potential to reshape African cities, but their generative potential remains to be seen.

Similarly, the productive capacity of these projects, i.e., their implications for production regimes, remains elusive. Rather than speculative investments driven by the political interest of local elites (Croese 2018), a productivist focus would strategically identify those economic sectors in which competitive advantage, internal market deepening, and opportunities for import substitution could be developed. Urban governance must be reconceptualized as part of a broader program of structural transformation to achieve this. According to Turok (2013: p. 66):

> possible examples of technologically realistic products [that African cities could produce] include fertilizers, chemicals, plastics and other petroleum products, construction materials, plant and equipment, pipes, electrical cables, pylons, buses and railway rolling stock.

New spatial instruments such as SEZs, eco-industrial parks, and others may play a part in this, but the strategic vision must be broader, involving the beneficiation of resources, for example, and the development of linkage and multiplier effects which may be achieved through these (Kaplinsky and Morris 2016). Fundamentally then, this comes down to nature and matters of state.

Although couched in the rhetoric of attracting investment and enhancing competitiveness, these fantasy urbanisms are driven mostly by consumption. However, since the new cities are often priced beyond the reach of the emerging middle class, such as it is (Melber 2022), these developments will substantially exacerbate social exclusion and disrupt existing consumption and production regimes, particularly those dependent on/by informal settlements and businesses. As van Noorloos and Kloosterboer (2018: p. 223) argue:

> The consumptive and supply-driven character of many projects so far (resembling gated communities for middle and higher classes), their insertion into "rurban" spaces with complex land governance arrangements, and their tendency to implement post-democratic private-sector-driven governance will make them at best unsuitable for solving Africa's urban problems, and at worst they will increase expulsions and enclosures of the poor, public funding injustice and socio-spatial segregation and fragmentation.

In sum, given the material and lived realities facing majority populations in most of Africa's cities – particularly those living in informal settlements and slums – it is clear that fantasy urbanism will do little or nothing to ameliorate these conditions any time soon. Rather than addressing these problems, these projects mark a high-water mark in the age of neoliberal urbanization in Africa, one focused on hypermodern approaches to the creation of "world city" developments or heterotopias (McDonald 2008). They are visions far detached from the lived worlds of most Africans, operating in an alternative universe of sorts where futuristic imaginaries can erase extant urban problems through big-push modernization projects that are coupled with market forces. Grounding urban development to produce sustainable livelihoods for the majority of the city's inhabitants, rather than new forms of exclusion such as these, must be the primary goal of those struggling for a different, better, and more inclusive urban Africa.

Note

1 Although others contend that the real objectives of such projects are not necessarily to make the city more internationally competitive but to achieve domestic political legitimacy and stability (Croese 2018).

Chapter Five
A Generative Urban Informal Sector?

Introduction

The informal economy has come to be a major component of urbanization in Africa; one that plays a predominant role in the production and consumption regimes of most cities. Informal is generally understood as labor or work that is conducted outside of formal state regulations and tax systems. This does not mean it is work that is illegal, illicit, or entirely beyond the reach of the state: it is not in many cases given much of the urban informal economy operates in plain sight of the state and is by-and-large accepted as an essential provisioner of goods and services to consumers. However, and despite the vital role it plays for the everyday lives and livelihoods of African urbanites, informal enterprises and workers operate in often precarious conditions that make it difficult to accumulate capital and invest to upgrade goods, services, and production techniques. As a result, the urban informal sector (UIS) remains hampered by low levels of productivity, poor working conditions, and an ever-present threat of eviction or displacement from state authorities seeking to "clean up" central urban areas and roadsides.

The origins of the informal economy throughout urban Africa can be traced to the emergence of capitalist relations along the continent's foremost coastal settlements, which fed into the creation of an informal labor market, although urban crafts and apprenticeship had a long history predating the colonial era. Economic histories, and particularly labor histories, of the early colonial period detailed heterogeneous informal laborers (e.g., "canoemen," road construction and agricultural workers,

The Urban Question in Africa: Uneven Geographies of Transition, First Edition. Pádraig R. Carmody, James T. Murphy, Richard Grant and Francis Y. Owusu.

distribution agents, transportation workers, fisherfolk, metalworkers and repairers) (Gutkind 1989). The sector existed and evolved long before Hart's (1973: p. 69) so-called "discovery" of it in urban Accra in the 1970s. However, Hart's naming of it made the "working poor" (e.g., hawkers, tinkers, tailors, market and drink sellers, porters, barbers, waste collectors) more visible to policymakers who had often previously viewed it as a traditional, transitional, or residual sector which would disappear with modernization. Nowadays, on the contrary, informality is widely recognized and anticipated to expand as Africa's population is projected to double by 2050, and most jobs are expected to be in that sector (Mpofu 2021). Current estimates are that the urban informal economy accounts for 80.8% of all employment in African cities, including 96% of youth labor and 92% of women's labor (Guven and Karlen 2020). As such, it is a critical, vital source of livelihoods, consumer goods, and services in Africa's cities. Figures 5.1 and 5.2 provide typical examples of these activities in Dar es Salaam and Nairobi.

Africa's UIS is contested between two divides: informalities as a barrier to development or as a potential driver (Azunre et al. 2022). Conventional policy approaches focus on formalization as a means to incorporate informal enterprises and labor into regulatory and taxation systems in order to address their "dark sides" (e.g., lack of compliance, tax evasion).[1] However, formalization strategies often fail to acknowledge the structural reasons why they exist – by-and-large a function of the state and production regime failures to support domestic industry

Figure 5.1 Informal manufacturers (wood workers) in Dar es Salaam.
Photo credit: James T. Murphy (Author).

Figure 5.2   Informal retailers in Nairobi.
Photo credit: James T. Murphy (Author).

and/or spur employment opportunities in the formal sector. When understood in relation to this wider political economy, there is a "bright side" to informality manifest in its contributions to urban livelihoods, entrepreneurship, employment generation, innovation, and the affordability and availability of consumer goods and services (Kaplinsky and Kraemer-Mbula 2022). As the world approaches or has exceeded planetary boundaries, alternative framings of Africa's urban informal economies warrant consideration; particularly those that support and encompass sustainable livelihoods, social solidarity, and adaptive resilience.

Recently more positive assessments of the gateway potential of the informal economy have emerged from literatures on informal innovation, green slum urbanism, circular economy, and urban mining (Kraemer-Mbula and Monaco 2020; Cobbinah et al. 2021; Grant and Oteng-Ababio 2021; Kaplinsky and Kraemer-Mbula 2022). The growing role of ICTs is also tilting policy discussion toward deploying appropriate technological solutions to catalyze informal entrepreneurship (Antikainen et al. 2018). Sustainability framings highlight the fact that many informal enterprises conform to principles of the circular economy – namely recycling, reuse, and repurposing (Swilling 2011). Such practices provide "an opportunity space" to link informal and formal realms that can be leveraged to catalyze more inclusive and just sustainability transition toward "liveable urbanization" (Swilling 2016; Ramos-Mejía et al. 2018; Oates 2021; Peter 2021). Such linkages would legitimate and support the UIS as a core component of urban sociotechnical systems.

A sociotechnical systems perspective brings a more comprehensive perspective to bear on cities and the role that the UIS plays in their everyday functioning. The UIS is central to consumption, production, and infrastructure regimes, providing small-scale, low-cost infrastructures, technologies, and services that are well aligned with the socioeconomic and material conditions facing most urban residents. As such, it can form the basis for the development and diffusion of innovations that can help drive urban transitions (Peter 2021). Particularly relevant are sustainable/green solutions and offerings (products and services) that can support social innovation and local economic diversification, as we discuss in Chapter 9.

Despite its importance in/for African cities, sociotechnical transitions in informal economies remain a neglected area of inquiry, with some exceptions (e.g., Lawhon and Murphy 2012; Ramos-Mejía et al. 2018; van Welie et al. 2018; Larbi et al. 2021; Oates 2021; Peter 2021). The failure to address urban informality in transitions research is highly problematic given the scale and scope of the UIS, and the fact that this marginalized majority of urbanites in Africa should be a central concern of those seeking more inclusive, just, and distributive urban development. Nevertheless, a considerable challenge for African cities is how to shift from entrenched practices and development pathways to more open ones that address the needs and possibilities of the informal economy as a vital contributor to progressive, generative urban transitions.

Larbi et al. (2021: p. 1) emphasize that cities in Africa "should not simply reproduce technical sustainability solutions successfully introduced elsewhere but should leverage indigenous potential to chart a sustainability path that is sensitive to conditions in the local context." They posit that sociotechnical transitions need to be rooted in extant, locally embedded practices and systems which can be built on with government and international resources and support. Exogenous technologies (i.e., those produced outside Africa, e.g., mobile phones) can also support "informals" but development through innovation needs to be fundamentally generated by local creativity and grassroot economic activities. By doing so, the informal milieu is not suffocated, but valorized in terms of its ability to devise small-scale urban solutions. For example, water, sanitation, and energy-delivery services in most slums are provided by informal enterprises, cooperatives, and entrepreneurs who effectively and affordably fill the gaps left by municipal utilities.

This chapter examines the informality question as it relates to African cities today, and with respect to future possibilities and sustainability pathways. We first provide an overview of the UIS in Africa – its general scale, scope, and the challenges facing its development. The next section dives deeper into the everyday realities in the UIS, focusing specifically on the case of the Agbogbloshie slum in Accra, Ghana. Building off these empirics, we then situate the UIS in relation to our sociotechnical systems framework, with particular emphasis on its contributions to production, consumption, and infrastructure regimes. Following this framing, we examine the prospects for technology-led transitions for the UIS, particularly through 4IR technologies. Achieving such transitions demands creative collaborations among diverse actors and the penultimate sections reflect on the dynamics of achieving these in urban Africa today. The chapter closes with brief concluding remarks.

The Contours of Africa's Urban Informal Economies

Informal economies function as a key part of the structure of Africa's economies and are characterized by apprenticeships, cooperative organizations, a heavy reliance on social capital, limited technology, and low levels of fixed capital. Informality is ubiquitous in cities, hubs and concentrated (particularly retail) activities occur in prime locations with heavy pedestrian traffic, e.g., around food markets and industrial clusters, or in less visible sites (e.g., homes, small workshops) where production activities can be conducted with limited disruption. Informality also extends to larger firms operating informally and competing in scale and sophistication with large formal ones. Large informal enterprises differ from small or microscale firms in part because they can and do exploit complex networks of seemingly isolated informals, subcontracting production or services to them (Benjamin and Mbaye 2012; Oteng-Ababio 2012).

Reliable statistics on informality are sparse, derived from national survey samples based on "snapshots." A number of international organizations (e.g., WIEGO [Women in Informal Employment: Globalizing and Organizing] and the ILO [International Labour Organisation]) occasionally publish data on select African cities, and we draw on this data to present a general overview.[2] A recent estimate shows that informal enterprises in Africa generate about 76% of value added outside of agricultural activities (Chen and Beard 2018). Informal activities account for about 50% of GDP in most African countries, and as much as 60% in Nigeria and Zimbabwe (Mpofu 2021). Moreover, unrecorded trade by informals may account for between 11% and 40% of total African intra-regional trade (Mold and Chowdhury 2021).

Africa's informal sector has grown steadily in the postcolonial period. By the 1980s the size of informal employment was twice that of the formal sector and five and a half times by the 1990s (Baah-Boteng and Vanek 2020; Guven and Karlen 2020). Informal employment – including self-employment in informal enterprises and wage employment in informal jobs – is approximately 79% in African cities (WIEGO 2018). It varies and accounts for an 86% share in Kampala (Uganda), 83% in Lomé (Togo), and 19% in Cape Town (South Africa) (see Table 5.1). Major categories of informal employment are home-based enterprises (HBEs), market trade, street vendors, and waste collectors with a significant gender division of labor (WIEGO 2018). For example, waste picking is a predominantly male occupation, although women provide ancillary services, e.g., food/drinks, and young women are engaged as water carriers to put out fires at dump sites (Grant and Oteng-Ababio 2021).

The informal economy supports a wide range of employment arrangements including full-time, part-time, casual work, and family labor. Informal workers

Table 5.1 Percentages of informal employment in formal activities and formal employment in informal activities in select African cities.

City	Informal employment in formal activities	Formal employment in informal activities
Abidjan	28.3	2.8
Antananarivo	5.9	6.3
Bamako	23.3	1.8
Cotonou	31.2	6.0
Dakar	26.3	2.2
Niamey	27.8	3.1
Ouagadougou	24.3	3.6

Source: Adapted from Baah-Boateng and Vanek, 2020.

are also being employed in formal jobs is widespread ("straddling" or multi-modes of livelihood), while formal labor taking place in the context of the wider informal economy is negligible (Herarra et al. 2012). For example, around one-third of informal workers are employed in formal employment in Lomé (Togo) and Cotonou (Benin), but the share is much lower in Antananarivo (Madagascar) (WIEGO 2018). Synchronization – or lack thereof – of interchange between the formal and informal economy varies substantially depending on the degrees of integration, sectoral composition, market structures, and other contextual/place-specific factors (Choi et al. 2020). Film industries (e.g., Nigeria's Nollywood and Ghana's Kumawood) blend mixes of formal and informal practices, the latter via the sale of pirated recorded videos (Azunre et al. 2022) and screenings at informal venues and via free digital platforms, e.g., the Afrinolly App.

Tax revenues from informal activities are meager: estimates range between 2% and 6% of total tax revenue (Mpofu 2021). Nonetheless, many informals pay multiple levies to municipalities in licenses and fees (e.g., market fees, rentals), but their immediate infrastructure/services provision is deficient to such an extent that many services (e.g., water) are procured from private/informal providers. Chiefs, criminal syndicates, slumlords, youth vigilantes, and market cooperatives also often levy a variety of non-statutory taxes (Resnick 2021). Some market cooperatives utilize these funds to finance local waste collection, provide security and remit bulk payments to service providers. Such informal practices can create ambiguity over accountability when those collecting revenue and those responsible for service delivery are separate entities, hindering the ability of informals to ensure that the quality of services matches the price (Resnick 2021). More positively, the literature highlights market associations in Lagos (Nigeria) practicing good governance: policing the behavior of association members; punishing dishonest traders selling defective good; incentivizing information sharing about unreliable traders; and organizing boycotts of offenders (Stacey 2019; Grossman 2021). However, informal associations are, by and large, governed by, numerous *ad hoc*, idiosyncratic grassroots interventions that appear to be "unsustainable" and clientelist (Cobbinah et al. 2022).

Beyond their internal governance, informal enterprises and street traders have also sought to secure their rights to the city through claims on space and citizenship (Lindell 2009; Brown et al. 2010; Lindell et al. 2019). Such movements have in part been a response to attempts by the state to assimilate or integrate the informal sector into the formal urban economy through licenses, enclosures, and relocation strategies. As Kamete (2018) notes in Southern Africa, however, such strategies are often "pernicious" in that they are costly to, and unrealistic for, informals; particularly the most vulnerable. Informals' resistance to assimilation strategies has demonstrated the resilience of these livelihood strategies and highlighted the everyday political struggles through which urban space is governed and managed. We now elucidate such struggles and lived realities through the case of the Agbogbloshie settlement in Accra, Ghana.

Explicating the UIS Experience: Agbogbloshie Settlement, Accra

Agbogbloshie is a "notorious" unplanned slum area in the heart of Greater Accra (see Figure 5.3). The Agbogbloshie settlement has long been subject to intense political debate about its future. After independence, Nkrumah's "Master Plan for Accra" aimed to turn the lagoon environs into a recreational/tourism "green wedge" for public use (Akese 2019), but it never materialized. In recent years

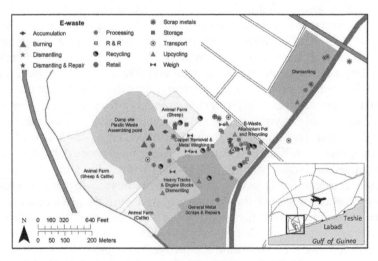

Figure 5.3   Agbogbloshie Settlement in Accra and E-waste Activities at their Zenith.

there has been intense speculation about Agbogbloshie's eventual future: cleaning and rehabilitating the site for a green/recreational area with land allocated for a district hospital; a real estate development zone or a return to local stool (traditional) land are all mentioned (Oteng-Ababio and Grant 2021).

The settlement was consolidated since the 1980s on vacant land, and its evolution is intertwined with influxes of Northern migrants (fleeing war) and others seeking a foothold in the city (affordable accommodation, informal work, and workspace) (Grant 2006). By 2020 it was a large settlement consisting of approximately 100,000 residents (Oteng-Ababio and van der Velden 2019), the largest informal food market and e-waste hub in the country as well as other informal activities, such as retailing of refurbished electronics, motor parts, and recycled building materials and timber (Grant and Oteng-Ababio 2021). Informal entrepreneurs engaged in numerous artisanal activities that center on unmaking and remaking, i.e., upcycling (e.g., turning car parts into dumbbells, roof-sheets into cookstoves, electronic waste into jewelry) (see Figure 5.4).

Figure 5.4 Informal Cookstove Manufacturer in Agbogbloshie.

Photo credit: Richard Grant (Author) and Martin Oteng-Ababio.

Informal reclamation of wetlands for residential development (utilizing saw dust, plastic bags, cardboard, plywood and other materials) depleted most of the green space in the environs (Cobbinah et al. 2021) and resulted in a denuded, dense, sprawling haphazard built environment with makeshift shacks, kiosks and other informal structures. In the absence of planning and modern infrastructure, self-organizing emerged, apportioning space for informal hubs in e-waste, automobile scrap, specialized food markets in onions, tomatoes, yams, truck repair, retail, and a timber yard (Oteng-Ababio and Grant 2021). Major deficits in service provision, even though tax collection (GRA) offices are located within the area, mean collective goods are largely provided by the residents themselves with assistance from community-based organizations (CBOs) and development partners (infrastructure regime). The area thus demonstrates splintered urbanism with its spatial and social polarization when compared to newer private enclaves and well-serviced, upscale areas.

Pursuing survivalist coping strategies, Agbogbloshie inhabitants made do, and lived and worked in precarious existences. Housing, marketplaces, and premises (consumption regimes) attracted little investment given that property rights in the settlement have been contested since 1984; subject to various rulings, threats of removal/relocation, and focused demolitions in flood-prone areas and along major thoroughfares. Elevated air and environmental pollution levels were documented with soil and water bodies heavily contaminated, and inhabitants suffering related elevated health risks (Daum et al. 2017). Workers, nearby residents and especially children living in or near the sites of informal e-waste recycling are particularly exposed to a variety of dangerous chemicals that impact cognitive functions and increase the risk of respiratory diseases, cancer, and other ailments (Lebbie et al. 2021). Moreover, seasonal flooding along the banks of the Korle Lagoon kills several residents every rainy season and fire tragedies have worsened (Stacey et al. 2021). Lack of primary and secondary storm drains, coupled with poor sanitation provisioning systems, exacerbates drainage, wastewater, and public health challenges. Decongestion initiatives, such as banning push carts, that sought to improve air quality and public safety did just the opposite, stimulating new forms of congestion, e.g., from motor taxis (*akoda*).

Agbogbloshie is depicted by the state and others as a "wasteland," "a hellscape" (Little 2019), "the most toxic site on the planet," (Akese 2019), "a heaven for criminality," and derogatorily referred to as "Sodom and Gomorrah" (the colloquial name of biblical origins for the informal settlement) (Environmental Justice Atlas 2020). Iconic images and alarmist public messages about the settlement solidify negative stereotypes taken up by public officials, nonresidents, and planners. The digital revolution has made it easier to circulate misinformation about the "dark side of development" in Agbogbloshie.[3] Indeed, extreme negative depictions in film, documentaries, social media, and NGO reports aestheticize decay while simultaneously erasing the settlement's histories and strong sense of community. Such representations stigmatize the area's inhabitants and ignore neglect Agbogbloshie's contributions to the city's economy by providing affordable housing, employment, and urban services (e.g., waste collection, water provisioning). The result is that the municipal government and policymakers alternate between benign neglect, piecemeal development interventions (typically with international donor or NGO funding), and top-down, intrusive exercises to decongest and eradicate the settlement.

The state's intransigence regarding what to do with the settlement has by-and-large excluded it from formal, forward-thinking plans for Accra's future. Political expediency has meant that government concentrated on infrastructure and upgrading projects in traditional Ga areas, older settlements, and new private developments to the total neglect of Agbogbloshie. Lack of finance, technical capacity, and leadership to champion pro-poor infrastructure solutions has sustained an anti-informal agenda that keeps the settlement stuck in a low-level equilibrium where poverty and material deprivations persist. This policy environment ignores alternative local development options that could catalyze Agbogbloshie's informal economy (production regime) to upgrade its activities and support more viable and resilient livelihood strategies for its residents. Also overlooked are the structural and material conditions that make it necessary to engage in survivalist work in unsafe conditions as the only viable livelihood option. These include an international political economy environment that enables the importation (i.e., dumping) of e-waste from the Global North into cities like Accra, and subsequent reexport of valuable fractions of e-waste as cheap inputs into new rounds of manufacturing abroad (Grant and Oteng-Ababio 2021; Fevrier 2022).

Several urban development projects were seeded in the area with NGOs and the German GIZ (*Deutsche Gesellschaft für Internationale Zusammenarbeit*) investing in initiatives to establish a formal recycling facility, upgrade aspects of informal work, and provide micro credit, machinery, protective gear, and training.[4] Most notable was the construction of the Agbogbloshie Recycling Centre (ARC), a formal e-waste processing facility funded by GIZ in collaboration with the Government of Ghana. However, this all amounted to a scattergun, piecemeal, and poorly coordinated approach that did not transform Agbogbloshie in any significant, widespread manner. Absent a major, state-sponsored redevelopment plan or upgrading program, one with buy-in from, and legitimated by, the settlement's residents, Agbogbloshie's residents immiseration persisted.[5]

Despite government and development partners' disparate e-waste initiatives, without notice, a combined regional/municipal team razed Agbogbloshie on July 1, 2021. Over the next week, demolition proceeded until the area was flattened, except for the ARC. Labeled a "Make Accra Work Again" initiative, the Greater Accra Regional Minister spearheaded the exercise to "sanitize" the central city and contribute to the place-marketing of Accra as "the cleanest city in Africa" (Boadu 2022, p. 1). The pandemic provided a global distraction to orchestrate removals and dissipate the informal sector. Receiving no coverage from major news outlets in the Global North, the demolition marked the end of an era (See Figure 5.5).

Figure 5.5   Razed Agbogbloshie and Fencing, 2023.
Photo credit: Richard Grant (Author) and Martin Oteng-Ababio.

An alternative market site to relocate the settlement's activities at Adjen Kotoku was built in 2012, some 33 km away on the outskirts of Greater Accra, but settlers refused to move, citing its unfavorable location (Oteng-Ababio and Grant 2021). Demolition prompted a new initiative from scrapyard owners, whereby members pooled resources to purchase a land parcel at Teacher Manet, some 121 km from Agbogbloshie, signaling a bottom-up shift to coordinate e-waste activities from a rural site. The splintering of the informal economy and the scattering of informal waste activities did not eradicate the activities that had been previously conducted at the site. Instead, it diffused these activities to nearby neighborhoods and sites in the urban periphery (Figure 5.6) with many informals desiring to be in the central city because of social networks and support. Abrupt relocation caused severe and uncontrolled effects on various areas, neighborhoods, and water bodies: in effect transferring environmental and congestion problems from one consolidated and self-organized site to numerous formative sites, many of them disorganized.

Beyond the need for major redevelopment initiatives that upgrade their built environments and basic services, settlements like Agbogbloshie need support for their informal economies such that they can transform into more sustainable, just, and productive communities. Informal enterprises and workers (e.g., metal-workers, waste pickers) should be viewed with a productivist lens (Azunre et al. 2021), as "resilient hyperlocal clusters of knowledge, expertise and capacity that perceive, bestow and manipulate value in spaces and materials where otherwise it would remain latent, invisible and intangible" (Osseo-Asare and Abbas 2019: p. 180). The UIS in Agbogbloshie created efficiencies in secondary use and repair, filled gaps in basic service provision (e.g., waste collection, water provision, social safety nets), and provided skills training (e.g., for artisans and repair technicians) that should not have been undervalued (*Azunre* et al. 2021). The prospects for

Figure 5.6   E-waste in Accra's urban periphery.
Photo credit: Richard Grant (Author) and Martin Oteng-Ababio.

generative urbanism in cities like Accra thus depend on the active integration and inclusion of informal settlement residents like Agbogbloshie's into development plans and policies. Such inclusion will demand political settlements that transcend the elite-driven, neopatrimonial, and splintering tendencies of urban governance in Africa today that allow the sweeping away of the urban poor so that urban poverty and immerisation are more occluded and away from social media and NGO gazes.

Any planned redevelopment of the area will accomplish little if it fails to tackle the urban development challenge at a sociotechnical system level; one that comprehensively integrates concerns about affordable housing, service provision, and employment. As of March 2023, the area is secured by a perimeter fence, the ARC is operating and incorporates a small portion of the informal e-waste sector, but the larger redevelopment of Agbogbloshie is still under consideration. Futuristic planning sketches of high-rise residential buildings, green spaces, and a district hospital have been published in *The Daily Graphic* (Boadu 2022), but the economic and COVID-19 crises and political backlash after demolition have curtailed redevelopment plans: there is presently a noticeable silence about Agbogbloshie's future (Tornyi 2023).

Situating Africa's UIS in a Sociotechnical Systems Framework

We argue that the sociotechnical systems approach developed in this book can offer a multidimensional perspective to better address challenges facing settlements like Agogbloshie; one that acknowledges/legitimates the UIS's role in the economy and which views it as a key contributor to sustainability transitions and "inclusive dualism" (Nattrass and Seekings 2019), rather than the repression of the sector. As described in Chapter 1, this framework views systems as constituted by three integrated/overlapping regimes related to production, consumption, and infrastructure. Regimes govern and guide the evolution of these urban processes through structures (e.g., rules, institutions, norms), inter-regime couplings (e.g., links between infrastructure and production), and multiscalar relations (e.g., to the global economy). These constitutive dimensions of regimes are visible (epistemologically) through the everyday practices (e.g., see the case of Agogbloshie above) through which urbanites go about carving out livelihoods, managing households, accessing basic services, and meeting their consumption needs. A "zooming in" on these practices and informal activities enables a subsequent "zooming out" to explore patterns and processes at the meso- and macrolevels (Nicolini 2009).

A distinct focus on production, consumption, and infrastructure regimes offers a means to understand how the UIS contributes to and sustains key functions in the city related to livelihoods, markets, and the maintenance and distribution of collective goods and services. By examining the practices and roles of informals in regimes, we can more fully appreciate and understand their embeddedness in African cities, and thus their potential role in urban transitions. Such an approach puts more emphasis on enabling "an operating space" for inclusion, to seed appropriate innovation and technology for experimentation rather than pernicious assimilation into formalized systems (Kamete 2018).

As noted above the UIS dominates urban regimes in African cities – supporting livelihoods, sustaining consumer markets, and delivering collective goods and services across a wide spectrum of residents. It is also a center of innovation, although this is often misunderstood (Fu 2020). Kaplinsky and Kraemer-Mbula (2022) highlight the innovative character of informal producers who operate under significant constraints in both input and product markets, and who by necessity are forced to innovate to survive. Innovations are commonly spurred by low-income consumers, spatially cut off from, or unable to afford, the output of formal firms. Localized responses to the needs of communities' consumption regimes are a driver of innovation, but informal entrepreneurs are not entirely detached from broader influences such as knowledge spillovers from local (formal) firms, technology transfers from donors, imports, and/or refurbished/customized equipment that can be incorporated into their production practices. For example, in the Kenyan woodworking industry, local machinery producers created hybrid technologies by combining Chinese and European machinery (Atta-Ankomah 2014).

Informality and small firm size militate against economies of scale, leading many informals to focus on specialized components rather than final goods (Atta-Ankomah 2014). This, and the geographical clustering of informal firms, enhances their innovative capabilities. For example, Jegede and Jegede (2018) highlight the spirit of openness in proximate firms in learning and sharing knowledge, and technological fixes within the informal Otigba hardware cluster in Lagos, as well as the Nigerian ICT sector more broadly. That said, there can be limitations to colocation in terms of the ability of informal enterprises to capture the value of novel innovations due to rapid imitation that can occur in clusters (Murphy 2003). Nonetheless, clusters do allow for specialization and the customization of production, leading to the creation of local market niches, some of which are scaled up by eventually connecting to formal support institutions (Bull et al. 2016). In some cases, exchanging information, experience, and tools, or jointly importing inputs, i.e., establishing collaborative rather than competitive relationships, spurs a process of open innovation, allowing informal firms to overcome the mere survival threshold (Kraemer-Mbula and Monaco 2020). For the most part, innovations tend to be incremental with reverse engineering and technology adaptation practices predominating (Fu 2020). However, and despite this innovative dynamism and potential, in most informal contexts these incremental improvements remain unsupported and unscaled.

Beyond production and consumption, the informal sector plays a key role in infrastructure regimes by providing basic services and collective goods to many/most urban residents. Informal infrastructure and service provision can be hard-wired into aspects of municipalities' *modus operandi* to reduce costs and fill gaps in service provision (e.g., waste collection and water services). African urban infrastructure regimes are characterized by decentralized low technology at the community and household scale that can be open to experimentation, without holding onto an expectation of city-wide functioning centralized infrastructure (i.e., the modern infrastructure ideal). Informals draw on indigenous knowledge (e.g., constructing water reserves) and low cost, easy-to-use technologies that can be implemented and or adapted by households, small firms, or communities (Frick-Trzebitzky et al. 2017; Holt and Littlewood 2017).

Informal innovations in infrastructure regimes are thus commonplace and vital in enabling low-income residents to access water, sanitation, energy and housing by improvising, making do, "fiddling," adopting and modifying existing solutions (Oteng-Ababio 2012). The net result is that infrastructure regimes in African cities are both fragmented and heterogeneous in terms of their spatial distributions, technologies, and service provisioning options (see van Welie et al. 2018). As such they are simultaneously well adapted to the needs, realities of informal communities and settlements yet often viewed as illegitimate/illegible to the state and formal infrastructure providers. Needed are innovative approaches that bridge these gaps while maintaining and building-up the informal sector's role in infrastructure regimes. Doing so will enhance the sector's prospects to contribute to generative urban transitions.

Transforming the UIS? ICTs, the 4IR and Makerspaces

Progressive transitions in African cities cannot be simply understood as radical transformations that formalize and modernize the informal economy. Weak domestic technological capabilities and inconsistent institutional policies mean that transitions are far more likely to be a "hard slog of competence building" (Rock et al. 2009: p. 242). Embracing and nurturing Africa's informal manufacturing traditions, styles of thinking, and social relationships is essential in this regard. Building on, rather than bypassing, existing capabilities and resources – tinkering, reinvention, indigenous knowledge, learning-by-doing, apprenticeships, and cooperative enterprises – and connecting with support networks (e.g., development organizations, NGOs, and makerspaces) to facilitate transitions is a more just, sustainable, and realistic strategy (Frick-Trzebitzky et al. 2017). A key challenge is the need to recognize and account for informal operating spaces; highly heterogeneous, often clustered, and yet simultaneously fragmented in tandem with other deficits that put the emphasis on low-cost innovations (Ramos-Mejía et al. 2018; Fu 2020).

In some domains technology has already disrupted informal behaviors. ICTs, in particular, have been highly transformative to African informal economies, leading to greater financial inclusion through digital payments, savings, and lending products; enhancing research and information gathering through internet access; supporting market expansion through networking activities; and facilitating new opportunities for the governance and regulation of urban markets (e.g., new registries and new taxpayers) (Larsson and Svensson 2018). For example, social media platforms such as Instagram, Twitter, and WhatsApp enable informals to advertise goods and services to a wider range of customers at minimal cost relative to brick and mortar premises (Larsson and Svensson 2018). Despite these gains however, ICTs have not yet been thickly or deeply integrated into informal production and consumption regimes in a manner that might spark knowledge economies (Murphy and Carmody 2015).

New, ICT-related challenges have surfaced in parallel with these positive developments. These include a heavier reliance on imports, burgeoning e-waste, cyber security challenges and new regulation challenges in terms of e-tax collection, data, and privacy. Government regulatory efforts, such as imposing regressive taxes on social media transactions, have met staunch resistance in several African countries. For example, Uganda's imposition of a 1% e-tax on the value of payments, transfers and withdraws, and a 200 Shillings tax on social media per day in 2018 triggered a 30% drop in internet users and a predicted reduction of US$750 million in GDP growth (Choi et al. 2020: p. 144). In Ghana, tax debates about a 1.75% e-tax culminated in punches being thrown in the national parliament in November 2021 as the new levy would disproportionately affect the poor and informal economy (The Guardian 2020: p. 1). Subscriber identity module (SIM) card registration has enabled data collection about hitherto uncounted informals and transactions, creating a registry that can be used to both support pro-poor interventions and also monitor/surveil informal enterprises. Huawei technologies, and the widespread use of Chinese TECHNO handsets, which account for 50% market share in East Africa, are also a concern (Larsson and Svensson 2018: p. 550).

All told, ICTs and other technological interventions need to be fit-for-purpose and aligned with existing informal practices and modes of governance in informal consumption, production, and infrastructure regimes. For example, an innovator in a makerspace in Nairobi is developing a *matatu* (minibus) tracking and cashless electronic payment system that can provide real-time data for commuters and transportation cooperatives (a.k.a. SACCOs [savings and credit cooperative organizations]) in Nairobi, and reduce operating losses due to the underreporting of fares (Murphy, interview). Digitization in combination with green economy interventions in the informal economy (see Chapter 9) has a good prospect for enhancing productivity growth, job creation, and sustainability while linking informals into the knowledge-based economy. At the same time, digitization will be highly disruptive, particularly for populations with low numerical and literacy skills. Subsistence activities that are unlikely to benefit from automation may face elimination and there will need to be training and job creation strategies to absorb this labor.

Perhaps one of the most pressing questions regarding the future of the UIS is whether and how it might become integrated with strategies to take advantage of the ongoing Fourth Industrial Revolution driven by informational capitalism, ICTs, AI, and robotics, in particular (see Chapter 2). 4IR technologies can support the informal sector by helping develop an information/knowledge-intensive skills base, assisting in data management and processing, and enhancing productivity through automation and improved management practices. Digitization can also assist in enabling access to basic services and collective goods for social security. Enhanced connectivity and interaction among parts, machines, and people may improve manufacturing design, production, outputs, and services, with potential for upgrading in national/regional value chains. 4IR innovations might further provide (informal) micro manufacturing firms with competitive advantages, creating products and services that are rare, inimitable, non-substitutable, and valuable (Serumaga-Zake and van der Poll 2021). In low-income environments, basic digital technologies such as web-based instructional videos, voice-activated tactile screens, and simple-to-use applications can empower low-skilled informal workers/community groups to perform higher-skilled tasks and access credit and insurance products with little collateral.

Related to the 4IR, the Makerspace Movement is spreading in several African cities with ties to more than 200 innovation hubs in the region (Ekekwe 2015). Makerspaces, e.g., Gearbox in Nairobi, see Figure 5.7, are physical spaces with tools, where individuals of different backgrounds design, prototype, and create manufactured works utilizing fit for purpose technologies for community impact. Makerspaces benefit from appropriate open source technologies, open design, and blueprints, enabling exogenous technologies to be adapted and reconfigured to meet local needs (Dougherty 2012). Informals have utilized Fab Labs to access 3D printing technology in Nairobi, Cape Town, Pretoria, and Soweto (Schonwetter and Van Wiele 2020).

Digital, 4IR technologies have enabled makerspace initiatives to connect to a virtual African network of "makers" since 2019 (Africamakerspace.net 2022). Open sourcing in combination with low-cost 3D printing can enable production of locally manufactured objects that might otherwise be infeasible to source due to import costs. Makers knowledgeable about one tool can aid large numbers of other innovators and vice versa: "one capable craftsman with a … 3D printer can provide improved manufacturing services and specialized components for hundreds of artisans; similarly, a technically literate artisan with a computer … can assist hundreds of … mechanics" (Waldman-Brown et al. 2014: p. 13) (See Figure 5.7). However, better alignment with informal manufacturing is still desirable.

Degrees of scaling in African makerspaces occur along several dimensions – upward (institutional integration and vertical integration), outward (i.e., geographical spread of a technology and horizontal integration), and downward (increasing participation and sharing values) (Armstrong et al. 2018). Armstrong et al. (2018) report maker communities in South Africa play an intermediary, semiformal role, as mediating entities between formal and informal elements of the country's innovation ecosystem.

Figure 5.7   Gearbox Makerspace in Nairobi.
Photo credit: James T. Murphy (Author).

Realizing a More Generative UIS: Collaborative Pathways for Transition

Efforts to link the formal and informal spheres are gathering some momentum in new blends of activities in several sectors, where state, NGOs, and informals come into contact in service provision (infrastructure regimes). Implementers are turning to collaborative and place-based approaches as a "new frontier" because of changing expectations of them bringing more success than conventional and neoliberal approaches (Pugel et al. 2022). For example, recycling networks now organize previously disenfranchized, self-organized waste pickers, encompassing a range of initiatives such as upcycling and repurposing waste, making informals legible and active participants in a more inclusive waste industry (José Zapata Campos et al. 2021). Moreover, wastepickers contribute significantly to environmental sustainability governance through their recycling efforts that, taken together, can transform waste management regimes at the city-scale (e.g., Kisumu Waste Actors Network (KIRAN) [Kenya] composed of forty-one heterogeneous groups [see José Zapata Campos et al. 2021: p. 5]). This is not to underestimate the challenge however, as the Dandora municipal open dumpsite in Nairobi poses a health risk to approximately a quarter of a million people (Kimani 2007 cited in Pelling et al. 2021).

Pathways toward collaborative approaches that bring together diverse entities such as these to solve complex problems are also emerging in water and sanitation where solutions build on skillsets of informal entities and enhance city-wide provisioning efforts (Pugel et al. 2022). Mitlin and Walnycki (2020) highlight the ways in which the state has learned from informal water service provision in Dar es Salaam, Harare, Blantyre, and Windhoek. In these cities experimentation at the neighborhood-level has resulted in informal provider practices (e.g., localized sales points such as kiosks) being tested and replicated by utilities. Water utilities and other public agencies supplying water are also experimenting, drawing on the approaches of informal suppliers, to find ways to extend their coverage into low-income and/or informal neighborhoods despite their legal status. Moreover, informal vendors and community organizations are drawn in as utilities experiment with new inter-agency configurations so that informal and formal water practices become less distinct.

In an analysis of eleven initiatives to strengthen water, sanitation, and hygiene (WASH) delivery in East Africa (Ethiopia, Kenya, and Uganda), researchers (Pugel et al. 2022) demonstrate that even though collaborative approaches can be contingent on context, a number of commonalities are observed in transition pathways. These include: the importance of government uptake; the need to demonstrate an "urgency for change"; evidence that the collaboration is a priority; the significance of "early wins"; the importance of flexibility given the volatility of informal contexts; and external donor support is vital in most instances. Coproduction of innovative responses too is essential for successful collaborations between the UIS, the state, and other actors. Linking sociotechnical approaches with mobility studies and ethnographic data from Dar es Salaam, Jacobsen (2021) demonstrates how coproduction plays an essential role for the functioning of the city's transport system. Coproducing the city's transport system is a hybrid process that entails combining local informal minibus practices and bus rapid transit (BRT). Despite global consultants' attempts to standardize the global BRT model and the use of its technologies like the intelligent transport system (ITS), implementing BRT has been uneven in Dar es Salaam and elsewhere (Sengers and Raven 2015). Coproduction thus needs to be seen as a flexible process whereby certain practices become more or less permanent even though they may have developed as temporary solutions, while other practices evolve and change over time.

Conclusion

A sociotechnical systems perspective enables a focus on gateway opportunities for informal entrepreneurship and innovation and highlights why geographic context matters greatly. This lens enables paying more attention to interactions, networks, collaborations, and collective arrangements central to the informal economy. Putting more power in the hands of communities, individuals, and informal groups within an urban sociotechnical system requires an appreciation of the UIS's innovation potential. Rethinking African urban informal economies means unsettling the dominant understanding of innovation as R&D-based, requiring heavy investment and large projects, toward a finer grained understanding of "under the radar innovation" that is learning-by-doing based, low cost, small-scale, cooperative, community centered, and demand-driven (e.g., by customers and business networks) (Fu 2020). "Small can be beautiful" and it deserves to be protected and nurtured through supportive policies and initiatives like Makerspaces (Kreamer-Mbula and Monaco 2020: p. 367).

The informal economy has a multitude of entrepreneurs and projects with significant potential for new ones to emerge with ICTs and the 4IR. Geels (2004) reminds us that transitions are the outcome of complex, mutually reinforcing, changes across several domains involving societal actors at multiple scales, and greatly shaped by intricacies of agency, power, and politics in transitions, but there are no prior examples of how these will unfold in informal environments. Despite all the moving parts and complexities, sociotechnical systems thinking enables to us to anticipate that action in one regime can engender reaction/stalemate/retreat in another regime, thus impacting the overall evolution of the urban system. Open collaboration, clustering, networks, learning-by-doing/experimenting, coproduction, and decentralized/customizable solutions are thus vital if the informal sector is to play a more inclusive/significant role in facilitating generative urban transitions in African cities.

Still, some contend the 4IR will lead to data and technological (re)colonization in Africa (Benyera 2021) and/or that it has little relevance to countries heavily dependent on agriculture, mining, and informal economies (Sutherland 2020). Such perspectives imagine that digitization will narrow the scope of African cities' participation in the global economy as larger benefits accrue to big technological firms located primarily in core economies and East Asia. To face these challenges, national and urban policy institutions (e.g., NUPs, see Chapter 2) will need to be substantially reconfigured to manage, harness, and enable collaborations between the informal and formal sectors, and other actors (e.g., planners, NGOs) able to support the development of innovative solutions to pressing urban challenges. In particular, there is critical need for mentoring and government support in the informal economy via policies to assist with accelerated adoption and subsequent use of 4IR technologies, both endogenous and exogenous. Makerspaces and political champions providing proactive leadership (e.g., Lagos' transformed mass transit system [Gorham et al. 2017]) to enable such transformations are essential and serve as harbingers of the types of change already in motion. A concerted effort will also need to be made on centering marginalized communities and experiences with ongoing technological change and to disseminate their creations widely so that they may also be blended into regional and national-scale innovation systems (Kraemer-Mbula and Monaco 2020).

More appropriate policies and supports for informals desperately need to be developed, tested, and disseminated. Presently little consensus exists about which policies to prescribe to promote informal innovation. This stems largely from dissenting views on the reasons for the existence of informality, the occluded ties between the formal and informal realms, the informal economy's poor relationship with the state and mainstream investors, and the data gaps. Lack of policy coherence also results from tensions among different levels of government, since economic development resources tend to be concentrated at the national and district/provincial level while local municipalities are generally responsible for urban management where the informal economy predominates (Fox and Goodfellow 2022; Kaplinsky and Kraemer-Mbula 2022). Adopting a systemic approach to innovation policy to better capture and share the benefits of its innovations requires widening the scope of innovation policy to include policy areas that directly affect informal economic actors (such as labor, welfare, urban planning, and social policies). It also implies expanding the reach of conventional innovation policy instruments such as grants for innovation, skills-upgrading programs, and initiatives that support interfirm collaborations to make them available to informal firms (Kaplinsky and Kraemer-Mbula 2022). Indeed, Charmes et al. (2018) posit that innovation in the informal economy may be entirely different, requiring different definitions, measurements, data, and lenses to assess and understand (Charmes et al. 2018). For example, not all transfers in informal economies are mediated by market dynamics: social, community, and other network rationalities coexist with these in highly significant ways.

After nearly a century of appreciating global technological systems and solutions such as the ubiquitous hard-smooth-shiny (and unsustainable) perfection of plastics, we need to embrace irregularity, imperfection, recycling, recombining and reinvention as they occur in African cities. Many of the projects and products that could spring from such framing are nascent and niche to informal economies. Critics will ask "how do you scale these up?" – but it is worth underscoring that this impulse toward growth and scale economies are a large part of the problem in terms of what/who counts in, or has a right to, the city. In informal Africa, grand solutions delivered by big businesses, tech giants, and external experts should be interchanged with the myriad of small-scale solutions, local experimentation, and co-learning processes (Jacobsen 2021). By doing so, a world dominated by globalized production in/through distantiated factories and supply chains might give way to one where distributed manufacturing is the norm; a potentially more generative trajectory for African cities.

Notes

1 Labor exploitation, livelihood insecurity, dangerous working conditions, and pollution are also common in informal economies (Guven et al. 2021).
2 While informality permeates multiple domains of city life (e.g., service provision, housing, land ownership and leasing, and finance), standardized comparable data are only available for categories of informal employment. Importantly, no reliable data exists on the deployment of technology in the informal economy, beyond uptake numbers of broadband, mobile phone, and fintech subscribers.
3 Such is the case especially with regard to the size and extent of e-waste dumping and contamination in Agbogbloshie, erroneously claimed and recycled as "the largest e-waste site in the world." Minter (2015) remarks on the conspicuously absent images showing huge stockpiles and volumes of e-waste in Agbogbloshie compared to Guiyu, China, employing 100,000 e-waste workers and covering 52 km^2 at its peak (Oteng-Ababio and van der Velden 2019).
4 European funding streams include EU funding of €1.2 million (2018–2022]) to formalize micro enterprises, disseminate best practices, and provide training; German government (€25 million) support to provide technical assistance; and Swiss funding of €6.1 million (2020–2023) for sustainable recycling of e-waste, including an initiative to teach informal recyclers to extract copper more efficiently without burning devices.
5 The cloak of the COVID-19 pandemic recently provided the Ghanaian government an opportunity to remake the area. Public attention to health issues and a need to reinvigorate a stalled economy led to a "Make Accra Work" initiative that sought "to make Accra the cleanest city in Africa" (Brown 2022). In 2021 a series of scheduled removals, with tacit community agreements from various leaderships, led to the relocation of the food markets to Adjen Kotoku, the transfer of the scrap market (but without space for workers' housing) to a 10 acre site (modest for accommodating the hub) at Kofi Kwei, 39 km to the northwest of the city and the removal of

approximately 1,000 evicted residents to peripheral sites at Adjen Kotoku and Amasaman with temporary structures to accommodate those removed. Many, however, opted instead to return to home villages in the north of Ghana. The government secured widespread public support by announcing that a portion of the site would be allocated for a major hospital and a new light industrial area, and that it would beautify the area and allocate land for green space (Brown 2022). No mention was made of upgrading the remaining residential settlement, however, one that continues to lack adequate housing and basic services.

Chapter Six
The Rise of the "Gig Economy" and the Impacts of Virtual Capital on African Cities (with Alicia Fortuin)

"Always skarreling" (hustling) – female Bolt [ride-sharing] driver, Cape Town.

The emergence and profusion of the Internet is transforming many dimensions of capital-labor relations in both formal and informal economies as new technologically-mediated platforms (e.g., Uber, Airbnb) are diffusing globally. These platforms are now the "dominant form of rentier in contemporary capitalism" (Sadowski 2020: p. 575 quoted in Anwar and Graham 2022: p. 33). They allow capital (i.e., corporations such as Uber) to deploy new infrastructures (e.g., ICTs) to intermediate in consumer markets (consumption regimes) and control labor in new service sectors (production regimes) (Heeks 2021). The net result is the emergence of new forms of "virtual capitalism" – so called "gig economies" – that enable transnational corporations to extract value from assets they do not own (e.g., automobiles) and from labor that is managed/controlled at a distance. Commercial platforms were once lauded as facets of the sustainable sharing economy. Over time there has been a deeper appreciation of their negative and relational effects, such as those that exacerbate socioeconomic inequality in cities throughout the world (Heeks 2021).

This chapter explores the nature of the emerging gig economy and associated virtual capital in urban Africa, with a particular focus on its impacts on labor arrangements and the reconfiguration of consumption and production regimes. We assess how these are reconfigured in different locations and geographic contexts. Empirical material from a survey of "ride sharing" (Uber and Bolt) drivers

The Urban Question in Africa: Uneven Geographies of Transition, First Edition. Pádraig R. Carmody, James T. Murphy, Richard Grant and Francis Y. Owusu.
© 2024 John Wiley & Sons Ltd. Published 2024 by John Wiley & Sons Ltd.

in Cape Town is presented. Whether this hybrid (in)formal economy can be reformed to offer decent, stable work, or whether it is yet another obstacle to generative cities is explored. This is assessed by examining the major implications of current practices for urban regimes.

Defining the Gig Economy

Technology is always restructuring the nature of African cities (Mtetwa nd), but in recent decades the pace of technological change has accelerated globally,[1] speeding up the cycle of "rounds of economic restructuring" (Peet and Thrift 1989). In Africa the accelerating pace of digitalization; particularly in the so-called "fin-tech" sector – financial technologies, such as mobile payments and money transfers, among other services, is particularly significant in cities given the rapid and extensive uptake of mobile phones (Malm and Toyama 2021) and technology hubs across the continent (Oranye 2016). However, the rise of the gig economy and its mediation through ICTs has had the greatest impact on the nature of work and mobility in cities (Giddy 2019).

Gig work is where a worker is contracted to undertake one specific task ("gig"), such as giving someone a ride to where they want to go, mediated through an online platform (Anwar and Graham 2020b). According to the ILO "gig jobs are classified under temporary employment with predetermined termination dates. And they could be fixed-term, task-based contracts, seasonal, or casual jobs" (cited in Kolawole 2020). In some cases, gig work is part of the so-called "sharing economy," where people are meant to share their cars ("ride sharing") or accommodation with others for payment through globally organized, digitally-enabled platforms such as Uber and Airbnb.

The gig economy's rise raises many concerns regarding digital workers, with respect to bargaining power, economic inclusion, intermediated value chains, and (generally lack of) social or economic upgrading (Graham et al. 2017).[2] More broadly, gig economy companies are reconfiguring the nature of labor markets and relations in African cities, enabling the rise of technologically-mediated, "disruptive" urbanism which has significant implications for the evolution of urban sociotechnical regimes (Maginn et al. 2018).

With respect to production regimes, conventional business models integrate three agency dimensions: capital, labor, and management, but virtual capitalist business models largely eliminate management as a social actor. Instead, management is undertaken by a combination of technology and customers, who rate the services they receive – what has been called algorithmic governance (Popan 2021). In the case of Uber "the app works as a 'telescopic prison', constantly watching drivers" (Geitung 2017: p. 59), including using facial recognition software to check who is driving. "We can see everything. We can monitor the drivers through the phone – when they accelerate, take a corner too fast, brake too roughly" (Uber executive quoted in Iazzolino 2021: p. 8). Although the gig economy also provides a source of livelihood, and in some cases status, particularly if properly regulated (Ayentimi et al. 2023).

The gig economy is then is a way of "extracting" value from (often) petty service producers, who may combine ownership of some capital, such as a car, with self-exploitation. Where other individuals or companies own the cars, rather than the drivers themselves, this puts further pressure on returns to labor and living standards – a form of globalized exploitation or poverty chains (Selwyn 2019). Paradoxically virtual capital operates transnationally, largely through third-party actors (e.g., Uber) who own/control the platforms, but remains nationally-based, with profits flowing offshore. In the South African and Kenyan cases, Uber fares initially transit through the Netherlands given its favorable business tax rates (Gedye 2015). Indeed, Uber avoided a legal challenge from workers in South Africa because the case was taken against the wrong subsidiary (Woodcock and Graham 2020). Importantly, this dynamic is enabled through reconfigured infrastructure regimes that prioritize ICTs as essential services, and consumption regimes that are increasingly dependent on practices that involve mobile phones, in particular.

According to Graham et al. (2017: p. 140) "a key feature of digital work platforms is that they attempt to minimise the outside regulation of the relationship between employer and employee... These issues are particularly acute when transactions cross national borders: as it becomes unclear which jurisdictions' regulations apply to the work being transacted." The neoliberal tactic whereby workers are discursively recast as "entrepreneurs of the self" (Foucault and Senellart 2008) is particularly relevant in this sector, whereby "insecurity becomes recast as freedom, self-exploitation reframed as 'being your own boss'" (Prentice 2018 cited in Parry 2018 quoted in Mallett 2020: p. 275).

Whereas the lexicon of the sharing economy implies equality between partners this is very far from the case as technological-near-monopolies (technopolies) emerge through network effects. For example, the more drivers who are on Uber, the faster the pickup will be, thus enabling the company to capture greater market share while doing relatively little to enhance the livelihoods of most of its drivers. All told, the rise of the gig economy implies an increase in precarity for many workers (in terms of wages, health, and safety standards); although some people also undertake gig work in addition to their main jobs – as a "side hustle," as part of the broader "zig, zag" (Jeffrey and Dyson 2013) or "hustle economy" (Thieme et al. 2021).

The Gig Economy in Africa

Because most people in African cities do not have formal sector jobs the gig economy is rising in importance. Although reliable data is nonexistent on the number of gig workers in Africa, BFA/Mastercard Foundation (2019) estimates up to 80 million people will be employed in SSA in digital labor by 2030, although this in not exactly coterminous with the gig economy, as it may also be subject to longer-term formal contracts. However the number of gig workers is significant, whatever it is exactly.

Numbers of registered workers or "independent contractors" for digital platforms are available. For example, Uber has 60,000 drivers registered on its application across the countries in which it operates in Africa (Mourdoukoutas 2017). There are approximately 12,000 Uber drivers in South Africa, for example, and almost a million "active riders" (Venter 2017); although other estimates put the figure as high as 5.3 million versus Bolt's 2.1 million (de Villiers 2018; Porteous and Morawczynski 2019).

Beyond Uber, there are many other areas of the gig economy in urban Africa and it is estimated that there are around 300 active digital platforms, employing nearly five million workers. These include platforms to hire domestic workers (Hunt and Samman 2020), and "non-physical" micro-work contracted through global platforms such as Upwork (Anwar and Graham 2020b). With respect to the latter, only about 6% of workers from Africa registered on Upwork ever get to make at least a dollar on it, showing how it is parasitic as the work of registration and gig search is never remunerated (Anwar and Graham 2020a).[3] Africa has about 120,000 registered freelancers on this platform; less than the Philippines, partly because of generally high broadband costs (Anwar and Graham 2022).

Those that can secure gigs often focus on menial tasks such as tagging images and videos of streetscapes to help train autonomous vehicles. In other cases, workers engage in search engine optimization in order to direct these to a client's website. Digital work such as this is part of what Ekbia and Nardi (2017) term "heteromation," the use of human labor in support of automated work, such as machine learning algorithms; labor that is often "invisible" and poorly compensated (Anwar and Graham 2020a). However, such work is raced, classed and gendered and may contribute to further urban splintering. In 2019, 92% of those who earned more than US $10,000 on Upwork in South Africa were "white" (Anwar and Graham 2022). Consequently, digitalization can make the world bumpier (Carmody 2014a) rather than "flat" as suggested by Thomas Friedman (2005).

Beyond these menial tasks, there are more positive trends associated with the gig economy. A survey of platform domestic workers in South Africa found that they earned between 45% and 50% more than the minimum wage for domestic workers, with most reporting being satisfied or very satisfied; although remuneration still fell short of meeting the minimum amount needed for a family of four to exceed the poverty line (Hunt and Samman 2020). This "premium" was related to ratings on the platform, among other factors, thereby providing a screening mechanism for employers. Of the 11 platforms in South Africa rated by the Fairwork Foundation, based on factors such as pay, contracts and working conditions, two of those offering domestic worker services scored 8 out of 10, while Uber and Bolt scored 4 and 1 respectively (Fairwork Foundation 2021).

Anwar and Graham (2021) also found that gigs paid better than local work for the majority of remote gig workers, while Hunt and Samann's (2020) noted that domestic workers felt that they had greater control and freedom in their work. Gig workers also engage in collective, individual, open, and hidden acts of resistance to platform control and price gouging, depending on context and nature of work. Physical gig workers are more able to organize, with taxi drivers and couriers tending to congregate at traffic junctions and restaurants (Tassinari and Maccarrone 2020). Moreover, and depending on the stage of work, their skills and reliability, remote gig workers also engage in bargaining with clients (Anwar and Graham 2021; Iazzolino 2021).

All told, the developmental impacts of different types of gig work vary based on local context and social background, such as education and skills, thus making generalizations difficult; even if certain commonalities appear as a result of the ways in which digital platforms work. Anwar and Graham (2021) argue that there are four primary dimensions through which gig platform work impacts lives and livelihoods of African workers: flexibility, freedom, vulnerability, and precarity. The extent to which each or a combination dominate workers' experiences depends on local context and competition (for the "physical" as opposed to remote gig economy); nature of and demand for their skills ("structural power"); the type of work and pricing policies and commissions of platforms, in addition to other costs, such as fuel.

Considered in relation to urban sociotechnical systems, the gig economy is having profound effects on the practices, modes of governance, and multiscalar relations constituting production and consumption regimes while relying heavily on infrastructure regimes that are reconfigured in ways that prioritize ICTs. With respect to production, the increasing reliance on platforms as livelihood strategies has, in effect, "semi-formalized" work for millions of urbanites who are employed in ways that are, at best, weakly regulated or monitored by the state. Governance in these regimes is now, by-and-large, achieved at a distance through transnational relations rather than conventional ties to proximate managers.

Consumption regimes have also evolved in response to platforms as mobile phone apps now play a central role in the everyday practices of consumers, particularly those related to transport and banking activities. Maintaining access to and paying associated fees and airtime costs for apps such as Bolt, Uber, and money transfer services (e.g., M-Pesa) is now a basic and growing need for consumers in African cities. The net result is that acts of consumption are increasingly intermediated through platforms able to extract value from afar. Ride-sharing platforms are emblematic of such transformations as we now demonstrate through the case of Cape Town, South Africa.

Ride Sharing and the Evolution of Cape Town's Sociotechnical Regimes

As intimated above perhaps the most iconic gig economy company globally is Uber – the "ride sharing," or self-proclaimed "technology" or "data" company. Uber is an American-based company with a US $78 billion valuation

(Cheng 2020) and has been instrumental in changing mobility in many cities around the world.[4] By 2017 "Uber was operating in 15 major African cities, with some 60,000 drivers in Egypt, Ghana, Kenya, Morocco, Nigeria, South Africa, Tanzania and Uganda" (Mourdoukoutas 2017). There are also a number of other "ride-sharing" apps such as Lyft, and Bolt, which also operate globally, in addition to African-owned/based ones, such as Little Cabs or An-Nisa Taxi, which caters exclusively for women and children in Kenya. In Africa, Uber and Bolt are currently the most widespread ride-sharing companies. Bolt (formerly Taxify), which is headquartered in Estonia, also now has operations in Kenya and South Africa and an "activation hub" in Nigeria. While there is work which examines the impacts of digital labor on workers (Graham et al. 2017), relatively little has been written about the implications of ride sharing for cities and work in Africa. We now do so through the case of Cape Town.

Cape Town is home to approximately four million people and is marked by the coexistence of "fabulous" wealth and deep poverty concentrated in the so-called "townships," which date from the apartheid era[5] (McDonald 2008); a spatial structure which has deepened in the (post)apartheid era (Levenson 2022). A deeply divided and racialized city, "the mother city" is sharply defined by a wealthy core on the Atlantic coast and behind Table Mountain the so-called Cape Flats: an amalgamation of various townships dominated by informal housing. While the city's core, its Northern and Southern corridors, and Somerset West are characterized by extravagant consumption, such as "super car" McLaren and Aston Martin dealerships, conditions in the Cape Flats are very different as pedestrian and shared public and informal transportation loom large.

In a context where human mobility is difficult for many of the poor, the City of Cape Town welcomed what has been termed electronic or e-hailing as another form of transport under the amendment of the National Land Transport Act of 2009, a subcategory of the metered taxi category under the Act. According to the Transport Manager, the City welcomes this transportation mode and fare competition between its operators (e.g., Uber and Bolt), regulating it through the issuance of Operating Licenses (interview June 2018). Unlicensed cars have proliferated, however, with Cape Town impounding several hundreds of unlicensed Uber cars in recent years (Van Zyl 2016). Uber subsequently paid R10,000 (US $700 approx.) fines to have the cars released, belying the claim it is not an employer. The City says it can only increase the number of licenses it disburses if Uber can demonstrate that there is both a demand for the service and that drivers can generate a profit "beyond making ends meet." In this contentious context, Uber has been reluctant to share their numbers of drivers with the City, or to specify who its car owners are.

Interviews of Uber and Bolt drivers were conducted in Cape Town in June 2018. Twenty-six drivers were interviewed, most of whom work for both Bolt and Uber. To capture a diversity of driver experiences and routes, we examined rides hailed using either the Bolt or Uber application in central Cape Town, a relatively high-income locale, and those from the low-income Cape Flats. During respective rides drivers were interviewed about their experience working through these companies. Employing an exploratory approach, we do not claim that these results are representative or statistically significant given the sampling method and relatively small sample size, but rather present the results as indicative.

Practices in Cape Town's Ride-sharing Regime

Gig workers operate under various conditions of precarity. Gig work is notorious for hiring "without regard for past employment and experience" and relying on "fast turnover and interchangeable workers" (Novitz 2021: p. 640). Uber, in general, charges a commission of 25% on each trip, whereas Bolt's rate is 15% of the accumulated fares for a week. Consequently, many drivers expressed a preference for working with Bolt rather than Uber. Uber justifies its higher fees based on costs associated with the continuous improvement of its app "in order for it to be seamless and efficient for riders and drivers so that we can market to riders and continue to create economic opportunities for the people of South Africa" (Uber South Africa spokesperson Samantha Allenberg quoted in de Villiers 2018).

A striking finding was the gendered nature of work. Twenty-five of the twenty-six drivers interviewed were male with the 26th being female (3.8% of the sample). This may relate partly to perceptions around gender and work, as taxi driving has traditionally been male-dominated globally,[6] and perhaps to issues of safety discussed later. Moreover, drivers were primarily of South African origin, although there were also drivers who came from the Congo and Zimbabwe.[7] On average drivers had been working in the industry for a relatively short period of time; nine and half months. Forty-two percent of respondents owned their own car. Of those who were using their own car, six bought the car using their own funds, whereas four others either used bank loans or hire-purchase agreements. Arrangements of drivers working for owners of vehicles have been noted elsewhere, in Ghana for example where:

> a big car-rental transport company owns a large fleet of cars which they have registered on Uber. These cars are then rented out to prospective drivers, while the Uber payment account is kept with the owner of the rental company. This is made possible because many of these drivers do not own cars and are desperately seeking some form of paid work. Drivers [also] pay a portion of their daily/weekly earnings to the rental company (Graham and Anwar 2018: p. 5).

Graham and Anwar (2018) further note that many of the drivers they spoke to experience hardship and long hours, with some sleeping in their cars over the weekend so that they could maximize time they could spend driving customers. According to one driver "the contract states that Uber can terminate you for any reason" (Munzvenga quoted in De Greef 2018).[8] The Cape Town situation is similar, where the average number of hours driving per week was 64, equating to approximately thirteen hours a day over a five-day week or almost eleven hours a day over a six-day week. Some of the drivers work more than seventy hours a week, representing a very high level of "self-exploitation" or what one driver refers to as "apploitation" (exploitation via mobile phone app) (cited in Taylor and Rioux 2018). In response to concerns about safety, Uber imposed a twelve hour shift limit on drivers in 2018, excluding breaks, although some drivers circumvent this rule by switching phones (Rosenblat 2018). Our results jibe with work conditions elsewhere, where most drivers make less than the minimum wage, after expenses, and are consequently forced to work long hours (Barnes 2018 cited in Chee 2018). In South Africa "if you get sick you still have to drive, otherwise you are missing out... I work from 7a.m. to 10pm, every day. More in weekends..." (Simbarashe, Uber driver, quoted in Geitung [2017: p. 32]).

An Uber survey in South Africa revealed 87% of drivers said one of the main reasons for joining the platform was "to be their own boss," whereas 85% reported they were "looking for more flexibility and to balance their home/work lives" (Simons 2019). However, the high number of average driving hours would suggest otherwise. This may be part of a more general dissimulation. As Taylor and Rioux (2018: p. 80) note:

> Uber drivers with a rating score below 4.6 or 4.7 out of five stars are very likely to be disconnected (i.e., fired) from the platform. Should we be surprised that a growing number of drivers offer free snacks and water to get high ratings and keep their jobs? Drivers do not hesitate to lie to their passengers when asked if they love their job, knowing full well that good ratings are based on the ability to uphold the illusion that the sharing economy is the tide that lifts all boats.[9]

We found similar results in our survey of Uber and Bolt drivers in Cape Town. Ninety-one percent of our polled South African drivers said earning more was their primary motivation for joining the platform. Drivers participated in a variety of occupations previously. For example, one driver, worked in debt counseling and another as retail shop assistant. Both the debt counselor and the shop assistant became drivers because of the flexibility of working independently and "working for yourself." A former driver at the airport highlighted that it wasn't that he particularly enjoyed being a driver, but rather that jobs are scarce. He said that he would like a more secure job, like working for the government in correctional services or as a traffic officer. Many drivers started driving for Uber because their family members (usually fathers or brothers) were already doing so. The latter speaks to the scarcity and temporary nature of much work in Cape Town and how it is often obtained through informal networks (Crankshaw 2014).

All told, while Uber makes claims it contributes to economic upliftment, the evidence in Cape Town indicates otherwise (Giddy 2019). Far from the inclusionary ethos of the "sharing economy," Cape Town's ride-hailing industry is characterized by highly exploitative labor conditions that by-and-large do not contribute significantly to social or economic upgrading. Instead, technological intermediation through the platform facilitates offshore value extraction, while heightening livelihood insecurity for most drivers.

Governing Ride-sharing: Power Asymmetries, Informal Contracts and Rating Schemes

With respect to governance, the ride-sharing regime operates through highly uneven, multiscalar power relations. To begin with, there are stark asymmetries embedded in platforms such as Uber. The transnational company imposes practical rules on South African drivers, such as the limit on the hours a driver can work, and takes a 25% commission from every trip. In return, however, the company is by-and-large unresponsive to the everyday concerns of drivers as it did not even have a contact number in case of difficulties.[10] The only way to contact Uber or Bolt was through an online connection, one that cost airtime; an added expense.

Drivers also faced a number of other obstacles such as those related to getting access to transport given that only, in the case of Uber, around 10% of drivers own their car (De Greef 2018). When a driver does not own a car s/he forms an agreement with a car owner, known as the Uber partner (hereafter partner), who holds the account with the company and sets performance targets for drivers to meet weekly.[11] Drivers maintain that partners set unrealistically high targets for the use of the car, ranging from US$190 to 250 per week (De Greef 2018). Often when the target is considered too high, and work is slow, the driver only works to reach the target and cover fuel costs, perhaps without breaks, but still works long hours. Some owners expect drivers to pay for service and maintenance of the vehicle, while others agree that the driver only pays for fuel and data costs. Also troubling is the fact that the vast majority of leased vehicles are owned by "white" South Africans – as high as 90% according to the Uber Drivers Guild (2018) – an indication that ride-sharing is governed in a manner that reflects and perpetuates the racialized division of wealth instantiated under colonialism and apartheid (Geitung 2017).

In one case a driver noted that he gave 40% of his takings to a garage that rented him his car, meaning he earned less that he had as a cab driver and worked longer hours (Pollio 2019). However he preferred Uber because of a lack of corruption and preferential treatment through call centers – "you cannot bribe a satellite" (Trevor quote in Pollio 2019: p. 760). This driver also had a taxi sign and worked illegally as a taxi driver until the next call from Uber – an example of a "transversal logic" (Caldeira 2017) opposed to that of the state. Some drivers also noted fuel savings by using Uber as they didn't have to drive around looking for customers. Consequently far from being solely "parasitic" Pollio (2019: p. 772) contends "the platform is also a connective technology whereby Uber drivers and others glean… 'marginal gains' in the transactional asymmetries of ride-sharing." Another study found that for most Uber drivers in Cape Town, many of whom are migrants and face local labor market constraints and barriers to entry, it was the best paying job that they have had (Stein 2021).

According to some of the drivers interviewed, as Uber does not formally employ them, if they end up in trouble the company does not have to take responsibility. This becomes a major concern if there is an accident or hijacking, for example. Uber is not accountable for any of the costs associated with insurance of the vehicle, medical costs, or the money that is lost due to the driver being unfit to work (interview, June 2018). On the other hand, many drivers commend Uber for their response rate and time to queries about issues such as riders who refuse to pay for a trip. Uber compensated drivers for unpaid trips by charging riders a cancellation fee of R25 (US \$1.7), which they receive.

Bolt protects drivers less because there are no cancellation fees for riders. Additionally, when riders refuse to pay for a trip the driver incurs the costs. According to respondents the response time to queries and complaints is extremely slow, with drivers sometimes going for months without a response (via email). Many drivers also mentioned the technicalities of the app as a big issue, as it's sometimes slow and takes a long time to even start a trip. This is problematic because clients often want the quickest trip possible, and consequently clients then give the driver a poor rating.

A low rating implies that the driver is not offering the client a good service, which is, in turn, problematic because activity scores and ratings determine whether drivers qualify for certain incentives. In the case of Uber, drivers with ratings above 4.7 are eligible for a discount on the commission charged. For Bolt, if a driver has an activity score (amount of trips a driver completes) of less than 90%, they can be deregistered. This may take several weeks to remedy, given the long response time from Bolt consultants. Consequently many drivers prefer Uber and many participants who drive for Bolt are in the process of obtaining their "slots" to drive for Uber as well.

An Uber "slot" is the driver profile that allows them to work with the company. However, this process can, in some instances, take up to two years, and, in addition, operating licenses need to be obtained from the City. Prior to a Commission on Mediation and Arbitration ruling, Uber drivers were suspended from the application for declining too many requests. However due to the ruling, Uber now permits drivers to decline as many trips as they wish.

Drivers from the sample remarked that although there are some subtle differences between the two applications, in effect, the companies offer similar experiences to drivers – putting all the responsibilities and unanticipated costs (car insurance, car maintenance, fuel hikes, data costs) on them, no employment contract protections, and long hours (De Greef 2018).[12] According to a presentation by the Uber Drivers Guild (2018) to the South African Parliament in Cape Town: Uber has "99% economic power over us and make policies that affects our life and continue to do so adversely." Worryingly, the organizers of the Guild were subsequently disconnected from the application (Geitung 2017).

Precarious Platforms: Safety Issues in Cape Town's Ride-sharing Economy

Beyond the practices and modes of governance associated with ride-sharing, other issues make it precarious as a livelihood strategy. Most significantly, drivers mentioned safety as one of the main challenges, particularly for rides hailed in the Cape Flats. In the past Uber and Bolt drivers have been mugged, robbed of their belongings, money, cell phones, stabbed, injured, hijacked and even killed (Dano 2018). Some drivers interviewed had experienced several incidents: trip being requested, only to get to the destination and be robbed. Replacement windscreens and bullet holes in drivers' car windows attest to past incidents and escapes.

Ironically one of the draws for riders using these services in South Africa is security, as drivers' locations are tracked by both phones and the platform. However, these apps also generate other insecurities. Thefts from Uber drivers became more common after the company started allowing cash payments in South Africa in 2016 (Geitung 2017) even though previously Uber promised drivers in an email communication that they would never have to drive with cash (Geitung 2017). Other new security risks for riders have emerged, e.g., hacking of personal information (Kamais 2019) and traffic accidents due to distracted drivers utilizing the interface (Acheampong 2021).

Issues of safety and work injuries have knock-on effects. A driver losing his/her phone lacks the means to make a living and funds are needed for replacement, if they don't have insurance on it. Drivers often cover the cost of vehicle repair, when the car is damaged as well as medical costs if injured, hospitalized, or forced to stay at home. Drivers have to settle hospital bills themselves: although in response to protests in 2018 in South Africa Uber began offering incentives through a rewards program for partners, including "fuel rebates, cellphone deals, maintenance and healthcare" (Rawlins 2018).

Neither Uber nor Bolt protects drivers from the issues that ensue following an injury or hijacking. When something happens to the driver it has "nothing to do with" Uber or Bolt because they are not technically employed by them. The female driver in the sample said that the issue of safety was a concern whether the driver was male or female, and that she was not in more or less danger because of her gender. A number of drivers mentioned the SOS button in the Uber App as an improvement to their safety on the road, although this merely alerts the security services that the driver is in danger, but it takes considerable time for them to arrive on the scene, often after the event.

With Bolt, drivers do not have access to photographs of clients and are thus unable to identify them when they request a ride, meaning "anyone" may request. Furthermore the Bolt app does not highlight the exact location the client is requesting from, but rather the address. If the driver is not familiar with the area he/she does not know where they are driving until they get to the destination. This is an issue in some areas in Cape Town and dangerous crime "hotspots" in specific locales. Some drivers suggest that Bolt and Uber should no longer operate in such areas to avoid violent incidents, although in effect this might represent a form of transportation redlining and accentuate urban inequalities by concentrating on wealthier areas and avoiding townships, as well as reducing drivers' incomes.

One driver suggested that Uber should remove the cash system completely and only allow card payments. In this way drivers would be safer because they would not have cash on them. However, other drivers felt that having the cash system helped to "put fuel in the car everyday," if they do not have their own credit or debit cards. Furthermore, with a card payment, Bolt takes the 15% commission immediately after the trip is completed, which is less advantageous to drivers in terms of providing them with working capital.

Ride-sharing and the Evolution of Sociotechnical Regimes in African Cities

Ride-sharing apps in cities like Cape Town are changing the nature of automobility in Africa. Whereas their services used to be largely restricted to the middle classes who could afford smart phones, this is now changing as three quarters of Rwandans now have these, for example (Moskvitch 2018).[13] Benefits include rider convenience, reduced drunk driving, the possibility of converting parking spaces to new uses, and potential environmentally friendly impacts as consumers buy fewer cars, although effects on traffic congestion and emissions in African cities are unknown (Rogers 2017). Moreover, e-hailing platforms accommodate passengers not served well by mainstream public transport such as after hours, public-holidays, weekends, and/or non-routine trips. They provide what the City (Cape Town) refers to as "the last mile home" service, where a commuter will travel home from work, but then has to get off at the bus stop or train station. The commuter will then request the Uber or Bolt to get home safely. In South Africa Uber data shows that many rides start within a radius of 200 meters of hubs for public transport – "suggesting Uber extends public transit networks" (Vermeulen 2017), thereby making urban consumption and infrastructure regimes related to transport more accessible and in effect coproducing a mobility solution for the urban poor.

Beyond positive outcomes such as these, ride-sharing reveals the darker side of the growing gig economy as an emergent facet of production regimes. By presenting themselves as technology companies Uber and Bolt discursively elide any employment relations with drivers. This represents a form of "virtu-real" accumulation, where the power relations and conditions involved in this "employment relation" become very difficult to contest (Carmody 2015). For example, strikes among drivers are difficult to organize, but not impossible, given the decentralized nature of the system and the fact that cars and drivers are crowd-sourced. There is also intense competition with and between tradi-tional taxis drivers and often poor relations among them, as evidenced by the so-called "taxi wars" in South Africa.[14] There have been protests against Uber from metered taxi drivers who are in direct competition with them, including extensive violence (Burke 2017). Uber fares are typically much cheaper than metered taxis and various requirements make it difficult for many taxi drivers to work for Uber, e.g., cars must be no more than five years old; generally cost-ing at least US $10,500 (De Greef 2018: https://www.uber.com/en-ZA/drive/resources/vehicle-requirements).

While cheaper fares are a benefit to consumers, there is little room for up-grading in Cape Town's ride-sharing economy as commissions and much of the profit flows offshore. Some drivers can put these services in competition with each other, in order to try to retain more value, and this may increase as more ride-sharing applications become available or widely used. However, presently there is a pronounced power imbalance given the way the ride-sharing markets are governed.

Not having a platform to air grievances remains one of the biggest challenges for drivers in Cape Town. Drivers have begun to fortify collective action through joining WhatsApp groups and through "The Movement" and the Drivers Guild. This sharing of information is a steppingstone to empowerment as newer drivers become privy to information they would not necessarily previously have had access to, like Uber's incentives. However, the seeming spatial "liquidity" of Uber (Ritzer 2010), mediated through the internet and mobile phones make organiz-ing difficult. Nonetheless, there have been some successes for drivers in terms of collective action, in Nairobi through the Digital Partners Society, and in Lagos through the Professional E-hailing Drivers and Partners Association (PEDPA) (Sperber 2020; Oluwole 2021).

Positive developments notwithstanding, ride-hailing gigs widen precarious employment or precarity, whereby work becomes increasingly unstable, uncer-tain and insecure, common, seemingly intractable features of informal economies in African cities (Kalleberg 2018). According to the World Bank's recent World Development Report (2019b) if workers are to be competitive with machines they must reskill. This may prove extremely challenging in transport. As a Western Cape government official interviewed emphasized the sharing economy "only works if you have skills," and it tends to disempower the unskilled (interview June

2018, Cape Town). It leads to short-termism and precarious work at odds with long-term decent work. The gig economy is leading to "a sharing of the scraps" in urban Africa.

Conclusion

African cities, like most of the planet's, have experienced a rapid, widespread uptake of new platforms through which individual consumers and service providers can now engage in/with markets, transnational corporations, and distanciated actors in the global economy. The so-called "gig" economy has taken off, particularly in relation to consumer-driven platforms and applications such as those associated with ride-sharing. As the Cape Town case highlights, the emergence of these new transactional spaces and semiformalized labor practices has not transformed extant urban regimes in ways that address the structural inequalities that have (re)produced forms of parasitic urbanization. Instead, new platforms have articulated, become integrated with these structural features (e.g., institutions, modes of governance) in ways that perpetuate them and, in some cases, accelerate and widen the scope for offshore value extraction. Utopian visions for digitally driven "leaps" to more just, inclusive, and distributive cities thus remain unlikely absent wider, deeper transformations to urban sociotechnical systems writ large.

It is difficult to contest the seemingly "placeless" power of platform-driven, virtual capital, which seeks to put "all into competition against all," thereby fostering a "race to the bottom."[15] As Sherman (2017) notes "no venture has ever raised more capital, grown as fast, operated more globally, reached as lofty a valuation – or lost as much money as Uber," bespeaking the impacts of financialization. Money is currently being made off the trading of stock rather than profits from production. However, companies like Uber must become profitable at some point to justify their market valuation. If not, then virtual capital will be just that.

But at what cost, and to who, will profitability be achieved? In the gig "on-demand" economy firms divest themselves of their responsibilities to employees (Herod 2018), reducing the structural power of labor.[16] This represents an undermining of any social contract between the parties, even more so than in the informal economy where personal relations predominate. For many workers dependent on platforms and gigs it is far from economically liberating and more akin to the "zigzag" economy (Jeffrey and Dyson 2013) where people do whatever they have to, including combining multiple modes of livelihood to survive (Mustapha 1992). Needed are new types of social protection for those working in the platform economy – such as "portable benefits" which travel with workers across gigs (Porteous 2019).[17] Others argue for the creation of "platform cooperatives," which are worker-owned and compete with branded, transnational platforms such as Uber, and which might offer better wages and working conditions (Graham and Anwar 2018), as has happened in Kenya among former Uber drivers (Iazzolino 2021). However, the embedded brand power and competitive advantages of transnationalized platforms may make alternative models difficult to sustain.

Absent such progressive changes it seems likely that the gig economy will be unable to drive urban transitions that widely improve the quality, security, and resilience of livelihoods in African cities, despite the fact they are becoming, and will continue to be for years to come, central to the governance and operation of production, consumption, and infrastructure regimes. Virtureal accumulation through governance-at-a-distance will remain the fundamental logic associated with platform capitalism, an ICT-enabled form of extraversion that continues long-standing patterns and legacies of expropriation and unequal exchange. A key contrast here being that, unlike prior modalities of exploitation (e.g., colonialism), the mechanisms driving "surplus value" extraction are invisible to the vast majority of Africans, built into the algorithms, servers, and apps that structure and control the flows (e.g., information, capital) and which intermediate labor and market relations.

Making platforms visible, more equitable, and governable in Africa, and by/for all Africans, is essential if the gig economy is to serve a progressively transformational role in shaping urbanization pathways. For this to happen regulatory and labor protections need to be delivered at global, national, and urban levels. As Novitz (2021) emphasizes, it remains unknown if gig work will become a short-lived interlude – a one-time "gold rush" technology, which while unregulated delivered a bonanza to platforms (and their investors), caused harm to African economies, urbanites, and their dependents. However the historical record shows that informal labor arrangements that are exploitative tend to endure in Africa. The lingering uncertainties of the pandemic, the absence of global governance of platforms, and African governments inability to adequately regulate the gig economy may mean that social change will be slow. Moreover, the general denial and absence of social protections in African societies will continue to drive urbanites into precarious situations where they work for themselves, but at enormous cost.

This is not to say that platforms and apps do not have a place or value in African cities. They do, particularly as ameliorative devices/technologies that enable urbanites to have better access to transportation, banking, and, increasingly, basic services such as energy.[18] Such benefits notwithstanding, app-driven, platform capitalism is presently unable to generate the kinds widespread, formal, and upgraded forms of employment needed to secure livelihoods and grow Africa's knowledge economies. There is no magic bullet here given that the developmental potential of platform capitalism in Africa depends on whether it can hold down and distribute value locally rather than further facilitating its offshoring. Needed are institutional changes such as more transparent regulatory environments that protect and support gig workers, and investments in innovative hubs and capabilities such that Africans can take greater control over the means of platform-based production in cities. This will demand a serious reconsideration of, and creative investments in, small-scale and informal enterprises, not simply a focus on attracting transnational platform firms to the region.

Notes

1 This has been driven by a variety of trends including Moore's law, which predicted that computing power per chip would double in each generation, minaturization, digitalization, technological convergence, bioengineering, and the other technologies of 4IR.

2 Acute under- and unemployment in Africa diminishes urban labor's bargaining power (Mahmood 2019). In general, temporary and casual staff such as those associated with gig work are much more difficult to organize into unions given their geographical dispersion and (often) precarity.

3 This is similar to Facebook and other social media platforms where users upload the content for free, while also providing their data which can be commercialized and monetized.

4 Uber has however been banned in certain cities and countries around the world over concern about some of its practices and that it presents "unfair competition" to taxi drivers. It is banned in Namibia because of "concerns over foreign profiteering and tax avoidance" (Moskvitch 2018). In discussion with a taxi driver in London it was noted that they must have licenses from the local authority to operate and comprehensive insurance, thereby raising their costs in comparison. Uber does however have commercial coverage for its drivers, when they are carrying fares (Rogers 2017). However, there was a recent court ruling in the UK that Uber is an employer and that consequently its drivers are entitled to the National Living Wage.

5 Of course the townships were not just the result of "natural growth" or "voluntary" in-migration but also forced removals under apartheid which rend the social fabric asunder (Pinnock 2016).

6 There are also specific initiatives to disrupt this. For example, Little Cabs in Nairobi which is an online ride-sharing platform offers customers the choice of a male or female driver and has seen a 13-fold increase in the number of women drivers in the past two years (Bhalla, 2018). It is estimated that women account for only 3% of the city's "e-taxi" drivers.

7 This may be over-reported as respondents may have been nervous about their immigration status. Professor Mike Morris estimates about 60–70% of drivers are Zimbabwean and 10–15% from the DRC (personal communication with Carmody 2019).

8 The exact language is "Uber may immediately terminate these Terms or any Services with respect to you, or generally cease offering or deny access to the Services or any portion thereof, at any time for any reason." (https://www.uber.com/legal/terms/za).

9 An Uber customer from Australia noted to me that while objectively he knows that the "sharing economy" is problematic, the fact that Uber drivers tend to be in better humor than regular taxi drivers is an incentive to use the service. This represents a form of "emotional labor" (Rogers 2017).

10   Uber did however with great fanfare announce a help phone number for drivers and riders in South Africa in late 2018 (Uber 2018). Drivers also expressed frustration about other issues. For example, on the Johannesburg "Uber Experience" Facebook page one post reads "Could anyone help to understand what is 'Document Unqualified'. I have been blocked for an Inspection Certificate. I have uploaded a new inspection from Dekra but every time it has been rejected. I have been asking what need to be done for the certificate to qualify but it seems I am talking to people that never completed their six years primary school. Must I wait until Monday for them to tell me what's wrong with the certificate?" https://www.facebook.com/groups/1635907093374900

11   There are also other ownership structures for cars. For example, groups of friends or family members may pool their money to buy a car and run it as many hours a day as possible. We are grateful to Professor Mike Morris for this observation.

12   For example, car insurance premia in South Africa doubled in price starting in 2015 (De Greef 2018).

13   This has meant that the country is now an attractive destination for inward investment from Volkswagen who are building an assembly plant there largely for the car/ride-sharing market.

14   Which was between drivers in the taxi mini-bus association.

15   Although there is sometimes a backlash against this. For example, the lower cost UberPop service was banned in the Netherlands and France for drivers who didn't hold (professional) licenses (Herod 2018).

16   Although this has been controversial with some lawsuits alleging drivers were misled by the company into believing they were employees and thereby eligible for reimbursement of expenses (Rogers 2017).

17   For example, GoJek in Indonesia adds the cost of social insurance contributions to its prices (Coupez 2017 cited in Hunt and Samman 2020).

18   As discussed above, Uber and Bolt are examples of transportation-based platforms. M-Pesa in Kenya is an iconic example of app-driven banking. With respect to energy, social enterprises – such as Paygo energy in Nairobi (https://www.paygoenergy.co) – provide platforms for helping consumers manage and access liquid petroleum gas (LPG) for cooking.

Chapter Seven
Making Cities Livable for All: Infrastructure and Service Provisioning Challenges

Introduction

Cities are much more than sites of production, and truly generative urban transitions must enhance the quality of life available to the majority of urban residents. Well-distributed and higher-quality collective goods and basic services are essential in this regard as they enable residents to live healthy, productive lives that facilitate social mobility. Infrastructures are thus essential contributors to residents' quality of life (the use values of cities) and the productivity of workers, firms, and industries (the exchange values of cities). Governance and delivery of these goods and services is understood here as occurring principally through infrastructure regimes. Infrastructure regimes shape, and are in turn shaped by, extant production and consumption regimes through their contributions to industrial productivity, costs of living, and the availability of capital (e.g., through tax revenues) to invest in the collective goods and basic services delivered by infrastructures. As such, couplings between infrastructure and other regimes play a central in determining the pace, scale, and scope of urban development processes. As Murphy and Carmody (2019) and Murphy (2022) show in the cases of Dar es Salaam and Nairobi, couplings can reinforce inadequate service distributions and significantly reduce the productivity of workers.

The Urban Question in Africa: Uneven Geographies of Transition, First Edition. Pádraig R. Carmody, James T. Murphy, Richard Grant and Francis Y. Owusu.

In general, urban infrastructures in Africa are woefully out-of-sync with the pace and scale of urban population growth in the continent today. Cities are by-and-large overly congested, sprawling, and splintered into enclaves of wealth and immiseration (slums). In such contexts, basic service provisioning systems do not adhere to the modern, integrated, and monolithic infrastructure ideal of one system to universally meet basic needs but are instead heterogeneous and fragmented with most residents making do through coping strategies, informal markets, and inefficient, *ad hoc* practices to meet personal and household needs (Jaglin 2008; Swilling 2011; Lawhon et al. 2018; van Welie et al. 2018). The net result is a negative impact on the quality of life available to urban residents and limited prospects for more efficient, productive, and competitive industries in cities (Castells-Quintana 2017). As this chapter explicates, Africa's urban infrastructure challenges are manifold and complex, demanding innovative solutions that can more evenly, justly address basic service, housing, and transport needs while contributing in strategic ways to the upgrading of industries, workers, and the competitiveness of cities in regional and global markets.

The chapter first describes the scope and scale of the challenges associated with Africa's urban infrastructure regimes. We then examine the governance features of these regimes, focusing on resource constraints, political priorities, and self-provisioning practices. We detail the splintered, fragmented, and heterogeneous nature of urban infrastructures and the challenges these create with regard to service provisioning. Splintered urbanization is a by-product of immanent, structural conditions and political economic priorities that place exchange value through transnational, extra-urban connectivity as a priority for states, donors, and private-sector actors. As a result, dominant actors prefer mega-infrastructure projects (e.g., national railways, large ports, motorways, new-build cities) over intra-urban efforts to improve the everyday living conditions facing majority populations. The chapter discusses these structural challenges and then closes with a call for systemic views that capture the interrelationships between infrastructure, consumption, and production regimes, and which recenter concerns about the use-values of cities for residents.

The Scale and Scope of the Collective Goods Challenge in African Cities

Basic services and collective goods that are delivered through vital infrastructures are lagging far behind the need for these in most cities in Africa. Population growth as a result of migration to, and natural increase within, cities is exacerbating an already bad situation by widening delivery gaps and making strategic planning extremely difficult. Even in Africa's more developed cities capital infrastructure investment can be out of sync with municipal revenue collection, and in decline. For example, in the eThekwini (Durban) Municipality spending in capital infrastructure declined from 18% of budget in 2015 to 9% in 2022/23 (The Durban Edge 2023). The steep decline in capital budget spending is due to human-made and natural disasters, especially flooding which requires increased capital investment into infrastructure repairs/upgrades. Water infrastructure damages associated with flooding in 2021/22 caused revenue collection from water consumption to fall by 12.8% further aggravating scarce municipal finances for development priorities (The Durban Edge 2023). Years of underinvestment in capital infrastructure magnify the infrastructure challenge in African cities and deficits are most clearly manifest in slums. At the same time, speculative private investments in luxury real estate are booming. As we discuss below, fragmentations such as these are an outcome of splintered, poorly planned cities with rather bleak distributions of vital services such as water, sanitation, housing, energy, and transport, particularly as these relate to informal settlements.

With respect to water, sanitation, and hygiene (WASH), urban areas in Africa are facing large deficits with respect to service delivery and management. According to UNICEF and WHO (2022a), about 40% of urban residents in Sub-Saharan Africa lack access to safely managed drinking water; 75% lack safely managed sanitation; and 70% lack basic hygiene services related to handwashing, food, and menstruation. Only 56% of African urbanites have access to piped water on their household premises and only 54% have water that is free from contamination (UNICEF and WHO 2022b). Given rates of population growth, particularly in informal settlements, the proportion of residents with safely managed water remained stagnant between 2015 and 2020 (UNICEF and WHO, 2022b).

Circumstances with respect to sanitation are even more dire, as only 16% of urban populations have sewer connections and 23% of waste is disposed of *in situ*. Pit latrines and informal coping mechanisms (e.g., open defecation/urination, "flying" toilets) remain commonplace as well (e.g., see van Welie et al. 2018). A recent GIZ (2019) report notes that while there have been some success stories with respect to piped water systems in particular, governance remains a challenge in many cities and there is an insufficient focus on addressing the needs of the poorest populations as the numbers with inadequate WASH services continue to rise.

Closely intertwined with the infrastructure challenges related to WASH are the housing conditions facing African cities, manifest most strikingly in the preponderance of slums. A 2018 World Bank estimate is that about 54% of all urban residents in SSA live in slums, a statistic that is only slowly, if at all, declining in contexts facing rapid population growth (World Bank 2022). Moreover, it is likely to have worsened due to the economic disruptions associated with the COVID-19 pandemic. Figure 7.1 and Figure 7.2 provide a sense of living conditions in two of Nairobi's slums – Mathare and Mukuru.

Conditions in most slums are precarious in terms of housing quality, safety, basic services, and the rights that slum dwellers have with respect to property and

Figure 7.1   Nairobi's Mathare Slum.
Photo credit: James T. Murphy (Author).

Figure 7.2   Drainage conditions in Nairobi's Mukuru slum.
Photo credit: James T. Murphy (Author).

rental arrangements. The vast majority of slum residents rent housing, oftentimes rooms or floorspace, frequently from landlords who have a tenuous, sometimes illicit control over the land which might be expropriated by the state for alternative uses (e.g., roads, formal investments).[1] As such, landlords are keen to earn a quick return on their properties and thus charge rents that are disproportionately higher given the quality of housing stock available (Bird et al. 2017; Talukdar 2018). This effectively results in a slum premium being charged to residents, particularly those seeking to live closer to the city center where formal employment opportunities as well as informal/casual work are more concentrated, and commute times significantly shorter/less costly as individuals can walk. In the case of Nairobi, this amounts to slum residents paying, on average, about 16% more for housing when quality adjusted (Talukdar 2018). Making matters worse, food in African cities is about a third more expensive than in comparator countries (Nakamura et al. 2016), partly as a result of oligopolies and collusion in fertilizer pricing (Roberts 2019).

Slum upgrading programs have tried to solve the housing crisis, but such initiatives are commonly isolated (i.e., to single communities rather than city-wide), foreign aid dependent, and hampered by city politics, insecure property rights, land conflicts, and insufficient participation by residents in planning, design, and implementation (Muchadenyika and Waiswa 2018; Doe et al. 2020). Further complicating matters is the fact that there is little available land for new, affordable housing developments in many cities given speculative real estate investments that often go unoccupied (Fox and Goodfellow 2018), land is often tied up in legal disputes, and because developers are generally disinterested and unincentivized to deliver affordable housing.

Energy delivery systems are more advanced in most cities and the World Bank (2022) estimates that nearly 80% of urban residents in Sub-Saharan Africa have electricity access. However, electrification rates do not tell the full story as many connections are illegal and outages and voltage fluctuations are frequent, e.g., 91.7% of grid-connected households experience more than four electricity disruptions a week in Rwanda (Koo et al. 2018). In slums, electricity distribution can be particularly difficult to provide with any certainty or consistency given the challenges of tracking usage and distribution. Informal systems often predominate, as they do with respect to water provisioning, commonly manifest as community-specific cartels that control and distribute electricity from transformers to slum dweller residences and informal workshops. Some utilities try to resist such work-arounds and in the process create hazardous situations, as when lower-voltage lines are placed above higher-voltage ones, a practice intended to make accessing power informally dangerous (de Bercegol and Monstadt 2018).

Given the costs of electricity, informal or formal, it is not commonly used for cooking thus meaning that charcoal and liquefied petroleum gas (LPG) predominate. Charcoal is cheap but problematic given the lack of adequate ventilation in slum households: its use long associated with upper-respiratory issues, particularly in women and children (Sanbata et al. 2014; Ezeh et al. 2017). LPG is cleaner but is typically imported, its price is directly linked to oil, and its distribution is often governed by foreign companies who control the distribution and filling of gas cylinders (Christley et al. 2021). As such, LPG is prone to price volatility which has significant implications given the poverty of most slum residents.

Transportation infrastructures within cities also remain wholly inadequate with traffic jams, air pollution, and congestion being major challenges (see Figure 7.3). Poor air quality is common with many cities' remaining below WHO standards given the particulate matter associated with diesel fuel (Rajé et al. 2018; Musah et al. 2020; Singh et al. 2020). Traffic congestion has significant implications for worker and economic productivity given wasted fuel and time. For example, in 2016 it was estimated that Nairobi's economy lost about $500,000 per day as a result of jams and congestion (Honan 2016). Losses from road traffic accidents, rapidly rising among the health burdens in Africa's cities, and the highest of any region of the world, are imposing a huge toll and financial burden on individuals, families, employers, and societies given limitations of insurance and social protection (Ryan-Coker et al. 2021). To partly address these issues, main artery roads in most cities have been upgraded gradually, but transportation planning remains rather haphazard and piecemeal, dependent upon donors for major upgrading projects. China, in particular, has contributed significantly to transportation infrastructures through the BRI but such investments tend to focus on inter-urban and transnational connectivity rather than intra-urban congestion and/or basic services for all (Alves 2013; Paller 2021).

Public transportation systems are multifaceted and dominated by informal, van/mini-bus-based paratransit systems (e.g., *matatu* [Kenya], *daladala*

Figure 7.3   Nairobi traffic jam.
Photo credit: James T. Murphy (Author).

[Tanzania], *danfo* [Nigeria], *trotro* [Ghana]) that operate on regular routes, but which are weakly regulated by municipal authorities (Klopp and Cavoli 2019; Xiao 2022). Such services are complemented by motorcycle taxis, conventional buses, auto rickshaws *(tuk-tuk)*, and, increasingly, app-based taxi and ride-sharing services (see Chapter 6). Light-rail and subway systems are poorly developed and/or nonexistent in most cities given the costs and logistics associated with their construction and implementation.[2] More promising has been the implementation of BRT systems, although the degree to which preexisting paratransit systems are integrated with these remains generally low (Klopp and Cavoli 2019). Given all the congestion and transport costs, walking still remains a logical, common, and predominant mobility choice, when possible (Sietchiping et al. 2012). Despite this reality, pedestrian walkways, safety measures, flyovers, and other supporting infrastructures are poorly developed and insufficiently invested in given the priorities of donors and city officials (Lukenangula and Baumgart 2020; Paller 2021).

With the exception of traffic congestion, wealthy and middle-class residents in African cities have been able to manage infrastructure deficits, often able to work from home through privatized solutions and/or by residing in enclaved (e.g., gated), well-serviced communities. As discussed in Chapter 4, new-build, often peri-urban cities have been on the rise, deemed as a desirable means for the wealthy to escape congested inner cities and avoid a reliance on municipal governments for basic services (Watson 2014; van Noorloos and Kloosterboer 2018). Such "solutions" however, fail to address the material realities and challenges facing majority populations forced to live in poorly serviced slums. In fact, for some planners, municipal leaders, and development agencies (e.g., World Bank 2009), slums are seen as short-term challenges associated with rapid urbanization; phenomena that will disappear with modernization and the rise of new, "smart" infrastructures in greenfield cities (interview with Kenyan planner).

Such cavalier perspectives notwithstanding, the reality is that slums are multigenerational communities that, in many cases, have existed for decades and which are unlikely to disappear through the growth of neoliberalized political economies. With respect to the development of cities, slums can be understood as poverty "traps" locked into low-level equilibria, even in cases where economic growth has expanded resource availability (Marx et al. 2013; Castells-Quintana 2017). Such equilibria are due in large part to the effects that inadequate infrastructure and poor services can have on long-term development. As Castells-Quintana (2017: p. 169) note:

> Access to basic services, in particular, is not just desirable per se in terms of quality of life for urban residents, but also in terms of capital accumulation and economic efficiency at national level, as they allow for the realisation of agglomeration economies and the control of congestion costs. The results provided suggest that investments that raise access to basic urban services, like sanitation, can have a non-negligible effect on long-run economic growth, especially for countries with high levels of urban concentration.

Given these circumstances, a key question is why infrastructure regimes and their governance in African cities have failed to address the highly uneven distributions of basic services and collective goods. Three tensions/issues are at the core of these challenges: governance through speculation, resource constraints, and political priorities; splintered urbanization; and structural and historical, political-economic conditions.

Governance of Infrastructure Regimes: Speculation, Resource Constraints and Political Priorities

African cities are experiencing what Fox and Goodfellow (2022) term "late" urbanization. In this context, cities have faced intense demographic pressures coupled with hyper-globalization and insufficient managerial capacity marked by *laissez-faire* approaches to urban planning. Urbanization has not occurred with large-scale industrialization that could generate significant formal employment, tax revenues and multiplier effects. Instead, urban-regional economic growth is by-and-large driven by consumption and capital generated through rural-based extractive sectors, agro-industries, and inward FDI that is often focused on real estate speculation. In the context of hyper-globalization and the liberalization of property markets, domestic and foreign capital (esp. from China and the Middle East) has flowed into some African cities as investors look for high returns on real estate (van Noorloos and Kloosterboer 2018).

In the case of Nairobi, favored speculative investments often include apartment blocks, petrol stations, car lots, and, in the case of larger investors, shopping malls and hotels (Murphy 2022). Speculative investments such as these, prioritized by municipalities and the investment arms of government, may deflect from other priorities such as the desperate demand for upgraded housing, and infilling of private projects means that urban land is not used for pro-poor needs. As has been observed in parts of Africa – e.g., Kigali and Addis Ababa – speculative practices often entail a *de facto* tax break for investors in that while the land itself is taxed, the buildings constructed on it are not; thus encouraging investors to build sooner rather than later. As Goodfellow (2017: p. 800) notes:

> Under such conditions and in the context of rapid economic growth, people with resources may be more inclined to speculate on buildings than on land itself. This is potentially even more damaging if it results in an oversupply of [inappropriate] buildings that does not match demand, a reduction in the availability of land for different uses and the sucking away of resources from productive investment.

The tying up of land for speculative consumption purposes, coupled with the lack of industrial development in the production regime, has greatly limited the land and tax revenue needed for infrastructure upgrades. While there are also other constraints, policies are lacking to prevent or reduce speculative practices which contribute to housing in cities becoming increasingly unaffordable. Worse yet, urban sprawl is raising slum premia or pushing lower-income residents to peri-urban locations far removed from their workplaces. Such spatial mismatches bode poorly for the prospects of social mobility among the poorest.

Adequate municipal finance is another key governance challenge that limits infrastructure upgrading. Informality exacerbates the revenue challenge as the vast majority of livelihoods are not taxed (Resnick 2021). Mpofu (2021) examined the literature on the links between the informal sector (IS) and tax revenues in Africa, highlighting that while the IS generates anywhere from 34% to 61% of GDP it contributes only 1.8 to 6% of national tax revenues in Ghana, Kenya, Nigeria, Tanzania, Zambia, and Zimbabwe. When considered in relation to cities and infrastructure, this greatly reduces the public resources that municipal governments have to invest in collective goods and basic services. Property taxes remain significant as a source of municipal finance, but tax systems remain limited by often outdated cadastral maps, low valuations, and inconsistent or weak collection systems (Franzsen and McCluskey 2017; Cirolia 2020). Moreover, as noted above, in some cities only land is taxed, not the buildings on it, thus further limiting revenues and incentivizing speculative, unproductive investments such as luxury apartments that may not be occupied in the near term (Goodfellow 2017).

Despite calls or policies for fiscal decentralization, national governments commonly maintain or exert significant control over budgets for municipal authorities; a by-product of what Fox and Goodfellow (2022) term "centripetal state politics." There are exceptions to this (e.g., fiscal devolution in Kenya) but by-and-large city governments have lacked the authority, capital, and capacity to implement infrastructure upgrades as national states have prioritized national over urban planning. The net result is that cities remain reliant on foreign aid and donors for most large-scale projects; actors whose priorities are typically focused on improvements that will enhance the attractiveness of cities for FDI, increase export and import flows, and serve geopolitical needs and priorities rather than those of the majority of urban residents (Goodfellow 2020). As Cirolia (2020: p. 4) notes:

> While often being given the policy mandate, [municipal governments] are not in control of the financial resources. These processes have led to fiscal fracturing among levels of government, departments, agencies, and actors involved in governance. Key revenue sources are ring fenced and allocated to national agencies and utility companies, donors and lenders dictate spending priorities through line departments, and local governments are constantly undertaking arduous fiscal accounting exercises which do little to increase real resource accountability.

The internationalization of infrastructure finance in Africa raises further concerns about the potential for the service delivery gaps facing the poor to be addressed any time soon. While domestic private finance accounts for only a small

fraction (14.7% in 2018) of infrastructure finance, foreign aid such as concessional loans and PPPs have played an increasingly significant role over the past
two decades (Goodfellow 2020). China too is a central actor in this regard, mobi-
lizing surplus capital in order to more deeply integrate African economies into its
production networks, markets, and geopolitics; albeit not in a unified, monolithic
manner (e.g., cf. Liu et al. 2020). For private finance and development banks,
infrastructure portfolios are viewed as potentially lucrative investments provided
African states play a risk-mitigation and mediating role for capital to ensure that
returns on investments are sufficiently high. PPP arrangements often rely on
revenue clauses and guarantees to ensure that investors get their desired returns;
often at the expense of increasing risks to public partners in Africa (Goodfellow,
2020). Needed are municipally controlled sources of finance that can be targeted
toward the priorities of residents and universal access to basic services rather
than profits for external investors (Turok 2016).

In response to provisioning failures in basic services and collective goods, the
majority of residents in most cities, particularly those in slums, self-govern and
self-provide them (Turok 2016; Baptista 2019; Grossman 2021). The results are
what Lawhon et al. (2018) term "heterogeneous infrastructure configurations"
manifest in informal, diverse, and variable strategies to access water, sanitation,
energy, and other vital services. Such strategies can include non-marketized coping mechanisms (e.g., open urination, see van Welie et al. 2018), the poaching of
services (e.g., illegal electricity connections, see Buyana 2022), and/or alternative
market mechanisms (e.g., private water sellers). As demonstrated in many African
cities, it is clear that monolithic, singular service systems for collective goods are
unlikely anytime soon, with heterogeneity remaining a key characteristic of water
(Blomkvist and Nilsson 2017; Stoler et al. 2019), sanitation (van Welie et al.
2018; Cherunya et al. 2020), energy (Baptista 2019; Njoroge et al. 2020), and
transportation (Rajé et al. 2018) infrastructure governance. Such adaptations
and the resilience of residents are quite remarkable given the difficulties of everyday life and the material limitations at work. That said, however, the injustice,
inequity, and immiseration that most residents face due to infrastructure deficits
is highly unsustainable and in need of creative, distributive solutions if Africa's
cities are to realize their economic and social potential.

Splintered Urbanization and the Challenge of Service Distribution

The governance of infrastructure regimes, and the heterogeneous configurations it
produces, reflects a key phenomenon shaping the urban question in Africa today –
what to do about splintered cities? The theory of splintered urbanization emerged
through the groundbreaking work of Graham and Marvin (2001). Focusing on
cities in the Global North, they argued that these are marked by spatially uneven
access to opportunities and benefits from the global economy, manifest particularly

in (im)mobilities related to capital, information, and transportation. The result is that contemporary cities are simultaneously constituted by hyper-globalized and hyper-localized spaces; the former associated with accumulation and wealth, the latter marked by socioeconomic stagnation. A major development challenge in this regard is how to enhance mobilities for all in part through investments in integrated and more inclusive infrastructures.

The concept of splintering has subsequently been deployed to understand and analyze African cities and their infrastructure distributions (Jaglin 2008; Odendaal 2011; Swilling 2011; Murphy and Carmody 2019; Murphy 2022). Such works show how infrastructure regimes in African cities function in highly exclusionary and uneven ways. As Swilling (2011, 2014) argues in his studies of Cape Town, the spatial segmentation of services has emerged in response to the shift toward "commodification" rather than universal access as the principle governing logic of collective goods and basic services. The result is that residents get what they can afford to pay for rather than what they need, often forced to turn to private, costly, informal, and/or self-provisioning options or to take up residence in new build cities if wealthy (Murray 2015; Fält 2019).

By its nature, splintering produces not only highly unequal cities but also complex, heterogeneous, polycentric infrastructure regimes that are difficult to manage, coordinate, and integrate. For example, van Welie et al. (2018) show how Nairobi's sanitation regime is made up of several subregimes or service-delivery options that produce a spatially fragmented regime across the city, varying not only in terms of settlement locations but also temporally (e.g., nighttime versus workday options). As Figure 7.4 shows, this produces a complex provisioning landscape that defies singular, centralized management solutions.

In contexts such as these, there is a need to first understand, document, and legitimate the everyday practices that residents rely on to access and maintain basic services and vital infrastructures. The links to the consumption regime are critical here, particularly the degree to which residents – especially those in precarious, costly tenure arrangements in slums – are able/willing to prioritize different aspects of service upgrading. A key concern here is to identify appropriate measures – affordable and those that are aligned with existing practices – that can be translated into policies and initiatives. This, in and of itself, is a major challenge given that most governments and utility companies are loathe to recognize or accept provisioning activities that elude, ignore, or bypass their direct control or revenue generating authority, and which may be illegal.[3] Instead, their emphasis often remains on the commodification of services through the modern infrastructure ideal (i.e., universal provisioning systems); a vision that is highly unrealistic in the medium term given the costs and pragmatics of accessing the finance for, and building such systems, particularly in informal communities. This is unfortunate in that it can discourage a willingness to meet low-income residents on their terms and to seek solutions that are better aligned with the practices and material realities they rely on and face.

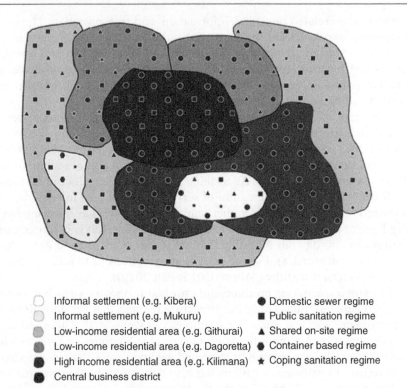

◯	Informal settlement (e.g. Kibera)	●	Domestic sewer regime
◔	Informal settlement (e.g. Mukuru)	■	Public sanitation regime
◓	Low-income residential area (e.g. Githurai)	▲	Shared on-site regime
◑	Low-income residential area (e.g. Dagoretta)	◉	Container based regime
◕	High income residential area (e.g. Kilimana)	★	Coping sanitation regime
◐	Central business district		

Figure 7.4   Conceptualizing Nairobi's splintered sanitation regime.
Source: van Welie et al., 2018 / With permission of Elsevier.

Decentralized, distributed solutions are emerging in some sectors that could serve as important, realistic solutions to the immediate challenges residents face. For example, Larsen et al. (2016) highlight several options for addressing WASH issues in Southern cities, including improvements to stormwater drainage, water-use productivity, wastewater treatment, and human waste management. Water purification technologies have evolved significantly, particularly with regard to point-of-use, household scale filtration technologies (e.g., see Dixit et al. 2019). Innovations have also emerged with regard to the provisioning of energy in slums, from off-grid solar power (e.g., see Rateau and Choplin 2022) to app-driven LPG delivery schemes and smart-metering technologies (e.g., see https://www. paygoenergy.co/cylinder-smart-meter). All told, technologies such as these have the potential to be better aligned with existing service provisioning practices and can thus improve material conditions in the short run. However, they do not amount to the kinds of immanent, structural transformations needed to provide long-term solutions to infrastructure gaps in African cities. Such changes are essential for sustainable and equitable infrastructure transitions but these remain difficult to imagine given the structural and political economic drivers shaping infrastructure regimes today.

Structural and Political Economic Drivers of Infrastructure Deficits in African Cities

Perhaps the most pressing structural challenge is to formally legitimate and legally recognize informal settlements, and some service provisioning practices that may not be governed or taxed by formal authorities at the present. While such recognition is an essential first step, it is currently difficult to imagine in many/most cities given it will demand that political elites and municipal authorities decentralize control over basic services in some areas and support investments that prioritize the needs of slum dwellers and informal settlements. Rather than seeing informality as a problem that will disappear through rapid modernization and economic growth, it needs to be understood as co-constitutive of the formal sector, often in regressive ways. Specifically, informal settlements can enable waged workers to live in close proximity to formal employment opportunities (e.g., see Bird et al. 2017), albeit with low wages and little chance for social mobility. The low quality of housing and reliance on informal, poorly distributed infrastructures for basic services has the effect of subsidizing low wages in the formal sector, while accelerating accumulation and the rent-seeking prospects for elites who provide limited, at best, tax revenues for widely accessible infrastructure upgrades.

As Wuyts (2001) argued years ago through the case of Tanzania, a large informal sector can help spur short-run economic vitality but not in a manner that is sustainable or conducive to long-run, productive structural transformations. This is particularly the case when the growth of domestic manufacturing industries is stagnant as imports become increasingly central as sources of wage goods such as food, clothing, and furnishings. Informality and the struggle to access and pay for basic services, coupled with the costs of congestion and public health challenges resulting from poor infrastructure, effectively undermine the productivity of urban-based workers. This consequently results in a regressive coupling between the infrastructure and production/consumption regimes in African cities; one that reinforces splintering and works against the prospects for generative urbanization.

These structural conditions are further entwined with the political-economic priorities of most African states today – to promote more rapid and deeper integrations in the global economy through trade and FDI. On one hand, the state and foreign capital's interest to connect the city's economy to global and regional markets has meant that there is a priority placed on big (often national) projects intended to improve and enhance global flows of commodities, information, and capital into city-regions. While there is little doubt that most African cities are much better connected to the global economy as a result, these infrastructure investments simultaneously facilitate nonproductive or counterproductive development outcomes as imports and speculative capital (esp. for luxury housing and retail space) flow more readily into African cities. In sum, transnational connectivity and exchange value trump basic need, equity, and justice considerations, thus meaning that gaps and inequalities with respect to collective goods and services remain poorly addressed.

Despite there being logical dimensions to the "go-global" approach, most African cities lack coherent, comprehensive, realistic, and well-financed strategies as well as capabilities to enable the kinds of infrastructure upgrades that can foster generative urbanization. There is a partiality at work here: a focus on externally funded, big-push, big-money showcase projects (see Chapter 4) that state officials and investors believe can rapidly jump-start economic-industrial-urban transformations, while also creating rent-seeking opportunities for elites. Such projects often seek to bypass or avoid the congestion, informality, and infrastructure deficits that mark most cities, striving instead to build smart, innovative, and/or green substitutes that are delinked from such problems. In one sense such optimism is refreshing and a direct challenge to the oft-negative assessments of the development challenges facing African cities today; the notion being that African cities should be viewed as sites for the realization of prosperous, modern, and globally significant futures with SEZ, greenfield cities, infrastructure megaprojects, and inward FDI leading the way. In practice, such heterotopic projects are chosen and implemented, if that, in a scattergun matter where boosterism and rent-seeking by elites trump just, distributive urban development concerns. Three projects – Accra's SkyTrain, Bagamoyo's Port, and Kenya's Standard-Gauge railway – further highlight the limits on such megaprojects as they relate to urban infrastructure regimes.

SkyTrain – Accra's Utopian Mega Infrastructure Project

Ghana's president, Nana Akufo-Addo, announced during the 2019 African Investment Forum the building of the first, for the continent, $2.6 billion SkyTrain in Accra. The project would be financed by the Ghana Infrastructure Investment Fund (GIIF), an independent fund set up by the government and the Investment SkyTrain Consortium of private companies, with the support of the African Development Bank. Couched in terms of sustainable mobility to help relieve the city's traffic and air pollution, Accra's SkyTrain would be a fully automated and highly efficient public mass transit system, using air propulsion technology to drive lightweight, high passenger volume vehicles to transport 380,000 people every year and create about 5,000 jobs. Such infrastructural projects are often presented as the symbols of the countries that host them, and the Accra Skytrain was no different – it was meant to signify a country taking flight as reflected in Ghana's economic growth (We Build Value 2019). Despite the euphoria that marked SkyTrain's launch, it is increasingly likely that this utopian project may never see the light of day. The project missed its initial start date of August 2020 and Ghana's minister of railway development, John Peter Amewu, recently noted that the project is too expensive given more pressing priorities: "I don't see a sky train being done in the next 3 to 4 years let's be very frank to ourselves" (quoted in Onukwue 2021). The reversal reflects the reality of Ghana's economic instability and the fact that the amount budgeted for the project, if invested in other infrastructures (e.g., roads), can benefit many more Ghanaians. Some see the SkyTrain's failure as a repetition of the 2010 $1.5 billion Accra Monorail Project that was expected to create 15,000 jobs but never went beyond the planning stages (Kuuire 2021).

The Bagamoyo Port Project, Tanzania

The Bagamoyo Port Project in Bagamoyo, Tanzania, was projected to be one of the largest government infrastructure projects in the country. The project was meant to involve the construction of the 1,700 hectare Bagamoyo SEZ. This US $10bn project was originally conceived as a joint venture between Tanzania, China, and Oman.[4] The port, expected to be the largest in East Africa, and the industrial zone, expected to attract over 700 enterprises, were seen as a means to ease congestion at the old port while supporting Tanzania's aspiration to become East Africa's leading shipping and logistics center (Africa Business Pages, nd).

Although the contracts for the construction of the port were signed in 2015, like other such projects around the continent, it remains stalled (BBC 2015; Mittal 2020). The Magufuli government suspended the project in January 2016 claiming it was too expensive and complex, although others attributed the suspension to opposition politicians and the private sector who saw the project as a waste of resources; instead supporting improvements to the existing Tanga, Dar es Salaam, and Mtwara ports (The Citizen 2016). The project was resumed in 2018 but halted indefinitely in 2019 because of the "exploitative and awkward" terms attached to the deal (Mittal 2020). There are indications that the current Tanzanian President, Hassan, has been in communications with Chinese officials and is looking for ways to resurrect the project (Moriyasu 2021). However, it seems that China is now focusing on port development, and a space launch facility in Djibouti, which already houses China's sole overseas naval base (Barton 2021; The Economist 2021). That said, the Tanzanian Ports Authority recently announced that construction would begin sometime in 2023 (TheAfricaLogistics 2022). While there is meant to be coordination on infrastructure development through the East African Community, in reality there is intense national level competition around connectivity (Walsh 2022).

Kenya's Standard-Gauge Railway (SGR)

One of Kenya's most significant, completed infrastructure projects to date is the multi-billion dollar, Chinese-funded SGR that connects Kenya's main port of Mombasa to Nairobi (see Figure 7.5). The 300-mile railway opened in October 2017 and the express train has reduced passenger travel time from 7 hours by bus to 4 hours and 30 minutes, with (rail) freight transport times reduced from 24 to 8 hours. The SGR was initially run by Afristar Operations, a subsidiary of the China Road and Bridge Corporation (CRBC), but this relationship came to an early end as Kenyan authorities terminated the contract five years early (in 2022) due to cost and debt concerns (Nyabiage 2021). Kenya Railways Corporation currently operates the line.

While welcomed originally as part of the Kenyan Government's Vision 2030 development plan, the SGR has been controversial both in terms of the US $2.5 billion of debt associated with its construction, and its impacts on the logistics and transportation industry (Mwangi 2019; Niba 2019; Tarrósy, 2020; Taylor 2020; Carmody et al. 2022a). When asked about the project, planners and other key informants in Nairobi were by-and-large skeptical, noting particularly that it was of lower quality compared with the railway linking Addis Ababa to Djibouti, that it was operating at a net loss, and that its actual costs were far greater (4 to 5 times) than expected due in large part to corruption, exaggerated land prices, and lack of transparency with regard to its financing and implementation. All told, the general sentiment was that despite being billed as a panacea for

Figure 7.5   Kenya's Standard Gauge Railway.
Source: Erasmus Kamugisha/ Wikimedia Commons / CC BY-SA 4.0.

industrial development, the SGR was too expensive, a "failure," and/or simply "not worth it" in the end.

Kenyan trucking companies and truckers too were unhappy with the SGR, particularly regarding mandates from the Kenya Port Authority requiring importers to use the SGR for freight shipments to Nairobi's Inland Container Depot (ICD), a policy that resulted in increased transport costs and scaled down operations, causing protests in Mombasa (Kitimo 2020) and the subsequent reversal of the policy by the new (Ruto) government. Given the controversies and poor performance, funds for the final sections of the railway to Uganda and onto South Sudan have yet to be granted by China, despite Kenya receiving a restructured repayment deal for the loans granted for approved/existing SGR lines (Mwangi 2019; Carrai 2021; Omondi 2021). Moreover, the planned extension of Kenya's SGR has been further jeopardized as strategic attention is now shifting to a potential alternative route that would extend the Djibouti-Ethiopia railway to Port Sudan; a project likely to garner significant interest from China if deemed feasible (Muchira 2020; Omondi 2021).

Achieving Infrastructure Transformations: Recentering Use-Value

One reason for the failure of the mega-projects stems from the fact that this approach fails to account for the challenges of productively aligning them with the situated realities facing established cities. Prioritizing a narrow set of features – commodity and capital flows, cost reclamation, profitability, and attractiveness to FDI – means that the focus of mega-infrastructure projects is almost exclusively on the city's exchange values and its potential to serve as a growth machine for national development (see Molotch 1976). How this emphasis articulates with the dominant features of existing urban infrastructure regimes is where the challenge lies – particularly considerations related to the precarious livelihood strategies and living conditions of residents. All told, the emphasis on mega-projects reflects extant infrastructure regimes that operate in a hollowed-out manner, incentivizing and supporting external connections in order to promote growth, global market expansion, and rent-seeking opportunities but without making substantive changes to the internal workings of the everyday/ ordinary city, particularly those associated with slums.

Recent studies of Dar es Salaam (Murphy and Carmody 2019) and Nairobi (Murphy 2022) have taken a more comprehensive view by analyzing the functioning, couplings, multiscalar relations, and development outcomes of urban sociotechnical systems in Africa. Viewed comparatively, and perhaps unsurprisingly, similar processes – namely urbanization without industrialization, splintering, and intraversion – are occurring in both places. Both cities, like most in Africa, can also be characterized as experiencing "late urbanization": high rates of population growth, speculative FDI and domestic investments in "unproductive" assets, centripetal state politics, and the splintering of collective good and basic service distributions.

In both cities, infrastructure policies and programs operate in a scattergun manner with the exception of consistently prioritizing economic liberalization and globalization through enhanced transnational trade, finance, investment, and import flows. Municipal governments lack financial or managerial capacity and infrastructure investments are focused more on the priorities of external funders (e.g., donors, PPP) rather than improving living conditions for the majority of residents.

The focus on transforming African cities into transnationalized growth machines in some ways reflects a singular emphasis/obsession with their exchange value. Missing here is a more holistic conceptualization of place-based development as manifest in the living conditions of residents, considerations of inequality, collective good provisioning systems, and the prospects for the least well-off to experience social upgrading. The sociotechnical systems approach deployed in this book seeks to address this gap – that is to integrate concerns about the use-value of city-regions with analyses of their ability to create exchange value through productive activities. Such an integration captures the development process in a more comprehensive manner by moving beyond the production regime and examining how it is shaped by consumption and infrastructure regimes that govern everyday provisioning practices. By doing so, it is possible to recognize that productivist success stories (e.g., economic growth) are often dependent upon inequality, poverty, and livelihood precarity for many; exclusions that can serve to subsidize globalized urban development, through cheap food provisioning in the informal sector for example (Santos 1979), yet which simultaneously make everyday living a struggle for far too many.

By explicitly considering "other" urban regimes – namely consumption and infrastructure – the systems approach demands a more comprehensive perspective on what cities do and how collective goods, amenities, and the quality of life available to their residents shape the prospects for sustainable, just, and distributive forms of development. In application, it calls for grounded, place-based research that goes beyond exchange value and economic growth in order to understand the life-worlds and everyday experiences of residents that reflect the city's use-values and the capacity for infrastructures to contribute to other development outcomes (e.g., see Pieterse et al. 2018). The quality of these experiences and the prospects for social upgrading, improved livelihoods, and welfare distribution through infrastructure upgrades being central indicators of successful urbanization.

Notes

1   For example, Mukuru, a large slum located near Nairobi's central business district and a traditional industrial area, recently experienced the demolition of 13,000 homes and the displacement of 40,000 residents to create space for a new expressway meant, in part, to ease traffic congestion from the airport to the city center (Ram 2021).

2 Exceptions include Addis-Ababa, Abuja, and in South Africa's major cities.
3 As noted above, energy utility companies may resort to rather extreme tactics to stop the "poaching" of services. See de Bercegol and Monstadt (2018) and Buyana (2022) for examples in the case of electricity.
4 The SEZ is funded by the Government of Tanzania and the State General Reserve Fund from Oman; the latter being part of a sovereign wealth fund (SWF) controlled by the Oman Investment Authority. China is constructing the port, and the industrial zone will be constructed by Oman and administered by the EPZ Authority of Tanzania.

Chapter Eight
The Wrath of Capital or Nature?
Threats to Cities from Climate to COVID-19

Introduction

Risk is the possibility or probability that something bad will happen such that an activity, system, infrastructure or investment will fail or fall short of expectations. Many see risk as being exacerbated by neoliberalization, the devaluation of labor, and/or exposure to climate change (Peck 2001; Leichenko et al. 2010). Risks are often determined by forces well beyond the direct control of individuals, states, planners, and investors particularly when they are associated with global phenomena such as climate change or the COVID-19 pandemic. The hazards (e.g., floods, droughts, heat waves) accompanying climate change have become more severe and frequent yet less predictable (Garthwaite 2021). Risk is being further amplified in urban contexts (Mora et al. 2013) and the unrestrained growth impetus of capitalism and its environmental impacts – what Parr (2013) refers to as the "wrath of capital."

Given their dense populations, complex-built environments, and importance as drivers of economic development, cities can be particularly vulnerable to risks and hazards, especially in cases where material and institutional weaknesses constrain urban management strategies. Such is the case in many African cities today, as they are double or even multi exposed to the vulnerabilities induced by rapid population growth, climate change, water scarcity (e.g., The Cape Town drought 2015–18), biodiversity loss, land degradation, and earthquakes in some instances, e.g., Accra,

The Urban Question in Africa: Uneven Geographies of Transition, First Edition. Pádraig R. Carmody, James T. Murphy, Richard Grant and Francis Y. Owusu.

Juba, and Kivu (see IPPC 2022 Africa report [Trios et al 2022] for a comprehensive discussion of climate-related hazards and the urban nexus), and the forces of globalization that can bring rewards for some, but often with huge risks for most (Rights and Accountability in Development 2021). The risks and hazards associated with climate change and public health issues, among others can be amplified significantly in African cities. Climate change can induce extremes of drought, flooding, and heat that threaten water supplies, displace residents, and reduce the productivity of laborers and small enterprises working in spaces that lack proper ventilation or cooling (Dougherty 2012). Diseases such as cholera, malaria, and COVID-19 can spread rapidly, particularly in informal settlements where waste, sanitation, and drainage systems are often wholly inadequate, and settlements can be dense. Absent effective planning, and the capital to invest in upgraded production and infrastructure regimes, African cities will remain highly vulnerable to such forces, and almost entirely reactionary and in desperate need of forward-thinking and context-sensitive strategies to manage heterogeneous circumstances (Cobbinah et al. 2019).

This chapter explores risks to African cities and their populations from the exacerbation of existing hazards (e.g., heat, sea level rise, flooding and drought), as well as new challenges such as the COVID-19 pandemic. We employ the concept of riskscapes to assess the geography of risk construction (proximate and distantiated) and its implications for urban regimes. Our analysis places particular emphasis on examining how "natural" threats could impact infrastructure regimes (e.g., through increased floods, heat), production regimes (e.g., public health and climate-driven impacts on worker productivity and industries), and consumption regimes (e.g., the quality of life and amenities possible/available to urban residents). We also discuss potential risk mitigation strategies and the challenges of implementing these.

The next section focuses on the geography of risks by defining them, discussing the concept of riskscapes and exploring its usefulness for understanding the layered dimensions of these associated with climate change dynamics and contemporary hazards, such as COVID-19. This is followed by a discussion of riskscapes in the context of African cities and the impacts of disaster risks on their sociotechnical regimes. The following section examines the impacts of the various dimensions of climate change on the sociotechnical regimes of African cities. We also explore "recent" threats, including Ebola and COVID-19, and their impacts. We end the chapter by exploring strategies for managing risk and resilience in African cities.

The Geography of Risk and Riskscapes

Risk is the probability that something bad will happen if exposed to a hazard.[1] Risk is exacerbated by precarity (or the precariousness of livelihoods). According to United Nations Office for Disaster Risk Reduction (UNDRR), disaster risk is the likelihood of loss of life, injury, or destruction and damage from a disaster in a given period of time. Disaster risk, therefore, is the combination of the severity and frequency of a hazard, the numbers of people and assets exposed to it, and their vulnerability to damage. Thus, the losses and impacts that characterize disasters usually have much to do with the exposure and vulnerability of people and places as they do with the severity of the hazard event (UN-DRR, n.d.).

> Risks can be extensive or intensive in nature. Extensive risk refers to the risk associated with low-severity, high-frequency events, mainly but not exclusively associated with highly localised hazards. Intensive risk denotes risk associated to high-severity, mid to low-frequency events, mainly associated with major hazards (United Nations Office of Disaster Risk Reduction 2015).

While intensive risk or disasters may attract media attention, extensive risk may also generate cumulative, substantial livelihood and other losses, which may ultimately be more harmful by virtue of not being insured, for example. An analogue to this is chronic food insecurity rather than famine – the former a type of "silent violence" (Watts 1983). Pressure may build through time and then be "released" through disaster (Blaikie et al. 1994).

Risk may also be proximate or distantiated. Morris et al. (2017) use proximal and distal pathways to illustrate the diverse climate change-induced risks in different geographic locations across timescales. According to them, proximal risk refers to risks to communities that occur within their locality or borders and in ways readily comprehensible to that population (including its policymakers). An example of proximal risk might include the situation in East Africa where climate change is projected to result in higher rainfall, as the atmosphere becomes more humid, which could lead to higher incidence of flooding if rain is concentrated (Cook et al. 2020). Distantiated risks impact communities through indirect routes and may be mediated by both natural and human systems. Risks can also be temporally distal because the extent of their effects will be experienced over time, or perhaps delayed for decades. An example of distantiated risk to cities would be that hydropower dams which supply electricity to them might dry up, or only work at very reduced capacity as a result of climate disruption (Falchetta et al. 2019).

In relation to geography, the concept of "riskscapes" or landscapes of risk has been employed to advance our understanding of climate change dynamics and contemporary events, such as COVID-19. Riskscapes are "temporal-spatial phenomena that relate risk, space, and practice" (Müller-Mahn et al. 2018: p. 197 c.f., 2020). They are "produced and reproduced when individuals and societies....inscribe knowledge and perception of potential risks and opportunities in space, and act accordingly" (Müller-Mahn and Everts 2013; Müller-Mahn et al. 2020: p. 2). Exposure to risk is seen as largely dependent on social, and relatedly, geographic positionality in political-economic, cultural, ecological, and sociotechnical systems (Müller-Mahn, 2013 Müller-Mahn and Everts 2013; Davies et al. 2020; Müller-Mahn et al. 2020).

This framing calls attention to interactions among risks and their "cumulative impact" across several dimensions of human life and the biophysical environment (Davies et al. 2020). For instance, climate change impacts often have social, economic, and physical dimensions, which make it very challenging to understand and manage the risks involved. The increased frequency and severity of the physical events generated by climate change affects the nature of risk, however, given we also need to consider the spatially diverse and temporally dynamic patterns of exposure and vulnerability (Davies et al. 2020). New threats, such as COVID-19, also tend to have more severe impacts on communities whose lives and livelihoods are already being threatened and are socially, politically, and economically marginalized. Moreover, the origins of these risks and the forces that sustain them also often operate on and across multiple spatial scales.

Riskscapes, Cities and Sociotechnical Systems

Table 8.1 summarizes the scope and scale of humanitarian emergencies in African cities between 2000 and 2015. Flooding (72 cities) and disease outbreaks (31) were, by far, the most common events. In the context of climate change and COVID-19, it is likely that such trends will intensify and be distributed more widely, while other threats, including drought, food crises, tropical storms, and fires become more commonplace. Extreme heat waves are also likely to play a more significant role in shaping riskscapes. More qualitatively, African cities present integrated but differentiated riskscapes. They are places where there is concatenation of economic, political, livelihood, health, security and other risks, but these are differentially distributed based on class, gender, geographic positionalities and disability, among others, with some people relatively secure while others are dispossessed (Buxton and Hayes, 2016). Differential exposure and resources generate uneven responses by creating or layering adaptation and se-curiscapes on top of riskscapes, such as in the case of Eko-Atlantic, a project that heightened flooding risks for slum dwellers in Lagos through a high-rise residential development for Nigerian elites (see Chapter 4).

Ongoing climate disruption and related emerging threats alone will increase risks for many, but the situation in African cities will be particularly acute as a result of rapid urbanization, poverty, and associated socioeconomic problems (Bird et al. 2017; Dos Santos et al. 2019). For most urban residents in informal settlements, risk exposure can/will be quite extreme and existential in nature. Poor-quality housing in marginal locations, coupled with limited

Table 8.1 Geophysical and epidemic-related disaster events requiring external humanitarian assistance in sub-Saharan Africa (January 2000-December 2015).

	Number of events	Number affected	Average affected per event	Affected urban area(s)
Flood	124	9,799,485	79,028	72
Disease outbreak	88	447,588	5,086	31
Storm/hail/wind	13	44,322	3,409	2
Cyclone/tropical storm	7	223,035	31,862	5
Volcanic eruption	5	140,558	28,111	1
Complex food crisis	4	39,525215	9,881,303	1
Drought	3	14,255,348	4,751,782	1
Landslide/mudslide	3	1,898	632	1
Wildfire	3	234,896	78,298	–
Earthquake	2	9,845,705	4,922,852	2
Insect infestation	2	46,220	23,110	–
Toxic pollution	2	48,118	24,059	2
Explosion	1	14,046	14046	1
Total	257	74,626,434	51,119	119

Source: Pharoah, 2016 / ActionAid International.

access to basic services such as sanitation and electricity, means that many will face potentially uninhabitable circumstances as temperatures rise and hazards, such as floods and/or heat-stressors become more frequent and severe (Raymond et al. 2020).

Considered in relation to our sociotechnical systems perspective, risks often articulate with, or impact, different regimes at the same time. For example, the COVID-19 virus is a risk to public health and healthcare infrastructures, consumer markets, public expenditure, and productivity and economic growth, among others. At the same time, it is also a distantiated risk in that new, more contagious, severe or deadly variants may emerge in distant locales, particularly as a result of low vaccination rates and vaccine inequity. The global structure of the pandemic, where some regions are oversupplied and others chronically undersupplied with vaccines, is implicated in the emergence of new variants and recursive vaccine hoarding and "boosting" in rich countries, allowing the cycle to repeat until the disease becomes endemic, or effective therapeutics become more widely available (Carmody and McCann 2022). In taking a sociotechnical systems view, it is possible to more comprehensively capture the constituent features, spaces, and practices that produce riskscapes, and to see how these shape, or are shaped by, core urban functions related to urban regimes.

Climate Change and Sociotechnical Regimes

Environmental challenges, both "internal" and "external" to cities, present a variety of threats to prevailing sociotechnical regimes. For example, if wet-bulb (humidity adjusted) temperatures become too high this may make cities effectively uninhabitable and outside work impossible; particularly likely in North Africa (Lewis 2021b). Such perturbations may result in "positive feedback" or deviation amplification not only in socio-environmental systems, but political ones. For example, climate change may be exacerbated by developmentalist and hydro-nationalist reactions to it and population growth, such as the construction of the Grand Renaissance Dam in Ethiopia which will restrict water flow to countries further down the course of the Nile. Egypt has repeatedly said it would use force to protect its water resources, if necessary, but this is perhaps unlikely given the potential for their poisoning upstream and consequently the incentives for cooperative rather than violent governance.[2]

Of all the existential risks facing the planet today, climate change is clearly the most pressing contributor to riskscapes. Nowhere on earth will be unaffected by global warming and its knock-on or direct effects in the atmosphere, biosphere, cryosphere, and hydrosphere. The ability to respond to climate change is very much a function of place-specific capabilities, resources, readiness, and strategies to mitigate its impacts and to enable transitions to new environments and economic development possibilities. As we detail below, many African cities are especially vulnerable to the uneven impacts of climate change through heat, sea-level rise, coastal erosion, flooding, and droughts. In the climate domain, their resilience is also in question.

Heat

Deadly heatwaves are likely to become more common across much of the continent (Birch et al. 2021). This may be further exacerbated by elevated indoor temperatures, if buildings are not shaded for example. One study found an indoor temperature ranges of between 22.2°C and 45.9°C for Accra in Ghana, with extreme high temperatures being potentially very dangerous to human health (Wilby et al. 2021). With higher temperatures there will be a need for more air conditioners, potentially generating more carbon emissions (Bassey 2012).[3] However, many will not have the resources to access, purchase, or regularly use air conditioners, particularly in informal settlements where housing and energy provisioning structures will not be capable of utilizing them.

Such outcomes will compromise all three urban regimes both directly and indirectly in a variety of ways. Widespread deaths from heatstroke would be a human tragedy in addition to undermining both production (making working conditions intolerable and thereby reducing productivity) and consumption in cities. The production and use of infrastructure might also be affected, for instance through the increased need for air conditioners for those who can afford them, with resultant strain on the use of hydropower or other electricity sources in many places (Falchetta et al. 2019). Furthermore, global warming will lead to more extreme weather events, making tropical storms more intense and dangerous, such as Cyclone Idai, which destroyed "90%" of Mozambique's fourth largest city, Beira, in 2019 (AfricaNews 2019) (see Figure 8.1). The longest-lived tropical storm on record with the highest cyclone accumulated energy ever recorded, Cyclone Freddy, hit the Southern African region twice in the same month in 2023, striking Madagascar particularly hard, causing extensive flooding and bringing two years' worth of rainfall in one month to parts of the region (Africa News, 2023: p. 1).

Sea Level Rise and Coastal Erosion

Both overabundance and scarcity of water also present potentially existential threats to some cities. Sea level rise and extreme weather pose severe threats to human health, safety, food and water security, and socioeconomic development. In particular, sea level rise presents an existential threat to many coastal cities. The western coast of Africa stretching from Mauritania to Cameroon has been identified as particularly vulnerable to coastal erosion and saltwater intrusion. Slums like Makoko, Lagos, built on stilts on reclaimed land are acutely vulnerable and could perish. Given the impacts of European colonization which led to the development of many primate cities on the coast, this is a particularly acute threat.

Figure 8.1   The aftermath of Cyclone Idai in Beira, Mozambique (2019).
Source: © European Union 2019 (Photographer: Christian Jepsen).

It is estimated that about 56% of the coastlines in Benin, Côte d'Ivoire, Senegal, and Togo are eroding, and this is expected to worsen in the future. The UN declared St. Louis in Senegal, a UNESCO World Heritage site with about 300,000 people, as the African city most threatened by rising sea levels. Saltwater and rising sea levels have destroyed houses, flooded streets, damaged crops, and displaced thousands in the city (Yeung 2019; Pronczuk 2020). Lagos, Nigeria, is also susceptible to damage from rising sea levels and coastal erosion, which has led to a decline in water quality, the destruction of drainage infrastructure, and an increase in incidences of water and vector-borne disease (Uwaegbulam 2019). Perennial flooding in Lagos has left many dead and scores displaced, with more than 2 million people directly affected by flooding and at least 69 people losing their lives in flood disasters in 2020 (Princewill 2021). As noted earlier, Eko-Atlantic is partly intended to stop the erosion of the Lagos coastline, but the physical changes this will induce may increase risk for nearby marginalized communities, without additional protective measures (Ajibade 2017).

Beyond the complexities of implementing mitigation measures against rising sea levels, the costs of doing so are exorbitant. For instance, it will require hundreds of billions of dollars to protect cities and villages from sea-level rise in West Africa alone (Hinkel et al. 2012). According to Sierra Leone's climate change response strategy, US $2,764 million could be mobilized from different sources to implement mitigation actions proposed in the plan (Government of Sierra Leone, nd). While these funds are meant to be partially sourced from the private sector and international climate finance, it is worth noting that the 2022 expenditure budget for the entire government of Sierra Leone was US $904 million (Government of Sierra Leone 2021).

Flooding

Another related impact of climate change is increased flooding with increased weather extremes. While many cities are flooded by major rivers that carry extreme flows of water from surrounding regions and even distant mountains, it may also arise locally within built-up areas from debris blocking streams and from overflowing sewers (Dube et al. 2022; Echendu 2022). A quarter of the world's population is at risk of flooding, with almost 90% of these being in low- and middle-income countries (Rentschler and Salhab 2020). The often-impermeable nature of urban ground surfaces exacerbates flooding risk as does the lack of adequate infrastructure – drainage systems, waste management facilities, and housing structures (Amoako and Inkoom 2018; Echendu and Georgeou 2021). Rapid urbanization, the inability to provide adequate housing, and poor planning have led to housing construction in flood-prone zones in many African cities, often without adequate infrastructure, especially drainage systems, making such areas more vulnerable and causing deaths every year.[4]

Flooding can have devastating effects on communities and livelihoods, especially marginalized communities and those who find subsistence in the urban informal sector. A World Bank study shows that flooding can have significant impacts on employment in African cities, thus highlighting a critical coupling between production and infrastructure regimes (Rentschler et al. 2019). The most vulnerable urban residents usually have less capacity and resources to recover from shocks (Salami et al. 2017; Amoako and Inkoom 2018). For instance, one flood in Ouagadougou, the capital of Burkina Faso, in 2009 resulted in 180,000 people being badly affected and 35,000 losing their homes, with a substantial majority being from one informal settlement (Dos Santos et al. 2019). When disasters strike, or if there are repeated low-intensity floods, this will exacerbate inhabitants' poverty through livelihood and asset destruction and health impacts.

Related to this, flooding can also significantly undermine and negatively impact infrastructure regimes. For instance, World Bank research mapped the channels through which regular flooding in Kinshasa, the Democratic Republic of Congo, impacts transport services, commuters' ability to reach their jobs, and the associated economic opportunity costs from travel delays (He et al. 2021). In Accra, the communities of Agbogbloshie and Glefe reported significant impacts on storm drains, communal toilets, schools, health facilities, and road access as a result of flood (Amoako and Inkoom 2018). Effective planning is frequently nonexistent and even when plans are developed, infrastructure implementation is often mismanaged, mired in corruption, and/or subject to "political meddling" that undermines upgrades (Echendu and Georgeou 2021; Echendu 2022).

Importantly, the riskscapes associated with flooding hazards in African cities are very much coproduced with informalization. That is, many of the same structural and other factors that produce informality and informal settlements, simultaneously create vulnerabilities to hazards like floods and the knock-on effects associated with them (e.g., disease, displacement, eviction). Here there is a direct link to the consumption regimes relied on by the majority of urban residents. As Amoako and Inkoom (2018: p. 2919) note:

> vulnerability to flood hazards in urban informal settlements in developing countries is a complex network of political and sociocultural factors rooted in their historical development and indigenous land management systems that together produce informal spaces.

The point of this is that people living in informal settlements, particularly those in flood-prone areas, are not simply passive victims but active agents claiming their rights to the city, albeit in those marginal spaces that are made available and affordable to them by regressive regulatory and planning environments. Absent significant investments and planning reforms that provide affordable access to higher quality locations, upgraded infrastructures, and improved livelihoods, the coproduction of vulnerability, risk, and informality will continue to plague African cities.

Drought

Water scarcity, particularly of potable water, is also a major issue in many cities. Only about a third of the urban population of Sub-Saharan Africa have piped water at home, down from 43% in 1990 (UNICEF and WHO 2015 cited in Satterthwaite 2017b). Potentially catastrophic water scarcity was dramatically illustrated in the recent past by a looming "day zero" in Cape Town when the municipal water taps would have run dry. In 2018 daily rations of water dropped to 50 liters per day per person, "with the spectre of 25 litres if supplies ran out on 'Day Zero'" (Kuper 2019, see Figure 8.2). This outcome reflected a severe multiyear drought, although it has been noted that for "people who live in shanty towns outside Cape Town without running water, it's always Day Zero" (Kuper 2019). The drought also affected other major cities in the region such as Zimbabwe's second city, Bulawayo. Residents there were required to flush their toilets at certain times to avoid fines (Bariyo 2019). Even the water flow in Victoria Falls or *Mosi-oa-Tunya* ("the smoke that thunders") was silenced in 2019 (Kinver 2019).

The impact of the drought in Cape Town is dramatically illustrated by Orimoloye et al. (2019) who found that between 2014 and 2018:

> land use dynamics witnessed drastic changes where vegetation, water body and bare surface decreased from 2095 to 141km^2, 616 to 167km^2 and 2337 to 1381km^2 respectively while built up and sparse vegetation increased from 5301 to 8191km^2 and 7382-7854km^2 during the period.

Land-use and land-cover changes thus contributed to city's riskscape and the Day Zero crisis arose even though Cape Town halved its water consumption from 2015 (Kuper 2019). The drought was only alleviated when rains came in June 2018 but before that, the reservoirs that served the city had dropped to around 20% of their capacity (Millington and Scheba 2021).[5]

According to Millington and Scheba (2021) the water crisis in Cape Town was as much a financial one as it was an environmental one, in line with Moore's (2015) thinking around the "double internality" of nature and capitalism. Moreover, it was resolved in regressive ways which increased socioeconomic inequality in the city.[6] This happened as a result of the general abolition of free basic water allowances, increases in tariffs, and the introduction of water management devices to monitor the free water allowance for "indigent" households. According to one interviewee in another study, the previous model of "cross-subsidization" of water, with the rich paying for higher volumes, was "sort-of pulled away from you because you no longer have those high volumes....to actually do the cross-subsidization" (Millington and Scheba 2021: 126). Thus the already unstable post-apartheid social contract was further undermined, in line with the general thrust of neoliberalization in the country (Ansari 2021).[7]

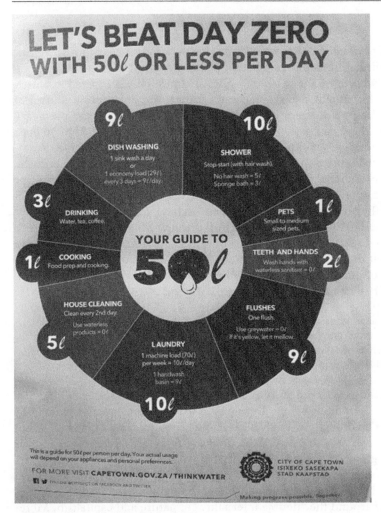

Figure 8.2   City of Cape Town, "Zero Day," flyer.
Photo credit: Richard Grant (Author).

Public Health Threats: Pandemics (Ebola and COVID-19)

"The pathogen is nothing, the terrain is everything." (Louis Pasteur)

In addition to those already existing, we cannot ignore the impacts of a "new" genus of threats in the form of epidemics and pandemics that have emerged recently.[8] An epidemic is "a widespread occurrence of an infectious disease in a community at a particular time" (Last 2001 quoted in Kelly 2011: p. 540).

For an epidemic to be designated, the reproduction (R) number must generally be above 1, or each person who catches it has to infect at least one more person. A pandemic is "an epidemic occurring worldwide, or over a very wide area, crossing international boundaries and usually affecting a large number of people" (Bonneux and Van Damme 2010, quoted in Kelly 2011: p. 540). We highlight Africa's experiences with two recent, devastating pandemics, Ebola Virus Disease (EVD) and COVID-19, to show how infectious disease outbreaks can have varying effects on the sociotechnical regimes of urban centers.

Ebola

Ebola is a rare and deadly disease and has had periodic outbreaks in different parts of Africa (first along the Ebola River in Zaire [present-day DRC] in 1976 and in 1979 in present-day South Sudan), with the most serious multicountry outbreak in West Africa (variously dated) from 2013 to 2016 that resulted in more than 10,000 deaths. Ebola had a significant impact on major cities in the region. For instance, the Ebola outbreak of 2014–2015 was concentrated in the capital cities of Guinea, Liberia, and Sierra Leone, where high population densities increased the scale of infection (Alexander et al. 2015). The case of Ebola shows that despite the existence of generally better health infrastructure in cities, this can paradoxically amplify risk. People in hospital are sometimes more likely to catch diseases such as COVID-19, Ebola, or "hospital bugs" as a result of the concentration of sick people, what is known as nosocomial infections, where risk is increased as a result of concentrations of sick people (Richards 2016). The Ebola epidemic thus might have been worse if there were more hospitals in the region. In fact, as the epidemic took hold, many hospitals in the region closed to avoid infections (Farmer 2020).

The spread of Ebola was also related to the quality of infrastructure regimes. For instance, the countries in the region varied in their ability to respond to Ebola – two of the worst affected countries were Liberia, which had a mere 90 doctors at the time, and Sierra Leone which was reported to have around 120 (Carmody 2014b). On the other hand, Nigeria's swift implementation of public health measures, including a rigorous tracking system, were sufficient to forestall a country-wide spread of this dreaded disease (Otu et al. 2018).

The Lagos city government played a key role in stopping the Ebola outbreak, operating as a local developmental state that was very effective in revenue management and service delivery (Cheeseman and de Gramont 2017; Idris and Fagbenro 2019). This shows that improved social infrastructure is vital to the development of "human capital" and economic development more broadly, in addition to forms of economic infrastructure. Unfortunately, the programs of economic reform promoted by Western donors in Africa over the last 30 years have largely focused on shrinking the African state. This is misplaced. Rather, what the Ebola crisis showed was the importance of building state capacity and accountability, particularly as it relates to vital collective goods and services (e.g., health, energy, water). Doing so can begin to address the general need to improve public health systems in the region and in locally appropriate ways (Buseh et al. 2015).

COVID-19

The most immediate pandemic threat to African cities has been COVID-19, a viral respiratory disease caused by a new coronavirus called SARS-CoV-2. The virus has killed millions of people, overwhelmed many health care systems, disrupted global trade, devastated economies, and changed the world in unprecedented ways through widespread mobility restrictions. Although the severity of impact caused by the virus varies widely, hardly any country escaped the impacts.[9] Africa has had a relatively low death rate from COVID-19 thus far, but the indirect impacts were severe in major cities, as lockdowns undermined informal livelihoods, among other things. In the absence of social security nets, people who earn their livelihood in the informal economy cannot effectively socially distance or self-isolate (Wilkinson 2020). As was highlighted above with respect to floods, informalization coproduces public health vulnerabilities as well.

The initial strategies for containing COVID-19 (wash hands, social distance, isolation, etc.) were difficult to adhere to in many of Africa's slums, where WASH and other basic services are often partial, mal-distributed, and informally governed (Van Belle et al. 2020; Onyishi et al. 2021). These urban areas also have more vulnerable populations with many preexisting conditions who are at higher risk. As a result, African cities have the potential for higher transmission rates – due to density, household, and social structures (e.g., sharing food), poor ventilation, livelihood imperatives, lack of water, and sanitation issues. However, despite having most of the attributes indicating a much higher expected severity, African countries had surprisingly many fewer cases of sickness and death from COVID-19, leaving researchers struggling to make sense of "Africa's anomaly" (Oppong 2020), although youthful demographics undoubtedly helps. However, the politics of global vaccine development and distribution means that African countries are also the least likely to have access to vaccines (Massinga Loembé and Nkengasong 2021). As of July 2022 only 39 vaccine doses had been administered per 100 people on the continent (Statista 2022), with only 17% of the population double vaccinated (Financial Times 2022).

The COVID-19 pandemic has had multifold, recursive impacts on cities not only through health but economic vectors such as the "bullwhip" effect, where supply chain becomes misaligned, resulting in substantial inflation and accompanying immiseration or a deepening of the poverty gap (Disney and Towill 2003). Production and consumption regimes have thus been hurt significantly with inflation, in particular, affecting those on low and fixed incomes. The pandemic also exposed the vulnerability in relying on the informal or gig economy (Otieno et al. 2020), unless it is entirely remote (Anwar and Graham 2022). Given the livelihood challenges facing the majority of urban households, and the nature of their work, technology-mediated home-based work is simply not an option for most Africans.

While COVID-19 has exposed the weaknesses inherent in production networks and supply chains, it can also create opportunities for African cities to renegotiate their engagement with the world economy. The pandemic particularly highlighted the risks inherent in overdependence on global supply chains. For instance, Africa imports 94% of its pharmaceuticals, thus raising critical concerns about the vulnerability of its public-health systems (OECD and UN-ECA 2020). As economies and companies seek to become less dependent on single suppliers for consumer goods, such as China, African countries and cities could become more attractive locations for producing such products, although processes of reshoring may militate against this (Barbieri et al. 2020; Carmody 2020). Moreover, as more companies continue to establish systems that enable staff to work offsite, and more workers also become accustomed to working offsite, it can speed up "outsourcing" of office work and expand noncore functions to African cities that have the infrastructure to support such activities. This can open new employment opportunities in some production regimes, although they are likely to be low level service jobs in the short/medium term.

Managing Risk and Resilience in African Cities

The challenges faced by Africa's rapidly growing cities are unique (Nagendra et al. 2018). The region's cities are growing at unprecedented rates, with much of the growth in informal settlements. Their growth is marked by riskscapes of multiple exposures – to climate change, COVID-19, fiscal austerity, poor social services, and intensified economic globalization. As a result, many residents in African cities continue to suffer from a high burden of disease, lack of economic opportunities, and extreme poverty in certain cases, which are exacerbated by the threat of "natural" disasters.

Of particular concern here is the impact that climate change will continue to have on urbanization pathways. Cities in Africa suffer from a general lack of capacity to develop and implement adaptation measures, due in large part to resource constraints. For example, it is estimated that the US city of Miami alone will need to spend billions of dollars to manage rising sea level in the coming decades (Miami-Dade County 2021). Compare this with Tanzania, a coastal country, that had an entire government budget of approximately US $1.5 billion in 2020 (calculated from TanzaniaInvest 2022). Beyond capital constraints, other deficits related to institutions, technological capabilities, political will, and multilevel stakeholder engagement in decision making, will further limit the ability to design and implement effective climate adaptation strategies.

As we argue, climate change-related disaster risks and risks associated with pandemics in Africa cities are strongly linked to underdevelopment. Since the relationship between disaster risks and various facets of underdevelopment are self-reinforcing, reducing risk and building resilience in urban areas requires tackling the developmental issues that underlie it. For example, increased poverty may feed into increased crime which may undermine infrastructure, such as that associated with copper wire thefts, common in South Africa. Reducing risk and building resilience in urban Africa thus requires concomitant improvements to infrastructure, basic services, and livelihoods in order to reduce vulnerability to hazards and enhance people's ability to recover from disasters. It also requires an integrated multi-sectoral approach to infrastructure regimes. For instance, failing systems can result in cascading impacts that disrupt the availability of clean water, electricity, and communications. Such cascading events combined with a high concentration of populations and investments at risk can quickly result in catastrophic impacts. In addition, since urban risk often results from a complex interaction of multiscalar pressures that extend beyond the administrative bounds of a given city, reducing risk and building resilience requires action across local, regional, and national levels (Pharoah 2016)

Reducing these risks and making cities resilient to disasters would also require a broader understanding about the possible nature, scale, and distribution of risks across the spectrum. For instance, the predominance of everyday, minor but recurrent disaster risks (extensive) over earthquakes, flooding, etc. (intensive) risk in African cities calls for more focus on the intersection between small, recurrent events and development, rather than a focus on the major events. For many low-income households in African cities with few physical assets, everyday risk and loss are often greater impediments. Moreover, identifying and acting on the risks of "small" disasters can reduce the risks and impacts from larger ones (Fraser et al. 2017).

Notes

1 According to Bannock et al. (2003: p. 374), risk is "a state in which the number of possible future events exceeds the number of events that will actually occur, and some measure of probability can be attached to them."
2 Former US President Donald Trump said Egypt would bomb the dam without negotiations (Addis 2020).
3 Although the West, in particular, owes Africa an ecological debt and it should not be forced to pay the price for the current global climate emergency.
4 Aljazeera has created a web documentary on the threats of flooding in Africa's megacities – see https://interactive.aljazeera.com/aje/2015/drowning_megacities/index.html
5 When they dropped to 13.5% Day Zero would have been declared. Some sources claim they did reach that level (HWM 2019).

6 According to Capra (1996 cited in Moore 2015) interconnected crises of ecology and economy are ultimately crises of perception as "capitalism" treats nature as something external to it which can be organized, commodified, regulated, and exploited, rather than seeing capitalism as a subset of nature.

7 Even though South Africa has substantial transfer payments Ansari (2021) makes the point that this is not in contradiction to neoliberalism and access to global financial markets indirectly sustains African National Congress rule through borrowing which allows for redistributive social security programs domestically.

8 Although some argue that emergence of the novel pathogens, antibiotic-resistant microbes, and pest infestations represents the natural world's response to the anthropogenic changes driven by capitalism in its pursuit of accumulation for accumulation's sake (Rice and Tyner 2021).

9 Except "remote" countries such as Tonga, which escaped until 2022, when there were fears that disaster relief after a volcanic eruption and tsunami brought it into the country (see Kwan 2022).

Chapter Nine
The Green Economy and African Cities

Introduction

The risks associated with global climate change have intensified efforts to restructure economies and development trajectories such that they are more environmentally sustainable. The impetus for promoting a global green agenda can be traced to the Brundtland Report *Our Common Future*, and was amplified in key international agreements since, such as Agenda 2030 for Sustainable Development; the Paris Agreement on Climate Change, Financing for Development; African Union Agenda 2063, and COP-22 and is espoused in policymaker circles as well as in many policy documents (UNECA 2020). The United Nations Environment Programme (UNEP) has played a leading role in shaping and promoting the green economy as "an engine for growth," generating jobs and eradicating poverty – defining it as "one that results in improved human well-being and social equity, while significantly reducing environmental risks and ecological scarcities" (UNEP, 2011: p. 1).

Green policies vary by country, and within countries and cities, with renewable energy, agro-processing, green manufacturing, green employment, green financing, and poor-poor development as typical emphases. More generally, green visions seek to enable inclusive, sustainable, resilient, and low carbon development, often promising a leapfrogging dynamic through rapid, discontinuous technological transformations. The COP-26 agreement, for example, surmises "it will turbo charge the uptake of green technologies by imposing worldwide standards and practices" (Harrabin 2021: p. 1).

The Urban Question in Africa: Uneven Geographies of Transition, First Edition. Pádraig R. Carmody, James T. Murphy, Richard Grant and Francis Y. Owusu.
© 2024 John Wiley & Sons Ltd. Published 2024 by John Wiley & Sons Ltd.

A plethora of green economy initiatives and innovations are being implemented at varying scales across Africa (Borel-Saladin and Turok 2013b; Swilling et al. 2016; Buseth 2017; Bergius and Buseth 2019). Several countries (e.g., Burkina Faso, Ethiopia, Kenya, Mauritius, Rwanda, Senegal, and South Africa) have developed forward looking national green economy policies, and green economy objectives are being added to spatial planning, subsector, and multi-sector policies (UNCTAD 2019a), including recent COVID-19 recovery plans. Among the most ambitious is the expansive "Great Green African Wall" traversing a strip that spans eleven Sahelian countries from Senegal in the West to Djibouti in the East of Africa. This 8,000-km-long (5,000-mile-long) and 15-km-wide strip when complete will be "the largest living structure on the planet," estimated to cost US \$33 billion (Great Green Wall Organisation 2022: p. 1), although the project is currently experiencing financial difficulties.

Considered comparatively to the West, African economies are already green in terms of their 3.8% share of global CO_2 emissions (Atlas 2022). However, Africa's green industrial base is not a major driver of socioeconomic development with current experiments only at an early stage (Okereke et al. 2019). At the city scale numerous and diverse arrays of urban-focused green initiatives are underway with major differences in ambition, scale, and scope. Larger-scale initiatives tend to be cross-cutting and multiscalar, implemented by national and municipal governments, international donors, PPPs (e.g., new-build ecocities; see Chapter 4), and environmental NGOs. Other, smaller projects are community-driven and/or individual green entrepreneurial efforts. Importantly, due to their varying scales and agendas, green initiatives deploy a wide and diverse range of project partners horizontally and vertically within countries, many of which are articulated with supporting organizations at international and regional scales. As a result, however, greening initiatives in Africa are by-and-large poorly coordinated or integrated with one another.

This chapter explores the nature of urban green economy initiatives on the continent and the extent to which they might fundamentally alter urban regimes such that sustainability transitions will be possible. The chapter proceeds as follows. First, we briefly elaborate on the green economy concept and its promise for advancing development in the Global South. We then sketch out the diversity and range of green economy initiatives in African national economies and highlight some common foci as well as differences between countries. We then turn to a discussion of green industrialization, which is a core focus of green economy interventions. In doing so we zoom in on South Africa's Western Cape Province (WCP) and the Atlantis Special Economic Zone (ASEZ) project – a high profile green manufacturing initiative aimed to kick-start a sustainability transition. We then shift to a discussion of the prospects for the urban informal sector (UIS) to be integral to green economy transitions. The chapter closes with reflections with respect the potential realization of greener economies in African cities.

The Green Economy and the Global South

The idea of a green economy has distinct connotations when considered in/for the Global South. In contrast to advanced industrial contexts, it is not seen as an antidote for a century-plus of "grow-first, clean-up later" trajectories, but an alternative model that might enable Southern places to bypass such pathways (Borel-Saladin and Turok 2013a; Georgeson et al. 2017). When idealized, it is viewed by some as a "win-win-win" or triple bottom line option that can deliver economic growth and expand welfare distributions in an environmentally responsible, sensitive manner (Barbier 2011; Loiseau et al. 2016; Lederer et al. 2018). It is thus an optimistic, futuristic, and modernist development imaginary that promises a new pathway for postcolonial countries to sustainably break free from dependencies, unequal exchange relations, and power asymmetries that limit their ability to benefit from economic globalization.

In reality, such transformational scenarios have rarely, if ever played out on a large/comprehensive scale in wealthy nations, let alone those facing high rates of poverty, structural inequalities, infrastructure challenges, legacies of colonial occupation, and/or low levels of industrialization. The green economy is thus an aspirational model for sustainable development; one that Southern states are increasingly pursuing in response to climate change, resource scarcities, local pollution, transnational incentives (e.g., reduction of emissions from deforestation and forest degradation [REDD+] programs, foreign aid), and development imperatives (e.g., the United Nation's 2015 SDGs). In this sense, the green economy is a very real thing; one that is having political, material, and environmental impacts throughout the South, albeit in highly uneven and inconsistent ways.

Following Georgeson et al. (2017: p. 1), the green economy can be understood as "an operational policy agenda to achieve measurable progress at the environment-economy nexus" (cf. Schmalensee 2012). Sustainable development is a core objective, measured, particularly in Southern contexts, by progress toward the SDGs. Green economy policies strive to achieve these through markets, investments, industries, institutions, and technologies that reduce carbon emissions, increase resource-use efficiencies, and make economies and societies more socially inclusive (United Nations Environment Programme [UNEP], 2011; Loiseau et al. 2016). An overarching objective is to shift or transform business-as-usual development pathways toward alternatives that can deliver greener, more distributive, and just societies (Georgeson et al. 2017). For some, such alternatives offer a significant opportunity for countries in the Global South to leapfrog beyond unsustainable development pathways (Caprotti and Bailey 2014).

In application, the green economy is an umbrella term under which a range of interventions, concepts, and fields are included: industrial ecology, circular economy, reuse/recycling, resource efficiency, life cycle management, and material flow management (Loiseau et al. 2016). In the Global South, green economy

initiatives are extended further, and often focused on, rural and extractive sectors and include carbon emission reduction payments (e.g., REDD+), ecotourism, biodiversity conservation, renewable energy production (e.g., ethanol), and sustainable agriculture (Brown et al. 2014; Buseth 2021). Such policies and projects often include a poverty-reduction agenda, linking green transitions to pressing socioeconomic needs and the SDGs (Lederer et al. 2018).

In discursive terms, green economy framings range from weak to strong versions. Weak versions do not question the endless need or capacity for economic growth, calling for market-led incentives to enhance resource efficiencies, provide substitutes for finite resources, and attract investments in new industries to produce and distribute green goods and services (Bina 2013; Borel-Saladin and Turok 2013a; Georgeson et al. 2017). Strong versions call for an emphasis on prosperity (i.e., well-being, happiness) through degrowth initiatives, steady-state economies, and structural and societal changes that can transform societies to be in harmony with nature (Bina 2013).

Beyond such binaries, Death (2015) identifies four Southern green economy discourses that are visible in various, and sometimes combined, forms: Green resilience, Green Growth, Green Transformation, and Green Revolution. *Green resilience* describes the call for technocratic, community-based responses to the risks, threats, and challenges accompanying climate change, resource scarcities, biodiversity loss, and insecurities with respect to basic needs (e.g., food, water). *Green growth* focuses on the prospects for "triple-bottom-line" development outcomes without disruptions to the structural features of capitalism. *Green transformation* is related to green growth perspectives but here greater emphasis is placed on "planetary and civilizational" concerns (e.g., global climate change) rather than entrepreneurs, industries, and markets (Death 2015: p. 2215). This discourse aligns well with developmental state narratives and ecological modernization given its emphasis on the close coordination between the state and private sector actors. Lastly, *Green revolution* views the green economy as a radical means to dramatically reconfigure economies and societies such that quality-of-life issues, welfare distributions, and nature-society balance matter more than growth. Emphasis here is placed on achieving prosperity through strategies and transformations that enable degrowth, steady-state or circular economies, autarky, environmental and social justice, and/or *buen vivir* (good life) (Bina 2013; Faccer et al. 2014; Death 2015; Loiseau et al. 2016).

To summarize, green economy agendas in the Global South are mobilized through a range of discursive framings. In reality, most countries draw on heterogeneous combinations of these frames to develop and justify green economy policies and initiatives. Therefore, it can be expected that the forms and places where the green economy can evolve in African cities will be variegated and uneven, and transition initiatives are likely to evolve and coexist with incumbent enterprises, industries, institutions, and established practices (Kirshner 2019).

Africa's Green Economy Experience to Date

Apart from South Africa, African economies are generally characterized by low emissions (Atlas 2022), but recent economic growth in African countries such as Nigeria (116 mtCO$_2$ in 2020) is changing this. Africa's emissions are mainly derived from the production of cement, coal-based liquids, petroleum, iron, steel, ammonia, and traditional manufactures (Jayaram et al. 2021). With rapid population growth expected, economic growth anticipated, and the emergence of more consumption-orientated middle-classes, emissions are likely to increase if corrective action is not taken. How to maintain low carbon intensity profiles while enhancing green industrialization and not adopting the high-emissions "grow-first" pathway is therefore a highly ambitious agenda.

Across Sub-Saharan Africa, green economy initiatives have realized modest and scattered levels of adoption (Brockington and Ponte 2015). As detailed below, South Africa is the exception here; a country with a mature manufacturing sector and a state that has promoted the green economy as a means to achieve industrial and social upgrading. Typically, however, African countries concentrate more on rural green economy initiatives related to agriculture, wildlife conservation, and primary-sector industries, reflecting the rural orientation of economies and demographic structures (Buseth 2017; 2021). Others (e.g., Ethiopia, Ghana, South Africa) adopt both rural and urban green economy initiatives and aim to link more sustainable agricultural, food production and renewable energy to efforts at green industrialization and more sustainable development pathways (PAGE 2021). In addition, several countries have embarked on greenfield urban development projects that have an element of greening/sustainability built into their design – "smart" cities that are being planned and built from scratch. As noted earlier, Chapter 4, these projects are primarily aspirational rather than practical initiatives, ones that have had little impact on the structure or functioning of economies in the region (Watson 2014, 2015; Murray 2015).

Most African cities and states prioritize production and infrastructure regimes in relation to the green economy, with limited attention to consumption regimes. Mauritius is an exception with its National Programme on Sustainable Consumption and Production (SCP) that aspires to change consumption patterns by promoting technological shifts and encouraging the adoption of more sustainable lifestyles. In addition, some countries have focused on incorporating green principles into general education. For example, Ghana targets primary and secondary schools to incorporate more sustainability thinking into the curriculum to build public support to transform unsustainable practices and environmentally unsound behaviors, e.g., dumping of e-waste, plastics, and other trash.

Despite there being variations, green economy policies in Africa have common emphases. There is an acknowledgment that improvements in economic performance have been accompanied by worsening CO$_2$ emissions, so countries aim to reduce dependence on fossil fuels and advance the development of renewables. Supplying greener infrastructure is also viewed as a preferred means to address service provisioning deficits and inefficiencies, while facilitating pro-poor development. Promoting green technologies and technology transfer is also seen as essential to generate efficiencies in critical infrastructures, spur domestic innovations, meet tightened international environmental standards, and conform to supply chain sustainability requirements. Different variegations of greening programs can be seen in the cases of Ghana, Tanzania, and South Africa.

Ghana is prioritizing waste as a strategic sector and is targeting green investment and donor support in formalizing aspects of recycling. Greening the waste sector is being focused on in major urban centers where training and upgrading of waste workers' skills, and the deployment of technological solutions in modern and (formal) facilities is underway. A good example here is establishment of the Agbogbloshie Recycling Centre in Accra where a central facility and supporting infrastructure (including an infacility medical clinic) are maintained (Grant and Oteng-Ababio 2021; see Chapter 5). Upcycling of waste is also occurring in other urban experimentations. For example, a multi-partner initiative in Accra designed, made, and installed "the first-ever bus shelter to be constructed from plastic waste" (Network 2022: p. 1) at Dzorwulu Junction (see Figure 9.1).

Tanzania's green economy experience is focused in rural areas where there has been an emphasis on coupling agricultural modernization with biodiversity

Figure 9.1   Dzorwulu Junction Bus Shelter in Accra.
Photo credit: Richard Grant (Author).

conservation; part of "a new green revolution in Africa" (Bergius and Bus-eth 2019). The focus is on developing growth corridors where modernized agricultural clusters are coupled with projects to protect wildlife and biodiversity given, in part, that (eco)tourism is a major economic sector (Buseth 2017). The underlying discursive framing of these initiatives emphasizes resource abundance as a growth opportunity, but one that is threatened by unsustainable livelihood practices of smallholders that cause degradation and scarcity in rural areas (Bergius and Buseth 2019; Bergius et al. 2020). The techno-optimistic solution to this problem is one that focuses on developing more productive and efficient ways to exploit nature by shifting agriculture to more capital-intensive, modern, and large-scale farming systems. In practice, such initiatives have been support-ed by private FDI and resulted in expulsions of smallholders and pastoralists from traditional lands (Bergius et al. 2020). There are thus highly significant concerns about justice and the distributional implications of Tanzania's "green economy"; issues that have made many distrustful of it (Brockington and Ponte 2015; Buseth 2017).

In South Africa, the green economy has had a more coherent articulation as part of a state project to promote green growth and industrial upgrading (Death 2014). Given the structural and other legacies of apartheid, greening policies also incorporate concerns about racial justice and inequality, striving to support Black-owned enterprises and Black communities (Swilling 2016; Baker and Sovacool 2017; Grant et al. 2020). With respect to industries, focus has been on the manufacture of renewable energy technologies (RETs) – solar and wind power in particular – and the development of ecotourism in rural areas (Baker and Sovacool 2017; Marcatelli 2018). For RETs, policies to attract FDI, coupled with procurement requirements that mandate the sourcing of components from South African firms, have been central to this green industrialization strategy; one that has been particularly promising in the Western Cape Province (Grant et al. 2020, see below). Ecotourism (esp. related to the development of private game parks and ranches) has also been a strategy, one that aims to provide an alternative to commercial farming, while upgrading rural livelihoods (Marcatelli 2018).

Despite having policy support from and legitimation by the state, South Africa's green economy has struggled to achieve significant economic, social, and environmental impacts. There are four principle challenges. First, entrenched political elites, a weak state, continued reliance on fossil fuels, powerful labor unions (esp. in extractive sectors), and the prioritization of rapid economic growth as a primary development objective have stalled a green transition (Swilling et al. 2016a Grant et al. 2020). Second, the development of domestic green indus-tries hinges on significant improvements to the skills of South African workers, yet policy support for labor upgrading has been rudimentary (Borel-Saladin and Turok 2013b; Baker and Sovacool 2017; Grant et al. 2020). Third, South Africa's economy – like most in Sub-Saharan Africa – has a large, growing infor-mal sector that has been ignored or excluded from greening strategies, raising concerns regarding its potential contribution to the structural inequalities that persist from the apartheid era (Smit and Musango 2015). Fourth, incentives for FDI and local sourcing of components have primarily benefitted foreign companies who continue to capture the bulk of the value added in the RET sector, while sourcing primarily low-value parts from South African firms, or bypassing procurement requirements altogether through loopholes (Swilling et al. 2015; Grant et al. 2020). We now elaborate further on the South Africa case, focusing on the development of the Atlantis Greentech Special Economic Zone in the Western Cape Province.

Green Industrialization through SEZs? South Africa's Atlantis GreenTech Zone

As special economic zones (SEZs) proliferate in Africa, the case has been made for the establishment of new-generation green industrial zones with more progressive attributes such as social amenities and environmentally friendly forms of production (Lopes and Willem te Velde 2021; UNCTAD 2021). The green economy tilt enables SEZs to move from being conventional industrial enclaves toward more industrial ecosystems marked by green infrastructure, green innovation, and green entrepreneurship. Lopes and Willem te Velde (2021) contend that green industries require infant industry support and protection so that they can be properly integrated into value chains, and urban and regional economies. Business incubators in green technologies such as Innovational Climate Centres (e.g., The Gauteng Climate Innovation Centre) and other innovation hubs are thus seen as critical support infrastructure (Gonsalves and Rogerson 2019).

In South Africa, the government defines the green economy as a "system of economic activities related to the production, distribution and consumption of goods and services that result in improved human well-being over the long term, while not exposing future generations to significant environmental risks or ecological scarcities" (Government of South Africa 2011: p. 4). Green economy strategies are now implemented at national, provincial, and municipal levels with the signing of a Green Economy Accord in 2011 as an important milestone. The Accord resulted in the equivalent of 4.67% of GDP being invested in 92 renewable energy projects by 2015, from "virtually a zero base in 2009" with the largest concentration of projects in the Western Cape Province (WCP) (Swilling et al. 2016a).

WCP and the city of Cape Town (CCT) have come together in an assemblage of urban and industrial policy entrepreneurs to help "leapfrog" or transition to infrastructure and production regimes able to support a green economy. The WCP Government launched the *Green Is Smart* roadmap in 2013, aiming to be "a pioneer, early developer" of green technologies and diversified green economic activities through the prioritization of "infrastructure-led growth" (WCG 2013). Around the same time, a second provincial agency, 110%Green, was created to bring together a mix of players to achieve environmental goals and mobilize civil society toward adoption of the green economy (Petrik 2016). These activities are aligned with the provincial OneCape2040 vision (WCP 2012): an ambitious plan to facilitate a transition toward an inclusive and resilient economic future for the province. Through these efforts, "South Africa is the world's fastest growing green economy," with the WCP hosting 60% of green project developers, two-thirds of all green manufacturing facilities, and 70% of all Renewable Independent Power Producer Programme (REIPPP) projects (Winde cited in FTWonline 2017; Wesgro, 2018 int.).

Emblematic of this progress is the Atlantis Special Economic Zone (ASEZ), an urban-based green industry initiative with potential to seed a transition in the WCP's production regime. Atlantis began as a so-called "new town," established in the 1970s by the South African apartheid government for evicted members of Cape Town's "colored" population and as a future industrial site on the outskirts of the city.[1] Designed to be a "coloured dream city," Atlantis was to "propel the development of the coloured (mixed-race) people by their participation in local manufacturing employment" (Stafford 2005: p. 35). At its height in 1985, approximately 119 manufacturing enterprises were located there, contributing 8,859 total manufacturing jobs; employment numbers that fell considerably short of expectations (Stafford, 2005). As industrial incentives expired in the mid-to-late 1980s, factories moved out, jobs disappeared, poverty increased, crime became rampant, and opportunities for economic advancement disappeared.

The redevelopment of Atlantis as a greentech SEZ commenced in 2011 with the goal of jumpstarting a regional green economy transition. Located approximately 45 km from Cape Town International Airport and 105 km from Saldhana port, its promoters contend that Atlantis has a comparative advantage in its proximity to large-scale logistical infrastructure and as a vital link to the West Coast corridor; an initiative which emphasized biodiversity to attract tourists (see Figure 9.2). Atlantis has specific locational advantages for manufacturing activities that rely on high-volume vehicular traffic in that it enables regional freight to circumvent the congested traffic of Cape Town, and workers traveling to Atlantis will benefit from shorter commuting times because of contra-traffic flows (DTI 2018 int.).

The ASEZ site is projected to create approximately 3,100 jobs by 2030 (GreenCape 2019: p. 8) and upgrading of the SEZ's physical infrastructure and labor market has already taken place through improvements to electricity, water management, telecommunication, and public transportation systems, and worker skills development in partnership with local high schools and a Technical and Vocational Educational Training College (Cape Peninsula University of Technology, particularly its South African Renewable Energy Technology Centre [SARTEC], the country's first renewable energy technology center). Moreover, since 2019 discussions and a feasibility study are ongoing with respect

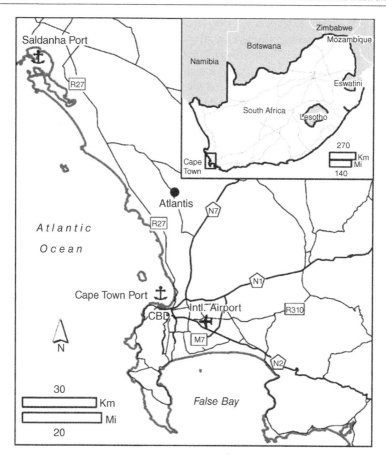

Figure 9.2   The Atlantis Green Tech SEZ location.
Source: Grant et al. 2020 / Cambridge University Press / CC BY 4.0.

to the development of an US$1.5 bn integrated liquid gas-to-power project in the Western Cape, that will include port facilities for the importation of Liquid Natural Gas (LNG) at Saldhana, as well as gas storage, transmission, and distribution infrastructures. The project is significant here in that its implementation may result in the conversion of Atlantis' Ankerlig power station from diesel to gas.

With respect to renewable energy infrastructure and industries, ASEZ is well situated with respect to policy support and investor interest. Because renewable energy providers in South Africa are required by law to foster local content creation, the establishment of a renewables components manufacturing hub is a priority for ASEZ. In doing so, a goal is to ensure that the SEZ serves as a linchpin of a broader structural green transformation (production regime transition) through supply chain linkages, innovation, and entrepreneurship. Efforts to support local green entrepreneurship are being facilitated by the ASEZ-based South African Renewable Energy Incubator (SAREBI); over 180 entrepreneurs have been assisted since 2015 (Town 2019). SAREBI's Manufacturing Technology Centre provides factory space, machinery, tools, and testing facilities for LED (light-emitting diode) lights and solar water heating systems for entrepreneurs aiming to set up manufacturing plants for new products or components in the renewable energy/energy efficiency supply chain. One start-up, iSOLAR, has fulfilled orders for 900 solar water heaters for the CCT and the Cape Winelands District Municipality (Town 2019). Thus, the ASEZ project is creating new greentech opportunities with a range of localization spillovers, that is, via supply chain linkages and the development of new markets for locally produced goods and greentech services.

Prior to its official designation in July 2018, the project's development was slow and limited to four large greentech investors manufacturing wind towers, wind turbine internals, geotextiles for environmental engineering, and energy-efficient double-glazing products (GreenCape 2019). The slow pace and small numbers reflect concerns that the main ASEZ foreign investors have with respect to the political and economic risk environment facing South Africa. Specifically, these actors have stressed the need to restore transparent procurement processes and an independent judiciary, and to proceed cautiously with respect to wholesale land reform; essential assurances needed to restore investor confidence (110%Green 2019 int.). That said, the WCP's links to new domestic and export markets (i.e., its ties to other production, consumption, and infrastructure regimes) are anticipated to improve in the pandemic aftermath. As such, and in spite of the risks, the ASEZ project is viewed optimistically by boosters who expect it to be fully operational in the mid-2020s.

The long-term development of ASEZ is dependent on the integration of four strategies to facilitate a large-scale transition of the WCP's production regime. A first strategy is to develop an industrial symbiosis program, to use waste from firms and reuse it as production input in other businesses including SMMEs, some of which may be informally organized (GreenCape 2015). Despite the positives, linking formal firms, many of which are international, with informal economy firms is an awkward zone of engagement given their different modes of operation, scale, and conformity to regulations, among other things. A second strategy for the ASEZ focuses on getting Atlantis' community members and leaders to support the project such that its long-term prospects for success are enhanced. Given the failure of the apartheid-era Atlantis project, community mistrust toward the ASEZ and the government's ability to manage it remains high and in need of significant efforts to ensure buy-in (GreenCape 2019). A third strategy strives to increase and diversify flows of FDI into ASEZ, with some early successes already recorded such as a ZAR 300 million (US$20.3 million) investment by the Spanish wind tower manufacturer, Gestamp Renewables (GR). A fourth strategy promotes the ASEZ as a center for green energy manufacturing in the Southern African region, a sector that can help transform production, consumption, and infrastructure regimes beyond South Africa; in and of itself a relatively small market.

While these strategies are sound and complementary, the international market is highly competitive and South Africa's firms are nascent and presently in need of support through import substitution polices, government procurement initiatives, and export incentives if the ASEZ is to support a green transition (PAGE 2017: p. 210). Moreover, the "hard infrastructure" projects and production outcomes in ASEZ need to be complemented by initiatives to foster "softer" goals such as networks, partnerships, and capacity building, especially the development of managerial, technical, and operational skills in national firms and the labor force. Such developments are vital for the legitimation and expansion of green industries in the wider regional economy such that a green transition is possible. Achieving such an outcome is fraught, however, given the inherent tension between place-marketing and the promotion of specific sites and premises in the ASEZ, and the broader green transition that is affected by national politics, the macro economy, societal trends, business-as-usual services and industries, and developments in the global economy.

The coordination and implementation challenges here are myriad. While CCT and the WCP participate in coordinating policy efforts to advance the green economy, these agencies are not always in sync with the national government or trade unions, namely the Congress of South African Trade Unions (COSATU). While the stakeholder network is an innovative instrument to build community buy-in and provide valuable networks for resource management, an energy transition, and climate change adaptation, it may not be enough. Building broader trust and support for the green transition among the marginalized poor in the region is still only small-scale with specific initiatives focusing mainly on worker training programs (e.g., logistic supply training, commercial driver training). While these represent a beginning, they may be insufficient for addressing the links between the production regime where industry operates and the consumption and infrastructure regimes that "everyday" people are forced to contend with, particularly in townships and informal settlements. To realize a more transformational future, a revamped national education system emphasizing science and technology will be necessary in addition to other supports for historically marginalized groups.

Still more problematic is the economic reality that growth remains largely driven by nongreen sectors – that is, the entrenched, mainstream production regime. Decarbonizing the economy will result in a loss of jobs and threaten socioeconomic stability in places where coal-fired power stations, mines, and transport services play a central role in provincial economies (e.g., in Mpumalanga and Limpopo). The carbon energy-mineral sectors and their strong unions represent formidable obstacles to a green transition, as evidenced by the fact that South Africa's new energy plan envisages coal remaining dominant in the country's energy mix through 2030 (Winkler 2019). Consolidating broad-based, national-scale support that can overcome opposition from entrenched nongreen economic constituents will thus not be easy; absent an effective and resourced just transition strategy

There is thus, in South Africa, a very delicate balancing act between a green urban transition, social transformation nationally, and economic competitiveness internationally. In response to a question about whether ASEZ might attract FDI that would take incentives and use the zone for imports, one of the GreenCape officials said that "any tenant is the right type of tenant as long as they generate jobs" (GreenCape 2018 int.), even though only 478 direct jobs had been created by 2020. This intimates a strongly neoliberal approach to economic development – one that insufficiently perhaps inverts the prioritization between the economy and the environment and suggests that green industries serve as a relatively minor niche in relation to the incumbent industrial regime.

All told, while many of the elements are present in ASEZ the sum of the parts does not add up to a production regime transition that can enable more sustainable, just, and distributive development outcomes. Several positive synergistic pressures are evident, ranging from strong political-economic forces ostensibly resulting from South Africa's impending climate altered future, the elevation of renewable energy policies internationally and nationally, and, to a lesser extent, changing societal values. However, in spite of the new green pathway imagined, the entrenched fossil-mineral complex in the WCP and nationally has not been sidelined and green industries and energy systems remain somewhat peripheral and unable to disembed the dominant regime. Still, experimentation with innovative green technologies in ASEZ is a highly novel approach to the challenges of sustainable development with potentially exciting outcomes to migrate and upscale to the mainstream. However, we caution about expecting too much of green zones like Atlantis as means to transform urban, regional, and national economies.

Green Economy Transitions and the Urban Informal Sector (UIS)

The ASEZ is a large-scale, formal industrial development initiative designed to jump-start a green economy transition through a reorganization of greater Cape Town's production regime. However, the greening of economies in African cities demands parallel, complementary, and integrated projects to enroll and enable the informal sector, domestic consumers, and small enterprises to participate in sustainability transitions. This is extremely challenging given the ways in which informality and poverty complicate transition planning by creating a more diverse, heterogeneous, and spatially differentiated set of actors, practices, and sociotechnical regimes as detailed in Chapter 5. Larbi et al. (2021) highlight the many local factors that can inhibit the transition to urban sustainability including budgetary constraints, corruption, malfunctioning institutions, weak governance capacity, lack of education, low levels of technology, poor infrastructural development, lack of transparency in the policy process, and high levels of economic inequality. Developing and upgrading worker skills, and retraining the informal sector to help make it "greener," takes investment and time. Currently, the readiness of Africa's UIS to participate in such improvements remains low and highly uneven in its distribution.

Prominent among the suite of strategies prioritized by African governments include those to promote investment in renewable energy, waste recycling, public transit, circular economies, urban green spaces, adaptive reuse of buildings, and, especially, green technologies. Moreover, NGOs and international development organizations have been funding and training some members of poor communities to experiment with green technology and solutions. Open African Innovation Research (OpenAIR) network represents an increasingly growing archive of successful stories of innovation in informal settings. ICT (esp. mobile phone applications) are often a central feature of these innovations, offering a low-cost, convenient means to achieving greener outcomes through changes to the everyday practices associated with production, consumption, and infrastructure regimes. As argued by Mboup and Oyelaran-Oyeyinka (2019: p. 33–34).

> The use of ICTs along with the planning of compact cities with socially mixed neighbourhood and mixed land used (residential and commercial activities together) will reduce the emission of CO_2 through various channels such as: (1) reduce the demand for total motorized transport; (2) promote the use of "low-emission" transport modes such as walking, cycling, and public transport and; (3) use the most efficient fuel-vehicle technology system possible for all trips. ICT will also decongest large unplanned African cities with the creation of smart secondary urban centres without increasing the use of motorized means of mobility. ICT will also enable digital urbanization with green, walkable, liveable, healthy spaces. Digital urbanization will foster economic development without damaging the environment …

Utopian visions such as these aside, there are risks in using ICT including cybercrime, unsafe personal information, and loss of employment owing to machines taking over workers' jobs, which may shift more people into the already overcrowded informal economy. Moreover, resistance to change, and/or limited acceptance of new technologies due to fear of complexity may be a problem that limits the ability of informal entities to benefit from green technology.

Some green technologies are particularly suited to African poverty contexts in that they are predominantly decentralized or semi-decentralized, can operate independently, are scalable (e.g., micro grids), can be supplemental to bulk infrastructures, and are customizable to local contexts and configurations (Peter 2021). In some cases, they are lower cost, easy to install, service, and maintain, and require only basic skills, thus creating opportunities for informal small and microenterprises. Parts of the informal sector already participate in the green economy in terms of lower carbon footprints, organic waste management, rain-water collection, recycling, urban farming, and, in some cities, through the emergent use of solar energy, water-saving devices, and greener buildings, e.g., solar shacks (Smit and Musango 2015). Worth highlighting here is that the driver of green practices is often poverty rather than an explicit desire for sustainable urban development.

The characteristics of innovations, including green economy solutions, that offer potential for absorption into African urban contexts and informal settings are outlined in Table 9.1. Solar, waste, plastics, and food are the most active sectors for urban informal green innovation. Various mixes of endogenous and exogenous technological solutions are evident, oftentimes in combination. In East Africa, Ugandan and Kenyan entrepreneurs have won energy awards for solar prototypes and informal entrepreneurs have developed fruit and vegetable dehydrators to curb food waste. Some technological solutions are employed in multiple settings (e.g., rainwater harvesting, plastic waste into affordable housing, converting biomass into briquettes) in many cities in the region.

Individual cities have promoted innovations with respect to informal sector greening activities. The Kenyan solar power market has existed since the 1980s

Table 9.1 The main features of informal innovation in African cities.

Informal innovation drivers	General characteristics
Market-pulled	Labor-intensive processes and basic product characteristics reflect low-income consumer markets
Constraint-based	Forces innovation under conditions of scarcity and utilizes social capital
Inter-enterprise division of labor	Small firms induce specialization along the chain
Non-R&D based	Incremental innovations, custom input, learning on the job, not lab-based
Adaptation of existing technologies, and ICT	Access suppliers, customers, logistics, adaptation, reverse engineering/combining of equipment, adapting imports to local conditions
Intellectual property rights	Intellectual property rights are absent, and access to technology through spillovers and open exchanges
Knowledge spillover	Clusters, social networks, Diaspora, NGO and donor-infused
Fast diffusion in local systems	Social dynamics in informal settings result in sharing practices and cooperation in procuring inputs and accessing markets
Green economy proclivity	Extensive reuse, recycling and repurposing of waste, but harmful emissions
Geographical clustering	Central areas with high foot traffic, industrial areas, waste sites, contested urban lands

and thousands of technicians have been trained. Nairobi, in particular, has served as a leading light in solar power through companies such as M-Kopa. Ghanaian cities are making strides in greening the waste sector through the support of various collaborations among informals, the government and development partners (especially GIZ) that have increased waste-collection coverage in Accra from 75% to 90% and waste capture from 53% to 90%, saving the municipality US$5.46 million in annual operating costs (Oduro-Appiah et al. 2019). Supported informal e-waste processing enables valuable fractions, or types of waste, to be utilized as inputs into domestic industries (e.g., copper is smelted for use by domestic manufacturers) and/or exported for more sophisticated processing and use in secondary markets (Grant and Oteng-Ababio 2016). Beyond the Atlantis SEZ discussed above, Cape Town has promoted an industrial symbiosis program and incubation hubs geared toward supporting informal economy firms (Grant et al. 2020). Western Cape Province has formulated a comprehensive intervention roadmap that engages with informal economy firms in various opportunities across multiple sectors, and a Circular Economy Officer has been created to oversee coordination efforts (GreenCape 2021).

At the multicity level, an open data platform, *The Circle City Scan Tool*, is funded by ICLEI (local governments for sustainability), the Ellen McArthur Foundation, and Circle Economy. The platform is being piloted in Accra, Cape Town, and Nairobi to assist formal workers and informals in identifying circular economy opportunities on the basis of socioeconomic and material flow data, and to allow them to synergize collaborations. Several cities or companies with them (e.g., Cape Town, Kumasi) have experimented with designing and producing electric vehicles for African urban contexts, but none have been brought to market to date. International NGOs such as Slum Dwellers International (SDI) also take on multicity efforts, linking slum communities globally and facilitating the transfer of ideas and practices that can enhance the sustainability and resilience of informal settlements and economies (e.g., see Sverdlik et al. 2019).

In sum, the greening of the UIS in African cities remains in the very early stages given that the integration of informal workers into the green economy is at a rudimentary stage of policy support, despite the pro-poor rhetoric often accompanying greening policies (Hlahla et al. 2016; Petrik 2016). Beyond these policy shortcomings, and the problems that poverty contexts such as informal settlements create, there is also the challenge of selling "green" initiatives to individuals and communities who have understandably, given the track record, become quite skeptical of, or inured to, new models of development. Civic involvement is largely absent from green policymaking, meaning that buy-in from African urbanites at large remains weak. These issues broadly reflect the challenges to inclusive sustainability transitions that might address the structural realities that have produced splintered cities throughout the continent.

Conclusion

This chapter provided an assessment of the green economy in urban Africa focusing on its industrial and economic ramifications in the formal and informal sectors. Our analysis showed that there is no single path to green transitions, but multiple and differing ones based on levels of development, national priorities, existing legislation, social, environmental, and urban contexts, and multiscalar relations. Some countries focus on cost effective quick wins (e.g., Ghana's waste collection and upcycling programs), while other initiatives (e.g., South Africa's greening of industry, Tanzania's agrarian green revolution) are more orientated toward longer-term transitions. Importantly, the prospects for green economy projects can only be fully understood in relation to competing or differing policy agendas (e.g., the strategic/political importance of the coal mining industry in South Africa). Implementation challenges are also critical concerns given the need to develop coordination mechanisms between different stakeholders, and to access, sustain, and effectively deploy financial and other resources (e.g., technological capabilities) in order to enable sustainability transitions.

Despite these realities and concerns, innovations like the ASEZ can help create/play important linkages and demonstration roles provided they are tailored to the local context and able to link to domestic suppliers outside the zone (Frick and Rodríguez-Pose 2019). The global shift toward sustainability should present opportunities for the growth of the green economy sector in Africa – including renewable energy and storage, electric vehicles, green buildings, and waste recycling. Whether African economies can partake will depend largely on their extant industries and the availability of green financing mechanisms. Significant urban-industrial challenges include the lack of technical expertise and monitoring capabilities, the region's enormous informal sector, and inadequate institutional capacity and political will to govern, integrate, and guide sustainable development policies (PAGE 2021). Moreover, Africa has the biggest gaps in access to critical infrastructure compared to any world region (Rozenberg and Fay 2019) and adapting to climate change will only add to this challenge. While acknowledging such difficulties, the potential exists for African countries to pursue low-carbon industrial development, provided there are major improvements to the accessibility and cost of green(er) technologies and related FDI (Cooper et al. 2020; Peter 2021).

With respect to finance, there are huge shortfalls from both external and domestic sources. Only a small fraction of global climate finance flows to the region: for example, in 2013 Africa accounted for 4% of climate finance flows (US\$ 331 billion) (Marbuah, 2020). and the region's share of the global green bond market is miniscule (0.3%) (Tyson, 2021). Only Kenya, Namibia, Nigeria, Seychelles, and South Africa have issued green bonds, and Cape Town and Johannesburg are the only municipal green bond issuers in the region (Marbuah,

2020). Africa's nascent green bond markets need significant expansion in order to expand the provision of capital necessary for scaling innovations in low carbon development (Tyson 2021).

Ultimately, green transition pathways in African cities will not be uniform as they will entail institutional, market, and political realignments at different spatial scales. Within cities, such (re)alignments will need to produce sustainability inducing complementarities and couplings between production, consumption, and infrastructure regimes, while including/integrating the informal sector into such strategies. Disruptions will be inevitable in the process, as global demand patterns and sustainability requirements induce shifts away from fossil fuels and high emission activities; having particular significance for places and industries dependent on resource extraction and other "non-green" industries for their development (e.g., coal and timber producing areas). As a result, green growth will be needed to rebalance and compensate for the disruption and spatial unevenness. This could be derived by leveraging Africa's large renewable energy generation capacity and rich natural capital endowments in responsible and strategic ways in order to generate revenues and lay foundations for domestic green industrialization. African cities will need to play a central coordinating role in such dynamics, as well as leading the process of greening.

Currently, however, such transformations remain distant, hopeful futures rather than feasible presents. Skeptics argue that green initiatives are, at best, add-ons to, or extensions of, existing policies that promote the exchange-values of cities as the *sin qua non* development objective. Longer-term thinking and planning is essential in this regard: strategies that can realistically, pragmatically, and justly produce more sustainable, even, and progressive development outcomes while laying the groundwork for greener, generative urban transitions.

Note

1 Originally the area was called Dassenberg New Town, but it was renamed Atlantis in 1975.

Chapter Ten
Prospects for Generative Urbanism in Africa

Introduction

Urbanization is one of the meta-trends which has and will continue to dominate African development in the coming century. The urban question is fundamentally about whether cities in Africa can generate development outcomes and structural changes able to spur more just, even, and sustainable futures. The focus on cities stems from their transformative potential as centers of production, innovation, and consumption, and nodes for the intersection of diverse flows and relations to the global economy. It is through, within, and from cities, and urban processes, that new trajectories of development can emerge; transitions that will ideally shift material realities and the discourses about Africa in ways that elide business-as-usual narratives about underdevelopment, poverty, and stagnation.

The urban question is thus a highly complex one to answer or analyze in a straightforward and/or comparative manner. This concluding chapter takes stock of our findings, and then explores the potential to recalibrate, rethink, and effectively implement initiatives and policies that can facilitate generative urbanization. In exploring what this entails it focuses on the key constraints, governance challenges, and potential resilience strategies that are associated with, and needed to transform urban regimes in African cities. We focus on generalizable features rather than grand, universalized strategies that may be unsuitable or unrealizable in some places. The chapter closes by arguing that a shift toward more generative modes of urbanization in Africa demands a reconfiguration of regime governance structures and the political settlements associated with these, the centering of cities' use values as central policy objectives while recognizing the

The Urban Question in Africa: Uneven Geographies of Transition, First Edition. Pádraig R. Carmody, James T. Murphy, Richard Grant and Francis Y. Owusu.

need for economic resources, and a concomitant shift beyond the singular logic of growth and exchange value.[1] More broadly, we argue for conceptual rethinking of how we study and compare cities in Africa and beyond – as sociotechnical systems that function and guide urbanization pathways.

Assessing the Urban Question in Africa Today: A Multidimensional View

The book's chapters have documented ongoing dynamics and development outcomes in African cities today, deploying a sociotechnical perspective to examine multiple forces and their interactions with production, consumption, and infrastructure regimes. We have sought to account for both multiscalar factors (e.g., China, imports, climate change) and how regimes interact with and couple to one another in ways that shape urbanization pathways. The net result has been a series of insights regarding the urban question in Africa today which we now summarize as they relate to particular regimes and inter-regime couplings.

As detailed in a number of chapters, production regimes in African cities today face a series of significant challenges that need to be overcome if they are to generate widespread, good employment, social upgrading, innovations, and greener economies. Urbanization without industrialization is a common theme as manufacturing has stalled and consumption regimes play an outsized role in providing work, much of this in the informal sector. Transnational relations with China are significantly shaping inward FDI in SEZs and industries more generally, as well as import flows. The combined effect of these forces is that African manufacturers have struggled to compete in local and regional markets, effectively stalling progress with regard to MVA. In some places, manufacturing has grown but through the emergence of industrialized (FDI-driven) enclaves that are weakly linked or integrated with domestic supply chains. Multiplier and agglomeration effects are consequently not emerging and urban production regimes remain split into parallel, stagnated, and weakly integrated formal and informal sectors.

Addressing such challenges demands policy innovations and spatial planning strategies on a number of key fronts. NUPs offer one way forward but only if these begin to address the needs of burgeoning informal sectors in African cities by legitimating and investing in these economies and communities. Upgraded infrastructure regimes are an essential first step; one that can have the combined effect of making cities more livable while improving the productivity of labor and small enterprises. A key strategy here should be to create better alignments or couplings between production (esp. manufacturing) and consumption regimes and/or urban-regional markets such that the displacement effects accompanying import flows from the East can be mitigated by endogenous, African-based industrialization. As noted below, this will demand difficult political settlements that are quite contrary to the business-as-usual politics in African cities today; compromises that put the last first and transcend neo-patrimonial tendencies/ histories that have limited development progress.

Another political-economic challenge to improved, resilient, and generative sociotechnical systems relates to finance – that is, where the money will come from to pay for long-term investments in the capabilities, infrastructures, and markets needed to support urban transformations. In one sense, there is a chicken-egg situation here given the scale of informal economies and their limited contributions to tax revenues in cities. An arguably bigger problem, however, stems from the "centripetal state politics" that has effectively weakened the capacity of municipal or urban-regional governments to invest in and guide industrialization in ways that benefit the majority of urban residents. Instead, cities are seen as nodes or tools to drive national development projects; a hollowed-out strategy that focuses solely on the transnational exchange values of cities. Such a perspective – if coupled with neo-patrimonial, elite driven politics – leads to an emphasis on magic-bullet, mega-development projects such as enclaved cities, BRI projects, and large-scale logistics hubs and corridors that facilitate extraversion and intraversion rather than the holding down of value within cities through employment, tax revenues, domestic supply-chain linkages, and other multiplier effects. Such projects can only drive long-term urban development if their impacts extend well beyond their construction; a circumstance that has by-and-large not materialized.

Climate change and public health threats will further impact urban regimes in African cities, with potentially dire consequences with respect to quality-of-life concerns. The needs here are unsurprisingly most pressing as they relate to the majority of urban Africans living in slums with poor access to vital collective goods and basic services. In contexts marked by spatial fragmentation and splintering between the haves and have-nots, it is likely that climate change and public health crises will only exacerbate such inequalities as poorer residents are unable to afford the services, technologies, and infrastructures needed to ameliorate the effects of these hazards. It is yet unclear if, from where, and when the capital and political will might come from to develop effective plans to make cities more resilient (despite the Conference of the Parties of the United Nations Framework on Climate Change [COP] promises that have proven empty to date) in the face of these threats and in response to neoliberal globalization; circumstances that are creating multiple exposures to risk and vulnerability.

Beyond explicating these challenges, our analysis has also sought to highlight emerging opportunities and potentialities that might facilitate generative urbanization. As infrastructure regimes become more digitalized, new forms of ICT-enabled production and consumption have been made possible. Foremost has been the rise of platform capitalism that has helped to transform consumer transport and banking sectors, in particular. Such platforms and apps have led to improvements in consumption regimes – e.g., extending public transportation systems, enabling cash-free transactions – but they have not led to the formation of production regimes that empower workers and/or greatly reduce the precarity of informal livelihoods. As such, they have simply articulated with and become integrated into, existing structures and forms of governance; immanent features of African cities that (re)produce inequality and informality. Virtualized forms of transnational extraversion have too been enabled, furthering Africa's adverse incorporation into the world economy.

There are other emerging opportunities that show greater promise to facilitate generative and sustainable urban transitions. Digitalization and the so-called 4IR can offer new pathways for industrialization through technological upgrading in manufacturing and services. The 4IR can further facilitate the emergence of more sustainable urban regimes, helping give rise to green economies in Africa. Such (potential) transformations are only just beginning to take shape and in a highly uneven and scattergun manner – manifest principally in one-off projects such as new-build, smart cities, greentech SEZs, megaprojects to modernize/upgrade infrastructure regimes, and Digital Silk-Road initiatives that are more conducive to development in China than Africa. Missing are comprehensive, coordinated, and realistic strategies aimed to transform urban sociotechnical systems through complementary, progressive inter-regime couplings and multiscalar relations that are inclusive and supportive of, in particular, the informal sector. Absent such inclusions it is unlikely that big-push 4IR and green economy modernization programs will result in generative urbanization for most residents as they will instead perpetuate/exacerbate splintering and exclusionary development.

Realizing Generative Cities: Constraints, Capabilities, Governance and Resilience Strategies

What then can be done to realize generative urbanism in Africa today? Simply stated, there is no singular strategy but a need for place-based, context-specific solutions to regime, inter-regime, and the multiscalar challenges facing African cities. As such, a more pragmatic and productive approach is to focus on general features that need attention as key ingredients for more sustainable urban transitions. We argue that three features of urban sociotechnical systems/regimes need particular attention – capabilities, governance, and resilience strategies – given their significance in enabling urban actors to overcome, manage, and alleviate the constraints placed on them as a result of material limitations, power relations, structural and socioeconomic inequality, and risks, hazards, and vulnerabilities.

Drawing on time geography conceptualizations of the role that constraints play in enabling actors to coordinate and realize their activities in time and space, we focus on three types of constraint that can be addressed through regime-specific changes to capabilities, governance, and resilience strategies (Hagerstrand 1970; Pred 1977; Neutens et al. 2011; Miller 2017). Capability constraints stem from deficiencies in fundamental resources, skills, knowledge, and mobilities needed to address socioeconomic and environmental problems, and/or to upgrade industries, infrastructures, and livelihoods. Chief among these in the context of African cities are fiscal resources, finance, income, human capital, technological and other skills (e.g., planning), physical mobility (e.g., congestion/traffic challenges), and the (under)funding of universities, which are critical to economic transformation (AfDB et al. 2022). Coupling constraints are fundamentally about accessibility: that is the ability of urban actors (e.g., residents, planners, firms, etc.) to connect with the goods, services, resources, individuals, investors, and institutions that can enable them to meet their basic needs, manage everyday challenges, innovate, and improve their livelihoods. Authority constraints account for the rules, regulations, norms, hierarchies, and structural features that may obstruct, limit, and/or prevent urban actors from gaining access to resources or which limit their mobility in time and space. These relate to statutory and customary systems of regulation and socioeconomic organization stemming from formal state and municipal authorities as well as the informal rules/norms associated with gender, race, age, and other axes of differentiation.

Approaching urban challenges through the lens of constraints demands that planners and policymakers first assess what these are in relation to extant urban regimes. To do so, it is imperative to document the everyday, generalized practices through which firms, municipal agencies, and residents go about sustaining businesses, innovating, managing infrastructures, securing livelihoods, accessing basic services, and obtaining consumer and other goods in markets. The grounded, concrete understandings that practice-based analyses can bring will enable municipal leaders, donors, and development practitioners to identify capability, governance, and resilience strategy challenges that need to be addressed in order to facilitate more generative dynamics. Such information and documentation are particularly vital as they relate to the most marginalized residents in cities – namely those living in poverty, informal settlements, and/or with poor access to collective goods such as water, sanitation, and energy. Documenting such practices and their relationships to regime governance, multiscalar relations, and inter-regime couplings in African cities has been a core objective of this book. We now summarize some of the key challenges and potential strategies facing regimes with respect to capabilities, governance, and resilience strategies.

Production Regimes

Africa's urban production regimes face fundamental challenges that are impeding innovation, industrial upgrading, investment, the social upgrading of workers, and potential transitions toward the 4IR and green economy. These include important capability constraints related to knowledge, skills, human capital, finance, and infrastructure that demand state-sponsored interventions on a number of fronts (e.g., educational systems, subsidies, and innovation hubs). Coupling constraints limit the potential of urban production regimes particularly in terms of market access for African manufacturers and the ability to develop competitive assets that can integrate domestic firms into GPN/GVC that might offer prospects for industrial upgrading. Instead, the primary transnational couplings available to African firms are structural in nature – "characterized by unequal power relations and external dependence" (MacKinnon 2012: p. 238). The productive integration of the UIS with/into the formal economy is another pressing coupling constraint; one that must be creatively considered through initiatives able to extend supply chains and other industrial linkages such that production regimes become less fragmented.

Such concerns highlight the need for improved modes of production regime governance that can overcome authority constraints such as those facing UIS enterprises. Here it is essential for Africa's municipal leaders and state author-ities to legitimate the UIS as a structurally derived, essential component of the economy, not simply a problem that will go away through rapid growth and neo-liberalization. In this context, governance structures and systems need to be re-configured in ways that recognize the value-added of informal enterprises both in terms of their support for the livelihoods of residents, their capacity to meet local consumer good and basic service needs (couplings to consumption regimes), and their potential to serve as drivers of innovation and labor-intensive forms of industrialization. At the present, such recognition and support are unlikely given that production regimes in most African cities are governed with the principal aim of attracting inward FDI in large-scale, formalized, and export-oriented manufacturing and service industries. This approach is partial and limited in that it focuses solely on creating external exchange value through transnational couplings that are structural in nature, rather than also investing locally in the development of supply-chain linkages and other means through which the up-grading of domestic manufacturing and the UIS might be possible.

Transforming governance as it relates to production regimes can only occur through new political settlements within cities and between cities and transnational capital. At the city scale, municipal leaders and planners will need to create effec-tive means to include the UIS in their strategies to improve living conditions and capture more value locally through informal-formal sector supply-chain linkages. This will be a difficult pill to swallow in many contexts given it means legitimating informal enterprises and devising means to productively link them with the formal economy. Rather than viewing this as a surrender, such strategies should be seen as stepping stones toward more inclusive forms of industrial development that can, perhaps enable incremental, just forms of formalization. Big push, modernization strategies have not succeeded in eliminating the need for, or value of, the UIS thus further highlighting the need for transformed settlements with the state.

Investments in capabilities, the amelioration of coupling and authority con-straints, and transformation to governance structures are fundamental to making

Africa's production regimes more resilient in the face of the numerous geoeconomic, geopolitical, and climate-related challenges facing the planet today. Considered systemically, it is also critical to account for, manage, and govern the couplings between production, consumption, and infrastructure regimes. Specifically, consumption regimes – particularly the local markets for consumer or wage goods – can be better aligned with domestic manufacturing through initiatives to improve the capacities of local firms to make products that are competitive with imports both in terms of price and quality. Contra neoliberal dogma, such alignments can be facilitated through strategic limits on imports in those sectors where African firms have the potential to meet local demand, and/or by "obligating [the] embeddedness" (Liu and Dicken 2006) of FDI in consumer goods and mature industries; manifest in requirements that investors support the development of supply-chain linkages to the domestic economy and commit to labor upskilling initiatives.

With regard to infrastructure, it is essential for municipal governments and states to recognize the direct and indirect links between productivity and low-quality infrastructure. Black outs, poor roads, floods, and other hazards that stem from inadequate infrastructure within cities add significantly to the costs of manufacturing. Moreover, workers who face long commute times due to congestion may be forced to pay premia, thus reducing the multiplier effects associated with the production regime. Indirectly, workers forced to live in poorly serviced settlements are more likely to get sick due to poor sanitation, drainage, and housing conditions. This, in turn, has a knock-on effect in production regimes with regard to the productivity of labor.

Consumption Regimes

Cities are central places for consumption but these regimes are often overlooked, ignored with respect to planning and policy, and assumed to function principally and solely through the invisible hand of the market. Consumption patterns and capabilities are critical considerations in that they reflect key development indicators such as wages, purchasing-power-parity, savings rates, and market access. Key constraints on African urban consumers stem from low wages, poverty, and catch-is-catch-can livelihood strategies that result in precarious and volatile circumstances with respect to wage good provisioning possibilities. Although city residents do not typically experience the "lived poverty" levels observed in rural areas, they likely experience at least one shortage in a basic need (i.e., cash income, food, medicine, cooking fuel, or clean water) over the course of year (Mattes 2020). Deprivations such as these reflect capability and coupling constraints – the former manifest in low and/or volatile incomes, the latter a function of access to affordable basic services in the infrastructure regime. Such constraints are especially significant in informal settlements.

An increasingly critical and severe challenge for urbanites is housing affordability, a cost that consumes a significant portion of monthly earnings for most. Authority constraints related to planning regulations and property rights often limit the provisioning of affordable housing, especially in informal settlements where long-standing contestations over land rights may delegitimate investments (Agyemang and Morrison 2018; Chitengi 2018; Nkubito and Baiden-Amissah 2019). Moreover, there is a preference toward higher-end, elite-driven, and/or FDI-enabled investments in new-build, often speculative housing and other real estate investments that do little or nothing to alleviate constraints faced by the poorest residents (Goodfellow 2017). Absent significant reforms and dramatic efforts to provide affordable housing for all residents, the consumption and savings possibilities available to them will continue to be contrary to generative urbanization.

The governance of consumption regimes in African cities is by-and-large done in a *laissez-faire* manner beyond regulations on where/when markets are located, the licensing of retailers/wholesalers, controls over some import flows, and through periodic crackdowns or relocations of informal sector activities. First and foremost, imports play an outsized role in consumption regimes in African cities and there is a dire need for states to think more carefully and strategically about what this means for the volatility and sustainability of consumer markets. Moreover, there are additional concerns with respect to how imports of consumer goods shape production regimes and the ability of domestic manufacturers to compete in urban-regional markets.

Imports also shape and govern consumption regimes by further fragmenting markets along class lines. Posh shopping malls where imports dominate increasingly serve the needs of the wealthiest residents, while public and informal markets remain significant for lower-income residents. Supermarket chains abound as well, often foreign owned (e.g., ShopRite [South Africa], Carrefours [France]) and serving as anchor stores in malls and/or as stand-alone franchises that cater to an increasingly diverse array of customers depending on the brand. For consumers, such developments and the imports they enable have diversified their sources for household needs but the articulation of chain stores and large supermarkets with domestic producers/suppliers (production regime couplings) has been uneven as small-scale farmers and informal enterprises in particular struggle to meet the standards and requirements needed to develop linkages, especially when processed food or finished goods such as clothing/furnishings are involved (Barrientos et al. 2016; Andam et al. 2018; Das Nair et al. 2018; Kamau et al. 2019; Ragasa et al. 2020; Boimah and Weible 2023; Reardon et al. 2021). Strengthening and widening couplings between domestic consumption and production regimes should thus be a key focus of governance and resilience strategies for African cities.

With respect to the governance of real estate investments, many/most states and municipal governments privilege private sector development projects over public housing and/or slum upgrading; the latter of which relies on donor-sponsored financing and/or NGO-driven initiatives. As such, housing markets are governed/controlled by-and-large through private investors or, in the case of new-build cities, PPPs focused on attracting investors and upper- or middle-class residents. As Migozzi (2020: p. 641) notes with respect to mortgage markets in Cape Town:

> financialization operates by staying away from the urban poor and precarious neighborhoods, as market actors target the middle- and upper-income sections of society, where public servants and white residents are overrepresented.

Needed are both changes in governance structures – namely demand-side incentives, subsidies, and public-sector programs that can provide financing for the urban poor – in tandem with supply-side slum upgrading and housing projects. Importantly, such programs must be designed and implemented in ways that do not displace people from informal settlements, but which entail close collaborations with these populations and other actors (e.g., NGOs such as SDI) to facilitate uptake and enhance long-term resilience.

Another governance and resilience challenge for consumption regimes relates to the state's ability to help households avoid periodic shortfalls of income and to find new ways to save for future investments. This challenge is fundamentally about the resilience of consumption regimes for the urban poor. While there are obvious, direct connections here to production regimes and the jobs/livelihoods these support, waiting for the materialization of widespread, production driven formal or upgraded employment does little to ameliorate the present-day realities facing many residents with respect to costs of living. States can instead take a more proactive role in governing consumer demand and gap-filling through subsidies for food and other essential products, low-cost collective goods, and/or universal basic income (UBI) programs. Such initiatives can help the urban poor to better make ends meet while freeing up capital that can be saved for future investments in housing, education, and for emergencies, etc. Here ICTs and mobile/e-banking can play an important role in helping consumers to save money more easily, provided such systems can offer interest on savings and be prevented from supporting predatory tactics such as high-interest, short-term loans or gambling applications.

Explicit considerations of the constraints on consumers, and a rethinking of urban governance with an emphasis on markets and the demand-side factors facing households, can open the door for novel interventions to address the everyday provisioning challenges facing residents of African cities. Such concerns are fundamentally about use-value, quality-of-life, and welfare distributions; issues that should be made much more explicit in planning and development strategies. The resilience of African cities will not simply depend upon the ability of production and infrastructure regimes to drive development through agglomeration, industrial upgrading, and growth through exchange value; but will further stem from what the distributional consequences of such changes are as manifest in the life worlds available to all residents. We argue that these worlds, and the possibilities for social mobility and upgrading within/through them, can best be accounted for and compared as consumption regimes that demand interventions through plans, policies, and programs to address the urban question.

Infrastructure Regimes

Given the pace and scale of demographic transitions in urban Africa, and the subsequent congestion and informality that has accompanied these, there are enormous constraints facing planners and utility managers with regard to how to begin to address the challenges in a manner than can improve basic service distributions while making cities more economically productive. Capital is clearly a key constraint, as is widespread informality and informal settlements; factors that relate directly and significantly to the functioning of production and consumption regimes. The fiscal resources to fund upgraded infrastructure depend critically on land value capture and economic growth that can support employment opportunities and pull people out of a dependence on informal livelihoods and settlements to make ends meet. As such, infrastructure-production-consumption regime constraints and couplings are key considerations when thinking about resilience strategies and prospects for generative urbanization.

Authority constraints and the governance of infrastructure regimes, however, are just as critical, manifest in two key issues. First, there are the ways in which municipal leaders, technocrats, planners, and engineers in cities imagine infrastructure in the first place. Here we argue that there is a cognitive lock-in of sorts in the sense that these actors are constrained by the "modern infrastructure ideal" – that is an essentialized, universalized, and one-size-fits-all conceptualization of the kinds of service-provisioning systems cities should be investing in and distributing (Coutard 2008; Furlong 2014; Dalakoglou 2016). Such an ideal might be feasible in new-build, green-field city development, but it is woefully inadequate and unrealistic for the highly complex realities of burgeoning African cities today. Forcing "modernity" into contexts like informal settlements, or in postcolonial cities of millions that were designed/planned for hundreds of thousands of people, is incredibly costly, disruptive, and apt to result in widespread displacements of vulnerable populations. Needed in this regard is a rethinking of infrastructures not as singular sectoral regimes that operate identically everywhere, but as heterogeneous configurations of place-specific, service provisioning platforms and practices (Lawhon et al. 2018; van Welie et al. 2018).

The challenge in embracing heterogeneity is twofold. The first is how to legitimate and mobilize such a perspective among state and municipal leaders who may view it as a failing rather than a more realistic means to distribute services. Moreover, it may be perceived as legitimating or formally recognizing informal settlements and informal service procurement practices. Second, heterogeneity immediately raises concerns about justice and rights-to-the-city, manifest particularly in questions around who gets access to the modern ideal and who does not. These are thorny, contentious issues that will need to be worked out through negotiations and deliberations between states, civil society actors, social movements, and community residents if they are to be resolved in sustainable ways. Meaningful participation and dialogue are thus essential; an issue that will require municipal leaders and agencies to be more transparent, collaborative, and flexible in their engagements with the urban poor, in particular. Moreover, there needs to be an explicit commitment to realizing upgraded, adequate, affordable, and accessible basic services for all residents as a foundational goal for municipal governments.

A second governance and resilience challenge relates to the priorities of the state and international finance (e.g., from China) when it comes to desirable infrastructure investments. As noted earlier, there is a hollowed-out strategy at work here, one that privileges transnational flows and the exchange values of cities in the global economy over their internal functioning and the distribution of services to residents. Municipal and state leaders in Africa ultimately appear to be more accountable to transnational donors, inward FDI, and speculative investors in real estate, new-build cities, and megaprojects than they are to lower-income residents. It will thus be vital for cities to reorient their infrastructure regimes in ways that recenter the need for widespread access and distribution. Moreover, there need to be limits on rampant real-estate speculation that ties up land in unproductive ways, littering the landscapes of cities like Nairobi with low-occupancy or no-occupancy buildings constructed for (imagined) future elites. The splintering effects of such practices bode poorly for urban development, absent significant transformations to infrastructure governance cultures, structures, and desires.

In sum, infrastructure regimes play a critical, bridging role for urban socio-technical systems; undergirding production and consumption regimes through the provisioning of vital goods and services, and facilitating flows both within cities and translocally and transnationally. The urban question in Africa thus hinges significantly on the development and transformation of infrastructure regimes and the inter-regime couplings and multiscalar relations they facilitate. In the face of climate change, and the socioeconomic exposures accompanying economic globalization, they need to be reconfigured and governed in new ways if they are to adequately support distributive, sustainable, and resilient forms of welfare distribution and environment impact in the coming decades.

Reframing the Urban Question as a Sociotechnical, Systemic One

Beyond the empirical and policy-related findings, this book has examined the urban question in Africa through a multidimensional, systemic perspective. We developed and applied a conceptual framework that seeks to comprehensively capture the functions, processes, modes of governance, and multiscalar relations that shape both the exchange values of cities, and their use values as evident in the quality of life and amenities available to residents. Considering both aspects of what cities "do" is essential if we are to move beyond a productivist bias in urban-economic geography, one that often fails to understand urban-regional development as (ideally) a dynamic of social and environmental, not solely economic, upgrading: in other words, to balance concerns over agglomeration economies and exchange value with wider considerations regarding quality of life, rights to the city, and the use value of urban spaces and amenities for all residents.

Our sociotechnical systems approach sought to account for exchange and use value through an analysis of the consumption, production, and infrastructure regimes that govern how cities function on a day-to-day basis, and which create the immanent conditions that determine the pace, scope, scale, and directionality of development pathways. Thinking about urban development through the lens of regimes is not novel per se (e.g., cf. Stone 1993, 2015) but we advance such approaches through an emphasis on different functions and their interrelationships – namely production, industrial development, and job creation (production regimes); market formations, consumption, and welfare distribution (consumption regimes); and collective good and basic service provisioning (infrastructure regimes). In doing so we bring a robust political economy and relational perspective to bear on geography's engagement with the urban question; perspectives that all too often remain rather containerized at the territorial scale, and/or apolitical with respect to determinants of regional success or failure.

Relationally, we emphasized the multiscalar and inter-regime relations that are shaping urban transitions in Africa today. Multiscalar relations include inward FDI flows from emerging powers such as China into African cities, the role of foreign-owned ICT platforms in governing the everyday consumption practices of urban residents, and the role that imports are playing in shaping the prospects for endogenous industrial development. Inter-regime relations entail the functional couplings between infrastructure, production, and consumption activities which can obstruct progressive changes; such as when informal settlements and other low-quality infrastructures reduce both the productivity and purchasing power of workers. Such couplings, we argue, need to be central policy and planning considerations so as to overcome some of the inertial features of contemporary African cities (e.g., how poor use values negatively shape exchange value possibilities).

With respect to political economy, our focus on regimes relates to a concern – à la Khan (2010, 2018) and Goodfellow (2018) – about how these reflect city-specific political settlements manifest in governance configurations. For example, governance in many African cities is increasingly driven by a Dubai model of sorts – one where municipal leaders and elites focus on attracting speculative investments in nonproductive sectors such as retail space, new-build cities/communities, and luxury housing rather than on addressing the everyday challenges facing the majority of residents. Infrastructure investments are a key objective of this governance but the principal focus here is on enhancing the outward/

inward flows from/to the city – i.e., its ability to exchange in the global economy – rather than on basic services and affordable housing. In thinking about regimes as governance configurations that operate in functional realms of production, consumption, and infrastructure we sought to provide a more comprehensive perspective on contemporary capitalisms in Africa today; variegations that can be compared and contrasted with respect to particular regimes, regime couplings, and multiscalar relations.

Our approach further recognizes that capitalist cities are reflective of class, international political economy, transnational flows, and technological developments which structure and guide the evolution of urban systems (Soja 2010). Urban transitions are thus shaped by class relations and the inter-constitutive and dynamic tensions between capital and labor, given, in particular, their different interests in the distribution of wages versus profits. Historically as capital has developed it has sought to increase profits through reducing the power of labor through strategies such as union-busting, off-shoring, automation, and others (Braverman 1974; Herod 2018; Kalleberg 2018; Taylor and Rioux 2018). For example, new-build, utopian city projects reflect a strategy of creating global connections through local erasure; an inclusion/exclusion dialectic. However, given that all cities are "shared spaces" between different social classes (Santos 1979) segregation can never be completely achieved resulting in "frictions" (Tsing 2005), such as those associated with splintered urbanism. Importantly, class tensions such as these can form the basis for social movements in African cities to demand for basic services, employment opportunities, human rights, and affordable housing. The rise of such movements is essential if governance of urban sociotechnical regimes is to be made more transparent and capable of addressing the needs of the majority of residents forced to rely on precarious, UIS strategies. As Paller (2019: p. xi) notes:

> Informal norms of settlement and belonging continue to structure everyday politics in Ghana's cities, helping to explain the logics of political clientelism, elite capture of public goods, and ethnic politics. But they can also contribute to the development of legitimate and responsive representatives, public spheres of collective decision making and multi-ethnic life...

He further suggests urbanization could create a new public sphere which transcends colonially created and inherited ethnic divisions, although rapid urbanization and political liberalization, to date, have increased the importance of indigeneity and autochtony on the continent.

In closing, the empirical evidence and our conceptual approach reveal the complex mix of forces, functions, features, relations, phenomena, and technologies shaping urbanization pathways in Africa today. In one sense, it is a somewhat overwhelming range of variables to simultaneously consider or manage in developing and implementing policies and planning strategies that have been all too compartmentalized by conventional sector-wide approaches rather than intersectoral and multisectoral approaches. Moreover, there is no singular set of solutions to the urban question given the context-specific, contingent, and conjunctural features that will determine the viability and promise of particular policies. As Robinson (2006: p. 763) argued, we need to instead think about cities as relational and diverse in form and function, to move beyond essentializing archetypes that almost inevitably derive from the western experience.

> This would be an urban studies which is drawn to learn from cities everywhere – from a world of diverse, distinctive cities – and which is not limited to or fixated by the processes and places of the powerful....We should be able to appreciate the diversity of processes and activities which go on in specific cities, producing their distinctiveness, as well as the many different kinds of connections which are forged – often with extreme difficulty and uncertainty – beyond neighbourhoods, quarters, municipalities and city-regions.

The sociotechnical systems approach developed and applied here offers a way to maintain this openness to diversity while providing a means to capture and compare fundamental features, processes, relationships, and interdependencies that shape the development of all cities.

Also needed are more sustained studies of African cities that can facilitate productive, comparative analyses that will enhance and advance practical understandings of what is and is not working with respect to urban transitions. We believe that the focus on sociotechnical regimes offered here can do this. Moreover, it can enable African and other, non-Western, cities to "theorize back" in a systemic way at established, hegemonic Northern and Anglo-European ideas about cities and their development. We have sought to do this here through the varied experiences of cities in Africa. As detailed throughout, common themes, processes, relations, and challenges are apparent in the region but these can belie the impossibility for grand strategies to "fix" all African cities such as those offered up by the World Bank (2009), and/or the limits on approaches that essentialize the role of singular processes such as agglomeration as drivers of urban-regional development success (e.g., Scott and Storper 2015).

This book has provided a starting point for deeper, systemic, and comparative engagements with the urban question in Africa and the Global South more generally. Many questions remain unresolved, however, particularly regarding how urbanization pathways will unfold differentially; where more/less progressive systems of governance will emerge and why; whether development outcomes in African cities can move beyond their seemingly never-ending tendency toward greater inequality and splintering; and what kinds of urban experiments offer promising, pragmatic solutions for the pressing challenges detailed throughout this book. The future of Africa lies in its diverse cities, peoples and their development, and we hope this contribution will help to extend, expand, deepen, and diversify the dialogues around them.

Note

1 Africa may have much to learn from China's approach to "land-value capture," in terms of generating resources to enhance urban use values (Cain 2017) in this regard.

References

Aberg, J.H.S. and Becker, D. (2021). The world is more than a stage: Foreign policy, development and spatial performativity in Ethiopia. *Territory Politics Governance* 9 (1): 1–16.

Abubakar, I.R. and Doan, P.L. (2017). Building new capital cities in Africa: lessons for new satellite towns in developing countries. *African Studies* 76 (4): 546–565.

Acheampong, R. (2021). Societal impact of smart, digital platform mobility services - and empirical study and policy implications of passenger safety and security in ride-hailing. *Case Studies on Transport Policy* 9 (1): 302–314.

Acuto, M. and Leffel, B. (2021). Understanding the global ecosystem of city networks. *Urban Studies* 58 (9): 1758–1774.

Addis, G. (2020). Trump's Nile dam statement is declaration of war. *Ethiopian church group slams US President Donald Trump for saying Egypt will bomb Grand Ethiopian Renaissance Dam.* Available at https://www.aa.com.tr/en/africa/trumps-nile-dam-statement-is-declaration-of-war/2019951# (Accessed 13 March 2021).

Adu-Gymfi, Y. and Adjei, B. (2016). *Skills development, knowledge and innovation at Suame Magazine, Kumasi.* Open African Innovation Research. (Open AIR): Working Paper 16. Available at https://openair.africa/wp-content/uploads/2020/05/WP-16-Skills-Development-Knowledge-and-Innovation-at-Suame-Magazine-Kumasi.pdf (Accessed 13 March 2021).

Adunbi, A. (2022). *Enclaves of Exception: Special Economic Zones and Extractive Practices in Nigeria.* Bloomington: Indiana University Press.

AfDB (2018). *Africa's infrastructure: great potential but little impact on inclusive growth.* African Development Bank. Available at https://www.afdb.org/fileadmin/uploads/afdb/Documents/Publications/2018AEO/African_Economic_Outlook_2018_-_EN_Chapter3.pdf (Accessed 15 July 2019).

The Urban Question in Africa: Uneven Geographies of Transition, First Edition. Pádraig R. Carmody, James T. Murphy, Richard Grant and Francis Y. Owusu.
© 2024 John Wiley & Sons Ltd. Published 2024 by John Wiley & Sons Ltd.

AfDB, OECD, and UNDP (2016). *African Economic Outlook 2016: Sustainable Cities and Structural Transformation*. Paris: OECD Publishing.

AfDB, UNECA, and Sahel and West Africa Club (2022). *Africa's Urbanisation Dynamics 2022: The Economic Power of African Cities*. Paris: OECD Publishing.

Afenah, A. (2009). *Conceptualizing the effects of neoliberal urban policies on housing rights: an analysis of the attempted unlawful forced eviction of an informal settlement in Accra, Ghana*. Development Planning Unit, University College London. Available at http://www.bartlett.ucl.ac.uk/dpu/latest/publications/dpu-working-papers/WP139_Afia_Afenah_Internet_copy.pdf (Accessed 15 July 2022).

African Union (2014). *AU strategy for science, technology, and innovation for Africa 2024, STISA-2024*. Addis Ababa: African Union. Available at https://au.int/sites/default/files/newsevents/workingdocuments/33178-wd-stisa-english_-_final.pdf (Accessed 15 July 2022).

African Union (2015). *Agenda 2063: The Africa We Want*. Addis Ababa: African Union Commission.

AfricaNews (2019 March 18). *90% of Mozambican city of Beira destroyed by Cyclone Idai - Red Cross*. Africa News. Available at https://www.africanews.com/2019/03/18/90-per cent-of-mozambican-city-of-beira-destroyed-by-cyclone-idai-red-cross (Accessed 15 July 2022).

AfricaNews (2023). *Freddy could become the longest cyclone on record – UN*. Available at https://www.africanews.com/2023/03/10/freddy-could-become-the-longest-cyclone-on-record-un (Accessed 11 March 2023).

Agyemang, F.S. and Morrison, N. (2018). Recognising the barriers to securing affordable housing through the land use planning system in Sub-Saharan Africa: a perspective from Ghana. *Urban Studies* 55 (12): 2640–2659.

Ajibade, I. (2017). Can a future city enhance urban resilience and sustainability? a political ecology analysis of Eko Atlantic city, Nigeria. *International Journal of Disaster Risk Reduction* 26: 85–92.

Akese, G. (2019). *Electronic waste (e-waste) Science and Advocacy at Agbogbloshie: The Making and Effects of "The World's Largest E-Waste Dump"*. Newfoundland, Canada: Unpublished PhD thesis Memorial University.

Akindele, A. (2021 April 21). *Amazon to set up African headquarters in South Africa*. Premium Times, Available at https://www.premiumtimesng.com/news/more-news/456705-amazon-to-set-up-african-headquarters-in-south-africa.html (Accessed 15 July 2022).

Alexander, K.A., Sanderson, C.E., Marathe, M. et al. (2015). What factors might have led to the emergence of Ebola in West Africa? *PLoS Neglected Tropical Diseases* 9 (6): e0003652.

Alonso, W. (1960). A theory of the urban land market. *Papers in Regional Science* 6 (1): 149–157.

Altenburg, T., Chen, X., Lütkenhorst, W. et al. (2020). *Exporting out of China or out of Africa? automation versus relocation in the global clothing industry*. Discussion Papers 1/2020, German Development Institute / Deutsches Institut für Entwicklungspolitik. Available at https://ideas.repec.org/p/zbw/diedps/12020.html (Accessed 15 July 2022).

Alves, A.C. (2013). China's 'win-win' cooperation: unpacking the impact of infrastructure-for-resources deals in Africa. *South African Journal of International Affairs* 20 (2): 207–226.

Ambole, A., Musango, J.K., Buyana, K. et al. (2019). Mediating household energy transitions through co-design in urban Kenya, Uganda and South Africa. *Energy Research and Social Science* 55: 208–217.

Amin, A. and Graham, S. (1997). The ordinary city. *Transactions of the Institute of British Geographers* 22 (4): 411–429.

Amin, A. and Thrift, N.J. (1994). Globalization, institutional thickness and local prospects. *Revue d'Economie Régionale Et Urbaine* 3: 405–427.

Amin, S. and Pearce, B. (1974). *Accumulation on a World Scale: A Critique of the Theory of Underdevelopment*. New York and London: Monthly Review Press.

Amoako, C. and Inkoom, D.K.B. (2018). The production of flood vulnerability in Accra, Ghana: re-thinking flooding and informal urbanisation. *Urban Studies* 55 (13): 2903–2922.

Andam, K.S., Tschirley, D., Asante, S.B. et al. (2018). The transformation of urban food systems in Ghana: findings from inventories of processed products. *Outlook on Agriculture* 47 (3): 233–243.

Angelidou, M. (2015). Smart cities: a conjuncture of four forces. *Cities* 47: 95–106.

Anglo-American (2013). *Robotics for safer mining – a ground-breaking partnership*. Available at https://southafrica.angloamerican.com/our-stories/robotics-for-safer-mining-a-ground-breaking-partnership (Accessed 15 July 2022).

Ansari, S. (2021). *Neoliberalism and Resistance in South Africa: Economic and Political Coalitions*. Basingstoke: Palgrave Macmillan.

Antikainen, M., Uusitalo, T., and Kivikytö-Reponen, P. (2018). Digitalisation as an enabler of circular economy. *Procedia CIRP* 73: 45–49.

Anwar, M.A. and Graham, M. (2020a). Hidden transcripts of the gig economy: labour agency and the new art of resistance among African gig workers. *Environment and Planning A-Economy and Space* 52 (7): 1269–1291.

Anwar, M.A. and Graham, M. (2020b). Digital labour at economic margins: African workers and the global information economy. *Review of African Political Economy* 47 (163): 95–105.

Anwar, M.A. and Graham, M. (2021). Between a rock and a hard place: freedom, flexibility, precarity and vulnerability in the gig economy in Africa. *Competition and Change* 25 (2): 237–258.

Anwar, M.A. and Graham, M. (2022). *The Digital Continent: Placing Africa in Planetary Networks of Work*. Oxford and New York: Oxford University Press.

Arezki, R., Rota-Graziosi, R., and Senbet, L. (2015). Natural resources and capital flight: a role for policy? In: *Capital Flight from Africa: Causes, Effects, and Policy Issues* (ed. S.I. Ajayi and L.O. Ndikumana), 263–276. Oxford: Oxford University Press.

Armstrong, C., de Beer, J., Kraemer-Mbula, E., and Ellis, M. (2018). *Institutionalisation and informal innovation in South African maker communities*. Available at http://peer

production.net/wp-content/uploads/2018/06/Armstrong-De-Beer-Kraemer-Mbula-Ellis-final-JoPP-submission-7-May-18.pdf (Accessed 15 July 2022).

Armstrong, W. and McGee, T. (1968). Revolutionary change and the third world city: a theory of urban involution. *Civilisations* 18 (3): 353–378.

Arsene, C. (2014). Chinese employers and their Ugandan workers: tensions, frictions and cooperation in an African city. *Journal of Current Chinese Affairs* 43 (1): 139–176.

Atlas, G.C. (2022). *Global carbon atlas, 2021*. Available at http://www.globalcarbonatlas. org/en/content/welcome-carbon-atlas (Accessed 15 July 2022).

Atta-Ankomah, R. (2014). *China's Presence in Developing Countries' Technology Basket: The Case of Furniture Manufacturing in Kenya*. Milton Keynes: Open University.

Austin, G., Frankema, E., and Jerven, M. (2017). Patterns of manufacturing growth in Sub-Saharan Africa. In: *The Spread of Modern Industry to the Periphery since 1871* (ed K. O'Rourke and J. Williamson). 345–374. New York: Oxford University Press.

Ayentimi, D.T., Abadi, H.A., and Burgess, J. (2023). Decent gig work in Sub Sahara Africa? *Journal of Industrial Relations* 65 (1): 112–125.

Ayentimi, D.T. and Burgess, J. (2019). Is the fourth industrial revolution relevant to sub-Sahara Africa? *Technology Analysis and Strategic Management* 31 (6): 641–652.

Azunre, G., Amponsah, O., Takyo, S., and Mensah, H. (2021). Informality-sustainable city nexus. The place of informality in advancing sustainable Ghanaian cities. *Sustainable Cities and Society* 67: 102707.

Azunre, G.A., Amponsah, O., Takyi, S.A. et al. (2022). Urban informalities in sub-Saharan Africa (SSA): a solution for or barrier against sustainable city development. *World Development* 152: 105782.

Baah-Boteng, W. and Vanek, J. (2020). *Informal workers in Ghana: a statistical snapshot*. WIEGO Statistical Brief 20. Geneva: WIEGO. Available at https://www.wiego.org/sites/default/files/publications/file/WIEGO_Statistical_Brief_N21_0.pdf (Accessed December 15 2021).

Baeten, G. (2012). Neoliberal planning: does it really exist? In: *Contradictions of Neoliberal Planning: Cities, Policies and Politics* vol. 102 (ed. T. Tasan-Kok and G. Baeten), 205–211. The GeoJournal Library, Springer.

Baker, L. and Sovacool, B.K. (2017). The political economy of technological capabilities and global production networks in South Africa's wind and solar photovoltaic (PV) industries. *Political Geography* 60: 1–12.

Baker, T. and McGuirk, P. (2017). Assemblage thinking as methodology: commitments and practices for critical policy research. *Territory, Politics, Governance* 5 (4): 425–442.

Baldwin, R.E. (2019). *The Globotics Upheaval: Globalisation, Robotics and the Future of Work*. Oxford and New York: Oxford University Press.

Ballard, R. and Harrison, P. (2020). Transnational urbanism interrupted: a Chinese developer's attempts to secure approval to build the 'New York of Africa' at Modderfontein, Johannesburg. *Environment and Planning a-Economy and Space* 52 (2): 383–402.

Bannock, G., Baxter, R.E., and Davis, E. (2003). *The Penguin Dictionary of Economics*, 7e. London: Penguin.

Baptista, I. (2019). Electricity services always in the making: informality and the work of infrastructure maintenance and repair in an African city. *Urban Studies* 56 (3): 510–525.

Barbier, E. (2011). The policy challenges for green economy and sustainable economic development. *Natural Resources Forum* 35 (3): 233–245.

Barbieri, P., Boffelli, A., Elia, S. et al. (2020). What can we learn about reshoring after Covid-19? *Operations Management Research* 13 (3): 131–136.

Bariyo, N. (2019 December 14). A fine for a flush: drought leaves Southern Africa high and dry: a worsening water crisis ravages crops, livestock and even the continent's biggest waterfall; Zimbabweans contend with a new weekly ritual. *Wall Street Journal*, Available at https://www.wsj.com/articles/a-fine-for-a-flush-drought-leaves-southern-africa-high-and-dry-11576324800 (Accessed 26 May 2022).

Barnes, L. (2018 March 6). *New study reveals just how little Uber drivers make*. Think-Progress. Available at https://thinkprogress.org/uber-drivers-often-make-less-than-minimum-wage-according-to-new-study-912d388c3c82 (Accessed 26 May 2022).

Barrett, P. and Baumann-Pauly, D. (2019). *Made in Ethiopia: Challenges in the Garment Industry's New Frontier*. New York: New York University Stern Center for Human Rights.

Barrientos, S. (2022). Regional value chains in the Global South: governance implications for producers and workers? *Cambridge Journal of Regions, Economy and Society* 15 (2): 437–443.

Barrientos, S., Knorringa, P., Evers, B. et al. (2016). Shifting regional dynamics of global value chains: implications for economic and social upgrading in African horticulture. *Environment and Planning A: Economy and Space* 48 (7): 1266–1283.

Barton, B. (2021). Agency and autonomy in the maritime silk road initiative: an examination of Djibouti's Doraleh Container Terminal disputes. *The Chinese Journal of International Politics* 14 (3): 353–380.

Barton, B. (2022). *The Doraleh Disputes: Infrastructure Politics in the Global South*. Basingstoke: Palgrave Macmillan.

Bassey, N. (2012). *To Cook a Continent: Destructive Extraction and the Climate Crisis in Africa*. Cape Town and Oxford: Pambazuka.

Bathelt, H., Malmberg, A., and Maskell, P. (2004). Clusters and knowledge: local buzz, global pipelines and the process of knowledge creation. *Progress in Human Geography* 28 (1): 31–56.

Batty, M., Axhausen, K.W., Giannotti, F. et al. (2012). Smart cities of the future. *The European Physical Journal Special Topics* 214 (1): 481–518.

Bayart, J.F. and Ellis, S. (2000). Africa in the world: a history of extraversion. *African Affairs* 99 (395): 217–267.

Bbaala, P. (2015). Emerging questions on the shifting Sino-Africa relations:'win-win'or 'win-lose'? *Africa Development* 40 (3): 97–119.

BBC (2015 October 16). *Bagamoyo port: Tanzania begins construction on mega project*. BBC, Available at https://www.bbc.com/news/world-africa-34554524 (Accessed 6 January 2021).

BBC (2020 April 29). *Jumia: the e-commerce start-up that fell from grace.* BBC, Available at https://www.bbc.com/news/world-africa-52439546 (Accessed 6 January 2021).

Bedinger, M., Beevers, L., Walker, G.H. et al. (2020). Urban systems: mapping interdependencies and outcomes to support systems thinking. *Earth's Future* 8 (3): e2019EF001389.

Beegle, K., Chritianensen, L., Dabalen, A., and Gaddis, I. (2016). *Poverty in a Rising Africa.* Washington: World Bank.

Benazeraf, D. and Alves, A. (2014). *'Oil for housing': Chinese built new towns in Angola.* South African Institute of International Affairs, Policy Briefing 88, Global Powers and Africa Programme. Available at https://saiia.org.za/research/oil-for-housing-chinese-built-new-towns-in-angola/#:~:text=In%20Angola%2C%20China%20is%20also,housing%20shortfall%20in%20the%20country (Accessed 6 January 2021).

Benjamin, N.C. and Mbaye, A.A. (2012). The informal sector, productivity, and enforcement in West Africa: a firm-level analysis. *Review of Development Economics* 16 (4): 664–680.

Benjamin, N.C. and Mbaye, A.A. (2020). *The informal sector in Francophone Africa. The other side of weak structural transformation.* Brookings Institution, Available at https://www.brookings.edu/research/the-informal-sector-in-francophone-africa-the-other-side-of-weak-structural-transformation (Accessed 16 July 2021).

Benner, C. (2006). South Africa on-call': information technology and labour market restructuring in South African call centres. *Regional Studies* 40 (9): 1025–1040.

Benyera, E. (2021). *The Fourth Industrial Revolution and the Recolonisation of Africa: The Coloniality of Data.* London: Taylor and Francis.

Bergek, A., Jacobsson, S., Carlsson, B. et al. (2008). Analyzing the functional dynamics of technological innovation systems: a scheme of analysis. *Research Policy* 37 (3): 407–429.

Bergius, M., Benjaminsen, T.A., Maganga, F., and Buhaug, H. (2020). Green economy, degradation narratives, and land-use conflicts in Tanzania. *World Development* 129: 104850.

Bergius, M. and Buseth, J.T. (2019). Towards a green modernization development discourse: the new green revolution in Africa. *Journal of Political Ecology* 26 (1): 57–83.

Berry, B.J.L. (1967). *Geography of Market Centers and Retail Distribution.* Englewood Cliffs: Prentice-Hall.

BFA/Mastercard Foundation (2019). *Digital commerce and youth employment in Africa.* Report commissioned by the Mastercard Foundation. Available at https://mastercardfdn.org/research/digitalcommerce (Accessed 12 January 2021).

Bhalla, N. (2018). *Women cabbies hit Nairobi's roads as taxi-hailing apps mushroom.* https://www.reuters.com/article/us-kenya-women-taxi-drivers-idUSKBN1I300D (Accessed 26 May 2023).

Bina, O. (2013). The green economy and sustainable development: an uneasy balance? *Environment and Planning C: Politics and Space* 31 (6): 1023–1047.

Binz, C., Coenen, L., Murphy, J.T., and Truffer, B. (2020). Geographies of transition—from topical concerns to theoretical engagement: a comment on the transitions research agenda. *Environmental Innovation and Societal Transitions* 34: 1–3.

Birch, C., Jackson, L., Finney, D. et al. (2021). *Future changes in heatwaves over Africa at the convection-permitting scale*. The SAO/NASA Astrophysics Data System, Harvard University, Available at https://ui.adsabs.harvard.edu/abs/2021EGUGA.23.2596B (Accessed 16 July 2022).

Bird, J., Montebruno, P., and Regan, T. (2017). Life in a slum: understanding living conditions in Nairobi's slums across time and space. *Oxford Review of Economic Policy* 33 (3): 496–520.

Bishop, R., Phillips, J., Yeo, W.W., and Yeo, W. (eds.) (2003). *Postcolonial Urbanism: Southeast Asian Cities and Global Processes*. Psychology Press.

Black, A. and Yang, C. (2021). South Africa's special economic zones as destinations for chinese investment: problems and possibilities. In: *South Africa–China Relations* (ed. C. Alden and Y. Wu), 161–178. London: Palgrave Macmillan.

Blaikie, P., Cannon, T., Davis, I., and Wisner, B. (1994). *At Risk: Natural Hazards, People's Vulnerability, and Disasters*. Cham: Springer.

Blomkvist, P. and Nilsson, D. (2017). On the need for system alignment in large water infrastructure: understanding infrastructure dynamics in Nairobi, Kenya. *Water Alternatives* 10 (2): 283–302.

Boadu, K. 2022. Agbogbloshie redevelopment scheme. *The Daily Graphic*, April 20, 2022. Available at https://www.graphic.com.gh/news/general-news/ghana-news-agbogbloshie-redevelopment-scheme-ready.html (Accessed 10 March 2023).

Boamah, F. and Rothfuß, E. (2018). From technical innovations towards social practices and socio-technical transition? Re-thinking the transition to decentralised solar PV electrification in Africa. *Energy Research and Social Science* 42: 1–10.

Bodomo, A. (2010). The African trading community in Guangzhou: an emerging bridge for Africa–China relations. *The China Quarterly* 203: 693–707.

Boimah, M., and Weible, D. (2023). "We prefer local but consume imported": results from a qualitative study of dairy consumers in Senegal. *Journal of International Food & Agribusiness Marketing* 35 (2): 244-260.

Bond, P. (2006). *Looting Africa: The Economics of Exploitation*. Scottsville, South Africa: University of KwaZulu-Natal Press.

Bonneux, L. and Van Damme, W. (2010). Preventing iatrogenic pandemics of panic. Do it in a NICE way. *BMJ* 340: 1308.

Borel-Saladin, J.M. and Turok, I.N. (2013a). The green economy: incremental change or transformation? *Environmental Policy and Governance* 23 (4): 209–220.

Borel-Saladin, J.M. and Turok, I.N. (2013b). The impact of the green economy on jobs in South Africa: news and views. *South African Journal of Science* 109 (9): 1–4.

Bork-Hüffer, T., Rafflenbeul, B., Kraas, F., and Li, Z. (2014). Global change, national development goals, urbanisation and international migration in China: African migrants in Guangzhou and Foshan. In: *Megacities* (ed. A. Sorensen and J. Okataz), 135–150. Amsterdam: Springer.

Boschma, R., Coenen, L., Frenken, K., and Truffer, B. (2017). Towards a theory of regional diversification: combining insights from evolutionary economic geography and transition studies. *Regional Studies* 51 (1): 31–45.

Boschma, R. and Iammarino, S. (2009). Related variety, trade linkages, and regional growth in Italy. *Economic Geography* 85 (3): 289–311.

Boston University Global Development Policy Center (2022). *Chinese Loans to Africa database.* Available at http://bu.edu/gdp/chinese-loans-to-africa-database (Accessed 15 July 2022).

Boy, J.D. and Uitermark, J. (2017). Reassembling the city through Instagram. *Transactions of the Institute of British Geographers* 42 (4): 612–624.

Bräutigam, D. (2020). A critical look at Chinese 'debt-trap diplomacy': the rise of a meme. *Area Development and Policy* 5 (1): 1–14.

Bräutigam, D. and Xiaoying, X. (2011). African Shenzhen: china's special economic zones in Africa. *The Journal of Modern African Studies* 49 (1): 27–54.

Braverman, H. (1974). *Labour and Monopoly Capital: The Degradation of Work in the Twentieth Century.* New York: Monthly Review Press.

Brenner, N. (2015) Introduction: urban theory without an outside. In: *Implosions/Explosions: Towards a Study of Planetary Urbanisation* (ed. N. Brenner). Berlin: Jovis.

Brenner, N. (2018). Debating planetary urbanization: for an engaged pluralism. *Environment and Planning D: Society and Space* 36 (3): 570–590.

Brenner, N., Marcuse, P., and Mayer, M. (2009). Cities for people, not for profit. *City* 13 (2–3): 176–184.

Brenner, N. and Schmid, C. (2012). *Towards a theory of extended urbanization.* Working paper, Urban Theory Lab, Harvard GSD, Cambridge, MA and ETH Zurich.

Brenner, N. and Schmid, C. (2015). Towards a new epistemology of the urban? *City* 19 (2–3): 151–182.

Bretagnolle, A., Pumain, D., and Vacchiani-Marcuzzo, C. (2009). The organization of urban systems. In: *Complexity Perspectives in Innovation and Social Change* (ed. D. Lane, D. Pumain, S. Ernst van der Leeuw, and G. West), 197–220. Dordrecht: Springer.

Breul, M. and Diez, J.R. (2018). An intermediate step to resource peripheries: the strategic coupling of gateway cities in the upstream oil and gas GPN. *Geoforum* 92: 9–17.

Brockington, D. and Ponte, S. (2015). The green economy in the global South: experiences, redistributions and resistance. *Third World Quarterly* 36 (12): 2197–2206.

Brown, A., Lyons, M., and Dankoco, I. (2010). Street traders and the emerging spaces for urban voice and citizenship in African cities. *Urban Studies* 47 (3): 666–683.

Brown, E., Cloke, J., Gent, D. et al. (2014). Green growth or ecological commodification: debating the green economy in the Global South. *Geografiska Annaler: Series B, Human Geography* 96 (3): 245–259.

Brown, N. (2022 April 21). Agbogbloshie redevelopment scheme ready. *Assase Radio 99.5,* Available at https://asaaseradio.com/agbogbloshie-redevelopment-scheme-ready (Accessed 11 May 2022).

Buchholz, M. and Bathelt, H. (2021). Models of regional economic development: illustrations using US data. *Zeitschrift Für Wirtschaftsgeographie* 65 (1): 28–42.

Bull, C., Daniels, S., Kinyanjui, M., and Hazeltine, B. (2016). A study of the informal metalworking sector in Nairobi. In: *The Informal Economy in Developing Nations–Hidden Engine of Innovation* (ed. E. Kraemer-Mbula and S. Wunsch-Vincent), 100–145. Cambridge and New York: Cambridge University Press.

Burke, J. (2017). Violence erupts between taxi and Uber drivers in Johannesburg. *The Guardian*, Available at https://www.theguardian.com/world/2017/sep/08/violence-erupts-taxi-uber-drivers-johannesburg (Accessed 11 May 2022).

Burns, R., Fast, V., Levenda, A., and Miller, B. (2021). Smart cities: between worlding and provincialising. *Urban Studies* 58 (3): 461–470.

Buseh, A.G., Stevens, P.E., Bromberg, M., and Kelber, S.T. (2015). The Ebola epidemic in West Africa: challenges, opportunities, and policy priority areas. *Nursing Outlook* 63 (1): 30–40.

Buseth, J.T. (2017). The green economy in Tanzania: from global discourses to institutionalization. *Geoforum* 86: 42–52.

Buseth, J.T. (2021). Narrating green economies in the global South. *Forum for Development Studies* 48 (1): 87–109.

Buxton, N. and Hayes, B. (eds.) (2016). *The Secure and the Dispossessed: How the Military and Corporations are Shaping a Climate-Changed World*. London: Pluto.

Buyana, K. (2022). Transgression in the energy infrastructure landscapes of cities. *Landscape Research* 48 (2): 1–13.

Cain, A. (2014). African urban fantasies: past lessons and emerging realities. *Environment and Urbanisation* 26 (2): 561–567.

Cain, A. (2017). Alternatives to African commodity-backed urbanization: the case of China in Angola. *Oxford Review of Economic Policy* 33 (3): 478–495.

Caldeira, T.P. (2017). Peripheral urbanisation: autoconstruction, transversal logics, and politics in cities of the global south. *Environment and Planning D: Society and Space* 35 (1): 3–20.

Campbell, E. (2007). Economic globalisation from below: transnational refugee trade networks in Nairobi. In: *Cities in Contemporary Africa* (ed. M.J. Murray and G.A. Myers), 125–147. Basingstoke: Palgrave Macmillan.

Capra, F. (1996). *The Web of Life: A New Scientific Understanding of Living Systems*. New York: Anchor Books.

Caprotti, F. and Bailey, I. (2014). Making sense of the green economy. *Geografiska Annaler: Series B, Human Geography* 96 (3): 195–200.

Carling, J. and Haugen, H.Ø. (2021). Circumstantial migration: how Gambian journeys to China enrich migration theory. *Journal of Ethnic and Migration Studies* 47 (12): 2778–2795.

Carmody, P. (1998). Constructing alternatives to structural adjustment in Africa. *Review of African Political Economy* 75: 25–46.

Carmody, P. (2010). *Globalisation in Africa: Recolonization or Renaissance?* Boulder: Lynne Rienner Publishers.

Carmody, P. (2013). A knowledge economy or an information society in Africa? Thintegration and the mobile phone revolution. *Information Technology for Development* 19 (1): 24–39.

Carmody, P. (2014a). The world is bumpy power, uneven development and the impact of new ICTs on South African Manufacturing. *Human Geography* 7 (1): 1–16.

Carmody, P. (2014b). *The Ebola Outbreak - Is Africa Really Rising?* Available at https://www.tcd.ie/news_events/articles/the-ebola-outbreak-is-africa-really-rising/#.VIlk ktKsWuI (Accessed 11 May 2022).

Carmody, P. (2015). ICT4D and E-business. In: *International Encyclopaedia of Digital Communication and Society* (ed. R. Mansell, P.H. Ang, C. Steinfield et al.). London: Wiley-Blackwell. Available at https://doi.org/10.1002/9781118767771.wbiedcs063.

Carmody, P. (2017a). *Variegated capitalism in Africa. The role of industrial policy*, Available at http://roape.net/2017/01/04/variegated-capitalism-africa-role-industrial-poli cy (Accessed 23 July 2017).

Carmody, P. (2017b). Assembling effective industrial policy in Africa: an agenda for action. *Review of African Political Economy* 44 (152): 336–345.

Carmody, P. (2020). Meta-trends in global value chains and development: interactions with COVID-19 in Africa. *Transnational Corporations: Investment and Development* 27 (2): 143–155.

Carmody, P. and Hampwaye, G. (2010). Inclusive or exclusive globalisation: the impacts of Asian-owned businesses in Zambia. *Africa Today* 56 (3): 84–102.

Carmody, P. and Kragelund, P. (2016). 'Who is in charge?' State power, agency and Sino-African relations. *Cornell International Law Journal* 49: 1–24.

Carmody, P., Kragelund, P., and Riberedo, R. (2020). *Africa's Shadow Rise: China and the Mirage of African Economic Development*. London: Zed.

Carmody, P. and McCann, G. (2022). The new (ab)normal, endemic inequality and pandemic blowback. In: *COVID-19, the Global South and the Pandemic's Development Impact* (ed. G. McCann, N. Mishra, and P. Carmody). Bristol: Bristol University Press.

Carmody, P. and Murphy, J.T. (2017). The impact of China and South Africa in Urban Africa. In: *Foreign Capital Flows and Economic Development in Africa: BRICS versus OECD's Impact* (ed. E. Wamboye and E. Tiruneh), 29–49. Basingstoke and New York: Palgrave MacMillan.

Carmody, P., and Murphy, J. T. (2022). Chinese neoglobalisation in East Africa: logics, couplings and impacts. *Space and Polity* 26 (1): 20–43.

Carmody, P., Taylor, I., and Zajontz, T. (2022a). China's spatial fix and 'debt diplomacy' in Africa: constraining belt or road to economic transformation? *Canadian Journal of African Studies* 56 (1): 57–77.

Carmody, P. and Wainwright, J. (2022). Contradiction and restructuring in China's Belt and Road Initiative: reflecting on China's 'pause' in a go world. *Third World Quarterly* 43 (12): 2830–2851.

Carmody, P., Zajontz, T., and Reboredo, R. (2022b). From 'debt diplomacy' to donorship: China's changing role in global development. *Global Political Economy* 1 (2): 198–217.

Carrai, M.A. (2021). Adaptive governance along Chinese-financed BRI railroad megaprojects in East Africa. *World Development* 141: 105388.

Cartwright, A., Palmer, I., Taylor, A. et al. (2018). *Developing prosperous and inclusive cities in Africa – national urban policies to the rescue?* Available at https://newclimateeconomy.report/workingpapers/wp-content/uploads/sites/5/2018/09/CUT18_Africa_NatUrbanPolicies_final.pdf (Accessed 23 July 2021).

Castells, M. (1977) *The Urban Question: A Marxist Approach.* London: E. Arnold.

Castells, M. (2010). Globalisation, networking, urbanisation: reflections on the spatial dynamics of the information age. *Urban Studies* 47 (13): 2737–2745.

Castells-Quintana, D. (2017). Malthus living in a slum: urban concentration, infrastructure and economic growth. *Journal of Urban Economics* 98: 158–173.

Chabal, P. (2009). *Africa: The Politics of Suffering and Smiling.* London: Zed Books.

Charmes, J., Gault, F., and Wunsch-Vincent, S. (2018). Measuring innovation in the informal economy - formulating an agenda for Africa. *Journal of Intellectual Capital* 19 (3): 536–549.

Chaturvedi, S. (2016). The development compact: a theoretical construct for South-South cooperation. *International Studies* 53 (1): 15–43.

Chee, F. (2018). An Uber ethical dilemma: examining the social issues at stake. *Journal of Information Communication and Ethics in Society* 16 (3): 261–274.

Cheeseman, N. and de Gramont, D. (2017). Managing a mega-city: learning the lessons from Lagos. *Oxford Review of Economic Policy* 33 (3): 457–477.

Chen, M. and Beard, V.A. (2018). *Including the excluded: supporting informal workers for more equal and productive cities in the Global South.* Available at https://www.wri.org/research/including-excluded-supporting-informal-workers-more-equal-and-productive-cities-global. (Accessed 15 July 2022).

Chen, X. and Myers, G. (2013 December-January). China and Africa: the crucial urban connection. *European Financial Review,* 50–55.

Cheng, M. (2020 November 6). Uber's market value has just reached an all-time high. *Quartz,* Available at https://qz.com/1928990/ubers-market-cap-surpasses-its-ipo-valuation (Accessed 15 July 2022).

Cherif, R. and Hasanov, F. (2019). *The return of the policy that shall not be named: principles of industrial policy.* Available from https://www.imf.org/en/Publications/WP/Issues/2019/03/26/The-Return-of-the-Policy-That-Shall-Not-Be-Named-Principles-of-Industrial-Policy-46710: (Accessed 15 July 2022).

Cherunya, P.C., Ahlborg, H., and Truffer, B. (2020). Anchoring innovations in oscillating domestic spaces: why sanitation service offerings fail in informal settlements. *Research Policy* 49 (1): 103841.

Chitengi, H.S. (2018). Regulations and housing informality in African cities: appropriating regulatory frameworks to factors that influence resilience. *Housing and Society* 45 (1): 14–41.

The Citizen. (2016). *Govt halts building of Bagamoyo Port.* https://www.thecitizen.co.tz/News/Govt-halts-building-of-Bagamoyo-Port/1840340-3025392-adiuyf/index.html. (Accessed 25 May 2023).

Choi, J., Dutz, M., and Usman, Z., (eds.) (2020). *The Future of Work in Africa: Harnessing the Potential of Digital Technologies for All.* Washington: Agence Francaise de Development and World Bank.

Choplin, A. and Franck, A. (2010). A glimpse of Dubai in Khartoum and Nouakchott, Prestige Urban projects on the margins of the Arab world. *Built Environment* 36: 64–77.

Christaller, W. (1966 [1933]). *Central Places in Southern Germany*. Englewood Cliffs: Prentice Hall.

Christley, E., Ljungberg, H., Ackom, E., and Nerini, F.F. (2021). Sustainable energy for slums? using the sustainable development goals to guide energy access efforts in a Kenyan informal settlement. *Energy Research and Social Science* 79: 102176.

Cilliers, J. (2018). Made in Africa: manufacturing and the fourth industrial revolution. *Africa in the World Report 8*, Institute for Security Studies.

Cirolia, L.R. (2020). Fractured fiscal authority and fragmented infrastructures: financing sustainable urban development in Sub-Saharan Africa. *Habitat International* 104: 102233.

Cissé, D. (2013). South-South migration and Sino-African small traders: a comparative study of Chinese in Senegal and Africans in China. *African Review of Economics and Finance* 5 (1): 17–28.

Cissé, D. (2021). *As migration and trade increase between China and Africa, traders at both ends often face precarity*. Washington DC: Migration Policy Institute (MPI). Available at https://www.migrationpolicy.org/article/migration-trade-china-africa-traders-face-precarity (Accessed 10 July 2022).

City of Cape Town and Western Cape Government (CoCT and WCP) (2012). *OneCape 2040: The Western Cape Agenda for Joint Action on Economic Development*. Cape Town: City of Cape Town and Western Cape Government.

Clark, D. (2019). Deindustrialization of Sub-Saharan Africa. *Global Economy Journal* 19 (2): 1950001.

Clémens, R. (1955). Le développment des sciences sociales et le Congo Belge. *CEPSI Bulletin* 31: 87–99.

Cobbinah, P.B., Asibey, M.O., Boakye, A.A., and Addaney, M. (2022). The myth of urban poor climate adaptation idiosyncrasy. *Environmental Science and Policy* 128: 336–346.

Cobbinah, P.B., Asibey, M.O., Opoku-Gyamfi, M., and Peprah, C. (2019). Urban planning and climate change in Ghana. *Journal of Urban Management* 8 (2): 261–271.

Cobbinah, P.B., Asibey, M.O., Zuneidu, M.A., and Erdiaw-Kwasie, M.O. (2021). Accommodating green spaces in cities: perceptions and attitudes in slums. *Cities* 111: 103094.

Cochrane, P. (2021) Dubai, the Business capital of Africa. *Middle East Eye*, Available at https://www.middleeasteye.net/news/uae-dubai-africa-business-capital (Accessed 15 July 2022).

Coe, N., Hess, M., Yeung, H.W.C. et al. (2004). Globalizing regional development: a global production networks perspective. *Transactions of the Institute of British Geographers* 29 (4): 468–484.

Coenen, L., Benneworth, P., and Truffer, B. (2012). Toward a spatial perspective on sustainability transitions. *Research Policy* 41 (6): 968–979.

Collins, T. (2021 March 10). Flutterwave becomes Africa's fourth $1bn unicorn. *African Business*, Available at https://african.business/2021/03/technology-informa tion/flutterwave-becomes-africas-fourth-1bn-unicorn (Accessed 15 July 2022).

Cook, K.H., Fitzpatrick, R.G., Liu, W., and Vizy, E.K. (2020). Seasonal asymmetry of equatorial East African rainfall projections: understanding differences between the response of the long rains and the short rains to increased greenhouse gases. *Climate Dynamics* 55 (7): 1759–1777.

Cooke, P. (2017). Complex spaces: global innovation networks and territorial innovation systems in information and communication technologies. *Journal of Open Innovation: Technology, Market, and Complexity* 3 (1): 1–23.

Cooper, A., Mukonza, C., Fisher, E. et al. (2020). Mapping academic literature on governing inclusive green growth in Africa: geographical biases and topical gaps. *Sustainability* 12 (5): 1956–1968.

Cooper, V. and Paton, K. (2021). Accumulation by repossession: the political economy of evictions under austerity. *Urban Geography* 42 (5): 583–602.

Corsni, L. and Moultrie, J. (2021). Distributed manufacturing and COVID-19: is crisis a window of opportunity for sustainable development in the Global South? *Strategic Design and Research Journal* 14 (1): 224–235.

Côté-Roy, L. and Moser, S. (2019). Does Africa not deserve shiny new cities? The power of seductive rhetoric around new cities in Africa. *Urban Studies* 56 (12): 2391–2407.

Coupez, A. (2017). *Sharing economy: a drive to success - The case of GO-JEK in Jakarta, Indonesia*. (Master's Thesis, Université Catholique de Louvain, Louvain).

Coutard, O. (ed.) (2002). *The Governance of Large Technical Systems*. London: Routledge.

Coutard, O. (2008). Placing splintering urbanism: introduction. *Geoforum* 39 (6): 1815–1820.

Coward, M. (2009). *Urbicide: The Politics of Urban Destruction*. London: Routledge.

Cramer, C. (2006). *Civil War Is Not a Stupid Thing*. London: Hurst.

Cramer, C., Oqubay, A., and Sender, J. (2020). *African Economic Development: Theory, Policy, Evidence*. Oxford and New York: Oxford University Press.

Crankshaw, O. (2014). Causal mechanisms, job search and the labour market spatial mismatch: a realist criticism of the neo-positivist method. *Journal of Critical Realism* 13 (5): 498–519.

Croese, S. (2016). *Urban governance and turning African cities around: Luanda case study*. Partnership for African Social and Governance Research Working Paper No. 018, Kenya: Nairobi.

Croese, S. (2018). Global urban policymaking in Africa: a view from Angola through the redevelopment of the Bay of Luanda. *International Journal of Urban and Regional Research* 42 (2): 198–209.

Cross, J. (2010). Neoliberalism as unexceptional: economic zones and the everyday precariousness of working life in South India. *Critique of Anthropology* 30 (4): 355–373.

Cugurullo, F. (2021). *Frankenstein Urbanism: Eco, Smart and Autonomous Cities, Artificial Intelligence and the End of the City*. London: Routledge.

Dahir, A. (2019 June 10). China's aid to African leaders' home regions nearly tripled after they assumed power. *Quartz Africa*, Available at https://qz.com/africa/1639750/chinas-aid-to-africa-favors-political-leaders-home-regions. (Accessed 15 July 2022).

Dalakoglou, D. (2016). Infrastructural gap: commons, state and anthropology. *City* 20 (6): 822–831.

Dano, Z. (2018 April 24). Uber driver shot three times by passengers. *Cape Argus*, Available at from https://iol.co.za/capeargus (Accessed 15 July 2022).

Das Nair, R., Chisoro, S., and Ziba, F. (2018). The implications for suppliers of the spread of supermarkets in southern Africa. *Development Southern Africa* 35 (3): 334–350.

Daum, K., Stoler, J., and Grant, R. (2017). Towards a more sustainable trajectory of e-waste: a review of a decade of research in Accra, Ghana. *International Journal of Environmental Research and Public Health* 14 (2): 135.

Davies, A., Hooks, G., Knox-Hayes, J., and Liévanos, R.S. (2020). Riskscapes and the socio-spatial challenges of climate change. *Cambridge Journal of Regions, Economy and Society* 13 (2): 197–213.

Davis, M. and Monk, D.B. (2007). *Evil Paradises: Dreamworlds of Neoliberalism*. New York and London: New Press.

Davis, J.C., and Henderson, J. V. (2003). Evidence on the political economy of the urbanization process. *Journal of Urban Economics* 53(1): 98–125.

de Bercegol, R. and Monstadt, J. (2018). The Kenya slum electrification program. Local politics of electricity networks in Kibera. *Energy Research and Social Science* 41: 249–258.

De Greef, K. (2018 September 12). Driving for Uber when you can't afford a car: in South Africa, extreme inequality means that drivers have a much more difficult time turning a profit with side-share service. *The Atlantic*, Available at https://www.theatlantic.com/business/archive/2018/09/uber-south-africa/567979 (Accessed 15 July 2022).

de Villiers, J. (2018 October 5). Uber drivers earn far less per trip than Taxify drivers in SA - here's how they compare, *Business Insider South Africa*, Available at https://www.businessinsider.co.za/how-uber-prices-compare-to-taxify-in-south-africa-2018-10 (Accessed 15 July 2022).

Death, C. (2014). The green economy in South Africa: global discourses and local politics. *Politikon* 41 (1): 1–22.

Death, C. (2015). Four discourses of the green economy in the Global South. *Third World Quarterly* 36 (12): 2207–2224.

DeLanda, M. (2006). *A New Philosophy of Society. Assemblage Theory and Social Complexity*. New York: Continuum.

Deleuze, G. and Guattari, F. (1988). *A Thousand Plateaus: Capitalism and Schizophrenia*. London: Bloomsbury Publishing.

Denton, F.G., Nkem, F.J., Bombande, M. et al. (2021). *Bridges of opportunity: partnering for Africa–Europe green development*. UNU-INRA, Available at http://collections.unu.edu/eserv/UNU:8127/GREAT_Pathways_____Discussion_Paper_July2021_4_.pdf (Accessed 15 July 2022).

Department of Trade and Industry, Chief, African Integration & Industrial Development, Interview with Gwynne-Evans, N. conducted by Pádraig Carmody, Cape Town, 6th of August, 2018.

Dias, M. (2021). Centralized clientelism, real estate development and economic crisis: the case of postwar Luanda. *African Geographical Review* 40 (3): 309–323.

Diawara, B. and Hanson, K. (2019). What does the evidence say about contemporary China-Africa relations? In: *Innovating South-South Cooperation: Policies, Challenges and Prospect* (ed. H. Beseda, E. Tok, and L. McMillan Polonenko), 217–242. Ottawa: University of Ottawa Press.

Disney, S.M. and Towill, D.R. (2003). The effect of vendor managed inventory (VMI) dynamics on the Bullwhip effect in supply chains. *International Journal of Production Economics* 85 (2): 199–215.

Dittgen, R. and Chungu, G. (2019). (Un)writing "Chinese Space" in urban Africa. of city-making, lived experiences and entangled processes. *China Perspectives* 4: 4–16.

Dittgen, R. and Chungu, G. (2023). A 'Chinese' street (un)scripted and (re)imagined, *Africa Development* 48 (1): 113–140.

Dixit, F., Barbeau, B., Mostafavi, S.G., and Mohseni, M. (2019). PFOA and PFOS removal by ion exchange for water reuse and drinking applications: role of organic matter characteristics. *Environmental Science: Water Research and Technology* 5 (10): 1782–1795.

Dobler, G. (2008). From Scotch whisky to Chinese sneakers: international commodity flows and new trade networks in Oshikango, Namibia. *Africa* 78 (3): 410–432.

Dobler, G. (2009). Solidarity, xenophobia and regulation of Chinese businesses in Oshikango, Namibia. In: *China Returns to Africa* (ed. C. Alden, D. Large, and R. Soares de Oliveira), 237–255. London: Hurst.

Dobson, J. (2017 April 6). Making sense of the global infrastructure turn. *The Conversation*, Available at https://theconversation.com/making-sense-of-the-global-infrastructure-turn-73853 (Accessed 15 July 2022).

Doe, B., Peprah, C., and Chidziwisano, J.R. (2020). Sustainability of slum upgrading interventions: perception of low-income households in Malawi and Ghana. *Cities* 107: 102946.

Dos Santos, S., Peumi, J.P., and Soura, A. (2019). Risk factors of becoming a disaster victim. The flood of September 1st, 2009, in Ouagadougou (Burkina Faso). *Habitat International* 86: 81–90.

Doshi, R. (2021). *The Long Game: China's Grand Strategy to Displace American Order.* Oxford and New York: Oxford University Press.

Dosso, M., Kleibrink, A., and Matusiak, M. (2022). Smart specialisation strategies in sub-Saharan Africa: opportunities, challenges and initial mapping for Côte d'Ivoire. *African Journal of Science, Technology, Innovation and Development* 14 (1): 121–134.

Dougherty, D. (2012). The maker movement. *Innovations: Technology, Governance, Globalization* 7 (3): 11–14.

Dube, K., Nhamo, G., and Chikodzi, D. (2022). Flooding trends and their impacts on coastal communities of Western Cape Province, South Africa. *GeoJournal* 87: 453–468.

Duranton, G. (2015). Growing through cities in developing countries. *The World Bank Research Observer* 30 (1): 39–73.

Duranton, G. and Puga, D. (2004). Micro-foundations of urban agglomeration economies. In: *Handbook of Regional and Urban Economics*, vol. 4 (ed. J.V. Henderson and J.-F. Thisse). Amsterdam: Elsevier.

The Durban Edge (2023). *Are we really improving Ethekwini's revenue collection by investing in public infrastructure*. Available at https://opencitieslab.gitbook.io/durban-edge-infrastructure-and-revenue (Accessed 13 March 2023).

Echendu, A. and Georgeou, N. (2021). 'Not going to plan': urban planning, flooding, and sustainability in port harcourt city, Nigeria. *Urban Forum* 32 (3): 311–332.

Echendu, A.J. (2022). Flooding in Nigeria and Ghana: opportunities for partnerships in disaster-risk reduction. *Sustainability: Science, Practice and Policy* 18 (1): 1–15.

The Economist (2021 December 9). *America worries about China's military ambitions in Africa*. Available at https://www.economist.com/china/2021/12/09/america-worries-about-chinas-military-ambitions-in-africa (Accessed 16 July 2022).

The Economist (2023). *The growth of Africa's towns and small cities is transforming the continent*. Available at https://www.economist.com/middle-east-and-africa/2023/03/09/the-growth-of-africas-towns-and-small-cities-is-transforming-the-continent?utm_source=substack&utm_medium=email (Accessed 9 March 2023).

Edwards, L. and Jenkins, R. (2014). The margins of export competition: a new approach to evaluating the impact of China on South African exports to Sub-Saharan Africa. *Journal of Policy Modeling* 36: S132–S150.

Ekbia, H.R. and Nardi, B.A. (2017). *Heteromation, and Other Stories of Computing and Capitalism*. Cambridge: MIT Press.

Ekekwe, N. (2015). Africa's maker movement offers opportunity for growth. *Harvard Business Review* 29.

Environmental Justice Atlas (2020). *Hazardous e-waste recycling in Agbogbloshie*. Accra, Ghana: Available https://ejatlas.org/conflict/agbogbloshie-e-waste-landfill-ghana (Accessed 12 January 2021).

Ezeh, G.C., Abiye, O.E., and Obioh, I.B. (2017). Elemental analyses and source apportionment of PM2. 5 and PM2. 5–10 aerosols from Nigerian urban cities. *Cogent Environmental Science* 3 (1): 1323376.

Faccer, K., Nahman, A., and Audouin, M. (2014). Interpreting the green economy: emerging discourses and their considerations for the Global South. *Development Southern Africa* 31 (5): 642–657.

Fairwork Foundation (2021). *Ratings: South Africa*. Available at https://fair.work/en/ratings/south-africa (Accessed 15 July 2022).

Falchetta, G., Gernaat, D.E.H.J., Hunt, J., and Sterl, S. (2019). Hydropower dependency and climate change in sub-Saharan Africa: a nexus framework and evidence-based review. *Journal of Cleaner Production* 231: 1399–1417.

Fält, L. (2019). New cities and the emergence of 'privatized Urbanism' in Ghana. *Built Environment* 44 (4): 438–460.

Farmer, P. (2020). *Fevers, Feuds and Diamonds: Ebola and the Ravages of History*. New York: Farrar, Staus and Giroux.

Farole, T. (2011). *Special Economic Zones in Africa: Comparing Performance and Learning from Global Experiences*. Washington: World Bank.

Fei, D. and Liao, C. (2020). Chinese Eastern industrial zone in Ethiopia: unpacking the enclave. *Third World Quarterly* 41 (4): 623–644.

Fevrier, K. (2022). Informal waste recycling economies in the Global South and the chimera of green capitalism. *Antipode* 1–22. https://doi.org/10.1111/anti.12841.

Financial Times. (2022). *Covid-19 vaccine tracker: the global race to vaccinate*. https://ig.ft.com/coronavirus-vaccine-tracker/?areas=gbr&areas=isr&areas=usa&areas=eue&areas=are&areas=chn&areas=chl&cumulative=1&doses=total&populationAdjusted=1. (Accessed 25 May 2023).

Florida, R.L. (2002). *The Rise of Rhe Creative Class: And How It's Transforming Work, Leisure, Community and Everyday Life*. New York: Basic Books.

Fosu, A.K. (2015). Growth, inequality and poverty in Sub-Saharan Africa: recent progress in a global context. *Oxford Development Studies* 43 (1): 44–59.

Foucault, M. (1984 October). Of other spaces: utopias and heterotopias. *Architecture /Mouvement/ Continuité*, Available at http://web.mit.edu/allanmc/www/foucault1.pdf (Accessed 16 July 2022).

Foucault, M. and Senellart, M. (2008). *The Birth of Biopolitics: Lectures at the College de France, 1978-79*. Basingstoke: Palgrave Macmillan.

Fox, L., Thomas, A., and Haines, C. (2017). Structural transformation in employment and productivity: what can Africa hope for?. *IMF Departmental Paper No. 17/02*.

Fox, S. and Goodfellow, T. (2022). On the conditions of 'late urbanisation'. *Urban Studies* 59 (10): 1959–1980.

Frantzeskaki, N., Broto, V.C., Coenen, L., and Loorbach, D., (eds.) (2017). *Urban Sustainability Transitions*. Oxford: Taylor and Francis.

Franzsen, R. and McCluskey, W. (2017). *Property Tax in Africa*. Cambridge, MA: Lincoln Institute of Land Policy.

Fraser, A., Leck, H., Parnell, S., and Pelling, M. (2017). Africa's urban risk and resilience. *International Journal of Disaster Risk Reduction* 26: 1–6.

Freire, M.E., Lall, S., and Leipziger, D. (2014). *Africa's urbanisation: challenges and opportunities*. The Growth Dialogue, Washington D.C., Working Paper No. 7. Available at http://www.growthdialogue.org/sites/default/files/documents/GD_WP7_web_8.5×11%20(3).pdf (Accessed 15 July 2022).

Frenken, K., Van Oort, F., and Verburg, T. (2007). Related variety, unrelated variety and regional economic growth. *Regional Studies* 41 (5): 685–697.

Frick, S.A. and Rodríguez-Pose, A. (2019). Are special economic zones in emerging countries a catalyst for the growth of surrounding areas? *Transnational Corporations Journal* 26 (2): 75–94.

Frick, S.A. and Rodríguez-Pose, A. (2022). Special economic zones and sourcing linkages with the local economy: reality or pipedream? *The European Journal of Development Research* 34 (2): 655–676.

Frick-Trzebitzky, F., Baghel, R., and Bruns, A. (2017). Institutional bricolage and the production of vulnerability to floods in an urbanising delta in Accra. *International Journal of Disaster Risk Reduction* 26: 57–68.

Friedman, T.L. (2005). *The World is Flat: A Brief History of the Globalized World in the Twenty-First Century*. London: Allen Lane.

FTWonline (2017). '*Green light for Western Cape green tech sector SEZ*. http://www.ftwon line.co.za/article/124543/Green-light-for-Western-Cape-green-tech-sector-SEZ. (Accessed 1 May 2018).

Fu, X. (2020). *Innovation under the Radar: The Nature and Sources of Innovation in Africa.* Cambridge: Cambridge University Press.

Furlong, K. (2014). STS beyond the "modern infrastructure ideal": extending theory by engaging with infrastructure challenges in the South. *Technology in Society* 38: 139–147.

Galtung, J. (1969). Violence, peace, and peace research. *Journal of Peace Research* 6 (3): 167–191.

Garthwaite, J. (2021). The shifting burden of wildfires in the United States. *Stanford News*. https://news.stanford.edu/2021/01/12/shifting-burden-wildfires-united-states. (Accessed 25 May 2023).

Gastrow, C. (2017). Cement citizens: housing, demolition and political belonging in Luanda, Angola. *Citizenship Studies* 21 (2): 224–239.

Gedye, A. (2015 February 20). Uber's SA competitors cry foul. *South African Institute of Taxation*, Available at https://www.thesait.org.za/news/217498/Ubers-SA-competi tors-cry-foul-.htm (Accessed 15 July 2022).

Geels, F.W. (2002). Technological transitions as evolutionary reconfiguration processes: a multi-level perspective and a case-study. *Research Policy* 31 (8–9): 1257–1274.

Geels, F.W. (2004). Understanding system innovations: a critical literature review and a conceptual synthesis'. In: *System Innovation and the Transition to Sustainability: Theory, Evidence and Policy* (ed. B. Elzen, F. Geels, and K. Green), 19–47. Cheltenham: Edward Elgar.

Geels, F.W. (2005). The dynamics of transitions in socio-technical systems: a multi-level analysis of the transition pathway from horse-drawn carriages to automobiles (1860–1930). *Technology Analysis and Strategic Management* 17 (4): 445–476.

Geels, F.W. and Schot, J. (2007). Typology of sociotechnical transition pathways. *Research Policy* 36 (3): 399–417.

Geitung, I. (2017). *Uber drivers in Cape Town: working conditions and worker agency in the sharing economy.* (Master's thesis). University of Oslo, Available at https://www.duo.uio.no/handle/10852/60423 (Accessed 15 July 2022).

Genus, A. and Coles, A.M. (2008). Rethinking the multi-level perspective of technological transitions. *Research Policy* 37 (9): 1436–1445.

Georgeson, L., Maslin, M., and Poessinouw, M. (2017). The global green economy: a review of concepts, definitions, measurement methodologies and their interactions. *Geo: Geography and Environment* 4 (1): e00036.

Gereffi, G. (2018). Protectionism and global value chains. In: *Global Value Chains and Development: Redefining the Contours of 21st Century Capitalism*, 429–452. Cambridge: Cambridge University Press.

Giannecchini, P. and Taylor, I. (2018). The eastern industrial zone in Ethiopia: catalyst for development? *Geoforum* 88: 28–35.

Giddy, J.K. (2019). The influence of e-hailing apps on urban mobilities in South Africa. *African Geographical Review* 38 (3): 227–239.

Gillespie, T. (2017). From quiet to bold encroachment: contesting dispossession in Accra's informal sector. *Urban Geography* 38 (7): 974–992.

Gillespie, T. and Schindler, S. (2022). Africa's new urban spaces: deindustrialisation, infrastructure-led development and real estate frontiers. In *Review of African Political Economy* 49 (174): 531–549.

GIZ (2019). *Access to Water and Sanitation in Sub-Saharan Africa*. Bonn: Deutsche Gesellschaft für Internationale Zusammenarbeit (GIZ).

Glaeser, E. (2013). *A world of cities: the causes and consequences of urbanisation in poorer countries*. Working Paper 19745, National Bureau of Economics Research, Available at https://www.nber.org/papers/w19745 (Accessed 15 July 2022).

Gleeson, B. and Low, N. (2000). Revaluing planning: rolling back neo-liberalism in Australia'. *Progress in Planning* 53 (2): 83–164.

Global Property Guide (2014). *Nigeria*. Available at http://www.globalpropertyguide.com/Africa/Nigeria (Accessed 15 July 2022).

Goetz, A. (2019). China and Africa: somewhere between economic integration and cooperative exploitation. In: *Innovating South-South Cooperation: Policies, Challenges and Prospects* (ed. E.T.H. Beseda and L. McMillan Polonenko), 173–216. Ottawa: University of Ottawa Press.

Gollin, D., Jedwab, R., and Vollrath, D. (2016). Urbanisation with and without industrialization. *Journal of Economic Growth* 21 (1): 35–70.

Gonsalves, M. and Rogerson, J.M. (2019). Business incubators and green technology. *Urbani Izziv* 30: 212–224.

Goodfellow, T. (2017). Urban fortunes and skeleton cityscapes: real estate and late urbanization in Kigali and Addis Ababa. *International Journal of Urban and Regional Research* 41 (5): 786–803.

Goodfellow, T. (2018). Seeing political settlements through the city: a framework for comparative analysis of urban transformation. *Development and Change* 49 (1): 199–222.

Goodfellow, T. (2020). Finance, infrastructure and urban capital: the political economy of African 'gap-filling'. *Review of African Political Economy* 47 (164): 256–274.

Goodfellow, T. (2022). *Politics and the Urban Frontier: Transformation and Divergence in Late Urbanizing East Africa*. Oxford and New York: Oxford University Press.

Goodfellow, T. and Huang, Z.L. (2021). Contingent infrastructure and the dilution of "Chineseness": reframing roads and rail in Kampala and Addis Ababa. *Environment and Planning A-Economy and Space* 53 (4): 655–674.

Gorham, R., Eijbergen, J., and Kumar, A. (2017 August 11). Lagos shows Africa the way forward (again). *World Bank Transport Blog*, Available at https://blogs.worldbank.org/transport/urban-transport-lagos-shows-africa-way-forward-again (Accessed 15 July 2022).

Government of Sierra Leone (2021 November). *FY 2022 Budget at a Glance*. Freetown: Ministry of Finance.

Government of South Africa (2011). *South Africa's green economy accord*. Available at https://www.gov.za/south-africas-green-economy-accord (Accessed 15 July 2022).

Graham, M. and Anwar, M.A. (2018). Two models for a fairer sharing economy. In: *The Cambridge Handbook of the Law of the Sharing Economy* (ed. N. Davidson, M. Finck, and J. Infranca), 328–340. Cambridge and New York: Cambridge University Press.

Graham, M., Hjorth, I., and Lehdonvirta, V. (2017). Digital labour and development: impacts of global digital labour platforms and the gig economy on worker livelihoods. *Transfer-European Review of Labour and Research* 23 (2): 135–162.

Graham, S. and Marvin, S. (2001). *Splintering Urbanism: Networked Infrastructures, Technological Mobilities and the Urban Condition*. Oxford: Psychology Press.

Grant, R. (2006). Out of place? Global citizen in local spaces: a study of the informal settlements in the Korle Lagoon environs in Accra, Ghana. *Urban Forum* 17 (1): 1–24.

Grant, R. (2009). *Globalizing City: The Urban and Economic Transformation of Accra, Ghana*. Syracuse: Syracuse University Press.

Grant, R. (2010). Working it out: labour geographies of the poor in Soweto, South Africa. *Development Southern Africa* 27 (4): 595–612.

Grant, R. (2015). *Africa: Geographies of Change*. Oxford and New York: Oxford University Press.

Grant, R., Carmody, P., and Murphy, J. (2020). South Africa's green transition? Sociotechnical experimentation in Atlantis special economic zone. *Journal of Modern African Studies* 58 (2): 189–211.

Grant, R. and Nijman, J. (2002). Globalisation and the corporate geography of cities in the lesser developed world. A comparative study of Accra and Mumbai. *Annals of the Association of American Geographers* 92 (2): 320–340.

Grant, R. and Nijman, J. (2004). The rescaling of uneven development in Ghana and India. *Tidjschrift voor Economishe En Sociale Geografie* 95 (5): 467–481.

Grant, R. and Oteng-Ababio, M. (2016). The global transformation of materials and the emergence of informal urban mining in Accra, Ghana. *Africa Today* 62 (4): 3–20.

Grant, R. and Oteng-Ababio, M. (2021). Formalising e-waste in Ghana: an emerging landscape of fragmentation and enduring barriers. *Development Southern Africa* 38 (1): 73–86.

Grant, R. and Thompson, D. (2014). City on edge: immigrant businesses and the right to the city in inner-city Johannesburg. *Urban Geography* 36 (2): 181–200.

Great Green Wall Organisation (2022). *The great green wall*. Available at https://www.greatgreenwall.org/about-great-green-wall (Accessed 15 July 2022).

GreenCape (2015). *Atlantis SEZ: Industrial Symbiosis Approach: Opportunities Identified*. Cape Town: GreenCape.

GreenCape. (2018). Project Executive and Project Officer, interview by Pádraig Carmody and Richard Grant, 18th of July, Cape Town.

GreenCape (2019). *Atlantis special economic zone for green technologies: annual report 2018/19*. Available at https://www.greencape.co.za/assets/Atlantis_SEZ_single_FA_webl.pdf (Accessed 15 July 2022).

Grossman, S. (2021). *The Politics of Order in Informal Markets: How the State Shapes Private Governance*. Cambridge: Cambridge University Press.

The Guardian (2020 December 21). *Punches thrown in Ghanaian parliament over electronic payment taxes*. Available at https://www.theguardian.com/world/2021/dec/21/punch es-thrown-ghana-parliament-electronic-payments-tax (Accessed 16 July 2022).

Guma, P. and Monstadt, J. (2021). Smart city making? the spread of ICT-driven plans and infrastructures in Nairobi. *Urban Geography* 43 (3): 360–381.

Gutkind, P.C. (1989). The canoemen of the gold coast (Ghana): a survey and an exploration in precolonial African labour history (Les piroguiers de la Côte de l'Or (Ghana): enquête et recherche d'histoire du travail en Afrique précoloniale). *Cahiers d'Études Africaines* XXIX (3–4): 339–376.

Guven, M., Jain, H., and Joubert, C. (2021). *Social protection for the informal economy*. Washington: World Bank. Available at https://openknowledge.worldbank.org/ handle/10986/36584 (Accessed 15 July 2022).

Guven, M. and Karlen, R. (2020). Supporting Africa's urban informal sector: coordinated policies with social protection at the core. *World Bank Blogs: Africa Can End Poverty* 3.

Hägerstrand, T. (1970). What about people in regional science? *Papers of the Regional Science Association* 24: 7–21.

Hallward-Driemeier, M. and Nayyar, G. (2018). *Trouble in the Making? the Future of Manufacturing-Led Development*. Washington: World Bank Group.

Han, A. and Freymann, E. (2021 January 6). Coronavirus hasn't killed Belt and Road. *Foreign Policy*, Available at https://foreignpolicy.com/2021/01/06/coronavirus-hasnt-killed-belt-and-road (Accessed 15 July 2022).

Hancock, T. (2017 August 28). Chinese return from Africa as migrant population peaks. *Financial Times*.

Hansen, K.T. and Vaa, M., (eds.) (2004). *Reconsidering Informality: Perspectives from Urban Africa*. Uppsala: Nordic Africa Institute.

Hardy, J. (1998). Cathedrals in the desert? transnationals, corporate strategy and locality in Wroclaw. *Regional Studies* 32 (7): 639–652.

Harrabin, R. (2021 November 2). *COP26: leaders agree global plan to boost green technology*. BBC, Available at https://www.bbc.com/news/science-environment-59138622 (Accessed 16 July 2022).

Harrison, P. and Yang, Y. (2015 December 9). Chinese urbanism in Africa. *Cityscapes*, Available at https://www.cityscapesdigital.net/2015/12/09/chinese-urbanism-africa (Accessed 2 March 2017).

Hart, G. (2002). *Disabling Globalisation: Places of Power in Post-apartheid South Africa*. Berkeley: University of California Press.

Hart, G. (2018). Relational comparison revisited: Marxist postcolonial geographies in practice. *Progress in Human Geography* 42 (3): 371–394.

Hart, K. (1973). Informal income opportunities and urban employment in Ghana. *The Journal of Modern African Studies* 11 (1): 61–89.

Hart, S.L. and Christensen, C.M. (2002). The great leap: driving innovation from the base of the pyramid. *MIT Sloan Management Review* 44 (1): 51.

Harvey, D. (1973). *Social Justice and the City*. London: Edward Arnold.

Harvey, D. (1989). From managerialism to entrepreneurialism: the transformation in urban governance in late capitalism. *Geografiska Annaler: Series B, Human Geography* 71 (1): 3–17.

Harvey, D. (2005). *Spaces of Neoliberalization: Towards a Theory of Uneven Geographical Development*. Stuttgart: Franz Steiner Verlag.

Harvey, D. (2008). The right to the city. *The New Left Review* 6 (1): 23–40.

Haugen, H.Ø. and Carling, J. (2005). On the edge of the Chinese diaspora: the surge of *baihuo* business in an African city. *Ethnic and Racial Studies* 28 (4): 639–662.

He, Y., Thies, S., Avner, P., and Rentschler, J. (2021). Flood impacts on urban transit and accessibility—A case study of Kinshasa. *Transportation Research Part D: Transport and Environment* 96: 102889.

Heeks, R. (2021). From digital divide to digital justice in the Global South: conceptualising adverse digital incorporation. *Proceedings of the 1st Virtual Conference on the Implications of Information and Digital Technologies for Development*, Available at https://papers.ssrn.com/sol3/papers.cfm?abstract_id=3907633 (Accessed 15 July 2022).

Herod, A. (2018). *Labor*. Cambridge: Polity.

Heron, T. (2008). Globalisation, neoliberalism and the exercise of human agency. *International Journal of Politics, Culture and Society* 20 (1–4): 85–101.

Herrera, J., Kuépié, M., Nordman, C.J. et al. (2012). *Informal sector and informal employment: overview of data for 11 cities in 10 developing countries*. Cambridge: Women in the Informal Economy Globalizing and Organizing (WIEGO), Available at www.wiego.org/sites/wiego.org/files/publications/files/Herrera_WIEGO_WP9.pdf. (Accessed 15 July 2022).

Hickel, J., Sullivan, D., and Zoomkawala, H. (2021). Plunder in the post-colonial era: quantifying drain from the Global South through unequal exchange, 1960-2018. *New Political Economy* 26 (6): 1030–1047.

Hidalgo, C.A., Klinger, B., Barabasi, A.L., and Hausmann, R. (2007). The product space conditions the development of nations. *Science* 317 (5837): 482–487.

Hinkel, J., Brown, S., Exner, L. et al. (2012). Sea-level rise impacts on Africa and the effects of mitigation and adaptation: an application of DIVA. *Regional Environmental Change* 12 (1): 207–224.

Hlahla, S., Goebel, A., and Hill, T. (2016). *Green economy: a strategy to alleviate urban poverty and safeguard the environment?* KwaZulu-Natal, South Africa. Paper presented at the Urban Forum.

Hodson, M. and Marvin, S. (2010). Can cities shape socio-technical transitions and how would we know if they were? *Research Policy* 39 (4): 477–485.

Holt, D. and Littlewood, D. (2017). Waste livelihoods amongst the poor–Through the lens of bricolage. *Business Strategy and the Environment* 26 (2): 253–264.

Honan, E. (2016 August 5). Nairobi looks to Africa's first bike-share scheme to tackle congestion. *Financial Times*, Available at https://www.ft.com/content/6133a0f0-5a5b-11e6-8d05-4eaa66292c32 (Accessed 15 July 2022).

Hoornweg, D. and Pope, K. (2017). Population predictions of the world's largest cities in the 21st century. *Environment and Urbanisation* 29 (1): 195–216.

Horner, R. (2020). Towards a new paradigm of global development? beyond the limits of international development. *Progress in Human Geography* 44 (3): 415–436.

Horner, R. and Hulme, D. (2019). From international to global development: new geographies of 21st century development. *Development and Change* 50 (2): 347–378.

Hoselitz, B. (1955). Generative and parasitic cities. *Economic Development and Cultural Change* 3 (3): 278–294.

Huang, Z. and Chen, X. (2016 June 22). Is China building Africa? *European Financial Review*, Available from http://www.europeanfinancialreview.com/?p=6110 (Accessed 24 July 2017).

Hughes, T.P. (1987). The evolution of large technological systems. In: *The Social Construction of Technological Systems: New Directions in the Sociology and History of Technology* (ed. W.E. Bijker, T.P. Hughes, and T.J. Pinch), 51–82. Cambridge: MIT Press.

Hui, A., Schatzki, T., and Shove, E. (2017). *The Nexus of Practices: Connections, Constellations, Practitioners*. London, New York: Routledge.

Hunt, A. and Samman, E. (2020). Domestic work and the gig economy in South Africa: old wine in new bottles? *Anti-Trafficking Review* 15 (15): 102–121.

HWM (2019 November 1). Cape Town: how day zero was averted. *HWM Global*, Available at https://www.hwmglobal.com/blog/2019/11/01/cape-town-how-day-zero-was-averted (Accessed 15 July, 2022).

Iacob, N., Friederici, N., and Lachenmayer, J. (2019). Operationalising relational theory of entrepreneurial ecosystems at city-level in Africa, Asia and the Middle East. *Zeitschrift Für Wirtschaftsgeographie* 63 (2–4): 79–102.

Iazzolino, G. (2021). 'Going Karura': colliding subjectivities and labour struggle in Nairobi's gig economy. *Environment and Planning A: Economy and Space*, doi:Artn 03 08518×21103191610.1177/0308518×211031916.

Idris, J. and Fagbenro, A. (2019). Lagos the mega-city: a report on how the metropolis handled an outbreak of the Ebola epidemic, In: *Socio-cultural Dimensions of Emerging Infectious Diseases in Africa: An Indigenous Response to Deadly Epidemics* (ed. G.B. Tangwa, A. Abayomi, S.J. Ujewe, and N.S. Munung). Amsterdam: Springer: 281–298.

Inclusive Development International. (2021). Taking stock of the Belt and Road Initiative. *China Global Newsletter | Edition 3*, https://www.inclusivedevelopment.net/china-global-program/china-global-newsletter-edition-3 (Accessed 25 May 2023).

Interview with Wesgro Investment officer, by Richard Grant and Pádraig Carmody, Cape Town, 21st of June 2018.

Ismail, F. (2019). A developmental regionalism approach to the African Continental Free Trade Area (AfCTA). *Journal of Reviews on Global Economics* 8: 1771–1785.

Jackson, T. (2014). Employment in Chinese MNEs: appraising the dragon's gift to Sub-Saharan Africa. *Human Resource Management* 53 (6): 897–919.

Jacobs, J. (1969). *The Economy of Cities*. New York: Random House.

Jacobsen, M. (2021). Co-producing urban transport systems: adapting a global model in Dar es Salaam. *Sustainability: Science, Practice and Policy* 17 (1): 47–61.

Jaglin, S. (2008). Differentiating networked services in Cape Town: echoes of splintering urbanism? *Geoforum* 39 (6): 1897–1906.

Jayram, K., Kendall, A., Somers, K., et al. (2021) Africa's green manufacturing cross-roads: choices for a low-carbon industrial future. McKinsey Sustainability.

Jeffrey, C. and Dyson, J. (2013). Zigzag capitalism: youth entrepreneurship in the contemporary global South. *Geoforum* 49: R1–R3.

Jegede, O. and Jegede, O. (2018 November 22-25). Determinants of innovation capability in the informal settings. *Paper presented at the 8th International Conference on Appropriate Technology*, Songha Center, Porto-Novo, Benin, Available at https://repository. hsrc.ac.za/handle/20.500.11910/13162 (Accessed 15 July 2022).

Jenkins, R. (2019). *How China is Reshaping the Global Economy*. Oxford and New York: Oxford University Press.

Jenkins, R. and Edwards, L. (2015). Is China 'crowding out' South African exports of manufactures? *European Journal of Development Research* 25 (5): 903–920.

Jeppsen, S. and Kragelund, P. (2021). Beyond 'Africa rising': development policies and domestic market formation in Zambia. *Forum for Development Studies* 48 (3): 593–612.

Jepson, N. (2019). *In China's Wake: How the Commodity Boom Transformed Development Strategies in the Global South*. New York: Columbia University Press.

Jessop, B. (1997). The entrepreneurial city: re-imaging localities, redesigning economic governance, or restructuring capital? In: *Transforming Cities* (ed. N. Jewson and S. MacGregor), 28–41. London: Routledge.

Joelsson, I. (2021). Risky urban futures: the bridge, the fund and insurance in Dar es Salaam. In: *African Cities and Collaborative Futures: Urban Platforms and Metropolitan Logistics* (ed. M. Keith and A. de Sousa Santos). Manchester: Manchester University Press.

Johns Hopkins University SAIS China-Africa Research Initiative (2021). *Chinese FDI Flow to African Countries*. Available at http://www.sais-cari.org/chinese-investment-in-africa_international_trade_in_goods_statistics (Accessed 15 July 2022).

Johnson, A. (2016). Post-apartheid citizenship and the politics of evictions in inner city Johannesburg. *CUNY Academic Works*, https://academicworks.cuny.edu/gc_etds/1566 (Accessed 25 May 2022).

Jones, A. and Murphy, J.T. (2011). Theorizing practice in economic geography: foundations, challenges, and possibilities. *Progress in Human Geography* 35 (3): 366–392.

Jordan, L., Hoang, A.P., Chui, C.H.K. et al. (2021). Multiple precarity and intimate family life among African-Chinese families in Guangzhou. *Journal of Ethnic and Migration Studies* 47 (12): 2796–2814.

José Zapata Campos, M., Carenzo, S., Kain, J.-H. et al. (2021). Inclusive recycling movements: a green deep democracy from below. *Environment and Urbanisation* 33 (2): 579–598.

Kalleberg, A. (2018). *Precarious Lives: Job Insecurity and Well-Being in Rich Democracies*. Cambridge: Polity.

Kamais, C. (2019). Emerging security risks of e-hail transport services: focus on Uber taxi in Nairobi, Kenya. *International Journal of Security, Privacy and Trust Management* 8 (3): 1–18.

Kamau, P., Thomsen, L., and McCormick, D. (2019). Identifying entry barriers for food processors to supermarkets in Kenya. *Scientific African* 6: e00189.

Kamete, A.Y. (2018). Pernicious assimilation: reframing the integration of the urban informal economy in southern Africa. *Urban Geography* 39 (2): 167–189.

Kaplinsky, R. (2008). What does the rise of China do for industrialisation in Sub-Saharan Africa. *Review of African Political Economy* 35 (115): 7–22.

Kaplinsky, R. (2013). What contribution can China make to inclusive growth in Sub-Saharan Africa? *Development and Change* 44 (6): 1295–1316.

Kaplinsky, R. and Kraemer-Mbula, E. (2022). Innovation and uneven development: the challenge for low- and middle-income economies. *Research Policy* 51 (2): 104394.

Kaplinsky, R. and Morris, M. (2016). Thinning and thickening: productive sector policies in the era of global value chains. *The European Journal of Development Research* 28 (4): 625–645.

Karaoguz, H. and Gurbuz, S. (2021). The political economy of Turkey-Africa relations. In: *Turkey in Africa: An Emerging Power?* (ed. E. Tepeciklioğlu and A. Tepeciklioğlu), 49–69. New York: Routledge.

Kazeem, Y. (2016). *Lagos is Africa's 7th largest economy and is about to get bigger with its first oil finds*. Quartz Africa, https://qz.com/africa/676819/lagos-is-africas-7th-largest-economy-and-is-about-to-get-bigger-with-its-first-oil-finds%23:~:text=But%20Lagos'%20success%20looks%20even,the%20continent's%20most%20promising%20economies (Accessed 3 June 2022).

Kearney (2019). *The 2019 Kearney global services location index*. Available at https://www.kearney.com/digital/gsli/2019-full-report (Accessed 15 July, 2022).

Keith, M. and de Souza Santos, A. (2021). Introduction: urban presence and uncertain futures in African cities. In: *African Cities and Collaborative Futures: Urban Platforms and Metropolitan Logistics* (ed. M. Keith and A. de Souza Santos). Manchester: Manchester University Press.

Kelly, H. (2011). The classical definition of a pandemic is not elusive. *Bulletin of the World Health Organization* 89 (7): 540–541.

Kemp, R., Loorbach, D., and Rotmans, J. (2007). Transition management as a model for managing processes of co-evolution towards sustainable development. *The International Journal of Sustainable Development and World Ecology* 14 (1): 78–91.

Kemp, R., Schot, J., and Hoogma, R. (1998). Regime shifts to sustainability through processes of niche formation: the approach of strategic niche management. *Technology Analysis and Strategic Management* 10 (2): 175–198.

Keshodkar, A. (2014). Who needs China when you have Dubai? the role of networks and the engagement of Zanzibaris in transnational ocean trade. *Urban Anthropology and Studies of Cultural Systems and World Economic Development* 43 (1/2/3): 105–141.

Khan, M.H. (2010). *Political settlements and the governance of growth-enhancing institutions*, mimeo. Available at https://www.researchgate.net/profile/Mushtaq-Khan-8/publication/265567069_Political_Settlements_and_the_Governance_of_Growth-Enhancing_Institutions/links/55f0b96a08ae0af8ee1d2e05/Political-Settlements-and-the-Governance-of-Growth-Enhancing-Institutions.pdf (Accessed 15 July 2022).

Khan, M.H. (2018). Political settlements and the analysis of institutions. *African Affairs* 117 (469): 636–655.

Kiely, R. (2020). *The Conservative Challenge to Globalization*. Newcastle: Agenda.

Kilby, P. (1975). Manufacturing in colonial Africa. In: *Colonialism in Africa, 1870-1960* (ed. P. Duignan and L.H. Gann), 475–520. Cambridge: Cambridge University Press.

Kimani, N. (2007). *Environmental Pollution and Impact to Public Health: Implication of the Dandora Municipal Dumping Site in Nairobi, Kenya*. Nairobi: Kutoka Network.

Kinver, M. (2019 May 2) Then and now: when silence descended over Victoria Falls. *BBC*, Available at https://www.bbc.com/news/science-environment-56902340 (Accessed 15 July 2022).

Kirshner, J., Baker, L., Smith, A., and Bulkeley, H. (2019). A regime in the making? examining the geographies of solar PV electricity in Southern Africa. *Geoforum* 103: 114–125.

Kitimo, A. (2020 January 14) As Kenya SGR cargo volumes increase trucker jobs reduce. *The East African*, Available at https://www.theeastafrican.co.ke/tea/business/as-kenya-sgr-cargo-volumes-increase-trucker-jobs-reduce-1434776 (Accessed 25 June 2020).

Klopp, J.M. and Cavoli, C. (2019). Mapping minibuses in Maputo and Nairobi: engaging paratransit in transportation planning in African cities. *Transport Reviews* 39 (5): 657–676.

Köhler, J., Geels, F.W., Kern, F. et al. (2019). An agenda for sustainability transitions research: state of the art and future directions. *Environmental Innovation and Societal Transitions* 31: 1–32.

Kolawole, O. (2020 September 15). The gig economy is a big boost, but still a different story in Africa. *Techpoint.africa*, Available at https://techpoint.africa/2020/09/15/africa-gig-economy (Accessed 25 June 2020).

Koo, B.B., Rysankova, D., Portale, E. et al. (2018). *Rwanda beyond Connections: Energy Access Diagnostic Report Based on the Multi-Tier Framework*. Washington: World Bank.

Korah, P.I. (2020). Exploring the emergence and governance of new cities in Accra, Ghana. *Cities* 99: 102639.

Korah, P.I., Osborne, N., and Matthews, T. (2021). Enclave urbanism in Ghana's Greater Accra Region: examining the socio-spatial consequences. *Land Use Policy* 111: doi:ARTN10576710.1016/j.lusepol.2021.105767.

Kraemer-Mbula, E. and Monaco, L. (2020). Informality and innovation: an avenue towards bottom-up industrialisation for Africa? In: *Research Handbook on Development and the Informal Economy* (ed. J. Charmes), 363–386. Cheltenham: Edward Elgar Publishing.

Kuo, L. (2015 August 16). African cities are starting to look eerily like Chinese ones. *Quartz Africa*, Available from https://qz.com/480625/photos-african-cities-are-starting-to-look-eerily-like-chinese-ones (Accessed 2 March 2017).

Kuper, S. (2019 March 29). Life after climate change: lessons from Cape Town. *Financial Times*, Available at https://www.ft.com/content/7889cb6e-501f-11e9-9c76-bf4a0ce37d49 (Accessed 25 June 2020).

Kuuire, J. (2017 March 18). What happened to Hope City? *Tech Nova*, Available at https://technovagh.com/what-happened-to-hope-city (Accessed 25 June 2020).

Kuuire, J. (2021 August 3) Will Ghana's "Skytrain" ever get off the ground? *Tech Nova*, Available at https://technovagh.com/what-is-the-state-of-ghanas-skytrain-project (Accessed 25 June 2020).

Kwan, R. (2022 February 21) 'We want one disaster, not two': Tonga struggles to keep Covid at bay. *NBC News*, Available at https://www.nbcnews.com/news/world/tonga-corona virus-volcano-covid-tsunami-eruption-lockdown-rcna13158 (Accessed 25 June 2020).

Lall, S. and Kraemer-Mbula, E. (2005). *Industrial Competitiveness in Africa: Lessons from East Asia*. London: ITDG.

Lall, S.V., Henderson, J.V., and Venables, A. (2017). *Africa's Cities. Opening Doors to the World*. Washington D.C.: The World Bank.

Lampert, B., Tan-Mullins, M., Chang, D., and Mohan, G. (2014). *Chinese Migrants and Africa's Development: New Imperialists or Agents of Change?* London: Zed Books Ltd.

Landrum, N.E. (2007). Advancing the "base of the pyramid" debate. *Strategic Management Review* 1 (1): 1–12.

Larbi, M., Kellett, J., and Palazzo, E. (2021). Urban sustainability transitions in the Global South: a case study of curitiba and accra. *Urban Forum* https://doi.org/10.1007/s12132-021-09438-4.

Large, D. (2021). *China and Africa: The New Era*. Cambridge: Polity.

Larmer, M. (2021). *Living for the City: Social Change and Knowledge Production in the Central African Copperbelt*. Cambridge and New York: Cambridge University Press.

Larsen, T.A., Hoffmann, S., Lüthi, C. et al. (2016). Emerging solutions to the water challenges of an urbanizing world. *Science* 352 (6288): 928–933.

Larsson, C.W. and Svensson, J. (2018). Mobile phones in the transformation of the informal economy: stories from market women in Kampala, Uganda. *Journal of Eastern African Studies* 12 (3): 533–551.

Last, J.M. (2001). *A Dictionary of Epidemiology*, 4e. Oxford; New York: Oxford University Press.

Lawhon, M. and Murphy, J.T. (2012). Sociotechnical regimes and sustainability transitions: insightsfrom political ecology. *Progress in Human Geography* 36 (3): 354–378.

Lawhon, M., Nilsson, D., Silver, J. et al. (2018). Thinking through heterogeneous infrastructure configurations. *Urban Studies* 55 (4): 720–732.

Lawhon, M. and Truelove, Y. (2020). Disambiguating the southern urban critique: propositions, pathways and possibilities for a more global urban studies. *Urban Studies* 57 (1): 3–20.

Lawson, T. (1997). *Economics and Reality*. London: Routledge.

Lawson, T. (2003). *Reorienting Economics*. London: Psychology Press.

Lebbie, T., Moyebi, O., Asante, K. et al. (2021). E-Waste in Africa: a serious threat to the health of children. *International Journal of Environmental Research and Public Health* 18 (16): 8488.

Lederer, M., Wallbott, L., and Bauer, S. (2018). 'Tracing sustainability transformations and drivers of green economy approaches in the global South. *Journal of Environment and Development* 27 (1): 3–25.

Lee, C.K. (2009). Raw encounters: Chinese managers, African workers and the politics of casualization in Africa's Chinese enclaves. *China Quarterly* 199: 647–666.

Lee, M. (2014). *Africa's World Trade: Informal Economies and Globalisation from Below.* London: Zed Books.

Lefebvre, H. ([1970] 2003). *The Urban Revolution.* Minneapolis: University of Minnesota Press.

Leichenko, R.M., O'Brien, K.L., and Solecki, W.D. (2010). Climate change and the global financial crisis: a case of double exposure. *Annals of the Association of American Geographers* 100 (4): 963–972.

Leithead, A. (2017 August 21). The city that won't stop growing: how can Lagos cope with its spiraling population? *BBC,* Available at https://www.bbc.co.uk/news/resources/idt-sh/lagos (Accessed 6 January 2021).

Lemanski, C. (2020). Infrastructural citizenship: the everyday citizenships of adapting and/or destroying public infrastructure in cape town, South Africa. *Transactions of the Institute of British Geographers* 45 (3): 589–605.

Lesutis, G. (2021 November 8). Kenya's mega-railway project leaves society more unequal than before. *The Conversation* Available at https://theconversation.com/kenyas-mega-railway-project-leaves-society-more-unequal-than-before-170969 (Accessed 15 July 2022).

Levenson, Z. (2022). *Delivery as Dispossession: Land Occupation and Eviction in the Post-apartheid City.* Oxford and New York: Oxford University Press.

Lewis, J. (2021b). 4 factors causing Middle Eastern countries to become uninhabitable. *Earth.org,* Available at https://earth.org/factors-causing-middle-eastern-countries-to-become-uninhabitable. (Accessed 15 July 2022).

Lewis, S. (2021a October 12). 5 out of 7 tech unicorns in Africa come from fintech. *FINTECH News Africa,* Available at https://fintechnews.africa/40003/fintech-nigeria/tech-unicorns-in-africa-come-from-fintech (Accessed 15 July 2022).

Lin, J. (2012). *New Structural Economics: A Framework for Rethinking Development and Policy.* Washington: World Bank.

Lin, J.Y. and Xu, J. (2019). China's light manufacturing and Africa's industrialisation. In: *China-Africa and an Economic Transformation* (ed. O. Arkebbe and J.Y. Lin), 265–281. Oxford and New York: Oxford University Press.

Lindell, I. (2009). 'Glocal' movements: place struggles and transnational organizing by informal workers. *Geografiska Annaler: Series B Human Geography* 91 (2): 123–136.

Lijphart, A. (1971). Comparative Politics and the Comparative Method. *The American Political Science Review* 65 (3): 682–693.

Lindell, I., Ampaire, C., and Byerley, A. (2019). Governing urban informality: re-working spaces and subjects in Kampala, Uganda. *International Development Planning Review* 41 (1): 63–84.

Lipton, M. (1977). *Why Poor People Stay Poor: A Study of Urban Bias in World Development*. London: Temple Smith.

Litonjua, M.D. (2008). The socio-political construction of globalisation. *International Review of Modern Sociology* 34 (2): 53–278.

Little, P. (2019). Bodies, toxins, and e-waste labour interventions in Ghana: toward a toxic postcolonial corporality? *Revista de Antropologi´a Iberoamericana* 14 (1): 51–71.

Liu, W. and Dicken, P. (2006). Transnational corporations and 'obligated embeddedness': foreign direct investment in China's automobile industry. *Environment and Planning A* 38 (7): 1229–1247.

Liu, W., Zhang, Y., and Xiong, W. (2020). Financing the Belt and Road Initiative. *Eurasian Geography and Economics* 61 (2): 137–145.

Loembé, M.M. and Nkengasong, J.N. (2021). COVID-19 vaccine access in Africa: global distribution, vaccine platforms, and challenges ahead. *Immunity* 54 (7): 1353–1362.

Loiseau, E., Saikku, L., Antikainen, R. et al. (2016). Green economy and related concepts: an overview. *Journal of Cleaner Production* 139: 361–371.

Loorbach, D. (2007). Governance for sustainability. *Sustainability: Science, Practice and Policy* 3 (2): 1–4.

Lopes, C. (2019). *Africa in Transformation: Economic Development in the Age of Doubt*. London: Palgrave Macmillan.

Lopes, C. (2020). The birth of the African lions. In: *The Rise of the African Multinational Enterprise (AMNE): Management for Professionals* (ed. E. Amungo), 79–100. Geneva: Springer.

Lopes, C. and Willem te Velde, D. (2021). *Structural transformation, economic development and industrialization in post-Covid-19 Africa*. Available at https://www.ineteconomics.org/uploads/papers/Lopes-te-Velde-African-industrialisation.pdf (Accessed 15 July 2022).

Lösch, A. (1954 [1940]). *The Economics of Location*. New Haven: Yale University Press.

Lukacs, M. (2014 January 21). New, privatized African city heralds climate apartheid. *The Guardian*, Available at http://www.theguardian.com/environment/true-north/2014/jan/21/new-privatized-african-city-heralds-climate-apartheid (Accessed 15 July 2022).

Lukenangula, J.M. and Baumgart, S. (2020). Futures of urban transport beyond the car: walkability in Dar es Salaam, Tanzania. In: *Transport Planning and Mobility in Urban East Africa* (ed. N. Appelhans, W. Scholz, and S. Baumgart), 161–190. London: Routledge.

MacKinnon, D. (2012). Beyond strategic coupling: reassessing the firm-region nexus in global production networks. *Journal of Economic Geography* 12 (1): 227–245.

MacKinnon, D., Dawley, S., Pike, A., and Cumbers, A. (2019). Rethinking path creation: a geographical political economy approach. *Economic Geography* 95 (2): 113–135.

Magableh, G.M. (2021). Supply chains and the COVID-19 pandemic: a comprehensive framework. *European Management Review* 18 (3): 363–382.

Maginn, P.J., Burton, P., and Legacy, C. (2018). Disruptive urbanism? Implications of the "sharing economy' for cities, regions, and urban policy. *Urban Policy and Research* 36 (4): 393–398.

Mahmood, M. (2019). The quality of jobs and growth in Sub-Saharan Africa. In: *The Quality of Growth in Africa* (ed. R. Kanbur, A. Noman, and J. Stiglitz), 76–110. Oxford and New York: Oxford University Press.

Mairfaing, L. and Thiel, A. (2013). The impact of Chinese business on market entry in Ghana and Senegal. *Africa* 83 (4): 646–669.

Mallett, R.W. (2020). Seeing the "changing nature of work" through a precarity lens. *Global Labour Journal* 11 (3): 271–290.

Malm, M. and Toyama, K. (2021). The burdens and the benefits: socio-economic impacts of mobile phone ownership in Tanzania. *World Development Perspectives*, https://doi.org/10.1016/j.wdp.2020.100283.

Marbuah, G. (2020). *Green bonds in Africa*. Stockholm Sustainable Finance Centre, Available at https://www.stockholmsustainablefinance.com/publication/green-bonds-in-africa (Accessed 15 July 2022).

Marcatelli, M. (2018). The land–water nexus: a critical perspective from South Africa. *Review of African Political Economy* 45 (157): 393–407.

Marcinkoski, C., (2017 July 24). Urban planners are irresponsibly designing risky mega-developments across. *The Architect's Newspaper*, Available at https://www.archpaper.com/2017/07/urban-planners-mega-developments-africa (Accessed 20 June 2022).

Markard, J. (2020). The life cycle of technological innovation systems. *Technological Forecasting and Social Change* 153: 119407.

Markard, J., Raven, R., and Truffer, B. (2012). Sustainability transitions: an emerging field of research and its prospects. *Research Policy* 41 (6): 955–967.

Marr, S. and Mususa, P. (2021). *The Practice and Politics of DIY Urbanism in African Cities*. London: Zed Books.

Marx, B., Stoker, T., and Suri, T. (2013). The economics of slums in the developing world. *Journal of Economic Perspectives* 27 (4): 187–210.

Mattes, R. (2020 March). Lived poverty on the rise: decade of living-standard gains ends in Africa. *Afrobarometer Policy Paper* No. 62.

Mauritius, Government of and UNCTAD (2020). *Industrial policy and strategic plan for Mauritius (2020-2025)*. Available from https://unctad.org/webflyer/industrial-policy-and-strategic-plan-mauritius-2020-2025 (Accessed 15 July 2022).

Mbaye, A.A., Golub, S., and Gueye, F. (2020). *Formal Land Informal Enterprises in Francophone Africa: Moving toward a Vibrant Private Sector*. Ottawa: International Development Research Centre.

Mbembé, J.A. and Nuttall, S. (2004). Writing the world from an African metropolis. *Public Culture* 16 (3): 347–372.

Mboup, G. and Oyelaran-Oyeyinka, B. (2019). Smart economy in smart African cities. In: *Smart Economy in Smart African Cities: Sustainable, Inclusive, Resilient and Prosperous* (ed. G. Mboup and B. Oyelaran-Oyeyinka), 1–49. Singapore: Springer.

McCann, E., Roy, A., and Ward, K. (2013). Assembling/worlding cities. *Urban Geography* 34 (5): 581–589.

McCann, E. and Ward, K. (2011). *Mobile Urbanism: Cities and Policymaking in the Global Age*. Minneapolis: University of Minnesota Press.

McCormick, D. (1999). African enterprise clusters and industrialization: theory and reality. *World Development* 27 (9): 1531–1551.

McDonald, D.A. (2008). *World City Syndrome: Neoliberalism and Inequality in Cape Town*. London: Routledge.

McFarlane, C. (2010). The comparative city: knowledge, learning, urbanism. *International Journal of Urban and Regional Research* 34 (4): 725–742.

McFarlane, C. (2011a). *Learning the City. Knowledge and Trans-Local Assemblage*. New York: Wiley-Blackwell.

McFarlane, C. (2011b). Assemblage and critical urbanism. *City* 15 (2): 204–224.

McKinsey Global Institute (2018 May 23). *Skill shift: automation and the future of the workforce*. Available at https://www.mckinsey.com/featured-insights/future-of-work/skill-shift-automation-and-the-future-of-the-workforce (Accessed 15 July 2022).

McMillan, M., Page, J., Booth, D., and Willem te Velde, D. (2017). Economic transformation: a new approach to inclusive growth. *Overseas Development Institute, Supporting Economic Transformation Briefing paper*, London: Available at https//set.odi.org/wp-content/uploads/2017/03/Economic-Transformation-New-Approach-SET-Briefing-Paper_FINAL.pdf (Accessed 15 July 2022).

Melber, H. (2022). Africa's middle classes. *Afrika Spectrum* 57 (2): 204–219.

Meth, P., Todes, A., Charlton S. et al. (2021). At the city edge: situating peripheries research in South Africa and Ethiopia. In: *African Cities and Collaborative Futures: Urban Platforms and Metropolitan Logistics* (ed. M. Keith and A.A.D.S. Santos). Manchester: Manchester University Press.

Miami-Dade County (2021). *Miami-Dade County sea level rise strategy*. Miami: Available at https://miami-dade-county-sea-level-rise-strategy-draft-mdc.hub.arcgis.com (Accessed 15 July 2022).

Migozzi, J. (2020). Selecting spaces, classifying people: the financialization of housing in the South African city. *Housing Policy Debate* 30 (4): 640–660.

Miller, H.J. (2017) Time geography and space-time prism. In: *International Encyclopedia of Geography: People, the Earth, Environment and Technology* (ed. D. Richardson, N. Castree, M.F. Goodchild et al.), Malden: Wiley Blackwell.

Millington, N. and Scheba, S. (2021). Day zero and the infrastructures of climate change: water governance, inequality, and infrastructural politics in Cape Town's water crisis. *International Journal of Urban and Regional Research* 45 (1): 116–132.

Minter, A. (2015). *Anatomy of a myth: the world's biggest e-waste dump isn't*. Available at https://politicadechatarra.wordpress.com/2015/06/17/anatomy-of-a-myth-the-worlds-biggest-e-waste-dump-isnt/ (Accessed 22 January 2021).

Mitlin, D. and Walnycki, A. (2020). Informality as experimentation: water utilities' strategies for cost recovery and their consequences for universal access. *The Journal of Development Studies* 56 (2): 259–277.

Mittal, P. (2020). Falling apart – a story of the Tanzanian Bagamoyo port project. *Observer Research Foundation*, Available at https://www.orfonline.org/expert-speak/falling-apart-a-story-of-the-tanzanian-bagamoyo-port-project (Accessed 15 July 2022).

Mkandawire, T. (ed.) (2004). *Social Policy in a Development Context*. Basingstoke: Palgrave Macmillan.

Mohan, G. (2021). Below the belt? territory and development in China's international rise. *Development and Change* 52 (1): 54–75.

Mohan, G. and Lampert, B. (2013 January 14-15). Chinese migrants in Africa: bilateral informal governance of a poorly understood South-South flow. *Unpublished draft paper presented for the UNRISD Conference* Geneva, Switzerland.

Mohan, G. and Tan-Mullins, M. (2009). Chinese migrants in Africa as new agents of development? an analytical framework. *The European Journal of Development Research* 21 (4): 588–605.

Mohseni-Cheraghlou, A. (2021). China and Sub-Saharan Africa trade: a case of growing interdependence. *Atlantic Council*, Available at https://www.atlanticcouncil.org/blogs/china-and-sub-saharan-africa-trade-a-case-of-growing-interdependence (Accessed 15 July 2022).

Mold, A. and Chowdhury, S. (2021 May 19). Why the extent of intra-African trade is much higher than commonly believed—and what this means for the AfCFTA. *Brookings Institute Blog, Africa in Focus*, Available at https://www.brookings.edu/blog/africa-in-focus/2021/05/19/why-the-extent-of-intra-african-trade-is-much-higher-than-commonly-believed-and-what-this-means-for-the-afcfta (Accessed 15 July 2022).

Molotch, H. (1976). The city as a growth machine: toward a political economy of place. *American Journal of Sociology* 82 (2): 309–332.

Molotch, H. and Logan, J.R. (1985). Urban dependencies: new forms of use and exchange in US cities. *Urban Affairs Quarterly* 21 (2): 143–169.

Monga, C. (2017). Industrialization: a primer. In: *Industrialized Africa - Strategies, Policies, Institutions and Financing* (ed. African Development Bank), 19–44. Washington: African Development Bank.

Moore, J.W. (2015). *Capitalism in the Web of Life: Ecology and the Accumulation of Capital*. London: Verso.

Mora, C., Frazier, A.G., Longman, R.J. et al. (2013). The projected timing of climate departure from recent variability. *Nature* 502 (7470): 183–187.

Moriyasu, K. (2021). Tanzania to revive $10bn Indian Ocean port project with China. *Nikkei Asia*, Available at https://asia.nikkei.com/Politics/International-relations/Indo-Pacific/Tanzania-to-revive-10bn-Indian-Ocean-port-project-with-China (Accessed 15 July 2022).

Morris, M. (2019). Personal communication with P. Carmody, August 5th.

Morris, G.P., Reis, S., Beck, S.A. et al. (2017). Scoping the proximal and distal dimensions of climate change on health and wellbeing. *Environmental Health* 16 (1): 69–76.

Moser, S., Cote-Roy, L., and Korah, P.I. (2021). The uncharted foreign actors, investments, and urban models in African new city building. *Urban Geography* https://doi.org/10.1080/02723638.2021.1916698.

Moskvitch, K. (2018 August 14). Volkswagen's got a radical plan to fix ride-sharing and car ownership. *Wired*, Available at https://www.wired.co.uk/article/volkswagen-car-sharing-rwanda-africa (Accessed 15 July 2022).

Mourdoukoutas, E. (2017). Africa's app-based taxis battle Uber over market share. *Africa Renewal*, Available at https://www.un.org/africarenewal/magazine/august-november-2017/africa%E2%80%99s-app-based-taxis-battle-uber-over-market-share (Accessed 15 July 2022).

Moyo, S. (2019). The scramble for land and natural resources in Africa. In: *Reclaiming Africa: Scramble and Resistance in the 21st Century* (ed. S. Moyo, P. Jha, and P. Yeros), 3–30. Singapore: Springer.

Mpofu, F.Y.S. (2021). Informal sector taxation and enforcement in African countries: how plausible and achievable are the motives behind? a critical literature review. *Open Economics* 4 (1): 72–97.

Mtetwa, E. (n.d.). The bloomery iron technologies of great Zimbabwe from AD 1000: : an archaeometallurgy of social practices. *Journal of Archaeological Science*. Available at http://urn.kb.se/resolve?urn=urn:nbn:se:uu:diva-334795 (Accessed 25 May 2023).

Muchadenyika, D. and Waiswa, J. (2018). Policy, politics and leadership in slum upgrading: a comparative analysis of Harare and Kampala. *Cities* 82: 58–67.

Muchira, N. (2020 June 16) Ethiopia eyes SGR route to port of Sudan. *The East African*, Available at https://www.theeastafrican.co.ke/tea/business/ethiopia-eyes-sgr-route-to-port-of-sudan-1443300 (Accessed 10 March 2023).

Müller-Mahn, D. and Everts, J. (2013). The spatial dimension of risk. How geography shapes the emergence of riskscapes. In: *Riskscapes: The Spatial Dimensions of Risk* (ed. Müller-Mahn), 22–36. London and New York: Routledge.

Müller-Mahn, D., Everts, J., and Stephan, C. (2018). Riskscapes revisited-exploring the relationship between risk, space and practice. *Erdkunde* 72 (3): 197–214.

Müller-Mahn, D., Moure, M., and Gebreyes, M. (2020). Climate change, the politics of anticipation and future riskscapes in Africa. *Cambridge Journal of Regions, Economy and Society* 13 (2): 343–362.

Murphy, J.T. (2003). Social space and industrial development in East Africa: deconstructing the logics of industry networks in Mwanza, Tanzania. *Journal of Economic Geography* 3 (2): 173–198.

Murphy, J.T. (2015). Human geography and sociotechnical transition studies: promising intersections. *Environmental Innovation and Societal Transitions* 17: 73–91.

Murphy, J.T. and Carmody, P.R. (2015). *Africa's Information Revolution: Technical Regimes and Production Networks in South Africa and Tanzania*. Malden and Oxford: Wiley-Blackwell.

Murphy, J.T. and Carmody, P.R. (2019). Generative urbanisation in Africa? a sociotechnical systems view of Tanzania's urban transition. *Urban Geography* 40 (1): 128–157.

Murray, M. (2015) City doubles: re-urbanism in Africa. In: *Cities and Inequalities in a Global and Neoliberal World* (ed. F. Miraftab, D. Wilson, and K. Salo), 92–109. New York: Routledge.

Musah, B.I., Peng, L., and Xu, Y. (2020). Urban congestion and pollution: a quest for cogent solutions for Accra city. *IOP Conference Series: Earth and Environmental Science* 435 (1): 012026.

Mustapha, A. (1992). Structural adjustment and multiple modes of livelihood in Nigeria. In: *Authoritarianism, Democracy and Adjustment: The Politics of Economic Reform in Africa* (ed. P. Gibbon, Y. Bangura, and A. Ofstad), 188–216. Uddevalla, Sweden: Scandinavian Institute for African Studies.

Mwangi, V. (2019 March 21). Kenya seeks sh368 billion loan from China to extend SGR, despite losses. *Soko Directory*, Available at https://sokodirectory.com/2019/03/kenya-seeks-sh368-billion-loan-from-china-to-extend-sgr-despite-losses (Accessed 20 April 2020).

Myabe, A. (2019). Supporting small informal business to improve the quality of jobs in Africa. *Brooking Institute policy brief*, Available at https://www.brookings.edu/wp-content/uploads/2019/10/Dualistic-Labor-Market_Ahmadou-Aly-Mbaye-1.pdf (Accessed 15 July 2022).

Myers, G. (2011). *African Cities: Alternative Visions of Urban Theory and Practice*. London: Zed Books.

Myers, G. (2014). From expected to unexpected comparisons: changing the flow of ideas about cities in a postcolonial world. *Singapore Journal of Tropical Geography* 31 (1): 104–118.

Myers, G. (2016). *Urban Environments in Africa: A Critical Analysis of Environmental Politics*. London: Policy Press.

Myers, G. (2018). The Africa problem of global urban theory: re-conceptualising planetary urbanization. In: *African Cities and the Development Conundrum* (ed. C. Ammann and T. Förster), 231–253. Leiden: Brill Nijhoff.

Myers, G. (2020). *Rethinking Urbanism: Lessons from Postcolonialism and the Global South*. Bristol: Bristol University Press.

Nagendra, H., Bai, X., Brondizio, E.S., and Lwasa, S. (2018). The urban south and the predicament of global sustainability. *Nature Sustainability* 1 (7): 341–349.

Nakamura, S., Hawati, R., Lall, S. et al. (2016). *Is living in African cities expensive?* Retrieved from World Bank Policy Research Working Paper No. 7641. Available at https://open knowledge.worldbank.org/server/api/core/bitstreams/1c2dd544-d7cc-571a-afb5-e2530eeb565e/content (Accessed 11 January 2021).

Nattrass, N. and Seekings, J. (2019). *Inclusive Dualism: Labour-Intensive Development, Decent Work, and Surplus Labour in Southern Africa*, 1e. Oxford: Oxford University Press.

Naudé, W. (2017). Entreprenuership, education and the fourth industrial revolution in Africa. *IZA Discussion Papers No 10855*.

Network, D.G. (2022 February 7). First plastic waste bus shelter commissioned. *Daily Guide Network*, *Available* at https://dailyguidenetwork.com/first-plastic-waste-bus-shelter-commissioned (Accessed 15 July 2022).

Neutens, T., Schwanen, T., and Witlox, F. (2011). The prism of everyday life: towards a new research agenda for time geography. *Transport Reviews* 31 (1): 25–47.

Newell, P. (2012). *Globalization and the Environment: Capitalism, Ecology and Power*. Cambridge: Polity.

Newman, C., Page, J., Rand, J. et al. (2016). *Manufacturing Transformation: Comparative Strategies of Industrial Development in Africa and Emerging Asia*. New York: Oxford University Press.

Ng'weno, A. and Porteous, D. (2018). Let's be real: the informal sector and the gig economy are the future, and the present, of work in Africa. *Center for Global Development*, 15: Available at https://www.cgdev.org/publication/lets-be-real-informal-sector-and-gig-economy-are-future-and-present-work-africa (Accessed 15 July 2022).

Niba, W. (2019 January 15). Will Kenya's Mombasa port be taken over by the Chinese. *RFI*, Available at http://www.rfi.fr/en/africa/20190114-kenya-mombasa-port-china-debt-default (Accessed 20 October 2019).

Nicolini, D. (2009). Zooming in and out: studying practices by switching theoretical lenses and trailing connections. *Organization Studies* 30 (12): 1391–1418.

Njoroge, P., Ambole, A., Githira, D., and Outa, G. (2020). Steering energy transitions through landscape governance: case of Mathare informal settlement, Nairobi, Kenya. *Land* 9 (6): 206.

Nkubito, F. and Baiden-Amissah, A. (2019). Regulatory planning and affordable housing in Kigali City: policies, challenges and prospects. *Rwanda Journal of Engineering, Science, Technology and Environment* 2 (1).

Novitz, T. (2021). Gig work as a manifestation of short-termism: crafting a sustainable regulatory agenda. *Industrial Law Journal* 50 (4): 636–661.

Nyabiage, J. (2021 March 14). Belt and Road Initiative: end of the line for China's Afristar rail firm in Kenya? *South China Morning Post*, Available at https://www.scmp.com/news/china/diplomacy/article/3125329/belt-and-road-initiative-end-line-chinas-afristar-rail-firm (Accessed 25 March 2021).

Oates, L. (2021). Sustainability transitions in the Global South: a multi-level perspective on urban service delivery. *Regional Studies, Regional Science* 8 (1): 426–433.

Obeng-Odoom, F. (2010). 'Abnormal' urbanisation in Africa: a dissenting view. *African Geographical Review* 20 (2): 13–40.

Obeng-Odoom, F. (2016). *Reconstructing Urban Economics: Towards a Political Economy of the Built Environment*. London: Zed Books Ltd.

Obeng-Odoom, F. (2017). Urban governance in Africa today: reframing, experiences, and lessons. *Growth and Change* 48 (1): 4–21.

Obobisa, E.S., Chen, H.B., Ayamba, E.C., and Mensah, C.N. (2021). The causal relationship between China-Africa trade, China OFDI, and economic growth of African countries. *Sage Open* 11 (4): doi:Artn2158244021106489910.1177/21582440211064899.

Odendaal, N. (2011). Splintering urbanism or split agendas? examining the spatial distribution of technology access in relation to ICT policy in Durban, South Africa. *Urban Studies* 48 (11): 2375–2397.

Oduro-Appiah, K., Afful, A., Kotey, V.N., and De Vries, N. (2019). Working with the informal service chain as a locally appropriate strategy for sustainable modernization of municipal solid waste management systems in lower-middle income cities: lessons from Accra, Ghana. *Resources* 8 (1): 12. Available at https://www.mdpi.com/2079-9276/8/1/12 (Accessed 15 July 2022).

OECD, United Nations Economic Commission for Africa, & African Development Bank (2022). *Africa's Urbanization Dynamics 2022*. Paris: OECD Publishing.

Ofosu, G. and Sarpong, D. (2021). The evolving perspectives on the Chinese labour regime in Africa. *Economic and Industrial Democracy* https://doi.org/10.1177/0143831×211029382.

Ogbonna, N. (2021 March 23). Can Chinese special economic zones revitalise Nigeria's manufacturing? *The Africa Report*, Available from https://www.theafricareport.com/74253/can-chinese-special-economic-zones-revitalise-nigerias-manufacturing (Accessed 15 July 2022).

Okereke, C., Coke, A., Geebreyesus, M. et al. (2019). Governing green industrialisation in Africa: assessing key parameters for a sustainable sociotechnical transition in the context of Ethiopia. *World Development* 115: 279–290.

Olesen, K. (2014). The neoliberalisation of strategic spatial planning. *Planning Theory* 13 (3): 288–303.

Oluwole, V. (2021 April 19). Why uber and bolt drivers in Lagos are on strike. *Business Insider Africa*, Available at https://africa.businessinsider.com/local/markets/why-uber-and-bolt-drivers-in-lagos-are-on-strike/jsn6ndz (Accessed 15 July 2022).

Omoegun, A. (2015). *Street Trader Displacements and the Relevance of the Right to the City Concept in a Rapidly Urbanising African City: Lagos, Nigeria*. PhD Thesis, Cardiff University.

Omokhodion, A. (2006). Globalisation and an African city: Lagos. *Ekistics* 73 (436/441) *Globalisation and Local identity* (January to December): 214–219.

Omondi, D. (2021 March 5). Costly project that divides Kenyans. *The Standard*.

Onukwue, A. (2021 November 25). Ghana's plan to build sky trains in Accra for $2.6 billion isn't happening after all. *Quartz Africa*, Available at https://qz.com/africa/2094653/ghanas-2-6-billion-skytrain-project-isnt-happening-after-all (Accessed 15 July 2022).

Onyishi, C.J., Ejike-Alieji, A.U.P., Ajaero, C.K. et al. (2021). COVID-19 Pandemic and informal urban governance in Africa: a political economy perspective. *Journal of Asian and African Studies* 56 (6): 1226–1250.

Oppong, J.R. (2020). The African COVID-19 anomaly. *African Geographical Review* 39 (3): 282–288.

Oqubay, A. (2015). *Made in Africa: Industrial Policy in Ethiopia*. Oxford: Oxford University Press.

Oranye, N. (2016). *Disrupting Africa: The Rise and Rise of African Innovation*. USA: Self-published.

Orimoloye, I.R., Ololade, O.O., Mazinyo, S.P. et al. (2019). Spatial assessment of drought severity in Cape Town area, South Africa. *Heliyon* 5 (7): e02148.

Osse-Asare, D. and Abbas, Y. (2019). Waste. *AA Files* 76: 179–183.

Otele, O. (2016). Rethinking African agency within China-Africa relations through the lens of policy. *The African Review: A Journal of African Politics, Development and International Relations* 43 (1): 75–102.

Oteng-Ababio, M. (2012). When necessity begets Ingenuity: e-waste scavenging as a livelihood strategy in Accra, Ghana. *African Studies Quarterly* 13 (1): 1–21.

Oteng-Ababio, M. and Grant, R. (2021). Ideological traces in Ghana's urban plans: how do traces get worked out in Agbogbloshie, Accra? *Habitat International* 83: 1–10.

Oteng-Ababio, M. and van der Velden, M. (2019). "Welcome to Sodom"- Six myths about electronic waste in Agbogbloshie, Ghana. *Blogging for Sustainability*, Available at https://www.smart.uio.no/blog/welcome-to-sodom.html (Accessed 21 January 2021).

Otieno, E., Stein, M., and Anwar, M.A. (2020). Ride-hailing drivers left alone at the wheel. In: *COVID-19 in the Global South: Impacts and Responses* (ed. P. Carmody, G. McCann, C. Colleran, and C. O'Halloran), 95–104. Bristol: Bristol University Press.

Otiso, K. and Carmody, P. (2023). Powering transport or transporting power?: the spatial political economy of Chinese railways in Africa. In: *Railway Renaissance: The Political Economy of Chinese Rail Projects in Africa* (ed. T. Zajontz, P. Carmody, M. Bagwandeen, and T. Leysens). London: Routledge.

Otu, A., Ameh, S., Osifo-Dawodu, E. et al. (2018). An account of the Ebola virus disease outbreak in Nigeria: implications and lessons learnt. *BMC Public Health* 18 (1): 1–8.

Page, J., Gutman, J., Madden, P., and Ghandi, D. (2020). *Urban economic growth in Africa. a framework for analyzing constraints to agglomeration.* Washington DC: Brookings Institute, Available at https://www.brookings.edu/wp-content/uploads/2020/09/20.09.28_urban_economic_growth_in_africa_FINAL.pdf (Accessed 15 July 2022).

Paller, J.W. (2019). *Democracy in Ghana: Everyday Politics in Urban Africa.* Cambridge University Press.

Paller, J.W. (2021). How is China impacting African cities? *Management and Organization Review* 17 (3): 636–640.

Parnell, S. and Pieterse, E.A. (eds.) (2014). *Africa's Urban Revolution.* London: Zed Books.

Parnell, S. and Robinson, J. (2012). (Re)theorizing cities from the Global South: looking beyond neoliberalism. *Urban Geography* 33 (4): 593–617.

Parr, A. (2013). *The Wrath of Capital: Neoliberalism and Climate Change Politics.* New York: Columbia University Press.

Parry, J. (2018) Introduction: precarity, class and the neoliberal subject. In: *Industrial Labour on the Margins of Capitalism: Precarity, Class and the Neoliberal Subject* (ed. C. Hann and J. Parry), 1–38. New York: Berghahn.

Partnership for Action on Green Economy (PAGE) (2017). *Green economy inventory for South Africa: an overview.* Available at http://www.un-page.org/files/public/green_economy_inventory_for_south_africa.pdf. (Accessed 15 July 2022).

Partnership on Action for a Green Economy (PAGE) (2021). *2021 Annual Report.* New York: PAGE.

Patey, L. (2020). *How China Loses: The Pushback Against China's Global Ambitions.* Oxford and New York: Oxford University Press.

Patorniti, N.P., Stevens, N.J., and Salmon, P.M. (2018). A sociotechnical systems approach to understand complex urban systems: a global transdisciplinary perspective. *Human Factors and Ergonomics in Manufacturing and Service Industries* 28 (6): 281–296.

Peck, J. (2001). *Workfare States*. New York: Guilford Press.

Peck, J. (2015). Cities beyond compare? *Regional Studies* 49 (1): 160–182.

Peck, J. (2017). Transatlantic city, part 1: conjunctural urbanism. *Urban Studies* 54 (1): 4–30.

Peck, J. and Tickell, A. (2002). Neoliberalizing space. *Antipode* 34: 380–404.

Peet, R. (1975). Inequality and poverty: a Marxist-geographic theory. *Annals of the Association of American Geographers* 65 (4): 564–571.

Peet, R. and Thrift, N.J. (1989). *New Models in Geography: The Political-Economy Perspective*. London: Unwin Hyman.

Pelling, M., Barcena, A., Leck, H. et al. (2021). Uncertain pasts and risk-sensitive futures in sub-Saharan urban transformation. In: *African Cities and Collaborative Futures: Urban Platforms and Metropolitan Logistics* (ed.M. Keith and A. de Sousa Santos). Manchester: Manchester University Press.

Peter, C. (2021). Social innovation for sustainable urban developmental transitions in Sub-Saharan Africa: leveraging economic ecosystems and the entrepreneurial state. *Sustainability* 13 (13): 7360.

Petrik, M. (2016). *A Review of the Green Economy in Cape Town: Local Policy in the Light of International Approaches*. Cape Town: (Master's thesis). University of Cape Town.

Pharoah, R. (2016). *Strengthening Urban Resilience in African Cities: Understanding and Addressing Urban Risk*. ActionAid International.

Phelps, N.A., Atienza, M., and Arias, M. (2015). Encore for the enclave: the changing nature of the industry enclave with illustrations from the mining industry in Chile. *Economic Geography* 91 (2): 119–146.

Phuluwa, H.S., Daniyan, I., and Mpofu, K. (2020). Sustainable demanufacturing model for promoting circular economy in the rail industry. *Procedia CIRP* 90: 25–30.

Pieterse, E. (2010). Cityness and African urban development. *Urban Forum* 21: 205–219.

Pieterse, E., Parnell, S., and Haysom, G. (2018). African dreams: locating urban infrastructure in the 2030 sustainable developmental agenda. *Area Development and Policy* 3 (2): 149–169.

Pigato, W. and Tang, W. (2015). China in Africa: expanding ties in an evolving global context. *World Bank Working Paper* 95161, Available at http://documents.worldbank.org/curated/en/241321468024314010/China-and-Africa-expanding-economic-ties-in-an-evolving-global-context (Accessed 17 July 2017).

Pinnock, D. (2016). *Gang Town*. Cape Town: Tafelberg.

Plummer, A. (2019). Kenya and China's labour relations: infrastructural development for whom, by whom? *Africa* 89 (4): 680–695.

Pollio, A. (2019). Forefronts of the sharing economy: Uber in Cape Town. *International Journal of Urban and Regional Research* 43 (4): 760–775.

Popan, C. (2021). Algorithmic governance in the gig economy: entrepreneurialism and solidarity among food delivery workers. In: *Cycling Societies: Innovations, Inequalities and Governance* (ed. D. Zuev, K. Psarikidou, and C. Popan). London: Routledge.

Porteous, D. and Morawczynski, O. (2019). *How the gig Economy could help power Africa's growth*. Available at https://www.weforum.org/agenda/2019/06/africa-s-gig-opportunity. (Accessed 15 July 2022).

The Post (Cameroon) (2005 July 25). *Chinese doughnuts producers perturb Bamileke traders*.

Pred, A. (1977). The choreography of existence: comments on Hägerstrand's time-geography and its usefulness. *Economic Geography* 53 (2): 207–221.

Prentice, R. (2018). From dispossessed factory workers to "Micro-entrepreneurs": the precariousness of employment in Trinidad's Garment Sector. In: *Industrial Labour on the Margins of Capitalism: Precarity, Class and the Neoliberal Subject* (ed. C. Hann and J. Parry), 289–308. New York: Berghahn.

Princewill, N. (2021 August 1). *Africa's most populous city is battling floods and rising seas. It may soon be unlivable, experts warn*. CNN, Available at https://www.cnn.com/2021/08/01/africa/lagos-sinking-floods-climate-change-intl-cmd/index.html (Accessed 16 July 2022).

Pronczuk, M. (2020 January 28). How the Venice of Africa is losing its battle against the rising ocean. *The Guardian*, Available at https://www.theguardian.com/environment/2020/jan/28/how-the-venice-of-africa-is-losing-its-battle-against-the-rising-ocean (Accessed 16 July 2022).

Pugel, K., Javernick-Will, A., Peabody, S. et al. (2022). Pathways for collaboratively strengthening water and sanitation systems. *Science of the Total Environment* 802: 149854. doi:https://doi.org/10.1016/j.scitotenv.2021.149854.

Qiang, C., Liu, Y., and Steenbergen, V. (2021). *An Investment Perspective on Global Value Chains*. Washington, DC: World Bank.

Ragasa, C., Andam, K.S., Asante, S.B., and Amewu, S. (2020). Can local products compete against imports in West Africa? supply-and demand-side perspectives on chicken, rice, and tilapia in Ghana. *Global Food Security* 26: 100448.

Rajé, F., Tight, M., and Pope, F.D. (2018). Traffic pollution: a search for solutions for a city like Nairobi. *Cities* 82: 100–107.

Ram, E. (2021 December 8). How Nairobi's 'road for the rich' resulted in thousands of homes reduced to rubble. *The Guardian*, Available at https://www.theguardian.com/global-development/2021/dec/08/how-nairobis-road-for-the-rich-resulted-in-thousands-of-homes-reduced-to-rubble (Accessed 10 March 2023).

Ramos-Mejía, M., Franco-Garcia, M.-L., and Jauregui-Becker, J.M. (2018). Sustainability transitions in the developing world: challenges of sociotechnical transformations unfolding in contexts of poverty. *Environmental Science and Policy* 84: 217–223.

Rankin, K.N. (2009). Critical development studies and the praxis of planning. *City* 13 (2–3): 219–229.

Rateau, M. and Choplin, A. (2022). Electrifying urban Africa: energy access, city-making and globalisation in Nigeria and Benin. *International Development Planning Review* 44 (1): 55–81.

Ravallion, M., Chen, S., and Sangraula, P. (2007). *New evidence on the urbanisation of global poverty*. Available at https://www.gtap.agecon.purdue.edu/resources/download/3430.pdf (Accessed March 10 2023).

Ravenhill, J. (1986). The Elusiveness of Development. In: *Africa in Economic Crisis*. (ed. J. Ravenhill), 1–43. Basingstoke: Macmillan.

Rawlins, L. (2018 June 19). *Uber, Taxify drivers demand higher percentage split*. IT Web, Available at https://www.itweb.co.za/content/RgeVDvPoOo5qKJN3 (Accessed 16 July 2022).

Ray, R., Gallagher, K., Kring, W. et al. (2020). *Geolocated Dataset of Chinese Overseas Development Finance*. Boston, MA: Boston University Global Development Policy Center. Online database.

Raymond, C., Horton, R.M., Zscheischler, J. et al. (2020). Understanding and managing connected extreme events. *Nature Climate Change* 10 (7): 611–621.

Reardon, T., Tschirley, D., Liverpool-Tasie, L.S.O. et al. (2021). The processed food revolution in African food systems and the double burden of malnutrition. *Global Food Security* 28: 100466.

Reboredo, R. and Brill, F. (2019). Between global and local: urban inter-referencing and the transformation of a Sino-South African Megaproject. *China Perspectives* 4: 9–18.

Redvers, L. (2012 July 3). *Angola's Chinese-built ghost town*. BBC, Available at https://www.bbc.com/news/world-africa-18646243 (Accessed 16 July 2022).

Rentschler, J., Braese, J., Jones, N., and Avner, P. (2019). *Three Feet Under: The Impact of Floods on Urban Jobs, Connectivity, and Infrastructure*. Washington: World Bank.

Rentschler, J. and Salhab, M. (2020 November 12). 1.47 billion people face flood risk worldwide: for over a third, it could be devastating. *World Bank Blog*, Available at https://blogs.worldbank.org/climatechange/147-billion-people-face-flood-risk-world wide-over-third-it-could-be-devastating (Accessed 16 July 2022).

Resnick, D. (2021). Taxing informality: compliance and policy preferences in Urban Zambia. *The Journal of Development Studies* 57 (7): 1063–1085.

Rice, S. and Tyner, J.A. (2021). Revanchist 'nature' and 21st century genocide. *Space and Polity* 25 (3): 347–352.

Richards, P. (2016). *Ebola: How a People's Science Helped End an Epidemic*. London: Zed Books.

Riddell, R. (1993). The future of the manufacturing sector in Africa. In: *Hemmed In. Responses to Africa's Economic Decline* (ed. T. Callaghy and J. Ravenhill), 215–247. New York: Columbia University Press.

Rights and Accountability in Development (2021). *The road to ruin: electric vehicles and workers' rights abuses at DR Congo's industrial cobalt mines*. RAID (UK), November. Available at https://www.raid-uk.org/sites/default/files/report_road_to_ruin_evs_cobalt_workers_nov_2021.pdf (Accessed 16 July 2022).

Ritzer, G. (2010). *Globalization: A Basic Text*. London: Wiley-Blackwell.

Roberts, S. (2019). (Re)shaping markets for inclusive economic activity. In: *The Quality of Growth in Africa* (ed. S.M.R. Kanbur, A. Noman, and J.E. Stiglitz). New York: Columbia University Press.

Robinson, J. (2004). In the tracks of comparative urbanism: difference, urban modernity and the primitive. *Urban Geography* 25 (8): 709–723.

Robinson, J. (2006). *Ordinary Cities: Between Modernity and Development.* London: Routledge.

Robinson, J. (2011). Cities in a world of cities: the comparative gesture. *International Journal of Urban and Regional Research* 35 (1): 1–23.

Robinson, J. (2013). The urban now: theorising cities beyond the new. *European Journal of Cultural Studies* 16 (6): 659–677.

Robinson, J. (2016). Comparative urbanism: new geographies and cultures of theorizing the urban. *International Journal of Urban and Regional Research* 40 (1): 187–199.

Robinson, J. (2022). *Comparative Urbanism: Tactics for Global Urban Studies.* London: Wiley.

Rock, M., Murphy, J.T., Rasiah, R. et al. (2009). A hard slog, not a leap frog: globalization and sustainability transitions in developing Asia. *Technological Forecasting and Social Change* 76 (2): 241–254.

Rodrik, D. (2014). The past, present, and future of economic growth. *Challenge* 57 (3): 5–39.

Rodrik, D. (2016). An African growth miracle? *Journal of African Economies* 27 (1): 1–18.

Rogers, B. (2017). The social costs of Uber. *Chicago Unbound* 82 (1): 85–102.

Rosenberg, J. (2005). Globalization theory: a post mortem. *International Politics* 42 (1): 2–74.

Rosenblat, A. (2018 March 2). Uber may have imposed 12-hour driving limits, but it's still pushing drivers in other troubling ways: the new policies from ride-hail apps seem more about dodging liability than ensuring safety. *Slate*, Available at https://slate.com/technology/2018/03/uber-may-have-imposed-12-hour-driving-limits-but-its-still-pushing-drivers-in-other-troubling-ways.html (Accessed 16 July 2022).

Rostow, W.W. (1960). *The Stages of Economic Growth, a non-Communist Manifesto.* Cambridge: Cambridge University Press.

Rotberg, R. (2020). *Things Come Together: African Achieving Greatness in the 21st Century.* Oxford and New York: Oxford University Press.

Roy, A. (2016). Who's afraid of postcolonial theory? *International Journal of Urban and Regional Research* 40 (1): 200–209.

Roy, A. and Ong, A., (eds.) (2011). *Worlding Cities: Asian Experiments and the Art of Being Global.* London: John Wiley and Sons.

Rozenberg, J. and Fay, M. (2019). *Beyond the Gap: How Countries Can Afford the Infrastructure They Need While Protecting the Planet.* Washington DC: The World Bank.

Ruddick, S., Peake, L., Tanyildiz, G.S., and Patrick, D. (2018). Planetary urbanization: an urban theory for our time? *Environment and Planning D: Society and Space* 36 (3): 387–404.

Ruggiero, S., Martiskainen, M., and Onkila, T. (2018). Understanding the scaling-up of community energy niches through strategic niche management theory: insights from Finland. *Journal of Cleaner Production* 170: 581–590.

Ryan-Coker, M.F.D., Davies, J., Rinaldi, G. et al. (2021). Economic burden of road traffic injuries in sub-Saharan Africa: a systematic review of existing literature. *BMJ Open* 11 (9): e048231.

Sabutey, E. (2021 October 26). 'Investment Hope City' hub for Ghana in offing, JoyOnline. Available at https://www.myjoyonline.com/investment-hope-city-hub-for-ghana-in-offing (Accessed 12 July 2022).

Sadowski, J. (2020). The internet of landlords: digital platforms and new mechanisms of rentier capitalism. *Antipode* 52: 562–580.

Sager, T. (2011). Neo-liberal urban planning policies: a literature survey 1990–2010. *Progress in Planning* 76: 147–199.

Salami, R.O., Giggins, H., and Von Meding, J.K. (2017). Urban settlements' vulnerability to flood risks in African cities: a conceptual framework. *Jàmbá: Journal of Disaster Risk Studies* 9 (1): 1–9.

Sanbata, H., Asfaw, A., and Kumie, A. (2014). Indoor air pollution in slum neighbourhoods of Addis Ababa, Ethiopia. *Atmospheric Environment* 89: 230–234.

Santos, M.L. (1979). *The Shared Space the Two Circuits of the Urban Economy in Underdeveloped Countries*. Methuen: Routledge.

Satterthwaite, D. (2017a). Will Africa have most the world's largest cities in 2100? *Environment and Urbanisation* 29 (1): 217–220.

Satterthwaite, D. (2017b). The impact of urban development on risk in sub-Saharan Africa's cities with a focus on small and intermediate urban centres. *International Journal of Disaster Risk Reduction* 26: 16–23.

Satterthwaite, D. (2021). *What do we don't know about Africa's 100 largest cities*. African Cities Research Consortium, Available at https://www.african-cities.org/what-we-dont-know-about-africas-100-largest-cities (Accessed 16 July 2022).

Schatzki, T.R. (2005). Peripheral vision: the sites of organizations. *Organization Studies* 26 (3): 465–484.

Schindler, S. (2017). Towards a paradigm of Southern urbanism. *City* 21 (1): 47–64.

Schindler, S. and Kanai, J.M. (2021). Getting the territory right: infrastructure-led development and the re-emergence of spatial planning strategies. *Regional Studies* 55 (1): 40–51.

Schmalensee, R. (2012). From "green growth" to sound policies: an overview. *Energy Economics* 34: S2–S6.

Schmid, C. (2015). Specificity and urbanization: a theoretical outlook. In: *The Inevitable Specificity of Cities* (ed. C. Diener, J. Herzog, M. Meili, and P.D. Meuron). Zurich: Lars Müller Publishers.

Schmid, C. (2018). Journeys through planetary urbanization: decentering perspectives on the urban. *Environment and Planning D: Society and Space* 36 (3): 591–610.

Schonwetter, T. and Van Wiele, B. (2020). Social entrepreneurs' use of fab labs and 3D printing in South Africa and Kenya. *The African Journal of Information and Communication* 26: 1–24.

Schot, J. and Geels, F.W. (2008). Strategic niche management and sustainable innovation journeys: theory, findings, research agenda, and policy. *Technology Analysis and Strategic Management* 20 (5): 537–554.

Schwanen, T. (2018). Thinking complex interconnections: transition, nexus and geography. *Transactions of the Institute of British Geographers* 43 (2): 262–283.

Scott, A.J. and Storper, M. (2003). Regions, globalization, development. *Regional Studies* 37 (6–7): 579–593.

Scott, A.J. and Storper, M. (2015). The nature of cities: the scope and limits of urban theory. *International Journal of Urban and Regional Research* 39 (1): 1–15.

Selwyn, B. (2019). Poverty chains and global capitalism. *Competition and Change* 23 (1): 71–97.

Selwyn, B. and Leyden, D. (2022). Oligopoly-driven development: the World Bank's Trading for Development in the age of global value chains in perspective. *Competition and Change* 26 (2): 174–196.

Sengers, F. and Raven, R. (2015). Toward a spatial perspective on niche development: the case of Bus Rapid Transit. *Environmental Innovation and Societal Transitions* 17: 166–182.

Senghaas, D. (1985). *The European Experience: A Historical Critique of Development Theory*. Leamington Spa: Berg.

Serumaga-Zake, J.M. and van der Poll, J.A. (2021). Addressing the impact of fourth industrial revolution on South African manufacturing small and medium enterprises (SMEs). *Sustainability* 13 (21): 11703.

Shapshak, Y. (2019 July 11). Africa's booming tech hubs are backbone of tech ecosystem, having grown 40% this year. *Forbes*, Available at https://www.forbes.com/sites/tobyshapshak/2019/07/11/africas-booming-tech-hubs-are-backbone-of-tech-ecosystem-having-grown-40-this-year/?sh=50d5108a24c2 (Accessed 16 July 2022).

Shepherd, B. and Twum, A. (2018). *Review of Industrial Policy in Rwanda. Data Review, Comparative Assessment, and Discussion Points*. London: International Growth Centre.

Sherman, L. (2017 December 14). Why can't Uber make money? *Forbes*, Available at https://www.forbes.com/sites/lensherman/2017/12/14/why-cant-uber-make-money/#5289215b10ec (Accessed 16 July 2022).

Sietchiping, R., Permezel, M.J., and Ngomsi, C. (2012). Transport and mobility in sub-Saharan African cities: an overview of practices, lessons and options for improvements. *Cities* 29 (3): 183–189.

Silver, J. (2015). Disrupted infrastructures: an urban political ecology of interrupted electricity in Accra. *International Journal of Urban and Regional Research* 39 (5): 984–1003.

Simone, A. (2001). On the worlding of African cities. *African Studies Review* 44 (2): 15–41.

Simone, A. (2004). People as infrastructure: intersecting fragments in Johannesburg. *Public Culture* 16 (3): 407–429.

Simone, A. (2022). *The Surrounds: Urban Life Within and Beyond Capture*. Durham, N. C.: Duke University Press.

Simons, B. (2019 March 21). *Africa's unsung 'industrial revolution' Centre for Global Development blog*. Available at https://www.cgdev.org/blog/africas-unsung-industrial-revolution (Accessed 16 July, 2022).

Singh, A., Avis, W.R., and Pope, F.D. (2020). Visibility as a proxy for air quality in East Africa. *Environmental Research Letters* 15 (8): 084002.

Smit, S. and Musango, J.K. (2015). Exploring the connections between green economy and informal economy in South Africa. *South African Journal of Science* 111: 1–10.

Smith, D.A. (1987). Overurbanization reconceptualized: a political economy of the world-system approach. *Urban Affairs Review* 23 (2): 270–294.

Smith, N. (1996). *The New Urban Frontier: Gentrification and the Revanchist City.* London: Routledge.

Smith, N. (2002). New globalism, new urbanism: gentrification as global urban strategy. *Antipode* 34 (3): 427–450.

Soja, E. (1976). *Spatial Inequality in Africa.* Berkeley: University of California Press.

Soja, E.W. (2010). Cities and states in geohistory. *Theory and Society* 39 (3): 361–376.

Solomon, S. and Iman, F. (2017 January 24). New African railways ride on Chinese loans. *VOA News,* Available at https://www.voanews.com/a/new-african-railways-ride-chinese-loans/3690287.html (Accessed 16 July 2022).

Songe, V. (2019 January 11). *Intra-African trade: a path to economic diversification and inclusion.* Brookings Institute, Available at https://www.brookings.edu/research/intra-african-trade-a-path-to-economic-diversification-and-inclusion (Accessed 16 July 2022).

Sonobe, T. and Otsuka, K. (2011). *Cluster-Based Industrial Development: A Comparative Study of Asia and Africa.* New York: Palgrave Mcmillian.

Sorrell, S. (2018). Explaining sociotechnical transitions: a critical realist perspective. *Research Policy* 47 (7): 1267–1282.

Sperber, A. (2020 November 29). Uber made big promises in Kenya: drivers say it's ruined their lives. *NBC News,* Available at https://www.nbcnews.com/news/world/uber-made-big-promises-kenya-drivers-say-it-s-ruined-n1247964 (Accessed 30 June 2022).

Splinter, E. and Van Leynseele, Y. (2019). The conditional city: emerging properties of Kenya's satellite cities. *International Planning Studies* 24 (3–4): 308–324.

Stacey, P. (2019). *State of Slum. Precarity and Informal Governance at the Margins in Accra.* London: Zed Books.

Stacey, P., Grant, R., and Oteng-Ababio, M. (2021). Food for thought: urban market planning and entangled governance in Accra, Ghana. *Habitat International* 115: 102400.

Stafford, C. (2005). *Apartheid Atlantis: A Planned City in a Racist Society.* (Honours Thesis). Stanford University.

Stark, L. and Teppo, A. (2022). Examining power and inequality through informality in urban Africa. In: *Power and Inequality in Urban Africa: Ethnographic Perspectives* (ed. L. Stark and A. Teppo). London: Zed.

Statista (2022). Number of administered coronavirus (COVID-19) vaccine doses per 100 people in Africa as of July 3, 2022, by country. *Statista,* Available at https://www.statista.com/statistics/1221298/covid-19-vaccination-rate-in-african-countries (Accessed 16 July 2022).

Steel, G. (2021). Going global–going digital. Diaspora networks and female online entrepreneurship in Khartoum, Sudan. *Geoforum* 120: 22–29.

Steen, M. and Hansen, G.H. (2018). Barriers to path creation: the case of offshore wind power in Norway. *Economic Geography* 94 (2): 188–210.

Stein, M. (2021). *Working for small change: investigating the livelihoods of ride-hailing drivers in Cape Town, South Africa*. (Master's Thesis). University of Cape Town.

Stoler, J., Brewis, A., Harris, L.M. et al. (2019). Household water sharing: a missing link in international health. *International Health* 11 (3): 163–165.

Stone, C.N. (1993). Urban regimes and the capacity to govern: a political economy approach. *Journal of Urban Affairs* 15 (1): 1–28.

Stone, C.N. (2015). Reflections on regime politics: from governing coalition to urban political order. *Urban Affairs Review* 51 (1): 101–137.

Storper, M. (1995). The resurgence of regional economies, ten years later: the region as a nexus of untraded interdependencies. *European Urban and Regional Studies* 2 (3): 191–221.

Storper, M., Kemeny, T., Makarem, N.P., and Osman, T. (2015). *The Rise and Fall of Urban Economies: Lessons from San Francisco and Los Angeles*. Stanford: Stanford University Press.

Storper, M. and Scott, A.J. (2016). Current debates in urban theory: a critical assessment. *Urban Studies* 53: 1114–1136.

Su, X. and Qian, Z. (2020). Neoliberal planning, master plan adjustment and over-building in China: the case of Ordos City. *Cities* 105: 102748.

Surborg, B. (2012). *The production of the world city: extractive industries in a global urban economy*. (Doctoral dissertation), University of British Columbia.

Sutherland, E. (2020). The fourth industrial revolution - the case of South Africa. *Politikon* 47 (2): 233–252.

Sverdlik, A., Mitlin, D., and Dodman, D. (2019). *Realising the multiple benefits of climate resilience and inclusive development in informal settlements*. International Institute for Environment and Development (IIED). Available at https://sdinet.org/wp-content/uploads/2019/10/2356_Realising_the_Multiple_Benefits_of__Climate_Resilience_and__Inclusive_Development_in_Informal_Settlements_FINAL.original.pdf (Accessed 16 July 2022).

Swilling, M. (2011). Reconceptualising urbanism, ecology and networked infrastructures. *Social Dynamics* 37 (1): 78–95.

Swilling, M. (2014). Contesting inclusive urbanism in a divided city: the limits to the neoliberalisation of Cape Town's energy system. *Urban Studies* 51 (15): 3180–3197.

Swilling, M. (2016). Africa's game changers and the catalysts of social and system innovation. *Ecology and Society* 21 (1): 37–50.

Swilling, M., Musango, J., and Wakeford, J. (2016a). Developmental states and sustainability transitions: prospects of a just transition in South Africa. *Journal of Environmental Policy and Planning* 18 (5): 650–672.

Swilling, M., Musango, J., and Wakeford, J. (2016b). *Greening the South African Economy: Scoping the Issues, Challenges and Opportunities*. Cape Town: Juta and Company.

Swyngedouw, E. (2004). Globalisation or 'glocalisation'? Networks, territories and rescaling. *Cambridge Review of International Affairs* 17 (1): 25–48.

Talukdar, D. (2018). Cost of being a slum dweller in Nairobi: living under dismal conditions but still paying a housing rent premium. *World Development* 109: 42–56.

Tang, X. (2020). *Coevolutionary Pragmatism: Approaches and Impacts of China-Africa Economic Cooperation.* Oxford and New York: Oxford University Press.

TanzaniaInvest (2022). *Tanzania Budget 2016–2022.* Available at https://www.tanzania-invest.com/budget (Accessed 11 October 2021).

Tao, N. (2015). *Urbanisation Flagship.* CNKI, Available at http://www.chinafrica.cn/africa_report/txt/2015-03/02/content_671736.htm (Accessed 16 July 2022).

Tarrósy, I. (2020). China's Belt and Road Initiative in Africa, debt risk and new dependency: the case of Ethiopia. *African Studies Quarterly* 19 (3–4): 95–28.

Tassinari, A. and Maccarrone, V. (2020). Riders on the storm: workplace solidarity among gig economy couriers in Italy and the UK. *Work, Employment and Society* 34 (1): 35–54.

Taylor, I. (2016). Dependency redux: why Africa is not rising. *Review of African Political Economy* 43 (147): 8–25.

Taylor, I. (2020). Kenya's new Lunatic Express: the Standard Guage Railway. *African Studies Quarterly* 19: 29–52.

Taylor, M. and Rioux, S. (2018). *Global Labour Studies.* Cambridge: Polity.

Taylor, P.J. (2005). New political geographies: global civil society and global governance through world city networks. *Political Geography* 24 (6): 703–730.

TheAfricaLogistics (2022 September 27). *Bagamoyo port construction now set for 2023.* Available at https://theafricalogistics.com/2022/09/27/bagamoyo-port-construction-now-set-for-2023 (Accessed 10 March 2023).

Thieme, T., Ference, M., and Stapele, N. (2021). Harnessing the 'hustle'. *Africa* 91 (1): 1–15.

Tomkinson, J. (2016). Beyond faith and fatalism in development discourse: global conditions and national development prospects in Ethiopia. *Paper presented at International Initiative for the Promotion of Political Economy Conference*, Lisbon.

Tornyi, E. (2023). *I'm charging my battery — Henry Quartey explains why he is silent.* Available at https://www.pulse.com.gh/news/local/im-charging-my-battery-henry-quartey-explains-why-hes-silent/k2hv6ez (Accessed 13 March 2023).

Town, I.C. (2019). *Success stories.* SA renewable energy business incubator. Invest Cape Town: Available at https://www.investcapetown.com/success_stories/sa-renewable-energy-business-incubator (Accessed 16 July 2022).

Trisos, C.H., Adelekan, I.O., Totin, E. et al. (2022). Africa. In: *Climate Change 2022: Impacts, Adaptation and Vulnerability.* Contribution of Working Group II to the Sixth Assessment Report of the Intergovernmental Panel on Climate Change (ed. H.-O. Pörtner, D.C. Roberts, M. Tignor et al.), 1285–1455. Cambridge, UK and New York, NY, USA: Cambridge University Press. Available at https://doi.org/10.1017/9781009325844.011. (Accessed 4 May 2023).

Truffer, B. and Coenen, L. (2012). Environmental innovation and sustainability transitions in regional studies. *Regional Studies* 46 (1): 1–21.

Truffer, B., Murphy, J.T., and Raven, R. (2015). The geography of sustainability transitions: contours of an emerging theme. *Environmental Innovation and Societal Transitions* 17: 63–72.

Tsing, A. (2005). *Friction: An Ethnography of Global Connection*. Princeton: Princeton University Press.

Turok, I. (2013). Linking urbanisation and development in Africa's economic revival. In: *Africa's Urban Revolution* (ed. S. Parnell and E.A. Pieterse), 60–81. London: Zed Books.

Turok, I. (2016). Getting urbanization to work in Africa: the role of the urban land-infrastructure-finance nexus. *Area Development and Policy* 1 (1): 30–47.

Turok, I. and McGranahan, G. (2013). Urbanization and economic growth: the arguments and evidence for Africa and Asia. *Environment and Urbanization* 25 (2): 465–482.

Tusting, L.S., Bisanzio, D., Alabaster, G. et al. (2019). Mapping changes in housing in sub-Saharan Africa from 2000 to 2015. *Nature* 568 (7752): 391–394.

Tyson, J. (2021). *Developing Green Bond Markets for Africa*. Policy Brief 3, Joint FSD Africa-ODI research program for financial sector development in Africa.

Uber (2018 December 10). Phone support to riders and drivers. *Uber Blog*, Available at https://www.uber.com/en-ZA/blog/introducing-phone-support (Accessed 16 July 2022).

UNCTAD (2019a). *Economic Development in Africa Report 2019*. Geneva: UNCTAD.

UNCTAD (2019b). *World Investment Report 2019: Special Economic Zones*. Geneva: UNCTAD.

UNCTAD (2021). *Handbook on Special Economic Zones in Africa: Towards Economic Diversification across the Continent*. Geneva: UNCTAD.

UNECA [United Nations Economic Commission for Africa] (2017). *Economic Report on Africa 2017: Urbanization and Industrialization*. Addis Ababa: UNECA.

UNECA (2020). *Political Economy of a Green Transition in Africa*. Addis Ababa: UNECA. Available at https://repository.uneca.org/handle/10855/43792 (Accessed 15 July 2022).

Unequal Scenes (2021). *Various locations in Africa*. Available at https://unequalscenes.com (Accessed 16 July 2022).

UN-Habitat (2010). *The State of African Cities 2010: Governance, Inequality and Urban Land Markets*. Nairobi: UN-Habitat.

UN-Habitat (2014). *State of the African Cities Report*. Nairobi: UN-Habitat.

UN-Habitat (2016). *World Cities Report 2016: Urbanization and Development: Emerging Futures*. Nairobi: UN-Habitat.

UN-Habitat (2020). *World Cities Report 2020: The Value of Sustainable Urbanization*. Nairobi: UN-Habitat.

UN-Habitat (2021). *National urban policy database*. Nairobi: UN-Habitat. Available at https://urbanpolicyplatform.org/national-urban-policy-database/#thematic-focus (Accessed 15 July 2022).

UNICEF and WHO (2015). *25 years progress on sanitation and drinking water, update and MDG assessment*. *WHO/UNICEF Joint Monitoring Programme*, New York: United Nations Children's Fund (UNICEF) and World Health Organization.

UNICEF and WHO (2022a). Global data on water supply, sanitation and hygiene (WASH). *WHO/UNICEF Joint Monitoring Programme*, New York: United Nations

Children's Fund (UNICEF) and World Health Organization. Available at https://washdata.org/data (Accessed 15 July 2022).

UNICEF and WHO (2022b). *Progress on Drinking Water, Sanitation and Hygiene in Africa 2000-2020: Five Years into the SDGs*. New York: United Nations Children's Fund (UNICEF) and World Health Organization.

UNIDO (2020). *African Industrial Competitiveness Report: An Overview of the Manufacturing Industry in the Region*. Vienna: UNIDO. Available at https://www.unido.org/sites/default/files/files/2021-02/African%20Industrial%20Competitiveness%20Report_0.pdf (Accessed 16 July, 2022).

United Nations Department of Economic and Social Affairs (UNDESA) (2018). *World Urbanisation Prospects 2018*. New York: UNDESA.

United Nations Development Programme [UNDP] (2021). *2015 Sustainable Development Goals*. New York: UNDP. Available at https://www.undp.org/sustainable-development-goals (Accessed 15 July 2021).

United Nations Environment Programme (UNEP) (2011). *Towards a green economy: pathways to sustainable development and poverty eradication*. Nairobi: UNEP. Available at https://www.unep.org/resources/report/towards-green-economy-pathways-sustainable-development-and-poverty-eradication-10 (Accessed 15 July 2022).

United Nations Office of Disaster Risk Reduction (2015). *Global Assessment Report on Disaster Risk Reduction (GAR) 2015: Making Development Sustainable: The Future of Disaster Risk Management*. New York: United Nations.

Upadhyaya, R. (2020). Kenya: 'Dubai' in the savannah. In: *The Political Economy of Bank Regulation in Developing Countries: Risk and Reputation* (ed. E. Jones), 218–238. Oxford: Oxford University Press.

Uwaegbulam, C. (2019 November 06). *How rising seas may wipe off Lagos, others by 2050*. The Guardian (Nigeria), Available at https://guardian.ng/news/how-rising-seas-may-wipe-off-lagos-others-by-2050 (Accessed 16 July 2022).

Van Belle, S., Affun-Adegbulu, C., Soors, W. et al. (2020). COVID-19 and informal settlements: an urgent call to rethink urban governance. *International Journal for Equity in Health* 19 (81).

Van der Laan, L. (1998). Changing urban systems: an empirical analysis at two spatial levels. *Regional Studies* 32 (3): 235–247.

Van der Panne, G. (2004). Agglomeration externalities: Marshall versus Jacobs. *Journal of Evolutionary Economics* 14 (5): 593–604.

Van der Zwaan, A.H. (1975). The sociotechnical systems approach: a critical evaluation. *The International Journal of Production Research* 13 (2): 149–163.

van Greunen, S. (2021). The city assemblage: a case of Windhoek, Namibia. *Cities* 119: 103374.

van Noorloos, F. and Kloosterboer, M. (2018). Africa's new cities: the contested future of urbanisation. *Urban Studies* 55 (6): 1223–1241.

Van Staden, C., Alden, C., and Wu, Y. (2020). Outlining African agency against the background of the Belt and Road Initiative. *African Studies Quarterly* 19 (3/4): 115–134.

van Welie, M.J., Cherunya, P.C., Truffer, B., and Murphy, J.T. (2018). Analysing transition pathways in developing cities: the case of Nairobi's splintered sanitation regime. *Technological Forecasting and Social Change* 137: 259–271.

Van Welie, M.J., Truffer, B., and Yap, X.S. (2019). Towards sustainable urban basic services in low-income countries: a Technological Innovation System analysis of sanitation value chains in Nairobi. *Environmental Innovation and Societal Transitions* 33: 196–214.

Van Zyl, G. (2016 July 18). Exclusive: Cape Town clamps down on Uber, Impounds 300 cars. *Fin24*, Available at https://www.fin24.com/Tech/News/exclusive-cape-town-clamps-down-on-uber-impounds-300-cars-20160718 (Accessed 16 July 2022).

Venables, A.J. (2009). Rethinking economic growth in a globalizing world: an economic geography lens. *African Development Review* 21 (2): 331–351.

Venables, A.J. (2010). Economic geography and African development. *Papers in Regional Science* 89 (3): 469–483.

Venables, A.J. (2018). Urbanisation in developing economies: building cities that work. *Region* 5 (1): 91–100.

Venter, I. (2017 November 9). Uber reaches almost 1-million users in South Africa. *Engineering News*, Available at http://www.engineeringnews.co.za/article/uber-reaches-almost-1-million-users-in-sa-2017-11-09 (Accessed 16 July 2022).

Vermeulen, J. (2017 September 27). *How many riders Uber has in South Africa*. Mybroadband, Available at https://mybroadband.co.za/news/motoring/230559-how-many-riders-uber-has-in-south-africa.html (Accessed 16 July 2022).

VOA News (2019 January 1). Kenya struggles to give life to futuristic 'Silicon Savannah' city. *VOA News*, Available at https://www.voanews.com/africa/kenya-struggles-give-life-futuristic-silicon-savannah-city (Accessed 13 July 2022).

Von Thünen, J.H. (1966, [1826]). *The Isolated State*. Oxford: Pergamon Press.

Vourlias, C. (2015 April 19). Lowered expectations for Ghana's Hope City? *Al Jazeera*, Available at http://america.aljazeera.com/articles/2015/4/19/lowered-expectations-for-ghanas-hope-city.html (Accessed 16 July 2022).

Waldman-Brown, A., Obeng, G., Adu-Gyamfi, Y. et al. (2014). Fabbing for Africa's informal sector. *Timbuktu Chronicles*.

Wall Street Journal (2012 June 20). Africans' protests highlight tensions in Guangzhou. *Wall Street Journal*, Available at https://blogs.wsj.com/chinarealtime/2012/06/20/africans-protests-highlight-tensions-in-guangzhou (Accessed 25 July 2017).

Walrave, B. and Raven, R. (2016). Modelling the dynamics of technological innovation systems. *Research Policy* 45 (9): 1833–1844.

Walsh, B. (2022). *Ugandan Agency within China-Africa Relations: President Museveni and China's Foreign Policy in East Africa*. London: Bloomsbury Academic.

Wan, Y., Zhang, L.J., Xue, C.Q., and Xiao, Y.B. (2020). Djibouti: from a colonial fabrication to the deviation of the "Shekou model,". *Cities* 97: 102488.

Wang, Y. (2022). Presidential extraversion: understanding the politics of Sino-African mega-infrastructure projects. *World Development* 158: 105976.

Wang, Y. and Wissenbach, U. (2019). Clientelism at work? a case study of Kenyan Standard Gauge Railway project. *Economic History of Developing Regions* 34 (3): 280–299.

Watson, V. (2014). African urban fantasies: dreams or nightmares? *Environment and Urbanisation* 26 (1): 215–231.

Watson, V. (2015). The allure of 'smart city' rhetoric: India and Africa. *Dialogues in Human Geography* 5 (1): 36–39.

Watts, M. (1983). *Silent Violence: Food, Famine, and Peasantry in Northern Nigeria.* Berkeley: University of California Press.

We Build Value (2019 December 11). *Africa's first SkyTrain: Ghana will build the first elevated train on the African continent.* We Build Value, Available at https://www.webuild value.com/en/infrastructure/ghana-skytrain-accra.html (Accessed 14 July 2022).

Wells, P., Abouarghoub, W., Petit, S., and Beresford, A. (2020). A sociotechnical transitions perspective for assessing future sustainability following the COVID-19 pandemic. *Sustainability: Science Practice and Policy* 16 (1): 29–36.

Werner, M. (2019). Geographies of production I: global production and uneven development. *Progress in Human Geography* 43 (5): 948–958.

Western Cape Government (WCG) (2013). *Green is smart: Western Cape green economy strategy framework.* Available at https://www.westerncape.gov.za/assets/departments/ transport-public-works/Documents/green_is_smart-4th_july_2013_for_web.pdf (Accessed 15 July 2022).

Wheatley, J. and Kynge, J. (2020 December 8). China curtails overseas lending in the face of a geopolitical backlash. *Financial Times,* Available at https://www.ft.com/ content/1cb3e33b-e2c2-4743-ae41-d3fffffa4259 (Accessed 17 July 2022).

WIEGO (2018). *Women and Men in the Informal Economy: A Statistical Picture (Third Edition).* Geneva: International Labour Office.

Wilby, R.L., Kasei, R., Gough, K.V. et al. (2021). Monitoring and moderating extreme indoor temperatures in low-income urban communities. *Environmental Research Letters* 16 (2): 024033.

Wilkinson, A. (2020). The challenge of COVID-19 in informal urban settlements and the need for co-produced local responses. In: *COVID-19 in the Global South: Impacts and Responses* (ed. P.R. Carmody, G. McCann, C. Colleran, and C. O'Halloran), 63–74. Bristol: Bristol University Press.

Williams, E. (1994). *Capitalism and Slavery.* Chapel Hill: University of North Carolina Press.

Williams, O. (2020 November 25). Zambia's default fuels fears of African 'debt tsunami' as Covid impact bites. *The Guardian,* Available at https://www.theguardian. com/global-development/2020/nov/25/zambias-default-fuels-fears-of-african-debt-tsunami-as-covid-impact-bites (Accessed 15 July 2022).

Winkler, H. (2019 October 29). South Africa's future energy mix: wind, solar and coal, but no nuclear. *The Conversation,* Available at https://theconversation.com/south-af ricas-future-energy-mix-wind-solar-and-coal-but-no-nuclear-111106 (Accessed 17 July 2022).

Wolf, C. (2016). China and latecomer industrialization processes in Sub-Saharan Africa: a case of combined and uneven development. *World Review of Political Economy* 7 (2): 249–284.

Wolf, C. (2017). Industrialization in times of China: domestic-market formation in Angola. *African Affairs* 116 (464): 435–461.

Woodcock, J. and Graham, M. (2020). *The Gig Economy: A Critical Introduction*. Cambridge: Polity.

Word Bank (2022). *World development indicators*. Available at https://data.worldbank. org/indicator/EN.POP.SLUM.UR.ZS (Accessed 9 January 2023).

World Bank (2009). *World Development Report: Reshaping Economic Geography*. Washington, D.C.: World Bank.

World Bank (2019a). *Achieving Africa's digital transformation is an ambition that requires game-changing cooperation*. Washington, DC: World Bank. Available at https://www. worldbank.org/en/news/feature/2019/05/06/achieving-africas-digital-transformation-is-an-ambition-that-requires-game-changing-cooperation (Accessed 15 July 2022).

World Bank (2019b). *World Development Report 2019: The Changing Nature of Work*. Washington: World Bank.

World Bank (2021a). *TCdata360*. Available at https://tcdata360.worldbank.org/ indicators/inv.all.pct?country=ZAFandindicator=345andviz=line_chartand years=1980,2024 (Accessed 15 July 2022).

World Bank (2021b). *Gross capital formation (% of GDP)*. Available at https://data.world bank.org/indicator/NE.GDI.TOTL.ZS (Accessed 15 July 2022).

Wright, I. (2013). *Are we all neoliberals now? Urban Planning in a neoliberal era*, unpublished manuscript prepared for the 49th ISOCARP Congress. Available at www.iso carp.net/Data/case_studies/2412.pdf (Accessed 15 July 2022).

Wuyts, M. (2001). Informal economy, wage goods and accumulation under structural adjustment theoretical reflections based on the Tanzanian experience. *Cambridge Journal of Economics* 25 (3): 417–438.

Xiao, A.H. (2022). The congested city and situated social inequality: making sense of urban (im) mobilities in Lagos, Nigeria. *Geoforum* 136: 312–320.

Yeung, P. (2019 April 8). *Climate change is already battering this west African city*. City-Lab: Bloomberg, Available at https://www.bloomberg.com/news/articles/2019-04-08/ coastal-senegal-braces-for-severe-climate-crisis (Accessed 16 July 2022).

Yonagbo, P. and Göransson, B. (2020). Constructing the national innovation system in Rwanda: efforts and challenges. *Innovation and Development* 12 (1): 155–176.

Yuan Sun, I. (2017). *The Next Factory of the World: How Chinese Investment Is Reshaping Africa*. Cambridge: Harvard Business Review Press.

Yuan Sun, I., Jayaram, K., and Kassiri, O. (2017). *Dance of the lions and dragons: how are Africa and China engaging, and how will the partnership evolve?* McKinsey Global Institute.

Zajontz, T. (2021). Debt, distress, dispossession: towards a critical political economy of Africa's financial dependency. *Review of African Political Economy*, online first https:// doi.org/10.1080/03056244.2021.1950669.

Zaywa (2021 August 12). UAE-Africa: building on a $50bln partnership. *Zaywa*, Available at https://www.zawya.com/mena/en/economy/story/UAEAfrica_Building_

on_a_50bln_partnership-ZAWYA20210812051551?utm_campaign=magnetandutm_
source=article_pageandutm_medium=recommended_articles (Accessed 16 July 2022).

Zhang, L.-Y. (2015). *Managing the City Economy: Challenges and Strategies in Developing Countries.* London: Routledge.

Zheng, H.W., Bouzarovski, S., Knuth, S. et al. (2021). Interrogating China's global urban presence. *Geopolitics* https://doi.org/10.1080/14650045.2021.1901084.

Ziso, E. (2018). *A Post State-centric Analysis of China-Africa Relations: Internationalisation of Chinese Capital and State-society Relations in Ethiopia.* Cham, Switzerland: Palgrave Macmillan.

Index

Note: page numbers in *italics* refer to figures and those in **bold** to tables.

The Urban Question in Africa: Uneven Geographies of Transition, First Edition. Pádraig R. Carmody, James T. Murphy,
Richard Grant and Francis Y. Owusu.
© 2024 John Wiley & Sons Ltd. Published 2024 by John Wiley & Sons Ltd.